More Praise for

Making Money Work

A Christian Guide For Personal Finance

"Bill is very knowledgeable about economics and finance. He has done an excellent job of relating this to biblical principles of stewardship and has made it user friendly by including computer software. I highly recommend this book for individual use as well as for study groups in churches." —Donald L. Hughes, Retired United Methodist Minister and Educator

"By choosing to exercise your free will in accepting Jesus Christ as your personal Lord and Savior, you make an 'investment' that pays 'dividends' throughout eternity. It is my hope that the purchase price of this book provides you with an unimaginable return on your investment throughout your lifetime." —Bill G. Page, Author of "Making Money Work (A Christian Guide For Personal Finance)"

MAKING MONEY WORK
A Christian Guide For Personal Finance

By: Bill G. Page

© 2005 Willie Glenn Page, Inc.

Making Money Work: A Christian Guide For Personal Finance © 2005 Willie Glenn Page, Inc.
All rights reserved.
ISBN – 0-9764905-0-1

No part of this book or software may be used in any form or by any means, or stored in a database or retrieval system whatsoever without written permission from the publisher with the exception of the stipulations in the Software License Agreement and brief quotations or references used in critical articles, reviews, books, sermons, speeches, lectures, or other talks. Written permission may be obtained from:

Making Money Work
P.O. Box 2605
Chapel Hill, NC 27515
www.MakingMoneyWork.us

This book and software is sold as is, without warranty of any kind other than the specifics outlined in the Software License Agreement. Neither expressed nor implied warranties of any kind are allowed including but not limited to warranties for the book's quality, performance, merchantability, or fitness for a particular purpose. Neither the author, editor, any contributors to the book, anyone quoted in the book, publisher, dealers, or distributors shall be liable to the purchaser or any other person or entity with respect to any liability, loss, or damage caused by or alleged to be caused by this book or software either directly or indirectly.

Several different Bibles are quoted in this book. Unless otherwise noted, scripture verses come from "*The New English Bible With the Apocrypha*" (Oxford University Press, London, 1970).
Brief verses from other Bibles quoted include:
The Soul Care Bible New King James Version (Thomas Nelson Publishers, Nashville, TN, 2001).
The Holy Bible Containing the Old and New Testaments (Cambridge University Press, cir. 1937, printed at The University Press, London).
Self-Pronouncing Edition, The Holy Bible Containing the Old and New Testaments Conformable to the Edition of 1611 Commonly Known as the Authorized or King James Version (The World Publishing Company, Cleveland, OH, and New York, 1952).
The following Bible versions are from the *Thompson Chain HyperBible* (Beacon Technology, Inc., Colorado Springs, CO, 1995):
The Holy Bible, New International Version (B. B. Kirkbride Bible Co. Inc. and the Zondervan Corporation, 1983).
The Holy Bible, King James Version (B. B. Kirkbride Bible Co. Inc., 1988).
The New American Standard Bible (The Lockman Foundation, 1988).
The Holy Bible: New International Version (The International Bible Society, 1984).
The Living Bible (Tyndale House Publishers, Wheaton, IL, 1971).
The Revised Standard Version of the Bible (The Division of Christian Education of the National Council of the Churches of Christ in the United States of America, 1971).

Microsoft Corporation owns Microsoft Excel and Microsoft Word.
Making Money Work is an independent entity from Microsoft Corporation and not affiliated with Microsoft Corporation in any manner.

Making Money Work: A Christian Guide for Personal Finance
Written by Bill G. Page, Edited by Reverend Don Hughes, Copy/Edit by Chapel Hill Press

About the Author

Bill G. Page joined Norcross First United Methodist Church in Norcross, Ga. in 1983. He served as a Stephen Minister and Stephen Minister Leader. He currently attends Orange United Methodist Church in Chapel Hill, NC. He is married to Lee Page and they have a daughter, Courtney, and a son, Justin.

He graduated from East Carolina University in Greenville, N.C., with a double major in Business Education and Distributive Education. He currently holds North Carolina teaching certificates in Basic Business Education and Marketing Education.

Bill spent 27 years working in sales and sales management with Colgate-Palmolive Company. He served as the 1999 president of the Food Manufacturers Sales Executive Club of Atlanta, Inc.

About the Editor

Don Hughes is an ordained United Methodist minister who has served as a full-time minister and also taught in the public school system. He holds a Master of Divinity degree from the Candler School of Theology at Emory University, a Master of Arts degree in Christian Education from Scarritt College, and a Bachelor of Arts degree in Psychology from the University of Tennessee. He has done additional graduate study at Emory University and the University of Georgia. Don is married to Mickey Hughes, and they have a son, Harold, and a daughter, Brenda, and two grandchildren.

Acknowledgments[1]

I would like to thank my wife, other family members, and friends including the Norcross First United Methodist Church "Library Room Emmaus Reunion Group" and the Norcross First United Methodist Church "Walk in Faith" Sunday school class for their prayers, encouragement, contributing ideas, and support. Without that support, this work would not have been accomplished. I would also like to thank the Reverend Don Hughes for his spiritual mentoring and his meticulous efforts in the editing of this book. Most of all, I would like to thank God for getting this work completed—in spite of my limitations.

Bill G. Page

---

[1] The opinions expressed by the author of *Making Money Work* do not necessarily reflect the opinions of others mentioned.

MAKING MONEY WORK
(A Christian Guide For Personal Finance)

MISSION STATEMENT

Making Money Work (A Christian Guide for Personal Finance) is a book and software program designed to help people make financial decisions based on God's principles. Extensive scriptural references are used as the basis for these principles. The software program is extremely user-friendly and saves people time and money as they analyze their personal financial decisions from eighth grade through death. *Making Money Work* has a strong biblical base and is a sensible, realistic, and easy-to-follow plan for personal finances.

Making Money Work has the goal of helping people develop a closer relationship with Jesus Christ while becoming better stewards of God's resources.

What the "Making Money Work" Logo[1] Symbolizes

- The fish symbol stands for Christianity.

- The white background inside the fish symbolizes the sinless perfect nature of Jesus Christ. It also symbolizes the sacrifice of Christ as a ransom for our sins during the crucifixion. For those that believe, our sins are forgiven.

- The Making Money Work portion of the logo is colored green to symbolize the money, finances, and resources God entrusts you with during your lifetime. It is enclosed within the fish to symbolize your stewardship of God's resources.

- The fish is gold-colored to symbolize life eternal for those who acknowledge God, confess their sins, and place their trust and faith in Christ to be Lord and Savior of their lives.

---

[1] View the file *What the MMW Logo Symbolizes* on the CD ROM to see the logo in color.

Making Money Work

"If any of you falls short in wisdom, he should ask God for it and it will be given him, for God is a generous giver who neither refuses nor reproaches anyone"—James 1:5.

Making Money Work is a building block type of instructional tool. It is important to understand each chapter before continuing sequentially on to the next chapter. The information learned in earlier chapters helps you with your understanding of financial principles in later chapters.

Contents

	Pages
1. The Ultimate Goal	1–14
2. Money Management Psychology	15–26
3. Tithing/Giving	27–43
4. Debt Management	44–65
5. The Magic of Compound Interest	66–75
6. Inflation—The Silent Thief	76–81
7. Saving/Goal Setting	82–98
8. Social Security	99–106
9. Taxes	107–115
10. Retirement Funds	116–128
11. Investments—Historical Returns	129–132
12. Abundance Thinking Versus a Scarcity Mentality	133–137
13. Investment Risks and Suggested Asset Allocation	138–141
14. Stocks	142–181
15. Mutual Funds	182–208
16. Bonds	209–226
17. Money Market Funds	227–230
18. Certificates of Deposit	231–233
19. Individual Retirement Arrangements (IRAs)	234–258
20. Annuities	259–266
21. Housing	267–285
22. Real Estate Investment Trusts	286–287
23. Futures Markets	288–289
24. Household Records	290–296
25. Checking Accounts	297–302
26. Keeping Track of Your Portfolio	303–308
27. Credit Cards	309–313

Contents

                                                                                                   Pages

28. Vehicles 314–342
29. College Expenses 343–357
30. Weddings 358–361
31. Life Insurance 362–373
32. Health Insurance and Disability Insurance 374–382
33. Automobile Insurance 383–395
34. Homeowner's/Renter's Insurance 396–402
35. Long-Term Care Insurance 403–412
36. Other Insurance 413–416
37. Wills, Trusts, and Estate Planning 417–440
38. Identity Theft 441–449
39. Grace, Faith, Purpose, and Peace 450–459
40. *Making Money Work* Website Address 461–461
41. Order Form for Additional Copies of MMW ... 462–463
42. MMW Scholarship Program 464–465
43. Bibliography 466–466
44. Index 467–476
45. MMW Copyright and Covenant Stipulations ... 477–479

LOAD THE *MAKING MONEY WORK* CD ROM WITH THE "MMW CALCULATORS" ONTO YOUR COMPUTER'S HARD DRIVE FOR USE WITH MICROSOFT EXCEL AND MICROSOFT WORD

For example, in the Microsoft Windows 98 version you might:
1. Place the *Making Money Work* CD ROM (Compact Disk Read Only Memory), which contains the "MMW Calculators", into your computer's disk drive (e.g., "D:" or "E:").
2. Single click with the left button of your mouse on "Start."
3. Single click on "Programs."
4. Single click on "Windows Explorer" or perhaps "Accessories" then "Windows Explorer."
5. Single click on your hard drive (e.g., "C:").
6. Single click on "My Documents" or on the folder where you would like to have the files stored.
7. Single click on "File."
8. Single click on "New."
9. Single click on "Folder."
10. Type in the name you would like for the folder you are creating (e.g., "Making Money Work").
11. Press "Enter."
12. Double click on the "My Documents" folder (or the main folder where you created the subfolder) to expand the subfolders.
13. Scroll to and double click on the "disk drive" (e.g., "D:" or "E:") to expand the subfolder.
14. Left click while holding down on the "MMW Calculators" folder and drag from the disk drive CD ROM to your newly created hard drive folder (e.g., "Making Money Work"). Release the left button on your mouse and wait for the files to be copied.
15. Double click on the new folder (e.g., "Making Money Work") to open the subfolder.
16. Double click on the "MMW Calculators" folder.
17. Double click on the calculator/file you would like to open (e.g., "SS10 Calculator—-Noncash Charitable Contribution.xls"). Click on "Enable Macros." Click the recalculate button after inputting your personal numbers—if the recalculation does not function and you receive an error message such as "The macros in this project are disabled," lower your security level to medium or lower (e.g., go to "Tools," "Macro," "Security," and click on "Medium").

For example, in the Microsoft Windows 2000 Professional version you might:
1. Place the *Making Money Work* CD ROM (Compact Disk Read Only Memory), which contains the "MMW Calculators" into your computer's disk drive (e.g., "D:" or "E:").
2. Single click with your left mouse button on "Start."
3. Single click on "Programs."
4. Single click on "Accessories."
5. Single click on "Windows Explorer."
6. Single click on the "Address" drop-down menu.
7. Single click on your disk drive (e.g., "D:" or "E:").
8. Single click on "My Documents."
9. Single click on "File."
10. Single click on "New."
11. Single click on "Folder."
12. Rename the "Folder" (e.g., "Making Money Work").
13. Press "Enter."
14. Single click your disk drive (e.g., "D:" or "E:").
15. Left click while holding down on the "MMW Calculators" folder and drag from the disk drive CD ROM to your newly created hard drive folder (e.g., "Making Money Work"). Release the left button on your mouse and wait for the files to be copied.
16. Single click on the new folder (e.g., "Making Money Work").
17. Double click on "MMW Calculators."
18. Double click on the calculator you would like to open (e.g., "SS10 Calculator—Noncash Charitable Contribution.xls").

19. Single click on "Enable Macros." Enter personal information, tab, and then press the "MMW Recalculation Button" or "Cntrl + m" to recalculate. If the recalculation does not function, lower your security levels to enable Macros—go to "Tools," "Macro," and "Security" settings.

For example, in the Microsoft Windows XP version you might:
1. Place the *Making Money Work* CD ROM (Compact Disk Read Only Memory), which contains the "MMW Calculators," into your computer's disk drive (e.g., "D:" or "E:").
2. Single click with your left mouse button on "Start."
3. Single click on "Programs."
4. Single click on "Accessories."
5. Single click on "Windows Explorer."
6. Single click on the address bar drop-down menu.
7. Single click on your disk drive (e.g., "D:" or "E:").
8. Single click on "My Documents" or the folder where you would like to store the information.
9. Single click on "File."
10. Single click on "New."
11. Single click on "Folder."
12. Rename the "Folder" (e.g., "Making Money Work").
13. Press "Enter."
14. Single click your disk drive (e.g., "D:" or "E:").
15. Left click while holding down on the "MMW Calculators" folder and drag from the disk drive CD ROM to your newly created hard drive folder (e.g., "Making Money Work"). Release the left button on your mouse and wait for the files to be copied.
16. Single click on the new folder (e.g., "Making Money Work").
17. Single click on "MMW Calculators."
18. Double click on the calculator you would like to open (e.g., "SS10 Calculator-Noncash Charitable Contribution").
19. Single click on "Enable Macros." Enter personal information, tab, and then press the "MMW Recalculation Button" or "Cntrl + m" to recalculate. If the recalculation does not function, exit all applications, re-enter, and then lower your security levels to enable Macros—go to "Tools," "Macro," "Security" settings and lower to "Medium" or lower, and then press "OK." For Microsoft Windows XP Professional Version 2002, go to "Tools," "Options," "Security," "Macro Security," select "Security Level @ Medium" or lower, and "OK."

To view in the formula bar the entire contents of cells in which you enter input into spreadsheets, click on "View" and "Formula Bar."

The disk drive files have been copied to your hard drive as "read-only" files. Read-only files can be viewed but not changed using the same file name. You may input your personal numbers in to the files and then save them using a "different" file name or you can remove the "read-only" designation from each file, input your personal information, and then save the file using the same file name. To remove the "read-only" designation from each file, complete the following steps:
1. **Left click on the individual file to select it.**
2. **Right click on the file.**
3. **Left click on "Properties."**
4. **Remove the "√" inside the "read-only" check mark box by clicking on it.**
5. **Click "Apply."**
6. **Click "Close."**
7. **The file is now ready to accept your personal input numbers and to be saved using the same filename.**

Caution: You will be using these files to input personal financial information—guard against identity theft by taking appropriate security measures. For example, keep your computer in a safe, locked, secure place. Use passwords to protect sensitive information. Load sensitive files to a CD and store the information in a safe, off-site location such as a bank safe-deposit box.

Calculators/Worksheets[1]

Document or Spreadsheet   **Open With**

1. What the MMW Logo Symbolizes .... Microsoft Word
2. File Folders .... Microsoft Word
3. SS10 Calculator-Noncash Charitable Contribution .... Microsoft Excel
4. SS12 Calculator-Liquid Assets Versus Current Liabilities .... Microsoft Excel
5. SS13 Calculator-Budget .... Microsoft Excel
6. SS14 Calculator-Loan Payment .... Microsoft Excel
7. SS15 Calculator-Compound Interest .... Microsoft Excel
8. SS16 Calculator-Retirement Savings Goal (In Today's Dollars) .... Microsoft Excel
9. SS17 Calculator-Taxable Equivalent Yield .... Microsoft Excel
10. SS18 Calculator-Investment Future Value .... Microsoft Excel
11. SS19 Calculator-Risk Assessment & Suggested Asset Allocation .... Microsoft Excel
12. SS20 Calculator-Stock Purchase, Sale, Split .... Microsoft Excel
13. SS21 Calculator-Mutual Fund Purchases & Sales (Unprotected WB) .... Microsoft Excel
14. SS22 Calculator-Present Value-Bond .... Microsoft Excel
15. SS23 Calculator-Annual Percentage Yield .... Microsoft Excel
16. SS24 Calculator-Traditional IRA Cost Basis .... Microsoft Excel
17. SS25 Calculator-Roth IRA Nondeductible Contributions .... Microsoft Excel
18. SS26 Calculator-Investment Future Value .... Microsoft Excel
19. SS27 Calculator-Mortgage Loan Estimate .... Microsoft Excel

---

[1] All calculations should be verified by your personal broker, accountant, lawyer, banker, and other personal financial institutions.

Calculators/Worksheets[2]

Document or Spreadsheet   **Open With**

20. **SS28 Calculator-Amortization** .... Microsoft Excel
21. **SS29 Calculator-Home-Property Improvement** .... Microsoft Excel
22. **SS30 Calculator-File Folders** .... Microsoft Excel
23. **SS31 Calculator-Household Inventory Form** .... Microsoft Excel
24. **SS32 Calculator-Annuity Comparison Estimator (SS Versus SS Leveling)** ... Microsoft Excel
25. **SS33 Calculator-Portfolio Allocation** .... Microsoft Excel
26. **SS34 Calculator-Lease Agreement (Vehicle)** .... Microsoft Excel
27. **SS35 Calculator-Vehicle Keep, Buy, or Lease Comparison** .... Microsoft Excel
28. **SS36 Calculator-College Costs and Savings** .... Microsoft Excel
29. **SS37 Calculator-Wedding Costs** .... Microsoft Excel
30. **SS38 Calculator-Life Insurance Needs** .... Microsoft Excel
31. **SS39 Calculator-Vehicle Insurance** .... Microsoft Excel
32. **SS40 Vehicle Accident Report** .... Microsoft Excel
33. **SS41 Calculator-Estate Planning Worksheets** .... Microsoft Excel
34. **SS42 Estate Plan Information Recap** .... Microsoft Excel

---

[2] All calculations should be verified by your personal broker, accountant, lawyer, banker, and other personal financial institutions.

The Ultimate Goal

Chapter 1

The Ultimate Goal

What do you think God felt as man spat in the face of His Son Jesus Christ, struck Him with their fists, flogged Him, forced a crown of thorns onto His head, and crucified Him (circa 33 AD)? Are you a parent? Do you have loved ones? What would you have done if you had witnessed someone abusing your son, daughter, or other loved one? God is omnipotent. God is almighty. God is all-powerful. God could have destroyed the entire world for man's sins against Jesus!

Back in Noah's time (circa 2950–2000 BC), God saw the world as corrupt. Noah was the only good man who walked with God. Because all men had lived corrupted lives on earth, God decided to destroy everything he had made except Noah, his sons, Noah's wife, Noah's sons' wives, and a male and female of all living creatures. Noah was instructed to build an ark. God sent rains to flood the earth. After the world had been destroyed, Noah built an altar to God and made offerings. God then said to himself, "*Never again will I curse the ground because of man, however evil his inclinations may be from his youth upwards. I will never again kill every living creature, as I have just done. While the earth lasts, seedtime and harvest, cold and heat, summer and winter, day and night, shall never cease*"—Genesis 8:21–22[1].

God fulfills his promises to man. So, when man persecuted Jesus, God did not choose

---

[1] Note: concerning the end-times of the world: "*And the present heavens and earth, again by God's word, have been kept in store for burning; they are being reserved until the day of judgement when the godless will be destroyed*"—2 Peter 3:7.

The Ultimate Goal

to destroy the world. God's purpose was to use Jesus to save the world! "*For God so loved the world, that he gave his only begotten Son, that whosoever believeth in him should not perish, but have everlasting life*"—John 3:16 (King James Version). You, as an individual, are of significant worth to God; otherwise, God would not have sacrificed His only Son for your sins. Through the crucifixion, God made a profound statement that He loves you enough to die for you. God brought nothing but good to man. Sin is a wrong that separates you from God. Man introduced vice[2] through Adam's original sin of eating from "*the tree of the knowledge of good and evil*"—Genesis 2:9.

We are all sinners in God's sight. The more we know about God's commandments, the more obvious it is to us that we do not obey them. The more we know about God's laws, the more obvious it is to us that we have been sinners, we are currently sinners, and we will always be sinners; however, we are forgiven sinners if we trust Jesus for our salvation. The inherent sin in our human nature makes it impossible for us to be good enough to obey all God's commands and earn our way to heaven.

We are not saved from sin by knowing God's commandments. God sent "*his own Son in a form like that of our own sinful nature, and as a sacrifice for sin, he has passed judgement against sin within that very nature, so that the commandment of the law may find fulfillment in us, whose conduct, no longer under the control of our lower nature, is directed by the Spirit*"—Romans 8:3–4. Through the death and resurrection of Jesus Christ, God pardoned our sins—even though we are guilty! We are forgiven sinners until

---

[2] God told Adam, "*You may eat from every tree in the garden, but not from the tree of the knowledge of good and evil; for on the day that you eat from it, you will certainly die*"—Genesis 2:16–17. Adam confessed to God, "*The woman [Eve] you gave me for a companion, she gave me fruit from the tree and I ate it*"—Genesis 3:12.

The Ultimate Goal

the day we die. We will never be perfect in action. You cannot earn forgiveness for your sins; forgiveness is yours by the Grace of God alone through Jesus Christ. "*And so I [Jesus] tell you this: no sin, no slander, is beyond forgiveness for men, except slander spoken against the Spirit, and that will not be forgiven*"—Matthew 12:31. Jesus Christ is capable of looking past the sin in each of us and recognizing the "saint" in each of us. By having faith in Christ to be your personal Savior from sin, confessing your sins, repenting your sins with a truly remorseful heart, and accepting God's forgiveness, you will be saved and share life eternal. "*If on your lips is the confession, 'Jesus is Lord,' and in your heart the faith that God raised him from the dead, then you will find salvation. For the faith that leads to righteousness is in the heart, and the confession that leads to salvation is upon the lips*"—Romans 10:9–10. Christ died to establish the eternal life for us that God intended. "*For all alike have sinned, and are deprived of the divine splendour, and all are justified by God's free grace alone, through his act of liberation in the person of Christ Jesus. For God designed him to be the means of expiating sin by his sacrificial death, effective through faith. God meant by this to demonstrate his justice, because in his forbearance he had overlooked the sins of the past—to demonstrate his justice now in the present, showing that he is himself just and also justifies any man who puts his faith in Jesus*"—Romans 3:23–26. Faith in Jesus Christ is a mental acceptance of God, a commitment to God, obedience to God, and trusting in God.

Acquittal of our sins is based upon the death and resurrection of Jesus Christ. "*We know that Christ, once raised from the dead, is never to die again: he is no longer under the dominion of death. For in dying as he died, he died to sin, once for all, and in living as he lives, he lives to God. In the same way you must regard yourselves as dead to sin*

The Ultimate Goal

and alive to God, in union with Christ Jesus"—Romans 6:9–11. Acquittal of our sins is not based on our own good deeds. We are sinners saved by Grace; that is the only way we get into heaven. Man's sin impedes the divine initiatives. God's redemption through Jesus Christ allows us to no longer be slaves of sin, but servants of God. When we put our trust and faith in Jesus Christ, then we can obey God and better follow God's commandments. It doesn't mean that you will never sin again. When you do sin, confess it immediately and then move forward to accomplish God's will for your life. Jesus Christ not only died for past sins, he died for all future sins as well. Pentecost was the descent of the Holy Spirit upon the apostles. Before Pentecost and the resurrection of Jesus Christ, Jesus was "with" the disciples. After Pentecost, Jesus was "within" the disciples. So it is with you today. When you accept Jesus Christ as your personal Lord and Savior, the Spirit of God lives within you. "*If the Spirit of him who raised Jesus from the dead dwells within you, then the God who raised Jesus from the dead will also give new life to your mortal bodies through his indwelling Spirit*"—Romans 8:11. This Spirit in you will change your life; you will never be the same again. This Spirit in your life allows you to take action so that you might accomplish God's will. Your faith, trust, belief, and commitment to Jesus Christ translate into the action of being a witness for Lord God! We do not have the Holy Spirit, the Holy Spirit has us. The Holy Spirit is not under our power; we are under the Holy Spirit's power. The Holy Spirit makes a change in your lifestyle immediately to improve your relationship with God and unites and draws Christians together. The Holy Spirit's purpose is the continuing presence of God in your life and provides the inner assurance of personal peace and joy. Also, the Holy Spirit provides outward motivation to act ethically and to be socially responsible. The Holy

The Ultimate Goal

Spirit enables you to make a "life" for yourself—not just a "living." In so doing, you "write" another Gospel with your life. You make the most of your life and value every moment. J. C. Wheakin near his death at age 77 said, "Life is short, especially if you live it to it's fullest."

God saves individuals. The choice is up to you as an individual—you, and you alone. God gives each individual the free will to accept his invitation to live within his love. "*Ask, and you will receive; seek, and you will find; knock, and the door will be opened. For everyone who asks receives, he who seeks finds, and to him who knocks, the door will be opened*"—Matthew 7:7–8. "*Here I [Jesus] stand knocking at the door; if anyone hears my voice and opens the door, I will come in and sit down to supper with him and he with me*"—Revelation 3:20. God's invitation is available to everyone. "*There is no question here of Greek and Jew, circumcised and uncircumcised, barbarian, Scythian, slave and freeman; but Christ is all, and is in all*"—Colossians 3:11. You can reject God's promise of companionship during this life and life eternal—the choice is up to you. God will honor your choice either way, even if your rejection results in evil. It is not God's responsibility to prevent our sins but to redeem us from our sins. Without the freedom of individual will, God's Grace and Love cannot be chosen! Calvary reveals the everlasting unconditional love of God. You may choose to turn your back on God; however, God loves you unconditionally and will never turn His back on you. Should you choose to turn around, God's love is there to welcome you with open arms. God said, "*I offer you the choice of life or death, blessing or curse*"—Genesis 30:19. God does not give up on waiting for our acceptance. God's Grace forgives you of your sins just as if the sins had never been committed—you cannot earn this forgiveness, you receive it; it is your free

The Ultimate Goal

gift from God! "*For it is by his* [God's] *grace you are saved, through trusting him; it is not your own doing. It is God's gift, not a reward for work done*"—Ephesians 2:8–9. Everyone has secular human faith. Everyone has the capacity to have religious faith. Religious faith is not something we acquire; it is something we respond to—given to us by God. Religious faith is a personal relationship with God that translates into the action of serving God. Serving God during your life on Earth equates to being saved now, not waiting until death. James W. Fowler states in his book *Stages of Faith* that "faith is a *verb*, it is an active mode of being and committing, a way of moving into and giving shape to our experiences of life." Religious faith enables the Christian follower to accept without proof the following:

1. God—the Father, Creator, and Provider
2. Jesus Christ—the Son of God, the Redeemer, the Savior of mankind
3. The Holy Ghost—the Holy Spirit, the Sustainer and Indwelling Spirit

Religious faith provides redemption and freedom. You are *justified* (released from the guilt of sin by God's forgiveness). You are *sanctified* (set apart from sin to achieve a sacred purpose). While you will never become perfect, you are constantly empowered by God to grow and learn and to become more Christ like.

There is no other decision anyone can make that is more important than the acceptance of God's gift of Grace and Love. The remainder of this financial guide will assist you in making numerous earthly decisions; however, all of these decisions are unimportant in comparison to the choice of accepting God's gift of eternal life. "*Set your mind on God's kingdom and his justice before everything else, and all the rest will come to you as well*"—Matthew 6:33–34. When you die, your material possessions, financial assets, real estate, and all other earthly property are taken from you. The courts might distribute some of your possessions to pay your taxes and debts. Some possessions might be given as

The Ultimate Goal

inheritance to your heirs. Some possessions might be given to charities. All you have left is your soul and the legacy of how you treated your fellow man while living your life on Earth. You will be held accountable for your actions here on Earth. How then do you prepare for this judgment day? If you have not done so, immediately bow your head, pray to God, confess your sins, accept Jesus Christ as your personal Lord and Savior from sin, and accept God's forgiveness. God wants you first, above all else. Your good works, charitable donations, and personal contributions to mankind are important, but you and your soul take precedence over all else in the Kingdom of God. In the book *The Search for Meaning* by Thomas H. Naylor, William H. Willimon, and Magdalena R. Naylor, the authors say, "We believe that the search for meaning is primarily concerned with the crafting of our soul—our only possession that can never be taken away even by death. While we are still alive, our soul is who we are. It is our being—our very essence." Regardless of whether you are rich, middle class, or poor, your soul is the only possession over which you have ultimate control. Two crucial concepts in the *Search for Meaning* book are "having" and "being." "For too many of us, if we looked back on our lives, we would see little more than an anxious series of accumulated things, a move from this year's 'new and improved' car model to the next, the rungs of an unending ladder of acquisitions. Ironically, even as we were accumulating, having, and getting, we were not having. Death is the great thief!" "*We brought nothing into the world; for that matter we cannot take anything with us when we leave*"—1 Timothy 6:7–8. Final death is separation of the soul from God. Believers are saved by Grace—God's unconditional free gift of love for the redemption of our sins and the sanctification and regeneration of our souls. Physical death in this world frees you of those material possessions that might have been holding on to you so that you can enjoy unencumbered eternal communion with God.

Life should be about "being." The Bible provides a blueprint for living your life—

The Ultimate Goal

especially the New Testament and the teachings of Jesus Christ. Jesus said, "*<u>Do not suppose that I have come to abolish the Law and the prophets: I did not come to abolish, but to complete</u>*"—Matthew 5:17. Read the Bible first. It is an important step in soul crafting. Contemplate the word of scripture in your heart. The fact is that life can be confusing. Religion can help guide you through ambiguous situations. We will never be able to fully understand the majesty of God's ways: however, He has given us guidelines by which to live and make decisions through the teachings of Jesus Christ that will guide us on the path of righteousness and life eternal. The Bible will provide the blueprint for living your life and the foundation so that you can deal with future decisions in a manner that is conducive to the will of God. Religion teaches us how to live.

When you have doubts about a decision you are faced with, pray to God for guidance. Barna Research Group, Ltd., found in a 1993 survey that 9 out of 10 adult Americans pray to God—6 out of 10 pray at least daily. A Princeton Religion Research Center study found the following about people who pray:

—94% feel more hopeful.
—62% feel divine inspiration or a feeling of being led by God.
—23% percent said they actually heard a voice or saw a vision as the result of prayer.

A Gallup poll of 688 Americans revealed the following:
—95% of the respondents said their prayers had been answered (although not always in the way they expected).
—86% said they actually got what they had asked for.
—86% believe praying made them better people.
—Most said prayer put them at peace.[3]

The purpose of prayer is not to "make everything right"; the purpose of prayer is to make you right for everything. The Spirit within you will assist you in accordance to God's will. In the book *The Will of God*, Leslie D. Weatherhead states, "the goal of all human

---

[3] *The Popularity of Prayer* by Gayle White, Atlanta Journal Constitution, Dec. 9, 1995 and Guideposts, January 1997.

The Ultimate Goal

endeavor is to fulfill God's purposes and to be one with him." Discerning the will of God can be difficult. Sometimes conflict arises when our individual wills come into conflict with God's will. Sometimes we second-guess God and think our will is what is best for us. The farther away from the source of your power you are, the weaker your spirituality becomes. The source of power for a Christian is complete surrender to Jesus Christ and an unconditional love of God. Anything that goes against the teachings of Jesus Christ is not conducive to the will of God. It usually helps to remove yourself from the situation when trying to determine God's will so that you are not tempted to take an easier route that is more pleasant to implement for yourself—or be tempted to take a course of action that benefits yourself. "*Look to each other's interest and not merely to your own*"— Philippians 2:4. Ask God how you can serve him in the middle of all this. Ask God to include you in His plans so that you might contribute to His Kingdom. Get closer to God until your will gets lost in God's will! Leslie D. Weatherhead says, "The guiding principle 'I will do God's will as far as I can see it' is one that answers a great many of our conflicts and therefore brings us peace and strength." An intimate, close, personal relationship with God is the number one priority in God's will for your life. Prayer, rest, meditation, study, and attending church help to develop this relationship so that you get to know, trust, and love God more and become closer to God.

Attending church helps the individual understand the counsel of God through the group experience. The group experience is better than an individual one because even the most mature person can benefit from the help of others. Even the person who feels insignificant has something positive to offer. The synergy of the group is always stronger than the efforts of an individual in isolation in absorbing God's counsel and discerning His will. Jesus said, "*For where two or three have met together in my name, I am there*

The Ultimate Goal

among them"—Matthew 18:20. God wants you to be the best that you can be in every circumstance every day. God's will is that you live up to your potential.

The Bible does not address all the specific questions or problems that will occur in your life; however, it can guide you in making decisions. For example, medical technology could not accomplish the things in the time of Jesus that it can accomplish today—such as organ transplants. Therefore, there are no biblical verses that specifically address the modern day medical wonders that can be accomplished by God through man. Armed with modern day knowledge and the direction that the Bible gives you, you can make decisions that will fulfill the will of God for your life. A personal example for myself involves the United Network for Organ Sharing (UNOS). UNOS is a nonprofit organization chosen by the U.S. Department of Health and Human Resources to operate the Organ Procurement and Transplation Network and to develop an equal access system for all patients on a waiting list for organs. The UNOS waiting list for organs is ever growing. As of March 16, 2004, they had the following waiting list for organs:

# Needed	Type of Organ
57,053	Kidneys
17,249	Livers
3,460	Hearts
3,909	Lungs
2,394	Kidney-Pancreas
1,559	Pancreas
185	Heart-Lung
184	Intestine
85,993	Total Transplant Registrations (84,001 Total Patients)

If someone is willing to donate the organs, medical technology now has the capability of improving or even saving more than 84,000 lives. How do you donate organs? Even if you have designated on your driver's license and carry a donor ID card, you must be in a

The Ultimate Goal

hospital on life-support systems. All efforts to save your life must have been exhausted. A physician must have conducted an EEG brain scan to determine that brain death has occurred. Your next of kin have to give permission for the procurement team to take your organs. While the Bible does not specifically address the issue of transplants, reading the Bible can give you guidance. The following verses had specific meaning to me regarding donating one's organs:

"*as her soul was in departing, (for she died)*"—Genesis 35:18 (King James Version)

"*So it is with the resurrection of the dead. What is sown in the earth as a perishable thing is raised imperishable. . . . sown as an animal body, it is raised as a spiritual body.*"—1 Corinthians 15:42–44

"*The Spirit alone gives life; the flesh is of no avail.*"—John 6:63

"*God is Spirit.*"—John 4:24

"*For the whole law can be summed up in a single commandment: 'Love your neighbour as yourself.'*"—Galatians 5:14

These verses to me meant that when you die, you leave your mortal body behind. The mortal body is merely the vessel for your soul. Your soul is claimed by God to become more godlike, and God is Spirit. You no longer need your old mortal body. What greater gift of love could you bestow on your fellow man than the gift of mortal life through the use of your organs? These scriptures could have an entirely different meaning to you. The Bible speaks through the Holy Spirit to different people in different ways. That's the reason it is crucial that you read the Bible for yourself. Read it with an open mind and an open heart—the Holy Spirit will then guide you in making your own personal decisions in regard to modern day questions. Your individual choices might even change as you age, gain experience, and gain knowledge—that's the reason to continue reading the

The Ultimate Goal

Bible your entire life. Circumstances can alter all things. The Bible might speak to you differently at different times in your life.

If you would like more information concerning organ donations, you can contact the following organization:

The Living Bank
P.O. Box 6725
Houston, TX 77265
www.livingbank.org
800-528-2971

Once you discern God's will, be proactive to implement it. Soul crafting is an ongoing art. We are constantly Christians under construction—learning and growing to improve our souls until the day we die. A Christian may stand on the "mountaintops of yesterday," but he is only at the "foothills of tomorrow." That is living your life to "be" rather than to "have." Naylor, Willimon, and Naylor phrase it wonderfully when they say, "Soul crafting is the point of life, the reason for being. In the end, that is all that remains." Religion prepares the soul for death! Human life is but a moment compared to eternity. "The fact is that as one grows older, one recognizes how central to all of life a proper theology is"—Anglican Archbishop Desmond Tutu[4]. Attend church; it will help you to become a better Christian and greatly facilitate the nurturing of your soul.

"*Where there is no vision, the people perish*"—Proverbs 29:18 (King James Version). The purpose of this financial guide is to enlighten your vision and help improve your personal finances using Christian principles. This guide is not intended to circumvent the advice of your financial service industry representatives; however, it is the belief of the writer that no one will take care of your money like yourself. The manual uses biblical verses as the basis for God-centered principles to enable you to make better financial

---

[4] Drusilla Menaker, Atlanta Journal-Constitution, telephone interview with Desmond Tutu.

The Ultimate Goal

decisions. God's principles do not change and should be the basis for our future decisions. God's principles are lighthouse beacons to bring you in from the storm. If we understand and utilize these God-centered principles, they will produce great results. To help you distinguish God's principles in this manual, all quotations from the Bible are *italicized* and <u>underlined</u>. The manual includes worksheets and software programs to help you calculate your financial decisions.

It is the enjoyment of learning, working, and accomplishment that gives meaning to life. This guide is not a get-rich-quick vehicle. Focus on the things you can control, and improve your own abilities. Be willing to make changes, which improve God's Kingdom. Try not to be fearful of change. Dr. Joseph B. Kennedy wrote the following in his poem titled "Perpetual Change":[5]

> Vast hope of endless scope is offered in PERPETUAL
> CHANGE. There is no end in failure or success
> Another chance to rise or fall presents itself
> At every dropping of the grain of sand.

Theologian Reinhold Niebuhr beautifully expressed change in his prayer: "God, give us grace to accept with serenity the things that cannot be changed, courage to change the things that should be changed, and the wisdom to distinguish the one from the other."[6] To paraphrase a thought from Sigmund Freud, change reminds us of ultimate change—death. Christians can accept change, even death, because they are armed with the knowledge that death in our human bodies is in reality the birth of our souls in eternal life. Christians can adapt to change in their lives because they are armed with the knowledge that change can build their souls and help prepare them for the eventual death of their human body. Change is a normal part of life. Crisis always involves change.

---

[5] Dr. Joseph Kennedy, Norcross First United Methodist Church Stephen Ministry training class handout, 1997.
[6] *Reinhold's Era: Life with a Public Theologian,* Magazine article by Gary Dorrier; The Christian Century, Vol. 121, February 24, 2004.

The Ultimate Goal

Christians, therefore, can even view crisis in their lives as a normal part of life. An expectation and acceptance of crisis as a part of life can develop in the Christian without a loss of faith or hope. It requires dedication and effort to make you as successful as possible with your financial well-being.

Chapter 2

Money Management Psychology

"*The love of money is the root of all evil*"—1 Timothy 6:10. Read the preceding verse again. Note that the verse does <u>not</u> say money is the root of all evil, it says the <u>love</u> of money is the root of all evil! Jesus said, "*How hard it is for the wealthy to enter the kingdom of God! It is easier for a camel to go through the eye of a needle than for a rich man to enter the kingdom of God*"—Luke 18:24–25. Joseph F. Girzone states in his modern day parable *Joshua* that "you become what you love, and when you love the things of this world you lower yourselves to the level of those things." A Christian loves God, not money. "*Do not live for money*"—Hebrews 13:5. A Christian lives for God, not money. Be attentive to loving the Blesser rather than the blessing. Be consumed with God first, then you will not be consumed with profit at the expense of your soul through the unfair treatment of other people. Staying focused on God helps you to keep from confusing your self worth with your net worth regardless of your financial situation. All people are worthy in God's sight—rich, poor, and in between. Money itself is neither good nor bad, the important issue is what is done with it—is it used as a vehicle to improve God's kingdom? There is not a sin in earning a lot of money if done justly; the important issue is what the Christian does with that money. "*Instruct those who are rich in this world's goods not to be proud, and not to fix their hopes on so uncertain a thing as money, but upon God, who endows us richly with all things to enjoy. Tell them to do good and to grow rich in noble actions, to be ready to give away and to share, and so acquire a treasure which will form a good foundation for the future. Thus they will grasp the life*

Money Management Psychology

which is life indeed"—1 Timothy 6:17–19.

While we may talk about "your money" in this financial guide, in reality all money belongs to God. "*God; his is the primacy over all created things. In him everything in heaven and on earth was created, not only things visible but also the invisible orders of thrones, sovereignties, authorities, and powers; the whole universe has been created through him and for him*"—Colossians 1:15–17 (New English Bible Version). "*God . . . is himself the universal giver of life and breath and all else*"—Acts 17:24–26. We are only stewards of God's money while we are here on earth. A steward is a manager of something that belongs to another. As stewards of God's money, we should do our best to manage our finances according to God's will. Part of God's will for our lives is that we do what is right. "*The man who is God fearing and does what is right is acceptable to (God)*"—Acts 10:34–35. "*How blest are those who hunger and thirst to see right prevail; they shall be satisfied*"—Matthew 5:6. "*But you, my friends, must never tire of doing right*"—2 Thessalonians 3:13. When you choose right over wrong, you choose God, and nothing pleases God more! When Satan tempts you, pray to God that the Holy Spirit fills you from within to such an extent that Satan cannot penetrate the temple of your body and God's Holy Fortress. We should conduct our lives according to God's commandments. God's laws cannot be compromised, bent, or amended. God said: "*You shall not make wrong use of the name of the Lord your God; the Lord will not leave unpunished the man who misuses his name. Remember to keep the sabbath day holy. You have six days to labour and do all your work. But the seventh day is a sabbath of the Lord your God; that day you shall not do any work, . . . for in six days the Lord made heaven and earth, the sea, and all that is in them, and on the seventh day he rested. Therefore the*

Money Management Psychology

Lord blessed the sabbath day and declared it holy. Honour your father and your mother, that you may live long in the land which the Lord your God is giving you. You shall not commit murder. You shall not commit adultery. You shall not steal. You shall not give false evidence against your neighbour. You shall not covet your neighbour's house; you shall not covet your neighbour's wife, . . . or anything that belongs to him"—Exodus 20:7–17. Let's look closer at the commandment "*Remember to keep the sabbath day holy. You have six days to labour and do all your work. But the seventh day is a sabbath of the Lord your God; that day you shall not do any work*." The founder of Chick-fil-A restaurants who established the business in 1946—Truett Cathy—made a policy that all Chick-fil-A locations would be closed on Sunday so that their employees would have time to attend church, worship God, spend time with their families, and rest. When one of their restaurant managers was asked if he thought the Sunday closing put them at a competitive disadvantage to restaurants that were open on Sundays, he replied, "I feel that God has blessed this chain because of the policy." A four-store highly successful Brazilian restaurant chain wanted to become Chick-fil-A franchises; however, they knew about the Sunday closing policy and had concerns about losing business. They decided to test one of their stores by closing it on Sundays—Sunday was the store's third best sales day of the week. The January following the store's Sunday closing resulted in net sales that increased by 14%! Chick-fil-A's philosophy is that it will generate more business in six days than others can generate in seven days. Chick-fil-A's corporate purpose is twofold:

1. To glorify God by being good stewards of all that is given to them
2. To have a positive influence on the people whose lives they come in contact with—both their customers and their employees

Money Management Psychology

Chick-fil-A is the nation's 2nd largest quick service chicken restaurant, has more than 1,100 outlets, and did more than $1.5 billion in sales in 2003. Obviously, Mr. Cathy's Sunday closing policy works for Chick-fil-A. What about the millions of Christians who work for other restaurants or businesses that are open on Sunday? The answer to that question depends on whether they are living within the spirit of the law or the letter of the law. The spirit of the commandment—"*that day you shall not do any work*"—is that you put God first in your life, you take the time to worship God, and you allow time for rest from work so that you may be spiritually regenerated. You must have time to reflect, meditate, have conversations with God, and to rest. The teachings of Jesus Christ take us the extra step from living within the letter of the law to living the spirit of the law. For example, "*the president of the synagogue, indignant with Jesus for healing on the Sabbath, intervened and said to the congregation, 'There are six working-days: come and be cured on one of them, and not on the Sabbath.' The Lord gave him his answer: 'What hypocrites you are!' he said. 'Is there a single one of you who does not loose his ox or his donkey from the manger and take it out to water on the Sabbath? And here is this woman, a daughter of Abraham, who has been kept prisoner by Satan for eighteen long years: was it wrong for her to be freed from her bonds on the Sabbath?*'"—Luke 13:14–16. Jesus said, "*It is therefore permitted to do good on the Sabbath*"—Matthew 12:12. Religious law does not work if the spirit of the law is not in your life. God "*also hath made us able ministers of the new testament; not of the letter, but of the spirit: for the letter killeth, but the spirit giveth life*"—II Corinthians 3:6 (King James Version). How then are you to make decisions concerning such matters in your individual life? Talk with

Money Management Psychology

God. Read the Bible. The Bible "speaks" to individuals in different ways. What is right for one individual may be different for another individual. It is up to you as an individual to decide what God is asking you to do. Living within the spirit of the law rather than the letter of the law sets you free to make a life for yourself rather than just a living. As spiritual power and inward Christian faith weakens, there is a natural tendency to place more emphasis on the outward law. When spiritual power is devoid, law will take over. You maintain your spiritual power by keeping the focus that God is first in your life and the center of your being. Obey and submit to God and be dependent on the Holy Spirit rather than just a "book of laws!"

As a footnote to this discussion, when Dan T. Cathy—Mr. Cathy's son and Executive VP and President of Chick-fil-A—was asked what he thinks of Christians that work in restaurants on Sundays, he replied, "We do not take a 'legalistic' approach to that" for if I did, it would be "somewhat hypocritical because I eat out on Sundays!"[1] If you are required to do "good works" on Sunday, make sure it is not at the expense of God, worship, family, and rest—make certain you take the proper time for these crucial elements for a successful life. A day of rest is to get you grounded in God and spiritually rejuvenated.

Part of God's will includes choosing a respectable profession in which to earn your living. "*Those who have come to believe in God should see that they engage in honourable occupations, which are not only honourable in themselves, but also useful*

---

[1] Dan T. Cathy, conversation with author at NFUMC UMM breakfast meeting, Feb. 11, 1996. Hoover's On-Line article by Zack Conzales, October 2004.

Money Management Psychology

to their fellow-men"—Titus 3:8–9.

This same principle applies to your investments—invest in companies whose output is concerned with Christian principles. All decisions within your realm of influence as an individual should be made according to Christian principles. As a Christian, it is important to work hard. "*Whatever you are doing, put your whole heart into it, as if you were doing it for the Lord and not for men, knowing that there is a Master who will give you your heritage as a reward for your service*"—Colossians 3:23–24. In preparation for Super Bowl XXXI, Reggie White, the Green Bay Packers star defensive end was quoted as saying, "I believe Christians should work harder because we represent something so much higher than ourselves. If I'm not working harder than anybody else, I'm making God look pretty bad."[2] "*The man who will not work shall not eat*"—2 Thessalonians 3:10. "*I passed by the field of an idle man, by the vineyard of a man with no sense. I looked, and it was all dried up, it was overgrown with thistles and covered with weeds, and the stones of its walls had been torn down. I saw and I took good note, I considered and learnt the lesson; a little sleep, a little slumber, a little folding of the hands in rest, and poverty will come upon you like a robber, want like a ruffian*"—Proverbs 24:30–34.

---

[2] Dave Kindred, Atlanta Journal-Constitution article, *White prefers talking God, playing football*, Jan. 25, 1997.

Money Management Psychology

Martin Luther made the point that God instituted work so mankind's needs would be met. Martin Luther said, "It is by our work in the secular world that the hungry are fed, the naked clothed, the sick healed, the ignorant enlightened, and the weak protected."[3] Martin Luther believed that through our work, God's people participate in the continuing care of the human race.

Your primary goal at work should be expressing your love for your neighbor by meeting the needs of God's people—money is a secondary side benefit. Money should not be the primary goal at work. The attitude of serving others differentiates Christians from other workers in the secular world who are at a job just for money. When serving others is your primary goal, the quality of your work is better and your dealings with people are fairer. Work is critical to your spiritual life and fundamental to the crafting of your soul. If you do good work, the soul benefits. If you do poor work, the soul suffers. The fabrication of one's soul in preparation for life eternal is the purpose of life on this earth. While it is important to work hard, it is also important to maintain a proper balance between worship, family, work, and play. This balance is crucial in order to be successful. We have the tendency to measure people by what they produce. One of the first questions we normally ask people we've just met is "Where do you work?" At least as important as our work lives is the ability to rest, pace ourselves, find beauty in nature and all of God's creations. This helps to provide a sense of balance in your life and helps to keep you at peace during the day. The next time you meet someone new, try asking them what they enjoy instead of where they work—you might end up defining the person

---

[3] Dick Doster, *Work: It's not just way to a paycheck*, Atlanta Journal-Constitution article, June 8, 2002.

Money Management Psychology

in a whole new light.

We need to be successful. Becoming successful is being the person God wants us to be. Worship and rest are critical to renew yourself spiritually so that you can contribute positively to God's kingdom. "*Whatever you are doing, do all for the honour of God*" —1 Corinthians 10:32. Most important is to seek God first! When Jesus was asked which is the greatest commandment, he answered, "*Love the Lord your God with all your heart, with all your soul, with all your mind. That is the greatest commandment. It comes first. The second is like it: Love your neighbour as yourself*"—Matthew 22:37–40. If you seek God first above all else during the good times in your life, when there is turbulence, God's love acts as the lighthouse beacon that directs you in from the storm. There will be pain, loss, suffering, and failures in your life. You will make mistakes with your finances. Suffering and mistakes can improve us and make us stronger. Suffering produces endurance, and endurance produces character, and character produces hope. "*And hope does not disappoint us, because God's love has been poured into our hearts through the Holy Spirit which has been given to us*"—Romans 5:5 (Revised Standard Version). Errors and suffering make us focus on situations that we would normally choose to avoid and thus can be beneficial in the ultimate building of our souls. If you know that there is meaning in suffering, you can endure anything. You can view mistakes either as a stumbling block or a stepping-stone to eternal life! In the book *Care of the Soul*, Thomas Moore says, "Problems and obstacles offer a chance for reflection that otherwise would be precluded by the swift routine of life." Thomas Moore also states, "The soul is partly in time and partly in eternity. We might remember the part that resides in eternity when we feel despair over the part that is in life." Rabbi Harold S. Kushner made the following

Money Management Psychology

comment concerning prayer and conversations with God: "Don't make my road a smooth road, give me the grace to walk it, no matter how rocky it is." We will never be perfect. Only the Father, the Son, and the Holy Spirit are perfect. "Perfection is more a process of striving than a state to be attained, so one's perfection is measured not by success in attaining a measurable goal but in attitudes constantly changing to ever more perfectly reflect the mind of God"—Joseph F. Girzone (*Joshua*). Rabbi Harold S. Kushner said, "I believe in a God who knows how complicated human life is, how difficult it is to be a good person at all times, and who expects not a perfect life but an honest effort at a good one."[4] We are imperfect people serving a perfect God.

A psychological profile was conducted on centenarians—people who are 100 years old or older. The study found that all centenarians had the ability to cope with loss, to incorporate loss into positive gain or knowledge, they had interest in achieving something, they were flexible, and they all had good humor. There are currently 50,000 Americans who are centenarians. These people have lived through two world wars, not to mention the numerous other conflicts around the globe, the rise and fall of communism, and countless changes in their own personal lives. Flexibility to adapt to change is important in everyone's life. By the year 2050, it is estimated that there will be 1.2 million centenarians in American—0.3% of the total population.[5]

Do not allow fear of failure or the fear of change to cripple you into inaction on your economic pilgrimage. After all, it is the very nature of humanity to improve things. God

---

[4] Harold Kushner, *You Don't Have To Be Perfect To Be Loved*, Parade Magazine article, September 8, 1996.
[5] Michael Gartner, *George Burns is 100? Big Deal!*, USA Today article, Volume 14, No.90.

Money Management Psychology

does not expect us to be perfect. God does expect us to try to live better than we do. When your burden from failures, mistakes, or disappointments becomes too great for you to bear, turn it over to God. No burden is too heavy for God's shoulders.

Jesus Christ is the basis upon which you build your life. Faith in Jesus Christ is a personal relationship with the Holy Trinity. When we have this relationship with the Holy Trinity, how are we to know what God wants us to do with our finances? Read the Bible. Obey God's commandments. "*It is not by hearing the law, but by doing it, that men will be justified before God*"—Romans 2:13. Pray for God's guidance when making your personal financial decisions. "*I tell you, then, whatever you ask for in prayer, believe that you have received it and it will be yours. And when you stand praying, if you have a grievance against anyone, forgive him, so that your Father in heaven may forgive you the wrongs you have done*"—Mark 11:24–25. "*In very truth I* [Jesus] *tell you, if you ask the Father for anything in my name, he will give it you*"—John 16:23. "*Be always joyful; pray continually; give thanks whatever happens; for this is what God in Christ wills for you*"—1 Thessalonians 5:16–18. Use God's commandments as the basis for your financial decisions. God's commandments have not changed since they were written. God's commandments will never change! The modern day financial strategies you read about in this manual may be subject to varying interpretations and applications depending on your own financial situation. This may require different personal decisions for different people; however, God's laws do not change. You should use the biblical verses quoted in this manual as the rock upon which to build your financial house. God said to Joshua, "*Be strong and resolute; observe diligently all the law which my servant Moses has given you. You must not turn from it to right or left, if you would prosper wherever*

Money Management Psychology

you go. This book of the law must ever be on your lips; you must keep it in mind day and night so that you may diligently observe all that is written in it. Then you will prosper and be successful in all that you do. This is my command: be strong, be resolute; do not be fearful or dismayed, for the Lord your God is with you wherever you go"—Joshua 1:7–9. "*What then of the man who hears these words of mine* [Jesus'] *and acts upon them? He is like a man who had the sense to build his house on rock. The rain came down, the floods rose, the wind blew, and beat upon that house; but it did not fall, because its foundations were on rock*"—Matthew 7:24–25. God's commandments are not intended to be a set of rigid laws that unreasonably restrict your freedom. They are guidelines for living your life—not constricting you—so that you may be free to grow and discover contentment. Laws cannot dictate contentment, nor legislate behavior. "All that God wants is that we love him and love one another and in doing that, find happiness"—Joseph F. Girzone (*Joshua*).

"*God will supply all your wants out of the magnificence of his riches in Christ Jesus*"—Philippians 4:19. Jesus said to his disciples, "*I bid you put away anxious thoughts about food to keep you alive and clothes to cover your body. Life is more than food, the body more than clothes. Think of the ravens: they neither sow nor reap; they have no storehouse or barn; yet God feeds them. You are worth far more than the birds! Is there a man among you who by anxious thought can add a foot to his height?*"—Luke 12:22–25. "*Set your mind upon his kingdom, and all the rest will come to you as well*"—Luke 12:31. God works many of his miracles through people. The essence of prayer is talking and listening to God in His presence. Through prayer, God can give you strength beyond your own. Prayer is not asking God to give something material to you. Prayer can

Money Management Psychology

help you know the hope of God for your calling. Prayer is asking God to empower you to use the abilities within yourself to accomplish the task before you so that you may be responsible for yourself. When you pray, pray as though 98% of the outcome depends on God. When you act, act as though 98% of the outcome depends on you.

> I am one,
> I am only one,
> I cannot do everything;
> but, I can do something.
> With God's help, I will do what I can do—Author Unknown.

Take to heart the words of Mother Teresa when she said:

> The fruit of SILENCE is Prayer
> The fruit of PRAYER is Faith
> The fruit of FAITH is Love
> The fruit of LOVE is Service
> The fruit of SERVICE is Peace.[6]

Information means nothing unless it provides you with an idea upon which you can act and have a positive impact on God's kingdom.

---

[6] Mother Teresa, included in letter to author, 1996.

Tithing/Giving

Chapter 3

Tithing/Giving

There are approximately 2,350 verses in the Bible that concern money and possessions. Around three-fourths of the parables from Jesus deal with money. Money is a common thread that permeates through different societies, different cultures, and different ages. Money is neither good nor evil. It is what we do with money that is important. Money can be fleeting—the whole tendency of our material possessions is to shackle us to this earth. Upon death, all material possessions will be left behind. God's unconditional love is the only secure promise in our lives.

God is the owner of all things, including your money. "*The earth is the LORD's and all that is in it, the world and those who dwell therein*"—Psalms 24:1. King David said, "*Thine, O LORD, is the greatness, the power, the glory, the splendour, and the majesty; for everything in heaven and on earth is thine; thine, O LORD, is the sovereignty, and thou art exalted over all as head. Wealth and honour come from thee; thou rulest over all*"—1 Chronicles 11–12. We are stewards who manage the resources entrusted to us by God. A steward has responsibility to the owner to manage those resources to the best of his or her ability. God wants us to prosper, to be successful, and to have rewards. The tithe belongs to God; it is our spontaneous response to the majesty of God. Jacob said, "*And of all that thou [God] givest me, I will without fail allot a tenth part to thee*"— Genesis 28:22. "*All good giving, every perfect gift, comes from above, from the Father of the lights of heaven*"—James 1:17. We should give cheerfully. The philanthropist Michael C. Carlos once said, "In this great country of ours, I do not consider it an obligation to give. I consider it a privilege."[1] When you give, give freely and

---

[1] Michael C. Carlos, *A Private Philanthropist,* Atlanta Journal-Constitution newspaper article.

Tithing/Giving

unconditionally. "*When you do some act of charity, do not announce it with a flourish of trumpets, . . . your good deed must be secret, and your Father who sees what is done in secret will reward you*"—Matthew 6:2–4. God gives his free gift of Grace unconditionally out of his love for you. You should give your tithe unconditionally out of your love for God. In sharing with others, we find fulfillment for ourselves and reason for being. When we give to a worthy cause, we make the world a better place. We can give without loving; but we cannot love without giving. Generosity is using material wealth for eternal spiritual growth.

"*You shall bring the choicest firstfruits of your soil to the house of the LORD your God*"—Exodus 34:26. Return to God what belongs to him first. Then, you can move on to the handling of the remainder of the finances. God has a promise for us: "*Bring ye all the tithes into the storehouse, that there may be meat in mine house, and prove me now herewith, saith the LORD of hosts, if I will not open you the windows of heaven, and pour you out a blessing, that there shall not be room enough to receive it*"—Malachi 3:10 (King James Version). Obedience out of love has a reward from the Master. God's resources are limitless. God wants to share those resources with you. "*Give, and gifts will be given you*"—Luke 6:38. The tithe does not just involve money. It also involves witness and service. God wants us to share our time, talent, and money. God can take a seemingly small contribution from man and compound it into huge benefits for mankind. John 6:1–13 tells the story about Jesus and his disciples on the shore of the Sea of Galilee. About 5,000 men were there to listen to Jesus. Everyone needed to be fed. A boy provided five barley loaves and two fishes. Jesus magnified the boy's seemingly small contribution and fed them all. Everyone ate as much as they wanted and afterward they filled twelve baskets with the uneaten barley loaves. The Lord has need of your tithe. God can multiply it infinitely. No matter how small your contribution, it can make all the

Tithing/Giving

difference in God's hands. Never underestimate the worth of your time, talent, and money to the Kingdom of God. God is powerful, and God can work miracles through you. "*Now he who provides seed for sowing and bread for food will provide the seed for you to sow; he will multiply it and swell the harvest of your benevolence, and you will always be rich enough to be generous*"—2 Corinthians 9:10–11. "*Sow bountifully, and you will reap bountifully*"—2 Corinthians 9:6. Jesus was quoted in Acts 20:35 as saying, "*Happiness lies more in giving than in receiving.*"

Is it realistic to think that poverty can be eliminated? Jesus said, "*You have the poor among you always*"—John 12:8. God does not expect you to give everything to the poor; God does expect you to do what you can. The Apostle Paul said, "*Give according to your means. Provided there is an eager desire to give, God accepts what a man has; he does not ask for what he has not. There is no question of relieving others at the cost of hardship to yourselves; it is a question of equality*"—2 Corinthians 8:12–14. Paul also said, "*Each person should give as he has decided for himself; there should be no reluctance, no sense of compulsion; God loves a cheerful giver*"—2 Corinthians 9:7. "*Faith; if it does not lead to action, it is in itself a lifeless thing*"—James 2:17. Faith in God should result in the sharing of your time, talents, and money. Giving is a means of sharing love. As God provides for us, we need to help those who are less fortunate. There is a God given urge within us to give. "*God so loved the world that he **gave** his only Son*"—John 3:16 (emphasis mine). It is not a gift unless it cost us something. When we give, we become more like God.

The average American household contributions, excluding households that made no donations, were as follows:

Tithing/Giving

Year	Amount of Contributions[1]	% of Household Income[1]	% of U.S. Households[1]
1987	$790	1.9%	71.1%
1989	$978	2.5%[1,2]	75.1%
1991	$899	2.2%[1,2]	72.2%
1993	$880	2.1%[1,2]	73.4%
1995	$1,017	2.2%	68.5%
1998	$1,075	2.1%	70.1%
2000	$1,620	3.2%	89%

Some other Independent Sector findings:
1. 69% of U.S. households contributed to charity; 27% of those contributing claimed a tax deduction.
2. Most volunteer time is concentrated in religious, educational, and youth development.
3. When the under-asked populations are contacted by charities, 85% respond; when not asked, only 44% give.

Some other findings from the Gallup Organization surveys:
1. In 1991, 51% of Americans did some volunteer work with an average of 4.2 hours per week.
2. Households with incomes less than $10,000 gave 4.3% of their income to charity in 1996; households with incomes between $40,000 and $50,000 gave 1.3%; households with incomes over $100,000 gave 3.4%—the lowest income group gave the highest percent of income (proof that giving is a matter of commitment versus a matter of surplus).

Also, according to the Gallup Organization findings, the following breakdown is where the contributions went to in 1989:

---

[1] Figures from Independent Sector, a nonprofit group conducting biennial surveys of giving (1997 information is not available).
[2] Gallup Organization survey results—error rate + or -3%.

Tithing/Giving

Areas That Receive Contributions

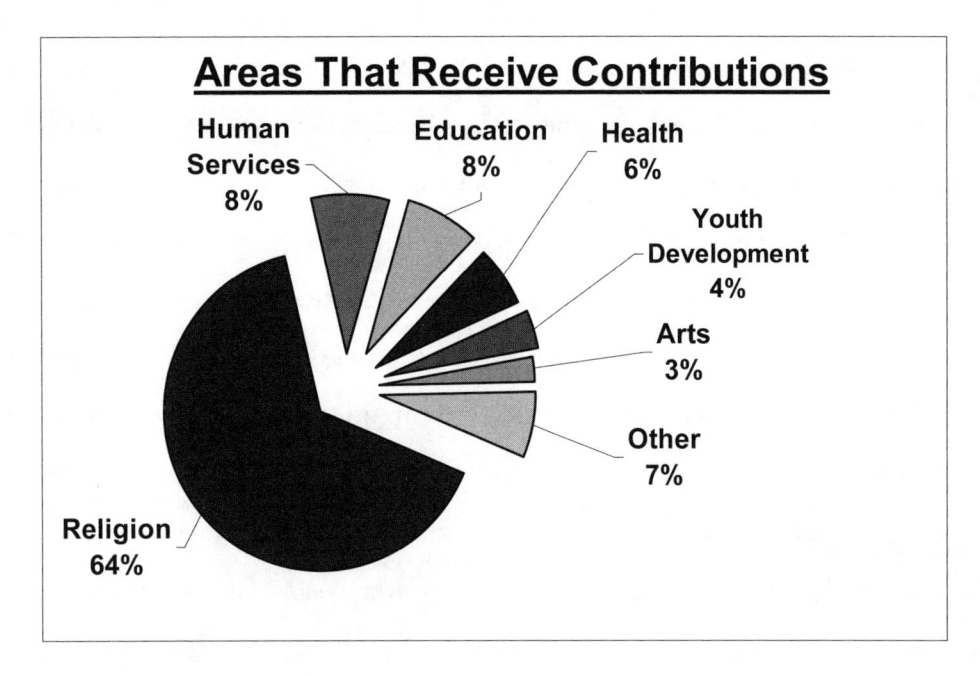

- Human Services 8%
- Education 8%
- Health 6%
- Youth Development 4%
- Arts 3%
- Other 7%
- Religion 64%

A good place to give is to your own church and other nonprofit, tax-deductible charitable organizations.

The aforementioned percentages indicate that the average household is well below the actual tithe percentage of 10% or more. A modern day strategy that can help increase contributions is called "the blessing of percentage giving." In percentage giving, you commit to put the Lord first in your life and first in your finances. You calculate what percentage of your income you gave to the Lord during the prior year—for example,1%, 2%, 3%, 5%, or more. Pray to God to seek guidance in what percentage the Lord would have you give in the coming year. Gradually, you strive to increase your prior year's giving a percent or two until you reach the tithe of 10% or more. Investing in the Lord is the most important investment you will ever make!

When you give, give unconditionally without expectations of receiving something in return. That does not mean that you should give unwisely. You should expect the receiving organization to accomplish as much good with your contributions as possible. That necessitates some preliminary investigation before making your contributions.

Tithing/Giving

The Internal Revenue Service recognizes more than 20 kinds of organizations that are not required to pay federal income taxes. Both tax-exempt and tax-deductible organizations are nonprofit. Donations to them are not necessarily tax deductible. Tax-exempt organizations might include chambers of commerce, labor unions, social clubs, sports clubs, and so on. These organizations are tax-exempt but not tax-deductible organizations. Unless an organization is a tax-deductible organization, you generally cannot deduct any of your contributions to them from your taxes. Tax-deductible organizations are also tax-exempt. There are more than 600,000 tax-deductible organizations—referred to as 501 (c) 3 organizations—nationwide. There are an additional 30,000 new tax-deductible organizations every year. Many tax deductible 501 (c) 3 organizations promote religious, scientific, or literary education activities; or fighting disease, hunger, cruelty to children or animals; or providing housing for the homeless. To be a charity, the organization must meet the Internal Revenue Service guidelines for a tax-deductible 501 (c) 3 organization, not just a tax-exempt status. Only then is your donation considered tax deductible. Charitable deductions can only be claimed by itemizing them on your tax return. You need written acknowledgement from any single charity for a donation of more than $250—cancelled checks are not sufficient to substantiate large contributions. It is the responsibility of donors by the time they file their taxes to obtain a written statement from the charity detailing their contributions unless the charity reports the information directly to the Internal Revenue Service. If your gift involves the donation of real estate or other property, you may have to get a formal appraisal for tax purposes.

You can only deduct charitable donations that have been made by December 31 of the deduction year. When calculating your charitable deduction, you must deduct the value of any benefit you might have received from the charity. For example, if you attend a

Tithing/Giving

fundraising dinner for a charity and you donate $200 and receive a meal valued at $50, the deductible portion of your donation would amount to $150. Charity donations can usually only be claimed when you purchase something if the donation amount exceeds the fair market value of the item purchased. For example, if you give an organization $25 for a box of candy that normally sells for $15, you are only entitled to a $10 tax-deductible donation. The Internal Revenue Service normally only considers the portion above the fair market value of the item to be tax deductible. Your time and labor are not deductible when helping a charitable organization; however, you should keep records of any out-of-pocket expenses such as transportation, parking, and phone bills that do qualify as charitable deductions. If you donate used items to a charity, you will be entitled to the fair market value of the goods, which is usually what they would sell for in thrift shops.

Giving <u>appreciated</u> assets such as stocks or mutual funds is a great way to get a bigger tax break than giving cash. In addition to getting a deduction for your charitable contribution, you avoid the capital gains tax on the appreciation. A gift of stock can be a more cost-effective way to make a charitable contribution than giving cash. For example, assume you donate stock worth $1,000 that you held for more than 1 year that originally cost you $200. The stock appreciated $800. Also, assume that you are in the 28% tax bracket and 15% capital gains tax bracket. The following is the effect of making a cash contribution versus making a stock donation:

Tithing/Giving

	Cash Gift	**Stock Gift**
Value of the Gift to the Charity	$1,000	$1,000
Income Tax Savings to the Donor	$280	$280
Capital Gains Tax Savings to the Donor	$0	$150
Total Tax Savings to the Donor	$280	$430
Cost of Gift to the Donor	$720	$570

By giving stock instead of cash, the donor saves $150 on the cost of the gift ($720 - $570 = $150); the donor avoids the tax on the gain he would have incurred had the donor sold the stock outright. If your brokerage holds the securities, instruct your brokerage to electronically transfer the securities to your charity. You may need to contact the charity to get their broker information, routing number, account number, and taxpayer identification in order to complete the wire transfer. Be sure you have held the appreciated assets for more than 1 year; otherwise, your gift will be limited to what you originally paid for the assets instead of the appreciated value. If the assets have lost value, it is better from a tax standpoint to sell the assets, claim the loss on your taxes, and then give a tax-deductible cash contribution to your charity.

For assistance in determining the benefits of making noncash versus cash donations, please complete the following steps:

1. Open the "SS10 Calculator-Noncash Charitable Contribution.xls" (Spreadsheet 10 Calculator).
2. Click "Yes" to enable macros, if necessary.
3. Fill in the required information in each white cell (you may tab from one white cell to another).
4. After completing the information in all of the white cells, press "Tab," then click on the "MMW Recalculation Button"—the spreadsheet will make the remaining calculations for you. You may also update calculations by pressing the "Ctrl + m" keys on your keyboard (the "m" stands for "Making Money Work") anywhere in the worksheet. Make a mental note of the "Ctrl + m" shortcut—it can be used with all the worksheets throughout this instructional tool. The "Ctrl + m" shortcut is extremely useful when working with larger worksheets.
5. After completing the form and making your contribution, save a copy of the form—it will assist you when completing your tax forms.

Tithing/Giving

Figure 3.1 Calculator to Determine Your Noncash Versus Cash Giving Benefits
Fill in the white cells (tab from cell to cell).

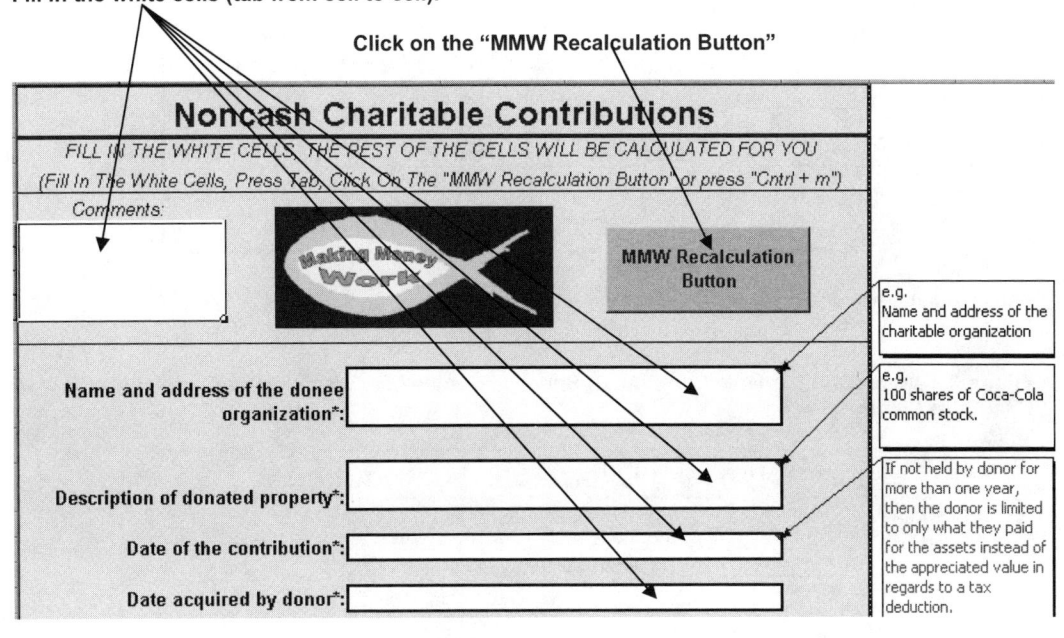

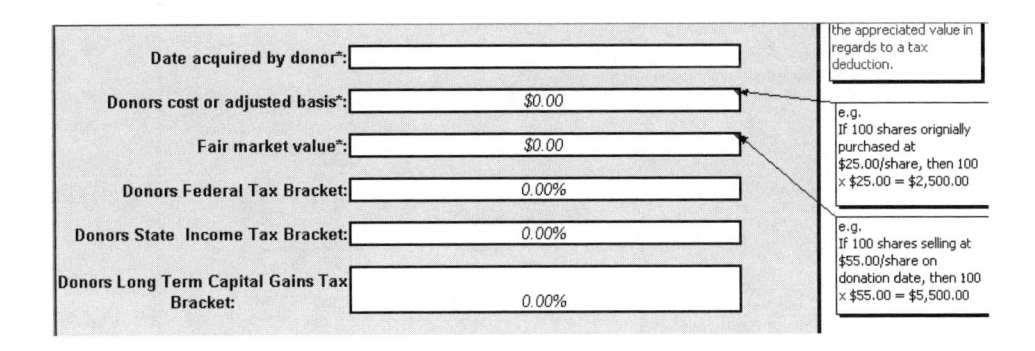

Click on the "MMW Recalculation Button"

Noncash Charitable Contributions

FILL IN THE WHITE CELLS. THE REST OF THE CELLS WILL BE CALCULATED FOR YOU
(Fill In The White Cells, Press Tab, Click On The "MMW Recalculation Button" or press "Cntrl + m")

Comments:

MMW Recalculation Button

e.g. Name and address of the charitable organization

Name and address of the donee organization*:

e.g. 100 shares of Coca-Cola common stock.

Description of donated property*:

Date of the contribution*:

Date acquired by donor*:

If not held by donor for more than one year, then the donor is limited to only what they paid for the assets instead of the appreciated value in regards to a tax deduction.

- - -

Date acquired by donor*:

Donors cost or adjusted basis*: $0.00

Fair market value*: $0.00

Donors Federal Tax Bracket: 0.00%

Donors State Income Tax Bracket: 0.00%

Donors Long Term Capital Gains Tax Bracket: 0.00%

the appreciated value in regards to a tax deduction.

e.g. If 100 shares originally purchased at $25.00/share, then 100 x $25.00 = $2,500.00

e.g. If 100 shares selling at $55.00/share on donation date, then 100 x $55.00 = $5,500.00

- - -

35

Tithing/Giving

	Sell Asset & Gift Net Proceeds	Compared To	Noncash Gift Of Asset Directly To The Charity
Original Value Of The Asset:	$0.00		$0.00
Income Tax Savings To The Donor (Federal & State):	$0.00		$0.00
Capital Gains Tax Savings:	$0.00		$0.00
Total Tax Savings:	$0.00		$0.00
Cost Of The Gift To The Donor:	$0.00		$0.00
Net Proceeds To The Charity:	$0.00		$0.00

(After Completing This Form, Save A Copy To Assist You When Completing Your Taxes; * Above Indicates Information Needed For Tax Preparation)

The calculator will complete these cells for you.

Figure 3.2 "Noncash Charitable Contribu (2) Sheet": Hypothetical Example of a Completed Noncash Charitable Contribution Form

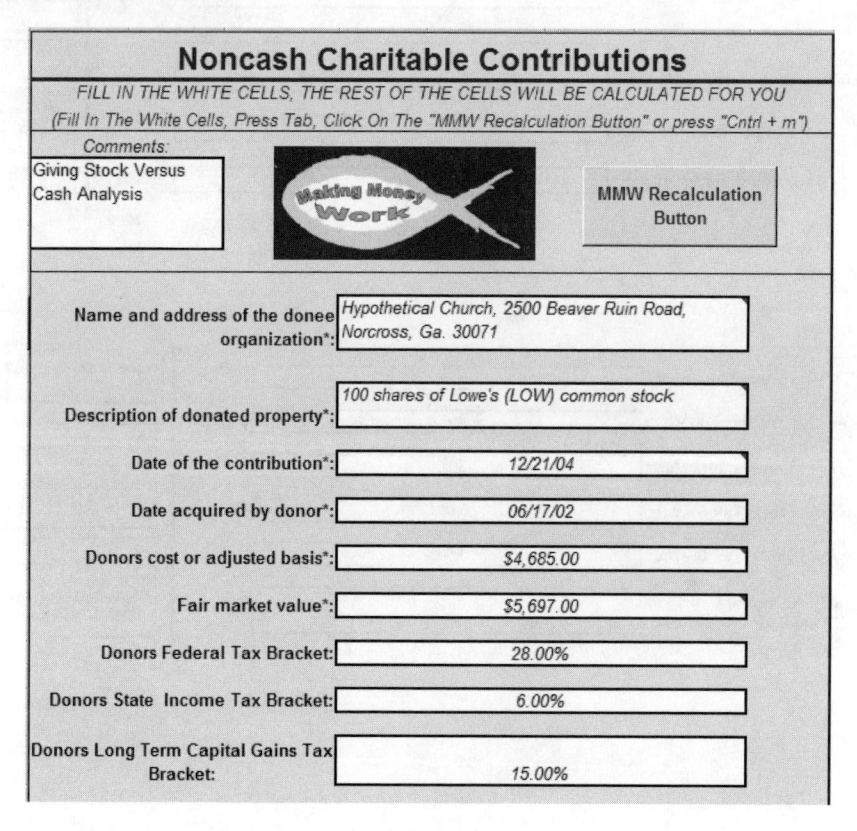

Noncash Charitable Contributions

FILL IN THE WHITE CELLS, THE REST OF THE CELLS WILL BE CALCULATED FOR YOU
(Fill In The White Cells, Press Tab, Click On The "MMW Recalculation Button" or press "Cntrl + m")

Comments: Giving Stock Versus Cash Analysis

MMW Recalculation Button

Name and address of the donee organization*:	Hypothetical Church, 2500 Beaver Ruin Road, Norcross, Ga. 30071
Description of donated property*:	100 shares of Lowe's (LOW) common stock
Date of the contribution*:	12/21/04
Date acquired by donor*:	06/17/02
Donors cost or adjusted basis*:	$4,685.00
Fair market value*:	$5,697.00
Donors Federal Tax Bracket:	28.00%
Donors State Income Tax Bracket:	6.00%
Donors Long Term Capital Gains Tax Bracket:	15.00%

Tithing/Giving

- - -

	Sell Asset & Gift Net Proceeds	Compared To	Noncash Gift Of Asset Directly To The Charity
Original Value Of The Asset:	$5,697.00		$5,697.00
Income Tax Savings To The Donor (Federal & State):	$1,936.98		$1,936.98
Capital Gains Tax Savings:	$0.00		$151.80
Total Tax Savings To The Donor:	$1,936.98		$2,088.78
Cost Of The Gift To The Donor:	$3,760.02		$3,608.22
Net Proceeds To The Charity:	$3,760.02		$5,697.00

(After Completing This Form, Save A Copy To Assist You When Preparing Your Taxes; * Above Indicates Information Needed For Tax Preparation)

The cost to the donor is less when giving the stock directly to the church.

The church receives more of the net proceeds when you give the stock directly to it.

Gifts of appreciated assets are not subject to capital gains taxes. The income tax itemizing donor receives an income tax charitable deduction for the full market value of the asset. Before making noncash gifts directly to your charity, consult your CPA, tax attorney, or other financial advisor regarding important tax implications for your situation.

Consider including God in your estate planning. It could be as simple as a provision in your will that 10% of the value of your estate be donated to the church holding your membership at the time of your death, or even 10% of your liquid assets.

Numerous agencies track charities to evaluate them on program spending as a percentage of income. These agencies can provide you with valuable information to help you make sure your donations go to honest charities that are efficient in getting help to the needy as opposed to spending excessive amounts of your contributions on executive salaries and administration. Experts consider the percentage of a charities' income that goes toward good works as the best indication of how efficiently the charity manages its resources. The National Charities Information Bureau has established standards calling for a minimum of 60 cents out of each dollar that a charity should be utilizing for true charity purposes. *Money* magazine ranked the largest 25 charities by the average

Tithing/Giving

percentage of their income spent on programs from 1993 to 1996:[2]

Number	Charity	Program Spending as % of Income	Number	Charity	Program Spending as % of Income
1.	American Red Cross	91.5%	14.	World Vision	78.5%
2.	Catholic Charities USA	87.7%	15.	March of Dimes	77.2%
3.	Salvation Army	85.8%	16.	Girl Scouts of the USA	76.8%
4.	Campus Crusade for Christ Intl.	83.9%	17.	Metropolitan Museum of Art	76.8%
5.	YWCA of the USA[3]	83.8%	18.	American Heart Association	76.6%
6.	Goodwill Industries International	83.4%	19.	American Lung Association	76.6%
7.	Nature Conservancy[4]	83.0%	20.	Boy Scouts of America	76.5%
8.	Planned Parenthood Fed. of America	80.5%	21.	Muscular Dystrophy Association	76.5%
9.	Habitat for Humanity International	80.4%	22.	American Cancer Society	70.2%
10.	Christian Children's Fund	80.3%	23.	Disabled American Veterans	58.5%
11.	National Easter Seal Society	79.8%	24.	ALSAC-St. Jude Children's Hospital	54.9%
12.	Boys and Girls Clubs of America	79.7%	25.	Shriners Hospitals	36.6%
13.	Focus on the Family	78.6%			

As you can see, program spending as a percentage of income among the top 25 recipients of donations ranged from 36.6% to 91.5%. The average of the 100 biggest groups was 78.4%. You may request that a charity send you their three most recent federal tax returns (Form 990) and/or their most recent annual report at no charge other than postage and copy cost in order to review their financial statements.

---

[2] Ellen Stark, Money Magazine, *Red Cross ranked most efficient of major charities*, Atlanta Journal-Constitution article, November 4, 1996.
[3] The data on YWCA was for the year 1995 only.
[4] Nature Conservancy program figures include land purchases.

Tithing/Giving

Reputable charities with nothing to hide are glad to provide you with written information on the charity's programs, goals, and finances. You may also want to check to see if your charity meets the standards of the leading agencies that keep track of national charitable organizations:

Name & Address	Phone Number	Website/Email
BBB Wise Giving Alliance 4200 Wilson Boulevard, Suite 800 Arlington, VA 22203-1838	703-276-0100	www.give.org give@cbbb.bbb.org
The American Institute of Philanthropy (AIP) 3450 Lake Shore Drive, Suite 2802 Chicago, IL 60655	773-305-0414	www.charitywatch.org aip@charitywatch.org
Also, for a religious charity, you can check with:		
The Evangelical Council for Financial Accountability Box 17456 Washington, DC 20041	800-323-9473	www.ecfa.org info@ecfa.org

The BBB Wise Giving Alliance gives useful charity organization reports from the National Charities Information Bureau and the Council of Better Business Bureaus' Foundation and its Philanthropic Advisory Service. The National Charities Information Bureau is a nonprofit organization that develops standards for charitable organizations, produces reports on national charities based on the standards, and informs the public regarding methods of assessing the performance of all charitable organizations. The American Institute of Philanthropy grades charities with letter grades such as "A," "B," "C," "D," and "F." The Evangelical Council for Financial Accountability believes that the general and administrative overhead percentage can be <u>a</u> measure but should not be <u>the</u> measure or "primary barometer to gauge the efficiency or effectiveness of a ministry." "Rather each organization is encouraged to define the accomplishment of its

Tithing/Giving

mission through accountable reports." Some organizations by necessity may have more overhead and administrative costs than others. A combination of reviewing the program spending as a percentage of income, the financial statements, and a review of the organization's mission accomplishments should give the donor a better gauge on a charitable organization's effectiveness. You may also check with your local Better Business Bureau and the Secretary of State's office; however, a charity's registration with the state does not guarantee it is legitimate. If the charity is not registered with the state, then there is a good probability it is not legitimate.

The following are some wise giving suggestions. Do not give cash. Make your check or money order out to the charity, not to the individual collecting donations. Only give out your credit card number or bank account number to charities you are certain are legitimate. Never give out personal information to unknown telephone or Internet solicitors or other strangers. Get a receipt to document your giving when preparing your taxes. Always get written materials from unfamiliar charities and research their legitimacy before donating. The Internal Revenue Service can disallow tax deductions made to fraudulent organizations for up to 2 years after you make the donation. It is important to do your homework up front or your donation could cost you more money later on. If you are solicited by phone by an unfamiliar charity, ask them to mail you their literature. If solicited on the street, ask for a brochure about the charitable organization. Gather the information from all solicitations, research the charities, and then decide which ones you choose to give donations. If solicited to buy products to help a good cause, ask what portion of the proceeds is actually donated to the charity. Sometimes the percentage can be quite small. If a solicitor is asking you to buy a candy bar for $5.00 and

Tithing/Giving

only $0.50 goes to the charity, your dollars will be better spent making a direct contribution to the charity yourself instead of possibly getting a product you do not want. If you receive a telephone solicitation, ask the telemarketer if he or she is a volunteer, a paid employee, or a professional fundraiser. If he or she is a professional fundraiser, definitely ask what portion of the donations actually goes to the charity—in many cases the percentage can be very small. Also ask if the Internal Revenue Service recognizes the donation as tax deductible. If not, your contributions are likely to be used more effectively elsewhere. Direct contributions to the charitable organization as opposed to the fundraisers might be a wiser use of your contributions. If you receive unordered items such as cards, stamps, address labels, or pens enclosed with a charitable appeal, you are under no obligation to pay for the items nor are you under any obligation to return the items.

If possible, volunteer to do some work for the organization before making a contribution so you can see if the organization is achieving its established goals and purposes.

If telemarketers or other solicitors use pressure tactics such as intimidation, threats, or repeated harassing calls, report them to your Better Business Bureau or report them to your state's attorney general. If you suspect an organization or offer to be fraudulent you might contact the following:

1. Government Guide: Consumer Protection Agencies, www.governmentguide.com (click on "Consumer Services," and then click on "Consumer Protection").
Provides information on federal, state, and local agencies involved in consumer protection and industry regulations.
2. National Fraud Information Center, 1-800-876-7060, www.fraud.org.
Provides information concerning misleading offers nationwide and what to do about them.

Tithing/Giving

3. Your Better Business Bureau, www.bbb.org.
4. The National Charities Information Bureau, 212-929-6300, www.give.org. Provides information on national charities.
5. The U.S. Postal Inspection Service, www.usps.gov/websites/depart/inspect/welcome.htm. Fights mail fraud.

God can accomplish great works through your generous support of charities that meet essential standards and are worthy of your contributions. You too will be blessed through the giving of your time, talent, and money. At sixteen years of age, William Colgate left home with all of his earthly possessions in a bundle he could carry in his hand. He told an old canal-boat captain that his father was too poor to support him. He also said he knew how to make soap and candles. The captain knelt and prayed for William and told him, "Someone will soon be the leading soap maker in New York. It can be you as well as someone else. Be a good man, give your heart to Christ, pay the Lord all that belongs to Him, make an honest soap; give a full pound, and I'm certain you'll be a prosperous and rich man." William arrived in New York City, he joined a church, and he gave one-tenth of his first dollar just as the captain had urged him to do. William gained employment, became a partner, and later became sole owner of the business. William increased his giving from 10 percent to 50 percent and eventually to 100 percent of his income. William Colgate gave millions of dollars away to charitable organizations. Today, Colgate-Palmolive does over $9 billion per year in sales.[5]

In January 1990, Brad Smith, a seminary intern at Spring Valley Presbyterian Church in Columbia, S.C., prayed, "Even as we enjoy the Super Bowl, we should be mindful of

---

[5] Southern Sensation, Colgate Southern Region Weekly Newsletter, Vol. 6, Issue #10, March 11, 1999.

Tithing/Giving

those who are without even a bowl of soup."[6] The prayer was inspiration for young people in the church to organize the "Souper Bowl." They asked each person in church who was planning to watch the Super Bowl football game to donate $1.00. The young people collected the donations in soup pots and then gave the donations to local ministries to help feed the hungry. The first year in Columbia, S.C., churches collected $5,700. By 1997, Souper Bowl had expanded to 50 states and Canada, 5,400 churches and other organizations, and raised $1.1 million. The Souper Bowl developed into a national organization with a board of directors and has raised more than $20 million for soup kitchens, food banks, and other charities. You can find more information about the Souper Bowl at www.souperbowl.org or by calling 1-800-358-7687.

When you give, you are the primary beneficiary because it is a reflection of what is in your heart. To paraphrase a thought from Winston Churchill, we make a living by what we gain; however, we make a life by what we give. Work to gain what you can, save as much as you can, and give all you can.

Making Money Work is not a nonprofit endeavor; however, at least 10% of any proceeds from this work will be donated to tax-exempt, tax-deductible, charitable organizations.

---

[6] Gayle White, *Pastor's prayer inspires donations on Super Sunday,* Atlanta Journal-Constitution, January 18, 1998.

Chapter 4

Debt Management

"Discharge your obligations to all men; pay tax and toll, reverence and respect, to those to whom they are due. Leave no claim outstanding against you, except that of mutual love"—Romans 13:7–8.

There can be *good* debt as well as *bad* debt. *Good* debt can be described as debt that helps you build equity or increase your net worth. For example, education loans usually are considered *good* debt because in the long run more education generally translates into higher earning power. Most people borrow money for a mortgage to get a home—if the home purchase was a wise investment that increases in value and adds to your net worth, then it would be considered *good* debt. Another example of *good* debt might be loans to run a small business—for example, if you borrow money at 7% and use that money to make a 15% or 20% return, then it would be considered *good* debt because you are using the loan to increase your net worth. *Good* debt includes loans that help to build your financial future.

On the other hand, *bad* debts are the ones that negatively impact your financial future. *Bad* debt might be described as obligations that last longer than the purchase item and ones that have no return toward increasing your net worth. Before making a purchase via a loan, ask yourself is this *good* debt or *bad* debt—will the debt help to increase my net worth or will it decrease my net worth? Avoid as much *bad* debt as possible. The Financial Planning Association suggests that total debt should not exceed 10–15% of your take-home pay—excluding mortgages. Many credit experts recommend that debt

Debt Management

should not exceed 25 percent of disposable income. Overindebtedness can push you to the maximum to repay your debt while still trying to maintain daily living expenses. A sudden unexpected event such as a job downsizing, divorce, a death in the family, an uninsured accident, theft, a large tax bill, or a major medical expense can have tragic results to your finances and result in a credit crisis. A major unexpected event combined with insufficient savings and insurance can easily result in a credit crisis. Assuming credit loans is something you want to avoid if at all possible. Few things are worth borrowing for. Avoid going into debt for rewards such as vacations or fancy restaurant meals; save for them and pay cash. Borrow as little money as possible and at the lowest interest rate possible.

Most debt can be avoided if you take action to live within your income. Consumer Credit Counseling Services stated that the number one cause of money problems with their nationwide clients was poor money management including impulsive spending. Practice *delayed gratification*—earn the money before you spend it. Save for purchases if at all possible until you can pay cash or use debit cards for them. When you borrow money, you pay interest plus the principal borrowed, so items purchased end up costing you much more than the original price. Practicing *delayed gratification* until you can pay cash saves you the added cost of the item and has less negative impact on your future net worth. Studies indicate that consumers generally spend about 25 percent less when they pay cash for items. This is due to the savings on interest charges and the fact that you waste less money on impulse purchases due to the temptation and convenience of credit cards. Many impulse purchases are for items you do not even need.

Debt Management

Forty percent of people pay off credit card purchases in full every month—the other 60 percent would benefit from making changes in their spending habits. If you purchase only what you can pay cash for, chances are you are in control of your financial life. You may be overextended if you cannot pay all of your debt—excluding mortgage—in 18 to 24 months. If you pay only the minimum amount due on your outstanding credit cards month after month, you might stay in debt indefinitely since most of the payment goes toward interest. You definitely have a credit problem if you cannot pay all of your monthly minimums. You should eliminate nonproductive, expensive debts as soon as possible.

Think of the money you earn in terms of $100.00 increments such as the following:

Income earned	**$100.00**
Order of expenditures:	
1. Tithe (example 10% to God)	$10.00
2. Savings (example: 10% to your 401K)	$10.00
3. Federal taxes (example: 28% Federal taxes)	$28.00
4. State Taxes (example: 6% to your state's tax program)	$6.00
5. FICA Taxes (example: 6.2% Social Security + 1.45% Medicare Insurance; or self-employed 12.4% Social Security + 2.9% Medicare = 15.3%)	$15.30
Total of above expenditures:	$69.30
5. Balance to spend on other items	$30.70

If you are spending $30.70 or less on the remaining portion of the $100.00 earned then you are living within your means and may or may not choose to complete a budget. Some people may choose to complete a budget so that they become even more efficient in

Debt Management

handling their personal finances. If you are spending $30.70 or more, then you will likely need to complete a budget to control your deficit spending habits.

If you are not currently living within your income, you need to change your old spending habits first. Any other debt management measures will be temporary aids at best without correcting the underlying problems in poor spending habits. Your entire family should develop the discipline to live within your means in order to prevent unmanageable debt.

One quick way to determine if you are overextended is to compare your liquid assets—available cash reserves—to your current liabilities—your near-term debts.

For assistance in determining your liquid assets versus your current liabilities ratio, please complete the following steps:

1. Open the "SS12 Calculator-Liquid Assets Versus Current Liabilities.xls" (Spreadsheet 12 Calculator). See Figures 4.1 and 4.2.
2. Click "Yes" to enable macros, if necessary.
3. Fill in the required information in each white cell (you may tab from one white cell to another).
4. After completing the information in all of the white cells, press "Tab," and then click on the "MMW Recalculation Button"—the spreadsheet will make the remaining calculations for you.

Debt Management

Figure 4.1 Calculator to Determine Your Liquid Assets Versus Your Current Liabilities
Fill in the white cells (tab from cell to cell).
Click on the "MMW Recalculation Button"

Liquid Assets Versus Current Liabilities Calculator

FILL IN THE WHITE CELLS, THE REST OF THE CELLS WILL BE CALCULATED FOR YOU
(Fill In The White Cells, Press Tab, Click On The "MMW Recalculation Button" or press "Cntrl + m")

Comments:

[MMW Recalculation Button]

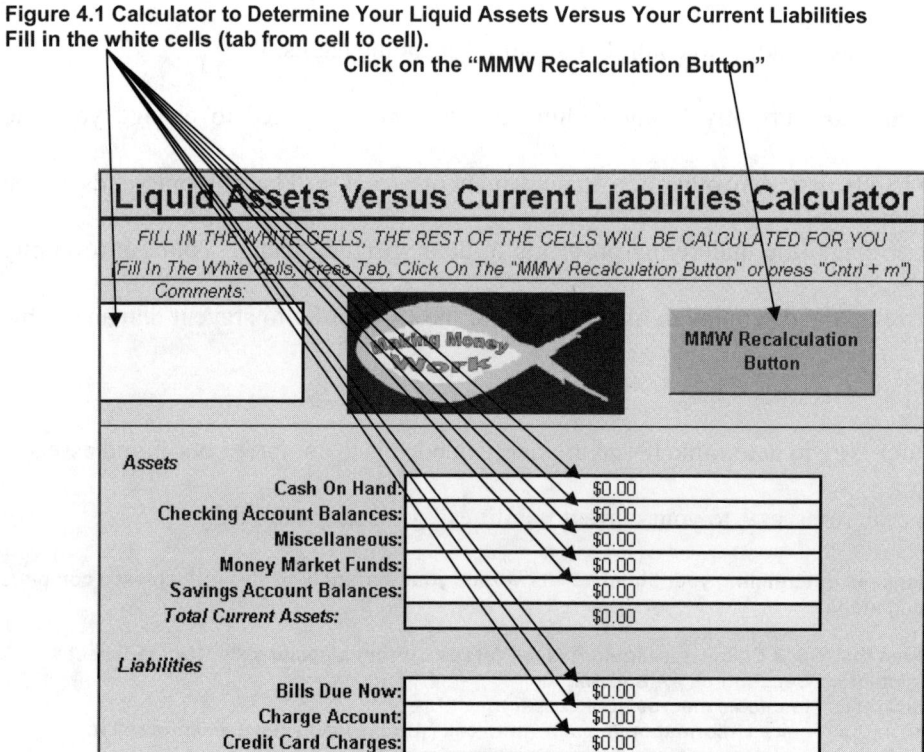

Assets
Cash On Hand:	$0.00
Checking Account Balances:	$0.00
Miscellaneous:	$0.00
Money Market Funds:	$0.00
Savings Account Balances:	$0.00
Total Current Assets:	$0.00

Liabilities
Bills Due Now:	$0.00
Charge Account:	$0.00
Credit Card Charges:	$0.00

Current assets should be 2 times greater than current liabilities. If they are not, you may need to take some steps to address your credit issues. Current liabilities that exceed current assets are a real danger signal. Other danger signals include: an inability to control your purchases, an inability to pay all your monthly minimums, having to choose which bills to pay, credit cards that are near their maximum limits, taking cash advances against your credit cards to pay other bills, credit balances that are increasing from month to month, having credit cards revoked due to exceeding their limits, adding new credit cards to increase your buying power, poor savings habits, compulsive shopping, living paycheck to paycheck, overdrawing checking or savings accounts, being unclear about your financial situation, and so on.

Debt Management

Figure 4.2 Hypothetical Example of a Completed Calculator to Determine Your Liquid Assets Versus Your Current Liabilities

Assets	
Cash On Hand:	$300.00
Checking Account Balances:	$2,000.00
Miscellaneous:	$0.00
Money Market Funds:	$10,000.00
Savings Account Balances:	$5,000.00
Total Current Assets:	$17,300.00

Liabilities	
Bills Due Now:	$1,000.00
Charge Account:	$3,000.00
Credit Card Charges:	$1,000.00
Current Installment Loans:	$500.00
Note Payments:	$800.00
Other Credit Lines:	$600.00
Miscellaneous:	$0.00
Total Current Liabilities:	$6,900.00
% Of Current Liabilities To Current Assets:	39.88%

Note: The % Of Current Liabilities To Current Assets Should Be Less Than 50%!

The "% Of Current Liabilities To Current Assets" should be less than 50%.

What should you do if you ascertain that you have a credit issue? Face the credit problem and take family measures to correct them. Stop purchasing with credit that increases your debts. If necessary, cut up your credit cards to curtail further indebtedness; or, if you have the ability to control credit card use, perhaps save one or two credit cards that are placed in a safe-deposit box for emergencies only. You might carry a few traveler's checks in your wallet for emergencies instead of credit cards. If you have difficulty controlling your spending because you buy for emotional reasons rather than actual need, consider contacting a support group such as Debtors Anonymous—http://www.debtorsanonymous.org/—these groups can help you correct spending habits and stop impulse buying.

Debt Management

Evaluate the problem. Determine how much you owe. List all your credit card balances along with their interest rates. Keep a daily log of all your spending for a month to see how much money you are spending on necessities versus nonessential items. Analyze your past spending—use your daily spending log, W-2 forms, prior year tax records, payroll check stubs, bank checking and savings account statements, and so on, to obtain the necessary information. Reviewing how you spent your income in the past can provide valuable information on improved spending plans for the future.

For assistance in determining your prior year spending habits, please complete the following steps:

1. Open the "SS13 Calculator-Budget.xls" (Spreadsheet 13 Calculator). See Figures 4.3, 4.4, 4.5, and 4.6.
2. Click "Yes" to enable macros, if necessary.
3. Click on the "Budget-Prior Year Actuals" sheet.
4. Fill in the required information in each white cell (you may tab from one white cell to another).
5. After completing the information in all of the white cells, press "Tab" and then click on the "MMW Recalculation Button"—the spreadsheet will make the remaining calculations for you.

Figure 4.3 Calculator to Determine Your Prior Year Actual Spending
Fill in the white cells (tab from cell to cell). Click on the "MMW Recalculation Button."

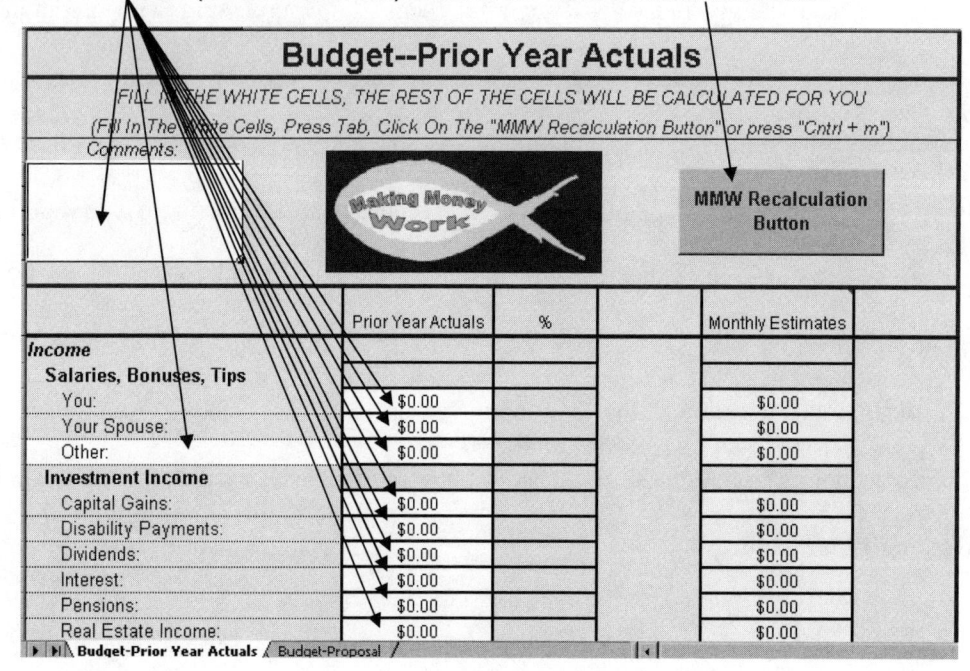

	Prior Year Actuals	%		Monthly Estimates	
Income					
Salaries, Bonuses, Tips					
You:	$0.00			$0.00	
Your Spouse:	$0.00			$0.00	
Other:	$0.00			$0.00	
Investment Income					
Capital Gains:	$0.00			$0.00	
Disability Payments:	$0.00			$0.00	
Dividends:	$0.00			$0.00	
Interest:	$0.00			$0.00	
Pensions:	$0.00			$0.00	
Real Estate Income:	$0.00			$0.00	

Debt Management

Figure 4.4

Note: "Total Housing Costs"—suggested allocation—less than 30% of income.

Note: "Total Transportation Costs"—suggested allocation—less than 18% of income.

Figure 4.5

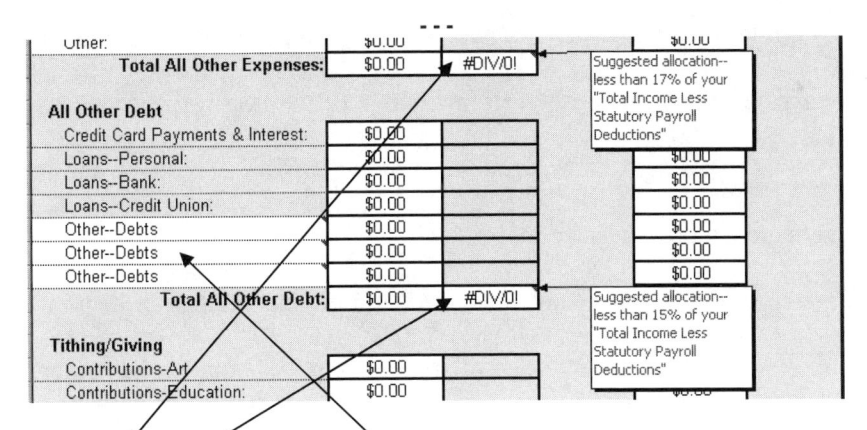

Note: "Total All Other Expenses"—suggested allocation—less than 17% of income.

Note: "Total All Other Debt"—suggested allocation—less than 15% of income.

Note: You may change the description of these white cells to accommodate your own personal budget descriptions.

Figure 4.6

51

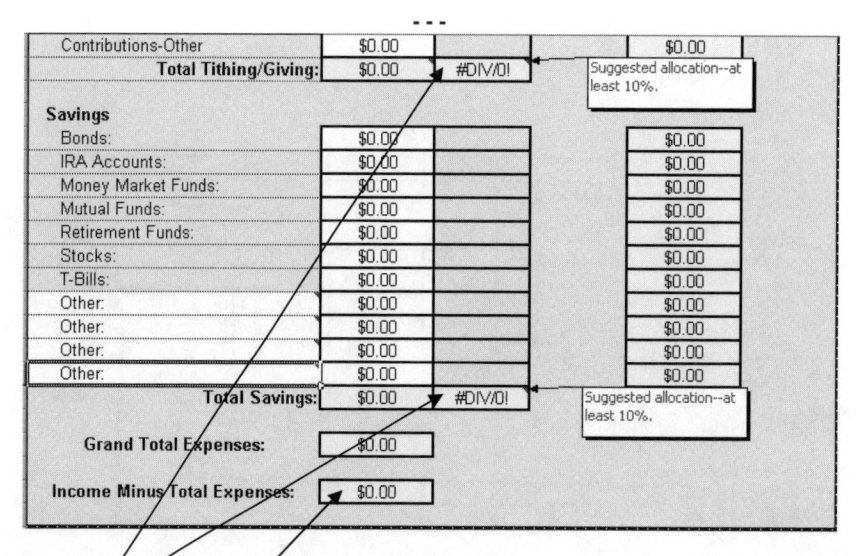

Debt Management

Contributions-Other	$0.00			$0.00
Total Tithing/Giving:	$0.00	#DIV/0!	Suggested allocation--at least 10%.	
Savings				
Bonds:	$0.00			$0.00
IRA Accounts:	$0.00			$0.00
Money Market Funds:	$0.00			$0.00
Mutual Funds:	$0.00			$0.00
Retirement Funds:	$0.00			$0.00
Stocks:	$0.00			$0.00
T-Bills:	$0.00			$0.00
Other:	$0.00			$0.00
Other:	$0.00			$0.00
Other:	$0.00			$0.00
Other:	$0.00			$0.00
Total Savings:	$0.00	#DIV/0!	Suggested allocation--at least 10%.	
Grand Total Expenses:	$0.00			
Income Minus Total Expenses:	$0.00			

Note: "Total Tithing/Giving"—suggested allocation—10% or more.

Note: "Total Savings"—suggested allocation—10% or more.

Note: If "Income Minus Total Expenses" is negative (cell will be in red), then you have urgent debt management issues to resolve.

Do not become discouraged if your past spending patterns require some adjustments. Recognizing your previous lifestyle patterns is one of the best ways to prepare for your future budget. Take corrective action to live within your income, reduce your dependence on credit, tithe/give more, and save more.

If you are spending beyond your income level, utilizing savings to help pay bills, or using credit for everyday living expenses, then changes should be implemented. "*The rich lord it over the poor; the borrower becomes the lender's slave*"—Proverbs 22:7. As mentioned earlier, the first step is to avoid incurring any additional debt. If you do not have the cash to pay for it, then do not buy it. You can increase your income, lower your spending, or use a combination of both to help resolve your budget issues. You might increase your income by working overtime, getting an additional job, having a yard sale,

Debt Management

or renting out a room. Use the extra income to increase monthly payments to each creditor. While setting up a written plan to pay off your existing debt, remember to work on a plan for savings. Your financial future depends on a systematic, regular savings plan that should include contributions from each paycheck. It is a learned discipline. After tithing, consider your savings plan the first bill you need to pay. If you are currently not saving anything, start out with 1% or 2% of your income and increase it each year until you achieve the goal of saving 10% or more. It is better to begin your savings with a small amount than to delay the savings habit because you think it is not enough. The best time to start saving is now. In fact, you should have 3 to 6 months worth of living expenses in savings available as an emergency fund. Debt reduction should occur in conjunction with building your savings for the future even if it means having to take longer to pay off your credit cards. In most cases, debt reduction should not come at the expense of future savings plans.

Living your life with less can make you happier and more financially secure. If your housing costs are exorbitant, consider moving to less expensive accommodations. Raise insurance deductibles on your home and automobiles to lower your premiums. Shop around for better rates on your insurance policies. In fact, it is a good idea to get at least three price comparisons on every purchase you make. Adjust the indoor temperature of your home to save on utility bills. Lowering the thermostat a few degrees in the winter and raising the thermostat a few degrees in the summer will not significantly affect your comfort level, and it will save you money on your bills. Cancel any unused premium cable TV channels or perhaps cancel cable TV altogether. Cancel the use of extra seldom

Debt Management

used telephone features. Control the use of long-distance telephone calls or cancel long-distance service with your phone company and use long distance calling cards instead.

In regard to reducing transportation costs, join a car pool or take mass transit to work to save gas and maintenance costs. New automobiles lose up to 60% of their value during the first three years. Consider buying used automobiles instead of new ones. Reduce your expenses by trading for a less expensive car that has lower monthly payments. Drive your car longer. You will save enough money to be able to retire around five years earlier by driving the average-priced car 10 years and then trading versus 3 years and then trading. Check your automobile's owner's manual for the recommended fuel octane level and purchase only the recommendation. Purchases of higher octane levels are unnecessary and a waste of money.

Reduce the number of times you eat out and your expenditures for entertainment. Trim expensive vacation plans. Use coupons for grocery purchases and look for sale items. Cut your food bill by purchasing fewer luxury items such as gourmet foods; purchase fewer more expensive convenience foods; buy in larger, more economic quantities; do more meal planning; and only purchase what is on the plan to eliminate purchasing nonessential impulse items. Take your lunch to work and drink water instead of soft drinks. You need water to survive—it is a necessity to live. Sodas are not essential to survival—they are luxury items that can be eliminated from your budget. Appreciate the fact that making minor adjustments to your spending can have huge effects on your economic well-being. For example, let's assume you save $3 per day taking your own lunch to work and drinking water instead of sodas and that you work an average of 215 days per year. You would save $645 annually. If you invest the $645 into your savings

Debt Management

plan and make 8% interest, in 30 years your change in lunch spending habits would equal to an additional $73,067.67 in your retirement savings plan! Look for additional minor adjustments you might be able to make in your spending habits. Keep track of all budget cost saving measures and apply the money to either your outstanding credit balances or your savings plan.

Make the largest payments toward your credit balances that you can afford each month—not the minimum. Pay off the credit cards with the highest interest rate charges first—not the ones with the highest outstanding balances. You might be able to switch your balances from high interest rate cards to lower interest rate cards. Ask your creditors if they have lower interest rates available—they may reduce your rate just to keep your business. If you have high credit balances that are close to your credit limits, pay them down before you apply for lower rate cards. High credit balances are red flags to low interest rate credit card issuers who might assume you present too much risk. Close any accounts you absolutely do not need before applying for lower rate cards. Some issuers total up the credit limit on all cards issued to the borrower to determine the potential liability. Some banks do not want their cards used for consolidating loans. Do not apply for more than 2 credit cards within any 6-month period—too many applications result in instant denial. A good place to check for credit card rates and other loans is www.bankrate.com. Carefully check the terms of the credit card for annual fees, late-payment penalties, and low interest rate introductory offers that quickly increase to higher rates. Cancel your old high interest rate charge cards to remove any temptation to use them again. Pay on time and stay within your credit limits to avoid any penalty rates.

Debt Management

Automatic payment plans can help—contact your bank or credit union to set up regular payments to creditors each month.

Getting out of debt requires commitment from everyone in the family. As you achieve steps in your debt reduction plan, celebrate the accomplishments with your family—it helps to motivate you to achieve even greater debt reduction.

For assistance in determining your proposed budget, please complete the following steps:

1. Open the "SS13 Calculator-Budget.xls" (Spreadsheet 13 Calculator). See Figures 4.7, 4.8, and 4.9.
2. Click "Yes" to enable macros, if necessary.
3. Click on the "Budget-Proposal" sheet.
4. Fill in the required information in each white cell (you may tab from one white cell to another).
5. After completing the information in all of the white cells, press "Tab" and then click on the "MMW Recalculation Button"—the spreadsheet will make the remaining calculations for you.

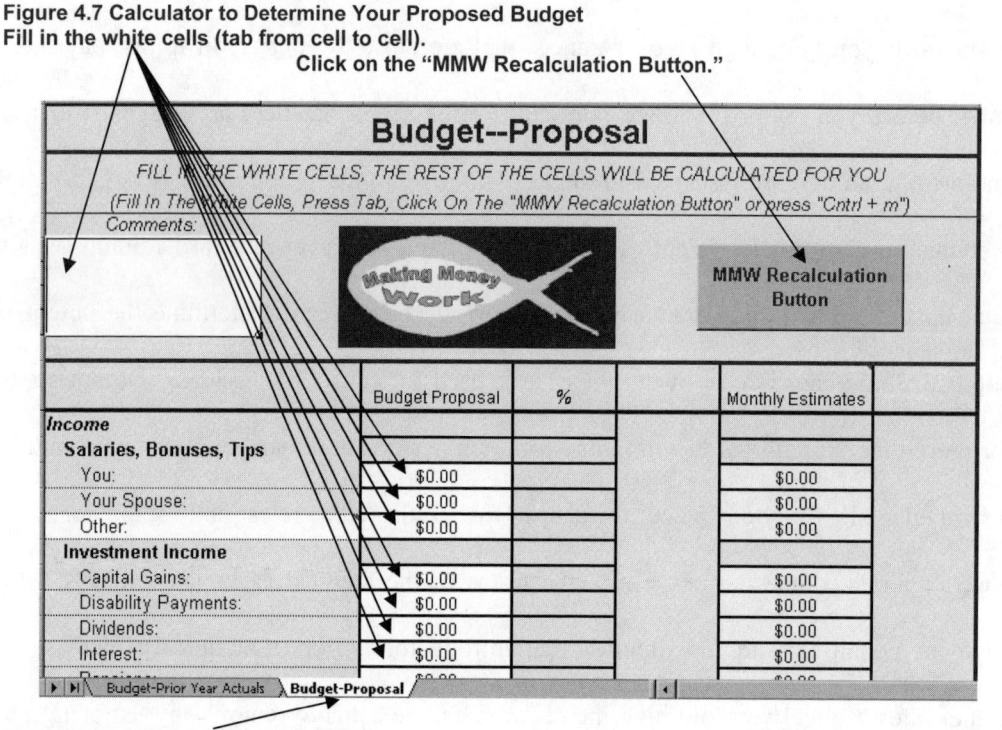

Figure 4.7 Calculator to Determine Your Proposed Budget
Fill in the white cells (tab from cell to cell).
Click on the "MMW Recalculation Button."

Click on the "Budget-Proposal" sheet.

Complete the information accurately and honestly utilizing any appropriate cost saving measures.

Debt Management

Figure 4.8

All Other Debt			
Credit Card Payments & Interest:	$0.00		$0.00
Loans--Personal:	$0.00		$0.00
Loans--Bank:	$0.00		$0.00
Loans--Credit Union:	$0.00		$0.00
Other--Debts	$0.00		$0.00
Other--Debts	$0.00		$0.00
Other--Debts	$0.00		$0.00
Total All Other Debt:	$0.00	#DIV/0!	$0.00

Please look at your "Total All Other Debt" (it should be less than 15%).

Figure 4.9

Other:	$0.00		$0.00
Other:	$0.00		$0.00
Other:	$0.00		$0.00
Total Savings:	$0.00	#DIV/0!	$0.00
Grand Total Expenses:	$0.00		
Income Minus Total Expenses:	$0.00		

Please look at your "Income Minus Total Expenses" (should not be negative). Suggestion: if you have a positive balance, use half of the money to pare debt and save the remaining balance.

If frugality and other cost cutting measures are insufficient to provide you with a positive balance on your "Income Minus Total Expenses," you will need to pursue other options regarding your debt problems.

You may wish to check your credit reports with all three major credit-reporting agencies since they do not share information with each other. Each agency can provide a report that shows how much you owe, to whom you owe it, and how well you've done in making the payments. There may be a small charge for the reports. You are entitled to a free report if you've been turned down for credit due to information contained in the credit bureau's files. It is a good habit to check your credit reports periodically—

Debt Management

especially before applying for loans. If your credit report contains an error, contact the credit bureau in writing to request a correction. The Fair Credit Reporting Act is the federal law that regulates consumer credit information. The law mandates that the credit bureaus investigate the validity of questionable information in your file. If the credit bureau made an error, it will amend your record. If the credit bureau refutes your claim, you may insert a rebuttal up to 100 words into your file. Credit information—excluding bankruptcies—is erased after 7 years.

You may get your credit information by contacting the following:

Name	Address	Phone	Website
Equifax Information Services LLC Center	P.O. Box 740241 Atlanta, GA 30374	800-685-1111	www.equifax.com
Experian National Consumer Assistance Center	P.O. Box 2002 Allen, TX 75013	888-397-3742	www.experian.com/consumer
Trans Union LLC Consumer Disclosure Center	P.O. Box 1000 Chester, PA 19022	800-888-4213 (if entitled to a free report—order via mail or online for a paid report)	www.transunion.com

Face your credit issues. If you are unable to pay bills, contact your creditors and explain the problems. Assure your creditors that you are eager to work with them and want to pay your balances. Negotiate a reasonable time frame with your creditors in which to pay your bills. Most creditors are willing to work out some type of payment plan.

It could be beneficial to get some credit counseling. The National Foundation for Consumer Credit offers free or low-cost credit counseling in every state—call 800-388-2227 for its automated 24-hour office location listings or visit its website at www.nfcc.org. The foundation deals with people encountering stressful financial situations. If it does not have an office conveniently located near you, then you may want

Debt Management

to try welfare organizations, military support centers, clergy, or legal aid societies for debt counseling guidance and support. Nonprofit credit counselors conduct a detailed analysis of your family's living expenses and debt. They create a budget and a repayment plan. The counselor may contact each of the family's creditors and reschedule the debt payments. The family may then agree to make one monthly payment to the counseling service. The counseling service then pays the creditors. Nonprofit credit counseling centers are funded by business community contributions. The business community benefits because individuals repay their debts instead of defaulting on their debts. Nonprofit credit counseling centers may charge their clients small fees based on the client's ability to pay.

Debt consolidation may help. If you roll all your outstanding debts into one large note with a single monthly payment, your debt issues may be easier to cope with. All previous creditors might be paid off. It simplifies bookkeeping and bill paying. You must close your old accounts and change your old spending habits for loan consolidation to work. Usually, two years after loan consolidation people are in deeper debt than before because they have not made the necessary changes in their underlying spending habits. It is the most common mistake credit abusers make. If you use debt consolidation, roll all accounts into a loan that has a lower interest rate than you had before on your accounts. With a lower interest rate, more of your money goes toward paying off the equity, and you pay your loans off faster. Pay at least as much each month as you were paying on all of your old bills. Beware of consolidation loans that stretch your payments over a longer period of time. They may offer a lower monthly payment than your current bills; however, you could end up paying more interest dollars due to the longer time frame.

Debt Management

Your total cost, not the monthly payment is what counts. Avoid trading short-term debt for long-term debt.

For example, assume you have the following credit card debts:

	Interest Rate	**$ Amount Owed**
Credit Card #1	14.75%	$598.23
Credit Card #2	17.90%	$1,092.98
Credit Card #3	18.74%	$496.75
Credit Card #4	23.99%	$2,789.20
Total Credit Card Debt:		$4,977.16

If it takes 1 year to pay each of the cards off individually, it would cost you the following amounts:

	Interest Rate	**Total $ Amount Paid With Interest**
Credit Card #1	14.75%	$647.10
Credit Card #2	17.90%	$1,201.83
Credit Card #3	18.74%	$548.61
Credit Card #4	23.99%	$3,164.79
Total Credit Card Debt:		$5,562.33

Now, let's assume you are able to negotiate a consolidation loan for the $4,977.16 at 14.40% interest to be paid off in 1 year:

	Interest Rate	**Total $ Amount Paid With Interest**
Consolidation Loan	14.40%	$5,373.87

You save $188.46 ($5,562.33 - $5,373.87 = $188.46) by utilizing one consolidation loan and paying off the other 4 credit cards.

For assistance in determining your own debt consolidation financials, please complete the following steps:

1. Open the "SS14 Calculator-Loan Payment.xls" (Spreadsheet 14 Calculator). See Figures 4.10 and 4.11.
2. Click "Yes" to enable macros, if necessary.
3. Click on the "Loan Payment Comparison By Year" sheet.
4. Fill in the required information in each white cell (you may tab from one white cell to another).
5. After completing the information in all of the white cells, press "Tab" and then click on the "MMW Recalculation Button"—the spreadsheet will make the remaining calculations for you.

Debt Management

Figure 4.10 Calculator to Determine Your Loan Payment Comparison by Year
Fill in the white cells (tab from cell to cell).
Click on the "MMW Recalculation Button."

Loan Payment Comparison By Year

FILL IN THE WHITE CELLS, THE REST OF THE CELLS WILL BE CALCULATED FOR YOU
(Fill In The White Cells, Press Tab, Click On The "MMW Recalculation Button" or press "Cntrl + m")

Comments:

MMW Recalculation Button

Loan Amount:	$4,977.16	Dollar Amount Of Loan
Interest Rate (i.e. 10% = 10.00%):	14.40%	Interest Rate For A Full Year
# Of Payments Per Year:	12	e.g. if 12 monthly payments/year, enter 12

Loan Term (# Of Years)	Loan Term (# Of Payments)	Amount Of Each Payment	Total Payments	Total Interest On The Loan
1	12	$ 447.82	$ 5,373.87	$ 396.71
2	24	$ 239.91	$ 5,757.83	$ 780.67
3	36	$ 171.08	$ 6,158.74	$ 1,181.58

Loan Payment Calculator \ **Loan Payment Comparison By Year** /

Click on the "Loan Payment Comparison By Year" sheet.

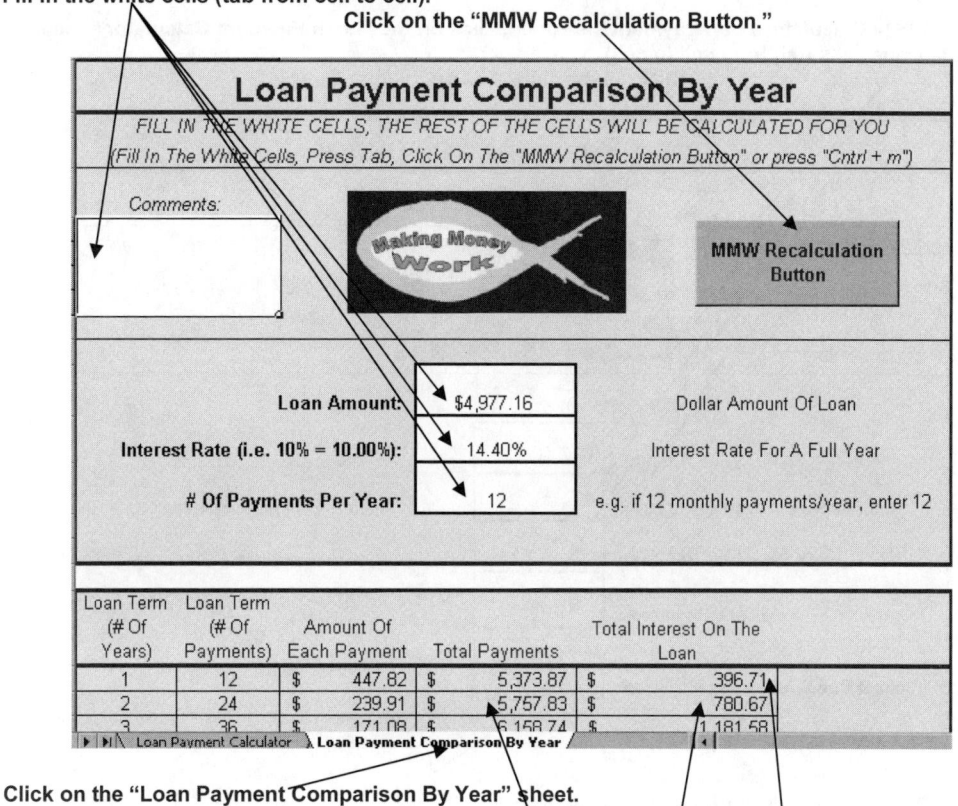

Note: If you pay the loan ($4,977.16 at 14.40%) off in 1 year it costs you $396.71 in interest.
Note: If you pay the same loan off in 2 years, it will cost you $780.67 in interest ($383.96 more than year 1; also note that in 2 years it would cost you $5,757.83 in total payments, which is more than the $5,562.33 originally planned to be paid in year 1 on your outstanding credit card balances).
A longer payback period, even at a lower interest rate, can cost you more money.

Use this calculator to determine your own outstanding debts and total payments on each. Then compare consolidation loans (e.g., check www.bankrate.com or your own bank, credit union, or financial institution) to determine if you can get a lower interest rate and a shorter payback period. Use the calculator again to determine if the consolidation loan will save you money. Do not forget to factor in any additional cost such as credit card annual fees, financial institution charges, or other loan fees.

Debt Management

Figure 4.11 Calculator to Determine Your Loan Payment

With the "SS14 Calculator-Loan Payment.xls" open, click on the "Loan Payment Calculator" sheet. Fill in the white cells (tab from cell to cell).
Click on the "MMW Recalculation Button."

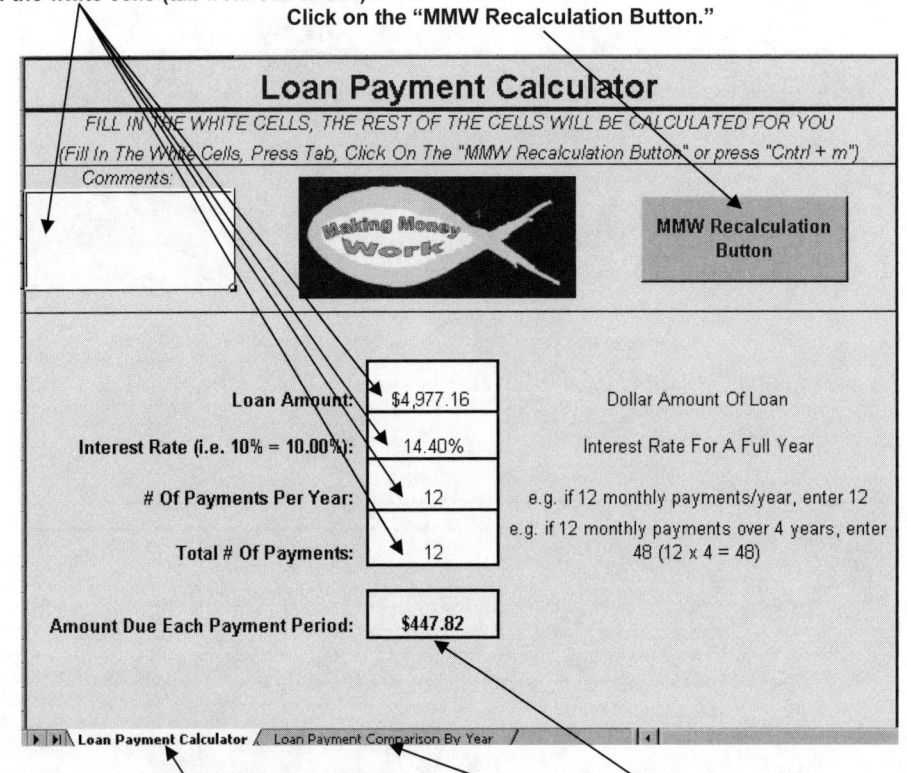

Click on the "Loan Payment Calculator" sheet.
Note: The "Amount Due Each Payment Period" for our example is $447.82. This calculator can be used to give you a quick reference on loans and the amount due each payment period, which is beneficial to know for budgeting purposes; however, the more important numbers are the "Total Payments" and "Total Interest On The Loan" found on the "Loan Payment Comparison By Year" sheet and calculator.

Check out your debt consolidation service with your state's attorney general's office or your local Better Business Bureau before conducting business with it. Before signing for any loan, always check to find out what would happen if you were to be late on your payments. Find out what portion of your consolidation loan goes to your creditors and how much is charged by the company as a service fee. Compare the interest rate charged by the debt consolidation service to your bank and credit union rate. Some debt

Debt Management

consolidation services are expensive and can do nothing more than create further debt for your family. Banks, credit unions, and finance companies offer consolidation loans designed to assist people in paying off their bills. These loans might require some type of collateral such as your automobile, a security, or your home. If you do not make your payments, you could end up losing your collateral. Be very careful in trading unsecured short-term debt such as credit card debt for long-term secured debt such as home equity lines of credit. Most lenders allow loans for only 80% of your home's value—homeowners would have to have 20% equity in their home before qualifying for loan funds. While home equity lines might provide lower interest rates and may be tax deductible, if you have turned unsecured credit card and installment debt into secured debt, your creditors can take your collateral if you go bankrupt. It is best to check with a lawyer and accountant before making your decisions.

Bankruptcy might be an extreme last resort if you have tried budgeting, decreasing your spending, increasing your income, credit counseling, and consolidating your debt and the measures still leave you without hope of being able to resolve your debt issues. Of all bankruptcies, 95% are personal bankruptcies. Personal bankruptcies occur primarily because people take on too much debt and do not have the savings to handle abrupt changes in their finances. The U.S. Bankruptcy Act of 1978 allows you to file a petition for a "straight" bankruptcy or seek "Chapter 13" protection. Under Chapter 13 protection, your basic assets are protected from claims while your old debts are regularly paid off with your future earnings—it is more favorable for the debtor than a straight bankruptcy. Any money left after paying off secured debt such as your mortgage goes toward paying off unsecured debt such as credit card or medical bills. "Chapter 7"

Debt Management

bankruptcy erases most nonpriority unsecured debts such as credit card bills. A straight bankruptcy discharges all your debts when you do not have a regular income—only limited certain debtor assets are protected from credit claims. Bankruptcy reports are carried in your credit bureau files for up to 10 years. Bankruptcy is the worst information that can appear on your credit report. Bankruptcy makes obtaining credit of any type nearly impossible. Bankruptcy filings normally rise or fall in conjunction with the percentage of debt payments as a percent of disposable personal income. The best solution for both you and others is to get control of your debts as a percentage of disposable income before you get into financial difficulty. Someone has to pay for the costs of bankruptcies. Fewer bankruptcies would result in more lending and lower lending rates for everyone. In short, if you do not pay your bills, it costs consumers who do pay their bills more money. "*Treat others as you would like them to treat you*"—Luke 6:31. Bankruptcy is provided by the law as a legal option for some protection from debts; it should only be chosen as an absolute last resort for those experiencing severe and unconquerable credit overextension financial difficulties. It is certainly not the best moral choice for those attempting to treat others as you would like to be treated yourself. Bankruptcy laws are instituted to help protect debtors experiencing catastrophic financial problems from a lifetime of indebtedness. Debtors should attempt to do everything within reason to satisfy their financial obligations to their creditors.

When Jesus was walking through Jericho, there was short man named Zacchaeus who wanted to see him. Zacchaeus was superintendent of the taxes, and he was very rich—most of the people considered Zacchaeus a sinner because he collected taxes. Unable to see Jesus due to the crowd, Zacchaeus climbed a sycamore tree. Jesus asked Zacchaeus to

Debt Management

come down from the tree and said that he wanted to stay with him. Zacchaeus told Jesus "*'Here and now, sir, I give half my possessions to charity; and if I have cheated anyone, I am ready to repay him four times over.' Jesus said to him, 'Salvation has come to this house today!'*"—Luke19: 8–10.

Chapter 5

The Magic of Compound Interest

"*Bring ye all the tithes into the storehouse, that there may be meat in mine house, and prove me now herewith, saith the LORD of hosts, if I will not open you the windows of heaven, and pour you out a blessing, that there shall not be room enough to receive it*"—Malachi 3:10 (Cambridge, London: Cambridge University Press Bible, 1937).

Chapter 3, "Tithing/Giving," acknowledged the importance of placing God first in your life and witnessing that faith through giving. Chapter 4, "Debt Management," addresses issues concerning "bad debt." Bad debt prohibits you from achieving financial success because it works against you. Bad debt's antithesis is compound interest"—a great ally in catapulting you toward achieving your financial goals. Through an understanding of compound interest, God can pour out a blessing upon you, which you will not be able to measure! Albert Einstein once called compound interest "the world's most impressive invention" and dubbed it the "eighth wonder of the world."[1] Compound interest means all the money you've invested earns interest and then the combined amount of the original investments plus your interest earns more interest. Compounding means interest added to interest. Compound interest does not produce linear growth like the pattern 1, 2, 3, 4, 5, 6, and so on; it produces geometric growth through compounding like the pattern 1, 2, 4, 8, 16, 32, and so on. Usually, the more frequently your money compounds when earning interest, the better. For example, daily compounding is

---

[1] Laurie Goering, *Making do with less may secure finances*, Chicago Tribune, January 1994.

The Magic of Compound Interest

normally better than monthly compounding, which is better than quarterly compounding, which is better than yearly compounding.

Simple interest is not compound interest at all. Simple interest is more linear in its growth nature. For example, let's assume you have $10,000 to invest. You find a bank certificate of deposit paying simple interest at 6% over a 5-year period. The formula for simple interest is as follows:

Simple Interest Earned = ID x R x T

Where:
ID = Initial Deposit
R = Rate (interest rate)
T = Time (number of years invested)

The math would work as follows:
Simple Interest = $10,000 x 6% x 5
$10,000 x 6% = $600 x 5 = $3,000 total earned in simple interest.

A basic formula for **compound interest** is as follows:

FV = ID (1 + R)^T, then FV – ID

Where:
FV = Future Value
ID = Initial Deposit
R = Rate (interest rate earned)
T = Time (number of years invested)

The math would work as follows:
$10,000 Initial Deposit, 6% interest Rate, 5-year Time period

Year	FV = $10,000.00 x (1 + 0.06)^5 **Formula Results By Year**	**Total Initial Deposit Plus Interest**
Year 1	$10,000.00 x (1 + 0.06)^1 = $10,600.00	$10,600.00
Year 2	$10,600.00 x (1 + 0.06)^2 = $11,236.00	$11,236.00
Year 3	$11,236.00 x (1 + 0.06)^3 = $11,910.16	$11,910.16
Year 4	$11,910.16 x (1 + 0.06)^4 = $12,624.77	$12,624.77
Year 5	$12,624.77 x (1 + 0.06)^5 = $13,382.26	$13,382.26
	Then	**Total Interest Earned**
	FV – ID = $13,382.26 - $10,000.00 = $3,382.26	$3,382.26

A more complete **compound interest** formula, which accounts for various compounding methods, is as follows:

The Magic of Compound Interest

$FV = ID(1 + R/N)^{NT}$, then $FV - ID$ = compound interest earned

Where:
FV = Future Value
ID = Initial Deposit
R = Rate (interest rate earned)
N = Number of times per year interest is compounded
T = Time (number of years invested)

Compound interest is geometric in its growth nature. The effect of the individual parts of the formula in combination with each other produces synergistic results in the outcome that are greater than the sum of its parts individually. In other words, small increases in any of the components can have a dramatic incremental effect on the total compound interest earned. As a comparison to the $3,000 **simple interest** earned in the $10,000, 6%, 5-year CD example above, let's assume you've researched 6 additional bank CDs that will give you the same 6% over 5 years. The only difference is that Bank 2 **compounds** interest annually (1 time per year), Bank 3 **compounds** interest semiannually (2 times per year), Bank 4 **compounds** interest quarterly (4 times per year), Bank 5 **compounds** interest monthly (12 times per year), Bank 6 **compounds** interest weekly (52 times per year), and Bank 7 **compounds** interest daily (352 times per year)—the typical CD. Which CD provides the best return on your money? The following chart compares the different scenarios:

The Magic of Compound Interest

Example	Type of Compounding	Interest Earned[2]
Bank #1 CD	Simple Interest (No Compounding)	$3,000.00
Bank #2 CD	Annual (1 time/year)	$3,382.26
Bank #3 CD	Semiannual (2 times/year)	$3,439.16
Bank #4 CD	Quarterly (4 times/year)	$3,468.55
Bank #5 CD	Monthly (12 times/year)	$3,488.50
Bank #6 CD	Weekly (52 times/year)	$3,496.25
Bank #7 CD	Daily (365 times/year)	$3,498.26

Simply by choosing the Bank #7 CD, which compounds interest *daily*, instead of the Bank #1 simple interest CD, you would make an additional $498.26.

The synergistic effects of the compounding formula can be further demonstrated by assuming you found another bank that would pay you **8%** on its CD instead of 6%. On the same $10,000 initial deposit at 8% over 5 years, compounding daily, you would earn $4,917.59—$1,419.33 more than the 6% daily compounded CD or $1,917.59 more than the Bank #1 simple interest CD at 6%! When investing, it pays to comparison shop for the most frequent compounding method and the best "risk tolerance acceptable" interest rate.

Some banks use the term "continuous compound interest." Continuous compound interest has a different formula than daily compounded interest; however, the results produce very little difference, if any. Another more dramatic example of the synergistic power of compound interest is as follows:

1. Assume you currently have $50,000 to invest.

2. Your current individual retirement account (IRA) is projected to earn 6%.

3. You are considering investing in a different IRA, which is projected to earn 8%.

4. You have 30 years before retirement.

---

[2] $10,000.00 invested at 6% over 5 years.

The Magic of Compound Interest

At 6% compounded daily, in 30 years your $50,000 would grow to $252,437.63. At 8% compounded daily, in 30 years your $50,000 would grow to $501,013.90—$248,576.27 more than the 6% scenario! That's the magic of compound interest! When you put compound interest to work for you, it is simply amazing how your money grows.

For assistance in determining your compound interest earnings, please complete the following steps:
1. Open the "SS15 Calculator-Compound Interest.xls" (Spreadsheet 15 Calculator). See Figures 5.1 and 5.2.
2. Click "Yes" to enable macros, if necessary.
3. Fill in the required information in each white cell (you may tab from one white cell to another).
4. After completing the information in all of the white cells, press "Tab" and then click on the "MMW Recalculation Button"—the spreadsheet will make the remaining calculations for you.

Figure 5.1 Calculator to Determine Your Compound Interest Earnings
Fill in the white cells (tab from cell to cell).
Click on the "MMW Recalculation Button."

Compound Interest Calculator

(This calulator assumes one initial deposit, a fixed interest rate, and no withdrawals of interest earned)

FILL IN THE WHITE CELLS, THE REST OF THE CELLS WILL BE CALCULATED FOR YOU
(Fill In The White Cells, Press Tab, Click On The "MMW Recalculation Button" or press "Cntrl + m)

Comments:

MMW Recalculation Button

Initial Deposit:	$10,000.00
Interest Rate (e.g. 6.75% = 6.75%):	6.00%
# Times/year interest is compounded:	365
Time (# of years invested):	5.00000

Daily = 365,
Weekly = 52,
Monthly = 12,
Quarterly = 4,
Semi-Annually = 2,
Annually = 1,
or other = your own #
(e.g. 360).

- - -

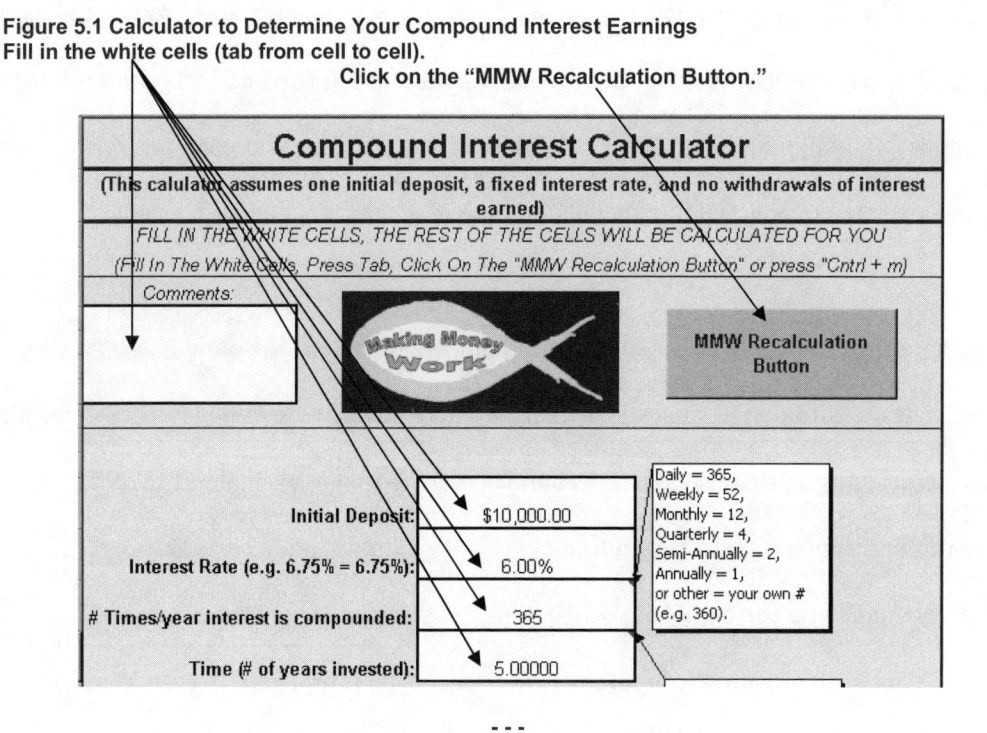

Figure 5.2 Calculator to Determine Your Compound Interest Earnings

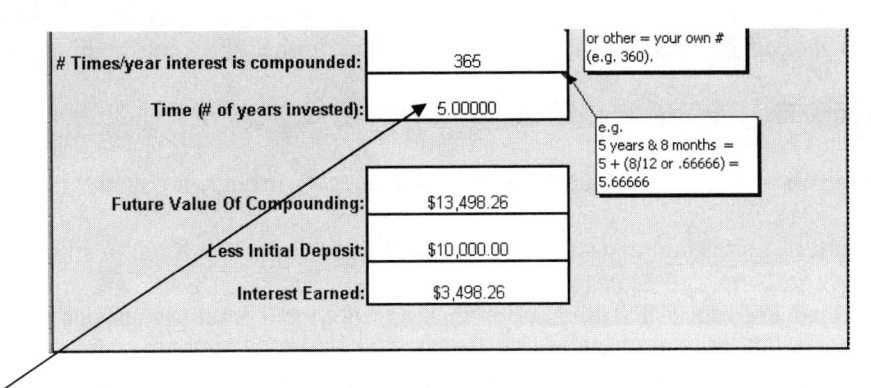

The Magic of Compound Interest

# Times/year interest is compounded:	365	or other = your own # (e.g. 360).
Time (# of years invested):	5.00000	e.g. 5 years & 8 months = 5 + (8/12 or .66666) = 5.66666
Future Value Of Compounding:	$13,498.26	
Less Initial Deposit:	$10,000.00	
Interest Earned:	$3,498.26	

Note: If your time period is 5 years and 8 months, enter the time as follows:
5 years + (8 divided by 12 = .66666) = 5.66666

Another useful tool in approximating the magic of compounding is the "Rule of 72." Albert Einstein is credited with discovering the compound interest Rule of 72 and said, "It is the greatest mathematical discovery of all time." The Rule of 72 is a mathematical way of approximating the number of years it takes an investment to double in value. You estimate the number of years for an investment to double by dividing 72 by the annual rate of return. For example, if you expect to earn a 10% return on your $10,000 investment, then 72 divided by 10 = 7.2 years for your investment to double in value to $20,000. It is a quick way to estimate returns also. For example, assume you are looking at lots with a real estate agent. The agent tells you the properties have doubled in value during the last 14 years. You could get a quick estimate of the increase per year in value by doing the following math: 72 divided by 14 = 5.14% per year.

The rule of 72 is not precise, but it is close for interest rates up to 15% and not too far off for rates up to 25%. The rule of 72 does not work as well with extreme numbers. For example, if you divide 72 by a 72% anticipated return, which equals 1, you would expect your money to double in one year. For your money to double in one year, it would take a 100% return, not a 72% return. If you are dealing with higher returns, it is more accurate

The Magic of Compound Interest

to use 76 instead of 72 as your guide. Usually the higher the return, the riskier the investment—this topic will be addressed in a later chapter.

When is the best time to get compound interest working for you? In a word, immediately. Let's assume Investor #1 puts $2,000 per year for 10 years in an investment and makes an 8% return and then stops making additional investments but leaves the accumulated money in the investment for another 20 years. Investor #2 delays investing for 10 years and then puts $2,000 per year in the investment making 8% for years 11 through 30. Which investor invests the most money, and which investor makes the most money? The following chart shows you what happens to each investor's money:

Year	Investor 1: $2,000/year for 10 years	Investor 1: Year-End Values @ 8%[3]	Investor 2: $2,000/year for years 10–30	Investor 2: Year-End Values @ 8%[4]
1	$2,000.00	$2,000.00	$0.00	$0.00
2	$2,000.00	$4,160.00	$0.00	$0.00
3	$2,000.00	$6,492.80	$0.00	$0.00
4	$2,000.00	$9,012.22	$0.00	$0.00
5	$2,000.00	$11,733.20	$0.00	$0.00
6	$2,000.00	$14,671.86	$0.00	$0.00
7	$2,000.00	$17,845.61	$0.00	$0.00
8	$2,000.00	$21,272.26	$0.00	$0.00
9	$2,000.00	$24,975.12	$0.00	$0.00
10	$2,000.00	$28,973.12	$0.00	$0.00
11	$0.00	$31,290.97	$2,000.00	$2,000.00
12	$0.00	$33,794.25	$2,000.00	$4,160.00
13	$0.00	$36,497.79	$2,000.00	$6,492.80
14	$0.00	$39,417.61	$2,000.00	$9,012.22
15	$0.00	$42,571.02	$2,000.00	$11,733.20
16	$0.00	$45,976.70	$2,000.00	$14,671.86
17	$0.00	$49,654.84	$2,000.00	$17,845.61
18	$0.00	$53,627.23	$2,000.00	$21,273.26
19	$0.00	$57,917.41	$2,000.00	$24,975.12
20	$0.00	$62,550.80	$2,000.00	$28,973.12
21	$0.00	$67,554.86	$2,000.00	$33,290.97
22	$0.00	$72,959.25	$2,000.00	$37,954.25
23	$0.00	$78,795.99	$2,000.00	$42,990.59
24	$0.00	$85,099.67	$2,000.00	$48,429.84

---

[3] Assumes deposits made at the end of the year with annual compounding.
[4] Assumes deposits made at the end of the year with annual compounding.

The Magic of Compound Interest

25	$0.00	$91,907.64	$2,000.00	$54,304.23
26	$0.00	$99,260.25	$2,000.00	$60,648.57
27	$0.00	$107,201.07	$2,000.00	$67,500.45
28	$0.00	$115,777.16	$2,000.00	$74,900.49
29	$0.00	$125,039.33	$2,000.00	$82,892.53
30	$0.00	$135,042.48	$2,000.00	$91,523.93
Total Investment:	$20,000 #1 Early Investor		$40,000 #2 Late Investor	
End Values:	$135,042.48		$91,523.93	
Total Earnings: (End Values Less Total Investment)	$115,042.48 #1 Early Investor		$51,523.93 #2 Late Investor	

The #1 Investor, who begins investing earlier, has only $20,000.00 out of pocket invested in his $135,042.48 savings. The #2 Investor, who waits until year 11 to begin investing, has $40,000.00 out of pocket invested in his $91,523.93 savings. The #1 Early Investor earns $115,042.48; the #2 Late Investor earns $51,523.93. The #1 Early Investor makes $63,518.55 more than the #2 Late Investor.

It is obvious from this example that the earlier you start saving for your retirement, the better. Making the contributions at the start of the year instead of the end could also increase the effects in this example. Getting an investment that compounds daily as opposed to annual compounding would also increase the effects.

If used wisely, God can richly bless you through the mathematical miracle of compound interest. And remember, when you are not invested, you are not compounding. The sooner you begin investing, the quicker you accumulate enough money to be able to do the things you would like to do in the future.

Jesus Christ told this parable: "*It is like a man going abroad, who called his servants and put his capital in their hands; to one he gave five bags of gold, to another two, to another one, each according to his capacity. Then he left the country. The man who had the five bags went at once and employed them in business, and made a profit of five bags,*

The Magic of Compound Interest

and the man who had the two bags made two. But the man who had been given one bag of gold went off and dug a hole in the ground, and hid his master's money. A long time afterwards their master returned, and proceeded to settle accounts with them. The man who had been given the five bags of gold came and produced the five he had made: "Master," he said, "you left five bags with me; look, I have made five more." "Well done, my good and trusty servant!" said the master. "You have proved trustworthy in a small way: I will now put you in charge of something big. Come and share your master's delight." The man with the two bags then came and said, "Master, you left two bags with me; look, I have made two more." "Well done, my good and trusty servant!" said the master. "You have proved trustworthy in a small way; I will now put you in charge of something big. Come and share your master's delight." Then the man who had been given one bag came and said, "Master, I knew you to be a hard man: you reap where you have not sown, you gather where you have not scattered, so I was afraid, and I went and hid your gold in the ground. Here it is—you have what belongs to you." "You lazy rascal!" said the master. "You knew that I reap where I have not sown, and gather where I have not scattered? Then you ought to have put my money on deposit, and on my return I should have got it back with interest. Take the bag of gold from him, and give it to the one with the ten bags. For the man who has will always be given more, till he has enough and to spare; and the man who has not will forfeit even what he has. Fling the useless servant out into the dark, the place of wailing and grinding of teeth!"'—Matthew 25: 14–30.

Everyone has different gifts. Each of us has different capacities for using those gifts. God expects you as an individual to make the best use that you can of all your

The Magic of Compound Interest

resources—your money, your time, and your talent. Limit borrowing, maximize saving. Invest to become an owner, not a loaner.

Inflation—The Silent Thief

Chapter 6

Inflation—The Silent Thief

Webster's dictionary describes inflation as "an increase in the volume of money and credit relative to available goods resulting in a substantial and continuing rise in the general price level." In other words, inflation can negatively affect your purchasing power. Inflation can be created when demand exceeds supply. Resources such as raw materials or skilled labor are scarce, and users of those resources bid aggressively for them, driving up production cost. Higher production cost results in higher consumer prices.

If the economy is growing too rapidly, orders for the manufacturer may exceed the traditional levels a normal supplier can maintain. The manufacturer then goes to outside suppliers for additional raw materials. As a result, the suppliers recognize the higher demand, and price discounts are no longer offered, which increases the manufacturer's production cost, which increases the consumer's purchase price. For example, let's say you have $1.00 saved this year. A manufacturer has been producing a product you have been purchasing for $1.00 at the grocery store. During the course of the coming year, the manufacturer experiences production cost increases and passes those increases along to you, the consumer. The next time you go to the grocery store, the same $1.00 item now costs you $1.03. Because of inflation, the item costs 3% more than it did a year ago. If you have not invested your money, making at or more than the rate of inflation, your purchasing power has actually declined because your $1.00 from last year will now only pay for 97% of the item's new cost. The real purchasing power value of your $1.00 has

Inflation — The Silent Thief

been diminished. Inflation can be described as an invisible thief—over time, it can erode the purchasing power of your money. Even fears of diminishing purchasing power have created actual inflation. Workers demand higher wages because they think price increases will erode their purchasing power. Producers demand more inventories to beat the surge in prices. The additional production further increases inflation.

The opposite of inflation is deflation. Webster's dictionary defines deflation as "a contraction in the volume of available money or credit resulting in a decline of the general price level." For example, you've saved $1.00. You've been purchasing an item at the grocery store for $1.00. During the course of the year, the manufacturer experiences reductions in production cost and lowers its price. The next time you go to the grocery store, the previous $1.00 item now only costs you $0.97. Your purchasing power has increased because your $1.00 now buys more. Periods of deflation have occurred only in 15% of the years from 1900 to 2001 in America's economy. Deflation is declining prices for goods and services while inflation is increasing prices for goods and services relative to your benchmark—in our example, $1.00.

If the economy is growing too strongly, it causes inflation. The U.S. Federal Reserve sets the discount rate it charges to banks. The federal funds rate is what banks charge each other for overnight loans. Any change in the federal funds rate is reflected in higher or lower bank prime lending rates. The bank prime lending rate is the benchmark rate for millions of consumer and business loans. The Federal Reserve may raise interest rates to restrain economic growth to help make inflation less likely. Higher interest rates make money more expensive to borrow. Higher costs discourage individuals and businesses from spending money, and decreased spending slows economic growth, which eases the

Inflation—The Silent Thief

pressure on inflation. This cycle may persist until economic growth and/or inflation stalls. Then the Federal Reserve might begin cutting interest rates to help speed the economy back up. Our economy is huge—you cannot speed it up or slow it down quickly like driving a sports car. It is more like driving a locomotive that never stops. The Federal Reserve attempts to brake the economic locomotive at the right time to keep inflation in check before it accelerates and then attempts to release the brake at the right time to keep the economy growing at a sustainable speed. Like driving a locomotive, "driving" the economy requires great skill in braking or releasing the brake before you reach your target. Nine to twelve months advance warning on economic conditions is necessary for the Federal Reserve to be effective in eliminating inflation problems. Most economists define the sustainable ideal speed as an annual gross domestic product, which is adjusted for inflation in the range of 2.5% to 3%. Like a locomotive that increases in speed until it is out of control, unchecked inflationary growth eventually derails, while noninflationary growth can go on and on.

Historical inflation rates for the United States economy for the years 1900 through 2000 are listed in Figure 6.1.

Figure 6.1 Historical U.S. Economy Inflation Rates

Year	Inflation Rate	Year	Inflation Rate	Year	Inflation Rate	Year	Inflation Rate
1900	1.00	1926	0.48	1952	2.26	1978	7.59
1901	0.99	1927	-1.42	1953	0.95	1979	11.28
1902	0.98	1928	-1.44	1954	0.31	1980	13.48
1903	2.91	1929	0.00	1955	-0.31	1981	10.36
1904	0.94	1930	-2.44	1956	1.56	1982	6.16
1905	-0.93	1931	-9.00	1957	3.38	1983	3.21
1906	1.89	1932	-10.44	1958	2.98	1984	4.37

Inflation—The Silent Thief

1907	4.63	1933	-4.91	1959	0.58	1985	3.54
1908	-1.77	1934	3.23	1960	1.72	1986	1.86
1909	-1.80	1935	2.50	1961	1.13	1987	3.66
1910	4.59	1936	1.22	1962	1.12	1988	4.12
1911	0.00	1937	3.61	1963	1.10	1989	4.81
1912	2.63	1938	-1.74	1964	1.37	1990	5.39
1913	1.71	1939	-1.78	1965	1.62	1991	4.22
1914	0.84	1940	1.20	1966	2.92	1992	3.01
1915	0.83	1941	4.76	1967	2.84	1993	2.98
1916	7.44	1942	10.80	1968	4.26	1994	2.60
1917	17.69	1943	6.15	1969	5.29	1995	2.76
1918	17.65	1944	1.45	1970	5.94	1996	2.96
1919	15.00	1945	2.38	1971	4.31	1997	2.35
1920	15.94	1946	8.37	1972	3.31	1998	1.51
1921	-10.83	1947	14.59	1973	6.20	1999	2.21
1922	-6.54	1948	7.87	1974	11.11	2000	3.38
1923	2.00	1949	-1.04	1975	8.98		
1924	0.00	1950	1.05	1976	5.75		
1925	2.94	1951	7.64	1977	6.62		

Note: The average inflation rate from 1900 through 2000 was 3.1893%.

For inflation rates from other years, check the following website:

http://www.eh.net/ehresources/howmuch/inflationq.php. You may check for forecasts on various stock indexes, interest rates, currency exchange rates, and general economy rates, including the U.S. Consumer Price Index and Inflation rates, at the Financial Forecast Center: www.forecasts.org.

The stock market usually bottoms out only when there is room for noninflationary growth in the economy. The stock market performs best after rare periods of deflation such as the year 1955. When inflation is low or falling such as the year 1993, the stock market performs better than average. When inflation is high or accelerating upward such

Inflation — The Silent Thief

as the year 1976, the stock market performs below average. For example, note the following Dow Jones Industrial Average price gains in the year after various inflation rates from 1946–1995:

Type of Period	Dow Jones Industrial Average Price Gain (Year After)
Deflation (prices declining)	+ 17%
Inflation 0% to 3% (prices increasing)	+ 10%
Inflation 3% to 5% (prices increasing)	+ 7%
Inflation 5% + (prices increasing)	+ 4%

Deflation and low inflation are beneficial for stock investors. High inflation is bad for stock investors. Over a period of years, volatile stock prices are less of a threat to your purchasing power than the threat of inflation.

Reread the parable told by Jesus from Matthew 25:14–30 in Chapter 5 or from your own Bible. The master had some harsh words for the servant who buried his one bag of gold in the ground. He called him lazy and a rascal. He told the servant that he should have put his money on deposit so it would have earned interest. The master had the bag of gold taken from the servant and then had the "useless" servant thrown into the dark. The parable relays some important modern day financial principles. Do not keep money at home, in a mattress, in a sock, or in a can buried in the yard. Most homeowner's policies only cover a few hundred dollars in cash. The federal government insures bank accounts up to $100,000. It is safer to keep your money invested as opposed to keeping it at home. Invest your money so it is earning interest. The servant had "saved" his Master's money by burying the one bag of gold in the ground; however, he had not invested it. A critical difference between saving and investing is recognizing the impact inflation can have on your investments. Using our $1.00 grocery store item example, let's say you have saved $1.00. You put the money into your bank checking account making 1%

Inflation — The Silent Thief

interest. Next year you now have $1.01. Now let's assume that inflation was 3% for the year. The cost of the item is now $1.03. Your investment is $0.02 less than the new purchase price. Your buying power has actually diminished. The difference between saving and investing then is purchasing power. Your earnings over time need to consistently exceed the rate of inflation, or like the servant in the parable, what you have will be taken away from you in the form of diminished purchasing power.

Saving/Goal Setting

Chapter 7

Saving/Goal Setting

The average American saves less than 5%. People in other industrialized nations such as Canada, France, and Japan save 11% to 15%. Just as your individual standard of living will decline in retirement without adequate savings, future generations of Americans will see their standard of living decline if the U.S. economy loses ground against global competition. It requires the efforts of individuals, families, corporations, and government to increase America's savings rate. This chapter focuses on things your family can accomplish to improve your savings rate.

In Aesop's fable about the grasshopper and the ant, the grasshopper ignored the potential for future difficult times and starved. The ant saved some food for the winter and was able to survive because of his foresight.

Saving money means accumulating funds for emergencies, seasonal expenses, short-term goals, and long-term goals. Like Aesop's grasshopper, you can use up all your resources now and have nothing later, or you can save for the future by spending a little less today, investing the savings, and then being able to spend a whole lot more in the future. Most Americans can do with less. According to Dr. Gregory A. Boyd in his book *Letters from a Skeptic*, Americans "make up about 7 percent of the population of the earth, but we consume over half its resources!"

After tithing/giving, your first order of business with your finances should be building your cash reserves for a bare minimum of three months living expenses for emergencies such as a job loss, unexpected medical expenses, repairs, and automobile maintenance.

Saving/Goal Setting

Six to nine months living expenses as an emergency fund is even better. Keep your emergency fund in an easily accessible liquid account. In fact, money you will need within five years should be kept in safe investments such as bank CDs, money-market funds, treasury bills, or mutual funds that purchase top-rated bonds maturing in one to three years. Money that you will not need within five years can be invested in the stock market. Saving and investing gives you comfort and a sense of security. Being in financial distress can create mental anxiety. Even if you never have to use your emergency fund for a "rainy day," it will provide funding for a "sunny retirement." Saving helps you to feel more secure about tomorrow, which makes you feel happier about today.

Saving should be considered a spending priority. The number one rule of saving for retirement is to begin saving immediately; the sooner you start saving, the longer your money will work for you. Every pay period, pay yourself by saving. Regardless of the amounts, savings should become part of your normal routine economic habits. When you save and invest, your money earns money for you. Saving consistency and discipline are keys to achieving good results. Automatic savings plans are a great way to insure your financial future. Automatic payroll deductions from work into your company's savings and investment plan or automatic payroll deductions sent to a credit union or other savings vehicle removes the temptation to spend the money on things other than savings. Avoiding having the money sent to you in the first place is the easiest way to save. If you receive unexpected funds from gifts, inheritances, income tax refunds, salary increases, bonuses, and so on, target as much of the funds as possible toward savings.

Saving/Goal Setting

How much do you need to save? You cannot know for certain; however, you can develop an estimate and establish financial goals. Most financial advisers estimate that you will need 70% to 80% of your preretirement income to maintain your current standard of living. You should need less than 100% because of the decline of some expenses upon retirement such as work transportation costs, work clothes, possible lower taxes, a mortgage that has been paid off, no longer having to save for retirement, and so on. Some financial advisers use the 20-to-1 rule of thumb. For example, if you need $50,000 per year to retire at age 65 and expect to live 20 years, you would need $50,000 x 20 = $1,000,000 in liquid assets for your retirement.

Develop a savings plan with the end in mind. Remember, planning is important—it was not raining when Noah built the ark. Your plan should be flexible and updated to account for recent developments. "Planning will never become an exact science. But it now can be less of a venture into the unknown. The future is a moving target. Planning can improve our aim"—IBM.[1] Only about 3% of the population establishes written goals. Most people who do set goals establish targets greater than they can achieve in one year and less than they can accomplish in ten years. Good goals are specific, quantifiable, written, realistic yet challenging, flexible, and have target completion dates. Most successful people have set written goals for what they would like to accomplish. Remember, things are actually created twice: first mentally and then physically.

Open the "SS13 Calculator-Budget.xls" (Spreadsheet 13 Calculator) you prepared in Chapter 4.

---

[1] Thomas H. Naylor, William H. Willimon, and Magdelena R. Naylor, *The Search For Meaning*, Abingdon Press, Nashville, TN, September 1994, page 120.

Saving/Goal Setting

Figure 7.1

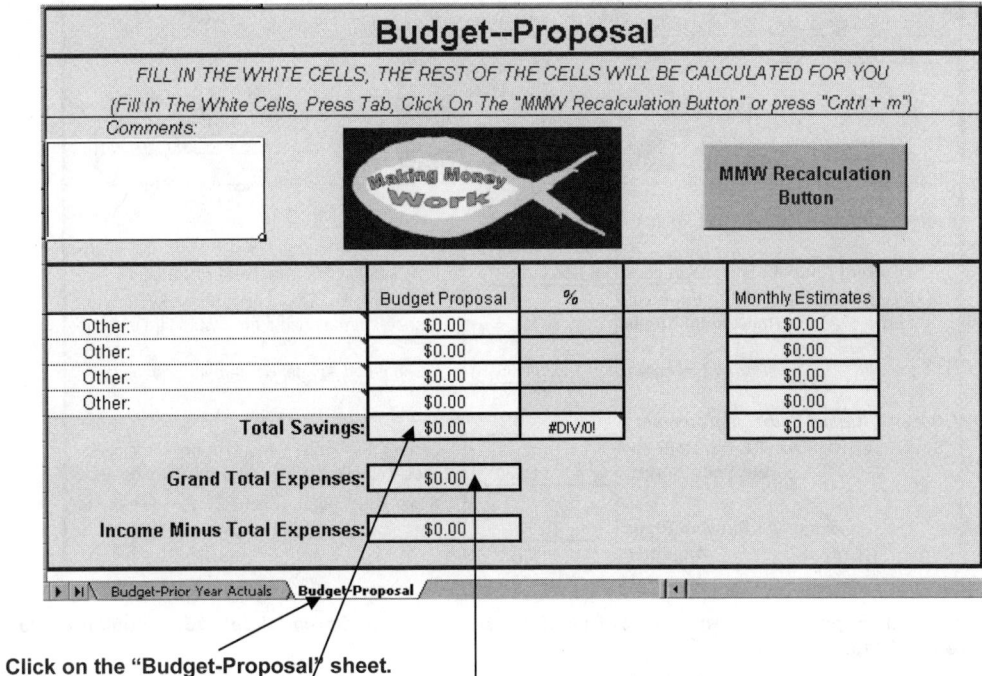

	Budget Proposal	%	Monthly Estimates
Other:	$0.00		$0.00
Other:	$0.00		$0.00
Other:	$0.00		$0.00
Other:	$0.00		$0.00
Total Savings:	$0.00	#DIV/0!	$0.00
Grand Total Expenses:	$0.00		
Income Minus Total Expenses:	$0.00		

Budget--Proposal
FILL IN THE WHITE CELLS, THE REST OF THE CELLS WILL BE CALCULATED FOR YOU
(Fill In The White Cells, Press Tab, Click On The "MMW Recalculation Button" or press "Cntrl + m")

Click on the "Budget-Proposal" sheet.

Make note of the "Grand Total Expenses" number in your personal budget.

Please enter this number or the number you feel is most accurate in the next spreadsheet—Retirement Savings Goal (In Today's Dollars) under "Current Annual Living Expenses."

Make note of the "Total Savings" number in your personal budget.

Please enter the "Total Savings" in the next spreadsheet—Retirement Savings Goal (In Today's Dollars) under "Total of Current Accumulated Savings."

For assistance in determining your retirement savings estimate, please complete the following steps:

1. Open the "SS16 Calculator-Retirement Savings Goal (In Today's Dollars)," (Spreadsheet 16 Calculator); see Figures 7.2a, b, c, and d.
2. Click "Yes" to enable macros, if necessary.
3. Fill in your own personal information in each white cell (you may tab from one white cell to another).
4. After completing the information in all of the white cells, press "Tab," and then click on the "MMW Recalculation Button"—the spreadsheet will make the remaining calculations for you.

Figure 7.2a Retirement Savings Goal—In Today's Dollars

Saving/Goal Setting

Retirement Savings Goal (In Today's Dollars)

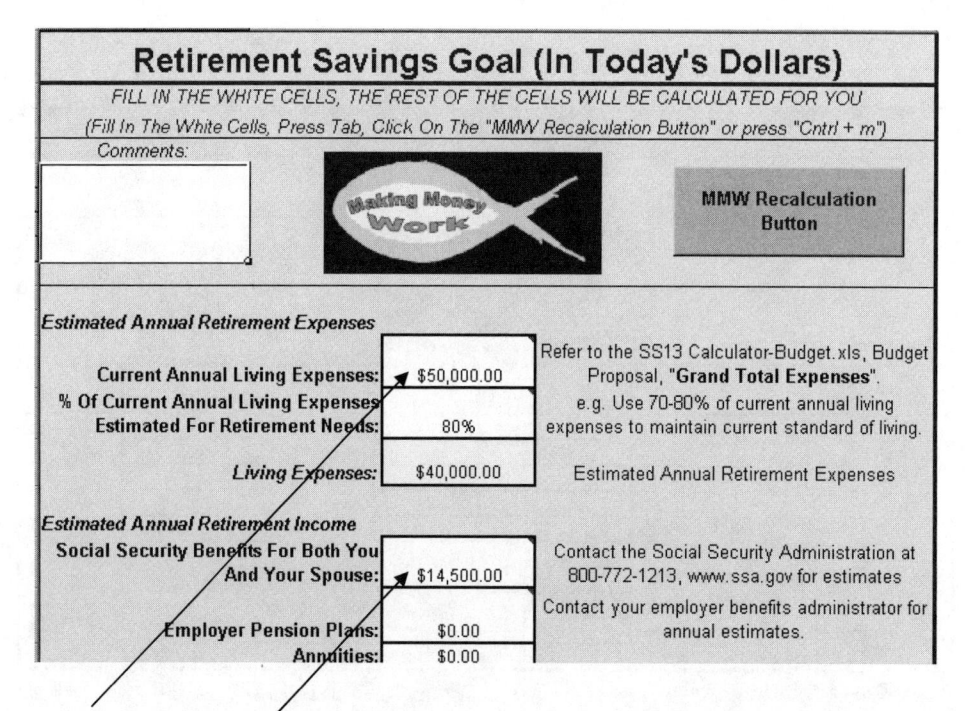

FILL IN THE WHITE CELLS, THE REST OF THE CELLS WILL BE CALCULATED FOR YOU
(Fill In The White Cells, Press Tab, Click On The "MMW Recalculation Button" or press "Cntrl + m")

Comments:

MMW Recalculation Button

Estimated Annual Retirement Expenses

Current Annual Living Expenses:	$50,000.00	Refer to the SS13 Calculator-Budget.xls, Budget Proposal, "Grand Total Expenses".
% Of Current Annual Living Expenses Estimated For Retirement Needs:	80%	e.g. Use 70-80% of current annual living expenses to maintain current standard of living.
Living Expenses:	$40,000.00	Estimated Annual Retirement Expenses

Estimated Annual Retirement Income

Social Security Benefits For Both You And Your Spouse:	$14,500.00	Contact the Social Security Administration at 800-772-1213, www.ssa.gov for estimates
Employer Pension Plans:	$0.00	Contact your employer benefits administrator for annual estimates.
Annuities:	$0.00	

"Grand Total Expenses" from "SS13 Calculator-Budget.xls" (Spreadsheet 13 Calculator) you prepared in Chapter 4.

Call the Social Security Administration (1-800-772-1213) to request a copy of your personal Social Security estimates. You may also visit the Social Security Administration website at www.ssa.gov for personal estimates—quick estimates, online estimates, or detailed estimates.

- - -

If you have average earnings, Social Security retirement benefits will only replace about 40% of your earnings. You will need to supplement your Social Security benefits with a pension plan, savings, or other investments. Social Security retirement benefits were never intended to be your sole means of support in retirement.

Douglas Bernheim—a Stanford University Professor—studied pension plans and estimated that 30% to 40% of employees have them. Companies have no legal obligation to provide pension plans. He also noted that when pension plans are available, they normally replace about 20% of the employees' needed income at retirement. You may

Saving/Goal Setting

contact your company's benefits administrator for a projection of your pension benefits at retirement, if available.

Figure 7.2b Retirement Savings Goal—In Today's Dollars

For help in Estimating Your "Life Expectancy (Number of Years)," refer to Chapter 7, Figure 7.3 ("Life Expectancy Rates") and Chapter 7, Figure 7.4 ("Life Expectancy Rate Projected").

Rental Income:	$0.00	
Part-time Income:	$0.00	
Other Income:	$0.00	
Total Income:	$14,500.00	Estimated Annual Retirement Income
Annual Retirement Shortfall:	$25,500.00	"Living Expenses" minus "Total Income"
Life Expectancy (Number Of Years):	90	Refer To Chapter 7, Figure 7.4, Table 2 Life Expectancy Rate Projected (Number Of Years)
Your Planned Retirement Age:	65	
Anticipated Number Of Years In Retirement:	25	
Real Rate Of Return Estimate		
Annual Investment Growth Estimate:	7%	Your personal estimate of your future savings growth rate/year.
Inflation Rate Estimate:	4%	Review to Chapter 6, Figure 6.1 Historical U.S. Economy Inflation Rates
Net Inflation Adjusted Rate Of Return:	3%	"Annual Investment Growth Estimate" minus the "Inflation Rate Estimate".
Assumed Return Factor:	17.41	Refer to Chapter 7, Figure 7.5, Table 3 (Assumed Return Factors).
Retirement Savings Goal (In Today's Dollars):	$443,955.00	"Annual Retirement Shortfall" x "Assumed Return Factor"

During the years 1926 through 2000, the large cap stocks averaged a 12.84% gain per year; long-term corporate bonds averaged 6.26% per year.[2]

Enter your personal estimate of future savings growth rate/ year.

Enter your personal inflation rate estimate. Refer to Chapter 6, Figure 6.1 ("Historical U.S. Economy Inflation Rates") and the Financial Forecast Center website at www.forecasts.org for references.

- - -

---

[2] John K. Paglia, Ph.D., FRM, CFM and Ivan C. Roten, *Using Asset Allocation Strategies to Recover from a Bear Hug,* Graziadio Business Report, Pepperdine University, www.gbr.pepperdine.edu, Summer 2002.

Saving/Goal Setting

Figure 7.2c Retirement Savings Goal—In Today's Dollars

"Total Savings" from "SS13 Calculator-Budget.xls" (Spreadsheet 13 Calculator) you prepared in Chapter 4.

Annual Savings Needed To Reach Retirement Goal (In Today's Dollars)		
Total Of Current Accumulated Savings:	$120,000.00	Refer to the SS3 Calculator-Budget.xls, Budget Proposal, **Total Savings**.
Pre-retirement Annual Investment Growth Estimate:	8%	Your personal estimate of your pre-retirement savings growth rate/year.
Inflation Rate Estimate:	4%	Review Chapter 6, Figure 6.1 Historical U.S. Economy Inflation Rates
Net Inflation Adjusted Rate Of Return:	4%	"Annual Investment Growth Estimate" minus the "Inflation Rate Estimate".
Number Of Years Away From Retirement:	20	e.g. Planned retirement age 65 - 45 (age now) = 20
Future Value Of Current Savings:	$262,934.78	Calculation assumes annual compounding.
Retirement Savings Goal (In Today's Dollars):	$443,955.00	"Annual Retirement Shortfall" x "Assumed Return Factor"--From Above
Retirement Goal Shortfall:	$181,020.22	"Retirement Savings Goal (In Today's Dollars) minus "Future Value Of Current Savings".
Assumed Discount Factor:	0.037	Refer to Chapter 7, Figure 7.6, Table 4 (Assumed Discount Factors).
Annual Savings Required To Meet Goal:	$6,697.75	"Retirement Goal Shortfall" x "Assumed Discount Factor"

Note: The actual dollar amount in your "Retirement Savings Goal" will be higher at retirement due to inflation. Values are approximations only for goal setting purposes.

For assistance in determining your "Assumed Discount Factor," refer to Chapter 7, Figure 7.6 ("Assumed Discount Factors").

Note: Adjust your "Annual Savings Required To Meet Goal" upward each year with inflation.

Suggestion: Update your "Retirement Savings Goal (In Today's Dollars)" annually to get a more accurate forecast of your retirement needs as conditions, savings, and forecasts change.

- - -

Figure 7.2 d Retirement Savings Goal—In Today's Dollars

Saving/Goal Setting

Enter your personal tax information.

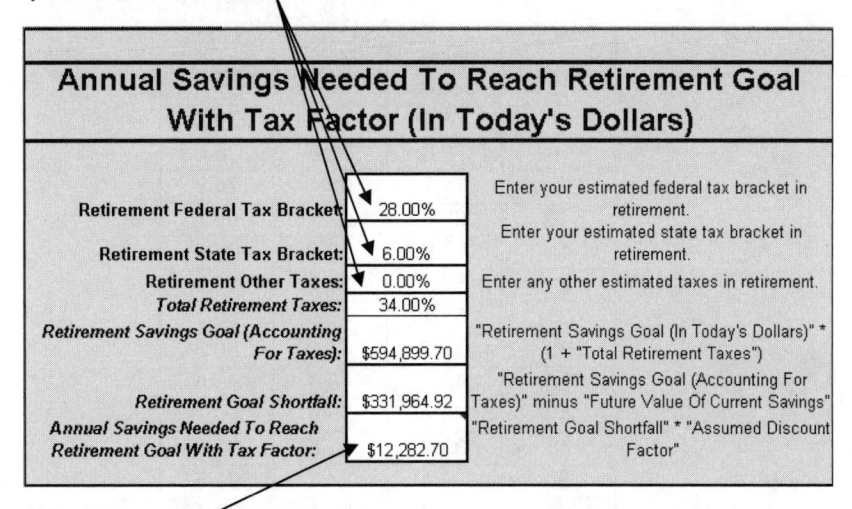

Annual Savings Needed To Reach Retirement Goal With Tax Factor (In Today's Dollars)		
Retirement Federal Tax Bracket:	28.00%	Enter your estimated federal tax bracket in retirement.
Retirement State Tax Bracket:	6.00%	Enter your estimated state tax bracket in retirement.
Retirement Other Taxes:	0.00%	Enter any other estimated taxes in retirement.
Total Retirement Taxes:	34.00%	
Retirement Savings Goal (Accounting For Taxes):	$594,899.70	"Retirement Savings Goal (In Today's Dollars)" * (1 + "Total Retirement Taxes")
Retirement Goal Shortfall:	$331,964.92	"Retirement Savings Goal (Accounting For Taxes)" minus "Future Value Of Current Savings"
Annual Savings Needed To Reach Retirement Goal With Tax Factor:	$12,282.70	"Retirement Goal Shortfall" * "Assumed Discount Factor"

Note: The calculator estimates the annual savings needed to reach your retirement goal to include taxes due.

Save enough so that no more than 6% of the "Retirement Savings Goal (Accounting for Taxes)" is needed in any one year to supplement your income from Social Security, pension funds, or other income. Using 6% of your principal will not hurt your portfolio too badly if you are diversified and invested wisely enough to average traditional market returns.

Figure 7.3 Life Expectancy Rates

Saving/Goal Setting

Age	Remaining Years of Life—All Races (1996 Data)[3]		
	Both Sexes	Male	Female
0	76.1	73.0	79.0
1	75.6	72.6	78.6
5	71.7	68.7	74.7
10	66.8	63.8	69.7
15	61.9	58.9	64.8
20	57.1	54.2	59.9
25	52.4	49.6	55.1
30	47.7	44.9	50.2
35	43.0	40.4	45.4
40	38.4	35.9	40.7
45	33.9	31.5	36.0
50	29.4	27.1	31.5
55	25.2	23.0	27.1
60	21.2	19.2	22.9
65	17.5	15.7	18.9
70	14.1	12.5	15.3
75	11.1	9.8	11.9
80	8.3	7.3	8.9
85	6.1	5.4	6.4

For more information about life expectancy rates, go to the National Center for Health Statistics Data Warehouse, a unit of the U.S. Department of Health and Human Services, Centers for Disease Control and Prevention website at:

http://www.cdc.gov/nchs/datawh/statab/unpubd/mortabs/lewk1.htm.

Please note that Figure 7.3 is a "snapshot" of statistical data in time. As knowledge, attitudes, nutrition, sanitation, lifestyle choices, and medical advances improve, life expectancy rates increase. For example, note the following information:

---

[3] Data from the National Center for Health Statistics Data Warehouse, a unit of the U.S. Department of Health and Human Services, Centers for Disease Control and Prevention.

Saving/Goal Setting

Life Expectancy at Birth in the United States[4]

Year	Male	Female
1960	66.6	73.2
1980	70.1	77.7
1990	71.9	79.0

During the period, 1960 through 1990, the U.S. male life expectancy from birth increased 5.3 years (7.957958% divided by 30 years = 0.265265267/year average increase). The U.S. female life expectancy increased 5.8 years (7.9234973 divided by 30 years = 0.264116577/year average increase). Life expectancy rates will continue to increase in the future. As people live longer, they are exposed to greater risk that they may outlive their financial resources.

While history is not necessarily representative of the future, you might use the 0.265 as a rough factor for life expectancy increases to get a better projection of your future life expectancy (number of years) as follows:

Figure 7.4 Life Expectancy Rate Projected

Explanation	Example	You
Year you plan to retire	2026	
Minus 1996 (year for information in Figure 7.3)	-1996	-1996
Total # of years	= 30	
x 0.265 rough projection factor	x 0.265	x 0.265 (or more)
Rough estimate in life expectancy increase	= 7.95	
Figure 7.3 (Life Expectancy Rates)—example of "age 65," "male"	+ 15.7	
Rough estimate of life expectancy rate after retirement	= 23.65	
Age at retirement	+ 65	
Life expectancy rate projected (number of years)	= 88.65	

---

[4] Tuljapurkar and Boe, based on World Health Organization mortality data, World Health Organization Mortality Database, www.ciesin.org.

Saving/Goal Setting

A word of caution: the 0.265 projection factor is based on historical increases, which have been more linear in their growth nature. Future life expectancy rates are more likely to increase dramatically. Steven Austad, a University of Idaho biologist, wrote a book called *Why We Age* and states, "The prospects of dramatically increasing human longevity are excellent." Steven Austad predicts 20- to 40-year life expectancy rate increases during the later part of this century.[5] Be liberal in your life expectancy predictions versus being too conservative. It is better to plan for more years than you will actually need in retirement than exposing yourself to the possibility of running out of funds for your retirement due to underestimating.

Enter your "Life Expectancy Rate Projected (Number of Years)" in the "**SS16 Calculator-Retirement Savings Goal (In Today's Dollars)**" beside "Life Expectancy (Number of Years)."

Figure 7.5 Assumed Return Factors[6]

To determine your assumed return factor, use your "Annual Investment Growth Estimate" minus your "Inflation Rate Estimate" to get your "Net Inflation Adjusted Rate of Return." For example, if you anticipate a 7% return on your savings for retirement and a 4% inflation rate, 7% - 4% = **3%** (Net Inflation Adjusted Rate of Return). Then determine the "Anticipated Number of Years in Retirement" = "Life Expectancy (Number of Years)" – "Your Planned Retirement Age." For example, 90 years life expectancy – 65 at retirement age = **30** years (Anticipated Number of Years in Retirement). In our example, look in the chart below under the **3%** column and **30** years to get your "Assumed Return Factor" of **19.60**.

---

[5] Stephen N. Austad, *Why We Age: What Science Is Discovering about the Body's Journey Through Life*, John Wiley & Sons, Inc., New York, March 1999.
[6] Source: *A Common Sense Guide to Planning for Retirement*, Fidelity Investments. Tables are end-of-year factors.

Saving/Goal Setting

Years	2%	3%	4%	5%	6%
1	0.98	0.97	0.96	0.95	0.94
2	1.94	1.91	1.89	1.86	1.83
3	2.88	2.83	2.78	2.72	2.67
4	3.81	3.72	3.63	3.55	3.47
5	4.71	4.58	4.45	4.33	4.21
6	5.60	5.42	5.24	5.08	4.92
7	6.47	6.23	6.00	5.79	5.58
8	7.33	7.02	6.73	6.46	6.21
9	8.16	7.79	7.44	7.11	6.80
10	8.98	8.53	8.11	7.72	7.36
11	9.79	9.25	8.76	8.31	7.89
12	10.58	9.95	9.39	8.86	8.38
13	11.35	10.63	9.99	9.39	8.85
14	12.11	11.30	10.56	9.90	9.29
15	12.85	11.94	11.12	10.38	9.71
16	13.58	12.56	11.65	10.84	10.11
17	14.29	13.17	12.17	11.27	10.48
18	14.99	13.75	12.66	11.69	10.83
19	15.68	14.32	13.13	12.09	11.16
20	16.35	14.88	13.59	12.46	11.47
21	17.01	15.42	14.03	12.82	11.76
22	17.66	15.94	14.45	13.16	12.04
23	18.29	16.44	14.86	13.49	12.30
24	18.91	16.94	15.25	13.80	12.55
25	19.52	17.41	15.62	14.09	12.78
26	20.12	17.88	15.98	14.38	13.00
27	20.71	18.33	16.33	14.64	13.21
28	21.28	18.76	16.66	14.90	13.41
29	21.84	19.19	16.98	15.14	13.59
30	22.40	**19.60**	17.29	15.37	13.76

Determine your own "Assumed Return Factor" and enter it in the "**SS16 Calculator-Retirement Savings Goal (In Today's Dollars)**" beside "Assumed Return Factor."

Figure 7.6 Assumed Discount Factors[7]

To determine your assumed discount factor, use your "Preretirement Annual Investment Growth Estimate" minus your "Inflation Rate Estimate" to get your "Net Inflation Adjusted Rate of Return." For example, if you anticipate an 8% return on your savings

---

[7] Source: *A Common Sense Guide to Planning for Retirement*, Fidelity Investments. Tables are end-of-year factors.

Saving/Goal Setting

prior to retirement and a 4% inflation rate, 8% - 4% = **4%** (Net Inflation Adjusted Rate of Return). Then determine the "Number of Years Away From Retirement" (e.g., planned retirement at age 65 – 45 [age now] = **20** years). In our example, look in the chart below under the **4%** column and **20** years to get your "Assumed Discount Factor" of **0.033**.

Years	2%	3%	4%	5%	6%
1	1.000	1.000	1.000	1.000	1.000
2	.495	.492	.490	.487	.485
3	.326	.323	.320	.317	.314
4	.242	.239	.235	.232	.228
5	.192	.188	.184	.180	.177
6	.158	.154	.150	.147	.143
7	.134	.130	.126	.122	.119
8	.116	.112	.108	.104	.101
9	.102	.098	.094	.090	.087
10	.091	.087	.083	.079	.075
11	.082	.078	.074	.070	.066
12	.074	.070	.066	.062	.059
13	.068	.064	.060	.056	.052
14	.062	.058	.054	.051	.047
15	.057	.053	.049	.046	.042
16	.053	.049	.045	.042	.038
17	.049	.045	.042	.038	.035
18	.046	.042	.038	.035	.032
19	.043	.039	.036	.032	.029
20	.041	.037	**.033**	.030	.027
22	.036	.032	.029	.025	.023
24	.032	.029	.025	.022	.019
26	.029	.025	.022	.019	.016
28	.026	.023	.020	.017	.014
30	.024	.021	.017	.015	.012
32	.022	.019	.015	.013	.011
34	.020	.017	.014	.011	.009
36	.019	.015	.012	.010	.008
38	.017	.014	.011	.009	.007
40	.016	.013	.010	.008	.006

Determine your own "Assumed Discount Factor" and enter it in the "**SS16 Calculator-Retirement Savings Goal (In Today's Dollars)**" beside "Assumed Discount Factor."

The American Savings Education Council developed the "Ballpark Estimate" worksheet, which gives you a basic idea of your retirement savings needs. They have an

Saving/Goal Setting

interactive version of the worksheet at www.asec.org. Use this worksheet as a second opinion to the one you completed in this manual. Also, you can contact the Certified Financial Planner Board of Standards at www.cfp-board.org for information on evaluating financial planners. Certified financial planners can conduct complete financial plans for you including meticulous retirement estimates. Financial planners are compensated in numerous ways. Always check to see how your planner is compensated. Make sure all fees are explained in advance before signing any agreements. Ask if the planner helps to implement the plan. A word-of-mouth referral with a good recommendation from someone who has used the financial planner can help to increase your trust level in selecting a planner.

Jesus said, "*Set your mind on God's kingdom and his justice before everything else, and all the rest will come to you as well. So do not be anxious about tomorrow; tomorrow will look after itself. Each day has troubles enough of its own*"—Matthew 6:33–34. If you make saving a part of your activities today, it will help to free you from financial anxieties about your standard of living tomorrow.

It has been said that if you do not know where you are going, no road will take you there. Now that you have developed a map with your financial end goal in mind, let's proceed with some directions on how to get you there.

First, let us take a brief look at some of the characteristics of prodigious savers—typical millionaires. This exercise is not for the purpose of accumulating treasures to be stored on earth, its purpose is to discover some of the techniques proven successful by others that should be useful to you in achieving your savings goal. Tom Stanley and William D. Danko spent more than 20 years interviewing thousands of millionaires

Saving/Goal Setting

concerning their lifestyle habits and wrote the book titled *The Millionaire Next Door*. They dispel the myth that the typical millionaire drives a Rolls-Royce automobile, lives in a multimillion-dollar mansion, owns a Rolex watch, and wears tailor-made suits. The typical millionaire is more likely to drive a secondhand General Motors car, live in a house with an average property value of $320,000, wear a watch costing less than $100, and buy suits off the rack for between $200 and $300—the suit was probably on sale. The single biggest characteristic typical millionaires exhibit is living within their means. They are prodigious savers, not prodigious spenders. Typical millionaires are frugal and save or invest much of their income. On average, typical millionaires save and invest 20% of their income versus the average American savings of less than 5%. They are debt-free and have no mortgage or automobile notes. Most millionaires have made their own fortunes in one generation—they did not win the lottery, win money on a TV game show, or pick the next Microsoft on the stock market. Many are self-employed in small businesses working in "dull-normal" areas such as pest control, paving contract work, or welding. Most millionaires work 45 to 55 hours per week. Most marry once and are still married. Most typical millionaires do not score well on their SATs for college and were not voted most likely to succeed while in high school. Most millionaires are self-made, receiving no inheritance and little financial aid from relatives. Typical millionaires do spend generously on service professionals who can help them plan their finances better such as estate planners, accountants, and lawyers who specialize in guarding property and wealth. They invest in education. They typically have a broker, but they make their own investment decisions. Typical millionaires achieved their results over time through discipline, hard work, and focus on their goals. The typical millionaire lives in a

Saving/Goal Setting

neighborhood where 75% of the residents are nonmillionaires. They generally do not stand out. The *Millionaire Next Door* book makes an important point—two people with the same income, similar positions in life, living literally next door to each other could differ to this extent: the first could be three paychecks from losing the house, and the other could be financially self-sufficient enough to live 10 years or more without any additional income. The difference between the two is their spending and saving habits.

The ministry of Jesus Christ is certainly not about materialism or accumulating excessive wealth. Christ's ministry is about loving God and serving your neighbor. *Making Money Work* is not about trying to help you become a millionaire who leaves excessive funds after your death. The first-century Romans had a proverb—"money is like seawater; the more a man drinks, the thirstier he becomes." *Making Money Work* hopes to help you achieve a degree of financial independence and security (savings) while serving your fellow man through effective use of your time, talent, and offering (tithing/giving).

Jesus told this parable, "*There was a rich man whose land yielded heavy crops. He debated with himself: 'What am I to do? I have not the space to store my produce. This is what I will do,' said he: 'I will pull down my storehouses and build them bigger. I will collect in them all my corn and other goods, and then say to myself, 'Man, you have plenty of good things laid by, enough for many years: take life easy, eat, drink, and enjoy yourself.' But God said to him, 'You fool, this very night you must surrender your life; you have made your money—who will get it now?' That is how it is with the man who amasses wealth for himself and remains a pauper in the sight of God.*"—Luke 12:16–21.

Saving/Goal Setting

Tom Stanley and William D. Danko make another point in their book, *The Millionaire Next Door*: it only takes one spender in the family to keep the family from accumulating wealth. When the typical millionaire dies, regardless of the amount of money left, it is all gone within a couple of generations because eventually the inheritance will end up in the hands of a spender who has not learned the proper financial management habits. Teach your children good money management skills.

Social Security

Chapter 8

Social Security

Your Social Security benefits are calculated on the earnings recorded under your Social Security number. Make sure your employer has the correct name on your Social Security card and the correct number in order for you to receive proper credit. If you work for an employer, the employer withholds Social Security and Medicare taxes from your paycheck, matches the amount you pay from your paycheck (you get all the benefit), sends the taxes to the Internal Revenue Service, and reports your earnings to Social Security. Self-employed people pay their own Social Security taxes (both the employee and employer rates) when they file tax returns. Then the IRS reports their earnings to Social Security. As you work, you earn a maximum of four credits per year. Most individuals need ten years of work or 40 credits to qualify for benefits—younger people may need less for disability or survivor benefits.

Social Security is not intended to be your sole income during retirement. It is intended to supplement income from pension plans, savings, or other investments. Your Social Security benefit is a percentage of your earnings averaged over most of your working life. You may call the Social Security Administration at 1-800-772-1213 to get a copy of your Personal Earnings and Benefit Estimate Statement. The statement estimates your retirement benefits, what you would be eligible to collect in disability benefits, and what your dependent survivors receive upon your death. The Social Security Administration also has interactive worksheets at www.ssa.gov, which can help you to determine your estimated benefits. It is a good idea to check your Personal Earnings and Benefit Estimate

Social Security

Statement at least every three years for errors. If a year's earnings have been omitted, you will have to send the Social Security Administration a copy of your W-2 Wage and Tax Statement form for the missing year and get them to correct their records. That is important because it can affect your future benefit payments.

Currently, reduced benefits can be collected at age 62. If you elect to begin taking reduced benefits, the reduction is permanent. The full retirement age is 65 for people born before 1938. The longer you wait to receive benefits between 62 and 65, the more money you will receive. About 70% to 80% of retirees take early benefits; however, if you do not need the money for living expenses, waiting to receive benefits will result in more money. The better your health and the longer you expect to live, the more sense it makes to delay receiving Social Security benefits. The full retirement age rises until it reaches 67 for people born in 1960 or later. People who postpone retirement get special credit for each month they are not receiving benefits until age 70. There are some reasons why you might not want to delay receiving benefits such as poor health, only having alternative sources of income from tax-deferred retirement plans, or having a long and full work history. If you have poor health, you may want to start receiving benefits as soon as possible to maximize your income. At most, 85% of Social Security benefits could be taxed versus 100% of money withdrawn from a tax-deferred retirement plan. If you have had a long and full work history, the extra money you pay into the Social Security system in your late fifties and early sixties will only yield a slight increase in your benefits.

Disability benefits can be paid at any age to those who have an impairment that prevents them from doing "substantial" work for a year or more. Disability benefits can also be paid to those suffering a condition that is expected to result in death.

Social Security

Family benefits might be available to your family members if you are eligible for retirement or disability benefits. These benefits might include your spouse if he or she is 62 years old or under age 62 if he or she is caring for a child under age 16. The benefits might include your children if they are unmarried and under age 18, under age 19 but still in school, or 18 or older but disabled. Ex-spouses could be eligible for benefits on the wage earner's record.

Survivor's benefits might include a surviving spouse age 60 or older, 50 or older if disabled, or any age if caring for a child under age 16. Survivor's benefits might also include unmarried children under the age of 18, under age 19 but still in school, or 18 or older but disabled. Survivor's benefits might also include your parents if you have been their primary means of support. Ex-spouses could be eligible for survivor benefits on the wage earner's record.

Medicare is a federal health insurance program for people age 65 and over. Medicare benefits involve hospital insurance and medical insurance. Usually, people who are age 65 and receiving Social Security automatically qualify for Medicare and are automatically enrolled in Medicare. You will receive your Medicare card three months before your enrollment date. People who have been getting disability benefits for two years generally qualify for Medicare. Other people must file an application. Medicare does not pay for hospital or medical expenses outside the United States. If traveling abroad, consider obtaining other insurance. For more information about Medicare, call 1-800-MEDICAR (1-800-633-4227) or go to www.medicare.gov.

Social Security

Supplemental Security Income Benefits (SSI) might be available to those people who have low income and few assets. Most people who qualify for SSI also qualify for Medicaid, food stamps, or other assistance.

The Social Security Administration will not start your benefits until you file your application. Apply for Social Security or SSI disability benefits when you become disabled or for survivors' benefits when a family breadwinner dies. File for retirement benefits in the January before you intend to retire, but not earlier than three months before you reach age 62. To file for benefits, call a Social Security representative at 1-800-772-1213 or visit a local Social Security office—check your local phone book for the location of an office nearest to you. You may need a copy of the birth certificate for each family member applying for benefits, a marriage certificate if your spouse is applying for benefits, your most recent W-2 Wage and Tax form, or your tax return if you are self-employed.

Social Security and Medicare tax rates have changed periodically over the years. In 2002, the Social Security tax rate was 6.2% and the Medicare (hospital insurance) tax rate was 1.45%. For most purposes, the two taxes are combined together (i.e., 6.2% + 1.45% = 7.65%) and referred to as payroll taxes or FICA (Federal Insurance Contributions Act). If you work for an employer, the employer matches your Social Security and Medicare taxes (i.e., in 2002, 7.65% + 7.65% = 15.30%) and sends the amount to the IRS. Self-employed people pay the combined rate and send the amount (e.g., in 2002, 15.30%) to the IRS. There is no earnings limit for Medicare taxes; however, there is a maximum taxable amount for Social Security. You do not pay any Social Security tax on earnings exceeding the maximum taxable amount. The maximum taxable amount increases each

Social Security

year depending on the national average wage increase. Figure 8.1, "Social Security and Medicare Taxes (Historically)," gives you an overview of the changes that have taken place prior to 2003.

Figure 8.1 Social Security and Medicare Taxes (Historically)

Social Security and Medicare Taxes (Historically)

Years	Employer and Employee Tax Rate	Self-Employed Tax Rate	Maximum Earnings Taxed Annually for Social Security
1937–1949	1.000%	Not Covered	$3,000.00
1950	1.500%	Not Covered	$3,000.00
1951–1953	1.500%	2.250%	$3,600.00
1954	2.000%	3.000%	$3,600.00
1955–1956	2.000%	3.000%	$4,200.00
1957–1958	2.250%	3.375%	$4,200.00
1959	2.500%	3.750%	$4,800.00
1960–1961	3.000%	4.500%	$4,800.00
1962	3.125%	4.700%	$4,800.00
1963–1965	3.625%	5.400%	$4,800.00
1966	4.200%	6.150%	$6,600.00
1967	4.400%	6.400%	$6,600.00
1968	4.400%	6.400%	$7,800.00
1969–1970	4.800%	6.900%	$7,800.00
1971	5.200%	7.500%	$7,800.00
1972	5.200%	7.500%	$9,000.00
1973	5.850%	8.000%	$10,800.00
1974	5.850%	7.900%	$13,200.00
1975	5.850%	7.900%	$14,100.00
1976	5.850%	7.900%	$15,300.00
1977	5.850%	7.900%	$16,500.00
1978	6.050%	8.100%	$17,700.00
1979	6.130%	8.100%	$22,900.00
1980	6.130%	8.100%	$25,900.00
1981	6.650%	9.300%	$29,700.00
1982	6.700%	9.350%	$32,400.00
1983	6.700%	9.350%	$35,700.00
1984	6.700%	11.300%	$37,800.00
1985	7.050%	11.800%	$39,600.00
1986	7.150%	12.300%	$42,000.00
1987	7.150%	12.300%	$43,800.00
1988	7.510%	13.020%	$45,000.00

Social Security

1989	7.510%	13.020%	$48,000.00
1990	7.650%	15.300%	$51,300.00
1991	7.650%	15.300%	$53,400.00
1992	7.650%	15.300%	$55,500.00
1993	7.650%	15.300%	$57,600.00
1994	7.650%	15.300%	$60,600.00
1995	7.650%	15.300%	$61,200.00
1996	7.650%	15.300%	$62,700.00
1997	7.650%	15.300%	$65,400.00
1998	7.650%	15.300%	$68,400.00
1999	7.650%	15.300%	$72,600.00
2000	7.650%	15.300%	$76,200.00
2001	7.650%	15.300%	$80,400.00
2002	7.650%	15.300%	$84,900.00

Medicare began in 1966. Medicare only had "maximum earnings taxed annually" during the following years: 1991, $125,000; 1992, $130,200; 1993, $135,000. There has been no maximum earnings taxed annually on Medicare since.

Figure 8.1 points out that the Social Security and Medicare tax system is an evolving, changing process. Expect changes to both in the future.

Let's assume it is year 2002, which has $84,900.00 "Maximum Earnings Taxed Annually for Social Security." Let's also assume you earned $100,000 working for an employer, exceeding the "Maximum Earnings Taxed Annually for Social Security." Your taxes would be computed as follows:

	Tax Rate		**Taxable Amount**		**Amount of Tax**
You for Social Security:	6.20%	x	$84,900	=	$5,263.80
You for Medicare:	1.45%	x	$100,000	=	$1,450.00
Your Total:					*$6,713.80*
Your Employer for Social Security:	6.20%	x	$84,900	=	$5,263.80
Your Employer for Medicare:	1.45%	x	$100,000	=	$1,450.00
Your Employer Total:					*$6,713.80*
Total SS/Medicare Taxes:					$13,427.60

Social Security

In 2002, the average monthly benefits were as follows:

Retired workers	$874
Retired couples	$1,454
Disabled workers	$815
Young widow and 2 eligible children	$1,764
Aged widow with no children	$841

Once again, check with the Social Security Administration (1-800-772-1213, www.ssa.gov) to get your personal estimates.

In 2002, the full retirement age for benefits was as follows:

Year of Birth	**Full Retirement Age**
1937 and before	65
1938	65 and 2 months
1939	65 and 4 months
1940	65 and 6 months
1941	65 and 8 months
1942	65 and 10 months
1943 through 1954	66
1955	66 and 2 months
1956	66 and 4 months
1957	66 and 6 months
1958	66 and 8 months
1959	66 and 10 months
1960 and later	67

In 2002, the reduced benefits for early retirement were as follows:

Social Security

Year of Birth	Retired Worker's Reduced Benefit Percent of Your Primary Insurance Amount for Early Retirement[1]				
	62	**63**	**64**	**65**	**66**
1937 and before	80.0%	86.6%	93.3%	100.0%	—
1938	79.1%	85.5%	92.2%	98.8%	—
1939	78.3%	84.4%	91.1%	97.7%	—
1940	77.5%	83.3%	90.0%	96.6%	—
1941	76.6%	82.2%	88.8%	95.5%	—
1942	75.8%	81.1%	87.7%	94.4%	—
1943 through 1954	75.0%	80.0%	86.6%	93.3%	100.0%
1955	74.1%	79.1%	85.5%	92.2%	98.8%
1956	73.3%	78.3%	84.4%	91.1%	97.7%
1957	72.5%	77.5%	83.3%	90.0%	96.6%
1958	71.6%	76.6%	82.2%	88.8%	95.5%
1959	70.8%	75.8%	81.1%	87.7%	94.4%
1960 and later	70.0%	75.0%	80.0%	86.6%	93.3%
(Decimals are rounded down)					

The only true "security," social or otherwise is for those who have faith in God. "*The inheritance to which we are born is one that nothing can destroy or spoil or wither. It is kept for you in heaven, and you, because you put your faith in God, are under the protection of his power until salvation comes.*"—1 Peter 1:4–5.

---

[1] The reduction factor to the primary insurance amount is 5/9 of 1% for each of the first 36 months prior to the full retirement age plus 5/12 of 1% for each month in excess of 36 for retired workers. Contact the Social Security Administration for spouse, widow(er), and disabled widow(er) early retirement reduction factors.

Taxes

Chapter 9

Taxes

Representatives of the lawyers and chief priests asked Jesus, "*Are we or are we not permitted to pay taxes to the Roman Emperor?*"—Luke 20:22. Jesus replied, "*Show me a silver piece. Whose head does it bear, and whose inscription? 'Caesar's,' they replied. 'Very well then, he said, 'pay Caesar what is due to Caesar, and pay God what is due to God*"—Luke 20:23–25. Jesus acknowledged the importance of paying taxes. Taxes support our road systems, infrastructure, education, law enforcement, and many other important public services. Note that Jesus told the representatives to pay Caesar what is "due" to Caesar—not more and not less, but what is "due." Franklin D. Roosevelt said, "Taxes, after all, are the dues that we pay for the privileges of membership in an organized society."[1]

If you are receiving a large refund from your tax filing for the end of the year, you have been overpaying your taxes throughout the year. That means the government has been using your money interest-free since collecting the tax. On the other hand, if you have been paying a large amount in taxes upon completing your tax return for the end of the year, you have not been paying the government enough taxes. The ideal situation is that the taxpayer should only owe the government a few hundred dollars at the end of the year. That way, you owe the government interest-free and have until midnight on April 15 to pay off the tax bills. To adjust your tax withholding to more accurately reflect what

---

[1] *Taxation Quotations,* Atlanta Journal-Constitution, April 11, 2004.

Taxes

is due to the government, ask your payroll department to help work out a more accurate estimate of your tax withholdings. You may also contact the Internal Revenue Service (1-800-829-1040) at www.irs.gov to download forms, publications, instructions, and frequently asked questions. IRS Publication 919 "How Do I Adjust My Tax Withholding?" is the form you'll need. In addition, www.paycheckcity.com is a website that has numerous calculators that deal with your paycheck, including determining withholding, links to withholding forms, and more.

While paying taxes is important for the government programs that benefit all citizens, you are wise to take advantage of the legally approved tax tactics that can lower your tax bills on a before-tax versus an after-tax basis. Your adjusted gross income can be adjusted by thousands of dollars per year by taking advantage of government approved programs such as employer savings plans that use pretax dollars or flexible spending accounts. Some employers offer flexible spending arrangements during a one-time-per-year sign-up period. Under flexible spending arrangements for services such as child care or elder care, employees can designate a portion of their salary to be deducted from their paychecks and deposited into a flexible spending account. Employees then draw on the account during the year to pay eligible expenses. Any salary set aside in the flexible spending account escapes income tax and Social Security tax. Once you sign up for the account, you cannot change the amount of your deductions from your paycheck unless you have some change in family status such as a divorce. It is important to accurately estimate the amount of money you will deposit into the account because any unused funds will be forfeited at year-end. This "use it or loose it" rule necessitates a conservative estimate on how much you think you will spend from the account in the

Taxes

coming year. Dependent care flexible spending accounts can be fairly well estimated based on last year's day care charges.

Setting aside a portion of your pretax income has a substantial effect on your taxes. For example, note the following hypothetical example of Employee #1 who does not take advantage of pretax savings or flexible spending accounts versus Employee #2 who does take advantage of pretax savings or flexible spending accounts:

	After Tax Employee #1 (No pretax advantages)	Before Tax Employee #2 (Takes advantage of pretax savings or flexible spending accounts)
Salary:	$50,000	$50,000
Federal Tax Bracket of 28%:	-$14,000 ($50,000 x 28%)	
State Tax Bracket of 6%:	-$ 3,000 ($50,000 x 6%)	
Total:	$33,000	
$5,000 in savings or flexible spending accounts:	-$ 5,000 (after tax)	-$ 5,000 (before tax)
Total:		$45,000
Federal Tax Bracket of 28%:		-$12,600 ($45,000 x 28%)
State Tax Bracket of 6%:		-$ 2,700 ($45,000 x 6%)
Net take-home income after taxes and savings or flex accounts:	$28,000	$29,700
Total taxes paid:	$17,000 ($14,000 + $3,000)	$15,300 ($12,600 + $2,700)

Note that Employee #2, who took advantage of the government's before-tax savings or flexible spending account tax advantages, saved $1,700 in taxes ($17,000 - $15,300 = $1,700) and had $1,700 more net take-home income ($29,700 - $28,000 = $1,700). Before-tax savings accounts and flexible spending accounts are great government-approved incentives to increase your savings, decrease your taxes, and increase your disposal income.

The government may also offer tax-free investments, which are municipal obligations or IOUs issued by local and state governments and governmental agencies to raise money for public projects such as roads and parks. The government pays you regular interest on

Taxes

your investment and then repays your principal when the obligations mature. In most cases, the interest earned on municipal obligations is exempt from federal income tax and, in many instances, exempt from local and state taxes as well. The interest paid on tax-free investments is usually lower than interest paid on taxable investments such as bank CDs or corporate bonds. You should compare the yields on tax-free investments to taxable investments taking into consideration the tax-free advantage. The taxable equivalent yield is the yield you would have to get on a similar taxable investment to equal the tax-free yield. The formula to calculate the taxable equivalent yield is as follows:

TEY = (IR on TFE) divided by (1 – YTFTB)

Where:

TEY = Taxable Equivalent Yield
IR = Interest Rate
TFE = Tax-Free Investment
YTFTB = Your Tax-Free Tax Bracket (e.g., Tax-Free Federal Income Tax Bracket + Tax-Free State Tax Bracket + Tax-Free Local Tax Bracket, if the investment is tax-free for all 3 tax areas).

For example, assume you have $10,000 to invest in the following similar risk investments and you are in the 28% federal tax bracket:

1. A 6% tax-free municipal bond

2. An 8% taxable corporate bond

Which provides you with the highest yield? Convert the tax-free yield to a "taxable equivalent yield" to compare as follows:

TEY = 6%/(1-.28) = 6%/.72 = 8.33%.

The taxable equivalent yield of 8.33% on the 6% tax-free municipal bond is .33% higher than the 8% taxable corporate bond. In this case, the lower interest rate on the tax-free

Taxes

bond leaves you with more investment income than the taxable bond on an after-tax basis. In addition, your investment may be exempt from state and local taxes. If also exempt from state taxes of 6%, the taxable equivalent yield would equate as follows:

TEY = 6%/1 - (.28 Federal Exemption + .06 State Exemption = .34) = 6%/.66 = 9.09%.

For assistance in determining your tax equivalent yields, please complete the following steps:

1. Open the "SS17 Calculator-Tax Equivalent Yields.xls"; see Figure 9.1.
2. Click "Yes" to enable macros, if necessary.
3. Fill in your own personal information in each white cell (you may tab from one white cell to another).
4. After completing the information in all of the white cells, press "Tab" and then click on the "MMW Recalculation Button"—the spreadsheet will make the remaining calculations for you.

Figure 9.1 Taxable Equivalent Yield

Fill in your information on the tax-free investment interest rate.
Fill in these cells only if your investment is tax-free in each.

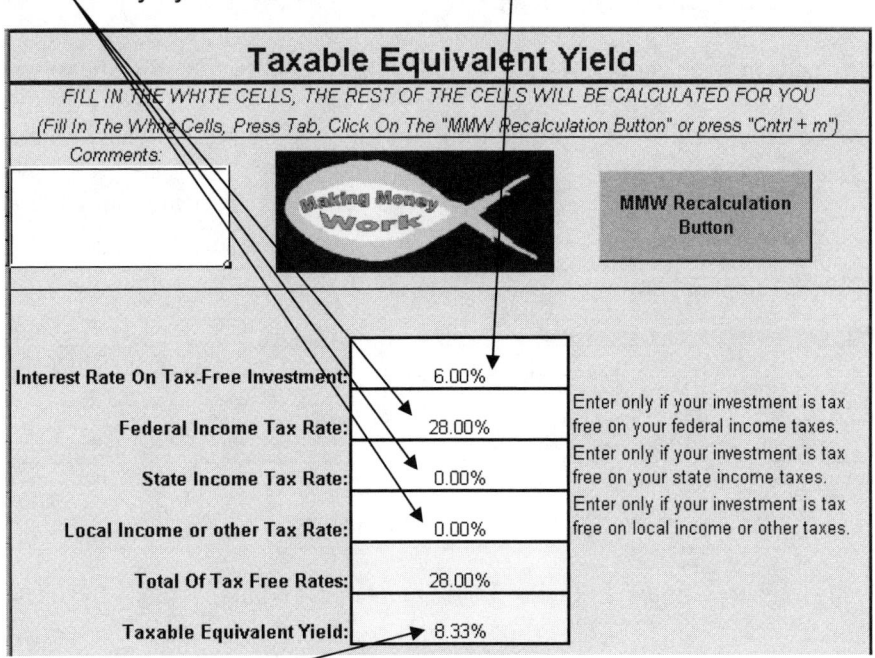

Taxable Equivalent Yield

FILL IN THE WHITE CELLS, THE REST OF THE CELLS WILL BE CALCULATED FOR YOU
(Fill In The White Cells, Press Tab, Click On The "MMW Recalculation Button" or press "Cntrl + m")

Comments:

MMW Recalculation Button

Interest Rate On Tax-Free Investment:	6.00%
Federal Income Tax Rate:	28.00%	Enter only if your investment is tax free on your federal income taxes.
State Income Tax Rate:	0.00%	Enter only if your investment is tax free on your state income taxes.
Local Income or other Tax Rate:	0.00%	Enter only if your investment is tax free on local income or other taxes.
Total Of Tax Free Rates:	28.00%
Taxable Equivalent Yield:	8.33%

This is the taxable equivalent yield you would need to get on a non-tax-free investment to equal your investment income on the tax-free investment.

There are three basic ways to invest for tax-free income:

1. Buy individual municipal bonds

Taxes

2. Invest in a fixed portfolio of bonds through a unit investment trust (UIT)

3. Purchase shares in a tax-free mutual fund

If you purchase individual municipal bonds, stick with bonds that are investment grade. Buy individual municipal bonds if you are planning to hold them to maturity. Buy enough municipal bonds to maintain a well-diversified portfolio. Most municipal bonds pay interest that is exempt from federal taxes. If you purchase bonds issued in your state of residence, the interest may be exempt from state or local taxes.

Unit investment trusts allow investors to purchase an interest in a fixed portfolio of diversified bonds, which are professionally selected but not actively managed. UITs offer a fixed rate of return and diversification.

Mutual funds provide continuous professional management and automatically diversify your investments, which helps to minimize your risk versus purchasing individual investments. Your risk tolerance should be considered when choosing mutual funds. The following chart may help you in selecting tax-free mutual funds:

Type	**Risk Category**	**Yield**	**Maturity**	**Share Price Fluctuation**	**Quality**
Money Market Funds	Most Conservative	Lowest	Shortest	None	Highest
Short/Intermediate Funds (5–15 years)	Conservative	High	Short/Intermediate	Low	High
Long-Term Funds (15–30 years)	Moderate	Higher	Long	Higher	Medium to High
High Yield Funds	Aggressive	Highest	Long	Highest	Low

Federally tax-free mutual funds hold municipal bonds issued by states and municipalities throughout the country. The income from these funds is usually exempt from federal income taxes. In addition, a portion of the income may be exempt from state and local taxes—usually the income generated from bonds issued in the state in which you reside. State tax-free mutual funds invest in municipal bonds issued by a single state.

Taxes

If you reside in the state, you normally get tax exemptions from federal, state, and local income taxes.

The higher your tax bracket, the more benefits you receive from investments that provide tax-exempt income. Tax-free investing can be very beneficial if you are in the 28% federal tax bracket or higher. For lower tax brackets, you may be better off investing in comparable-quality taxable investments and paying your taxes since tax-free funds usually have lower returns than comparable taxable funds. The important factor is not how much tax you avoid, but how much income you keep on an after-tax basis.

When considering taxes, think about short-term gains versus long-term capital gains. Profits from short-term investments (those held less than one year) are taxed at your regular income tax level. Capital gains from long-term investments (those held longer than one year) are currently taxed at a top rate of 20% (10% if you are in the 15% tax bracket). Length of investment holdings is determined from trade dates, not settlement dates. When possible, take advantage of the long-term lower tax incentive. Also, when you sell investments, you might be able to minimize taxes by selecting which investments to sell first if your investments were purchased at different times and different prices. If you do not specify which shares to sell, the IRS will make you assume on your tax return that the first shares you bought were the first shares you sold (FIFO—"first in, first out" accounting method). If your investments have steadily increased in value, FIFO usually results in the biggest taxable gain possible since the investments sold would usually be those acquired at the lowest price. You may use the "average cost" method of accounting, which still costs a lot in taxes. Once you choose the average cost method, you cannot switch to another accounting method when redeeming shares from your investment. You

Taxes

can also choose to sell the investments you acquired at the highest prices first to minimize taxes (HIFO—"highest in, first out" accounting method).

To compare theses three accounting methods, let's assume you purchased the following:

1,000 shares @ $10.45
1,000 shares @ $17.28
1,000 shares @ $21.69

Let's assume you've held all of the shares longer than one year (long-term capital gains of 15%). Also, let's assume you sold 1,400 shares @ $24.75 = $34,650.00 total sale. The following is a comparison of the three different accounting methods and the taxes due on each:

FIFO Method (first in, first out)	Average Cost Method	HIFO Method (highest in, first out)
1,000 @ $10.45 = $10,450.00	$10.45 + $17.28 + $21.69	1,000 @ $21.69 = $21,690.00
400 @ $17.28 = $ 6,912.00	= $ 49.42	400 @ $17.28 = $ 6,912.00
Total: $17,362.00	Divided by 3	Total: $28,602.00
Sold—	Average Cost = $ 16.47	Sold—
1400 @ $24.75 = $34,650.00	Share Sold x 1,400	1,400 @ $24.75 = $34,650.00
- $17,362.00	Total: $23,058.00	- $28,602.00
= $17,288.00	Sold—	= $ 6,048.00
x 15%	1,400 @ $24.75 = $34,650.00	x 15%
Taxes Due = $ 2,593.20	- $23,058.00	Taxes Due = $ 907.20
	= $11,592.00	
	x 15%	
	Taxes Due = $ 1,738.80	

Another way to minimize capital gains taxes is to sell some of your money-losing investments along with those that have appreciated in value. Losses on your investments can offset any capital gains you may have reaped on other investments. "Harvesting losses," means selling investment losses to offset the taxes you will need to pay by selling investments that return a profit to you.

Taxes

Pay taxes that are due; however, utilize tax tactics approved by the government. Defer taxes when possible so your investments can compound without the negative impact of taxes being taken out up front. Minimize taxes where you can to maximize investment income.

Retirement Funds

Chapter 10

Retirement Funds

Jesus said, "*Whoever wants to be great must be your servant, and whoever wants to be first must be the willing slave of all—like the Son of Man; he did not come to be served, but to serve, and to give up his life as a ransom for many*"—Matthew 20:26–28. God served you by sending himself in the form of Jesus Christ as a sacrifice for your sins that you might have life eternal. God wants you to serve your fellow man. Serving is a lifetime commitment to God. It does not end with your retirement from employment. Savings and retirement funds can help you achieve financial freedom so that you no longer have to work for money; however, Christians express their love for God by serving their neighbors all the days of their lives. Once you retire from your employment, you have more freedom to do volunteer work at church and in your community in order to serve others. The Bible does not talk about retiring. You never retire from being a Christian and sharing Christ's love. You never retire from serving God.

First, let's look at some retirement fund fundamentals that will help you get to the point that you can choose to retire from employment to pursue more volunteer work. If your employer offers a qualified tax-deferred retirement account, you might be able to have contributions to the plan deducted from your paycheck. Utilize before-tax contributions to your employee retirement plan as much as possible. Making before-tax contributions keeps you from paying taxes on the portion of your salary that you invest in the plan (tax deferral) and allows your earnings to grow tax-free until the money is withdrawn. This allows compounding interest to maximize your savings as much as

Retirement Funds

possible so your retirement nest egg will be much larger than savings accumulated on an after-tax basis. An amount of $166.67 per month saved in a tax-deferred savings plan over a 30-year period compounded at 8% annually would grow into a retirement nest egg of $244,692. Without the tax shelter, the same investment in a 28% tax bracket would only grow to $160,326. The annual payment of taxes on investments is one of the greatest factors deterring investment growth. Your retirement nest egg will be much larger the longer you can delay paying the taxes. In most cases, it is wise to set aside the maximum the law allows in employer-sponsored, tax-deferred retirement accounts. Upon retirement, you may even be in a lower income tax bracket and end up paying less in taxes. A word of caution: generally, if you withdraw your qualified tax-deferred retirement account funds prior to 59½ years of age, you have to pay regular income taxes on the withdrawal amount plus a 10% penalty for the early withdrawal. You are not subject to the 10% penalty if you receive payment as a lifetime retirement annuity, you die, or you become disabled.

Most employers match the contribution individual employees make to their retirement plans. For example, a typical employer plan might match $0.50 for every $1.00 employees put into their retirement plan up to a maximum of 6% of their annual gross pay. That's a guaranteed 50% immediate return on your savings! At a minimum, save enough funds in your company's retirement plan to harvest the maximum amount of employer matching contributions. The only time that might not be a good investment for you is when employers put their matching 50% into an investment with which you are not comfortable. If the investment is going into your company stock and your company is

Retirement Funds

on the verge of bankruptcy, your 50% matching contributions could be worth 0% in the future.

Contributing to your company retirement account with matching contributions should be your first priority in your savings plan. Begin participating in company-sponsored investing plans as soon as possible. Do not invest too much in your company's stock. Your company stock holdings should not exceed 10% to 15% of your total portfolio for diversification purposes. Diversification means distributing your assets among different kinds of securities in order to lower your risk of losses due to one investment loosing its value. A well-diversified portfolio not only is safer, but it will return more money over a long time frame. Rebalance your savings holdings periodically to insure proper diversification. Retirement savings is long-term investing that requires persistent, steady effort.

Try not to borrow from your retirement account if at all possible because you loose the earnings your money would have made if the funds had been left in the account. Any interest on your retirement account loan is paid back into your account; however, the interest is taxable. In addition, you have to have the discipline to pay the loan back; if you do not, then you are jeopardizing your future retirement. If you do not pay the loan back, you must pay regular income tax plus the early withdrawal penalty before age 59½. Some plans will not allow you to continue to make regular pretax contributions while you are repaying the loan—that means you miss out on the employer's matching contributions. If you change jobs and start to work for another employer, you will have to repay the loan in full within 90 days. You will have to pay taxes on the money twice because you are borrowing before-tax dollars and repaying the loan with after-tax money; then, when you

Retirement Funds

retire, you will pay tax a second time on the money you borrowed! While the loan may require that you pay yourself back with interest, the percentage of interest you pay the loan back with is typically less than the amount of interest you would have earned if the money had been left in your retirement savings account to begin with. In addition, your plan administrator might assess loan fees and other charges for you to borrow the money. More than likely, you are better off seeking other sources of loans—such as a home equity loan—than borrowing from your retirement account. Retirement loan interest is not deductible; home equity loan interest is deductible. Retirement account money is best left untouched.

What are some of the available retirement fund options? 401 (k) plans are offered to employees of taxable corporations. 401 (k) plans are savings plans named after the section of the Internal Revenue Code Section 401 (k) made into law by a 1978 act of Congress. The IRS determines specific features and limits of 401 (k) plans, and your employer determines the specific plan parameters. 401 (k) funds allow you to set up a tax-deferred investment account. Employees put up most or all of the money to be invested. More than 85% of the companies offering 401 (k) plans match contributions on varying scales—the policy depends on the individual company. Each company is responsible for setting up its own matching formula and its own cap level for matching employee contributions. A typical company match is $0.50 for every $1.00 the employee contributes up to a 6% of salary cap level. The total contribution level varies depending on your company's matching fund policies; however, most employees can devote up to 15% of their gross pay to their 401 (k)—highly paid employees may be subject to lower restrictions. For example, if your company matches up to 6%, you might receive free

Retirement Funds

matching contributions to the 6% level and then contribute another 9% on your own with no match to the 15% total limit. Employees pay no taxes on the contributions in their retirement account until withdrawal. Interest and dividends earned on the investments are free from taxes until withdrawal. Employees select how they want the contributions invested among the plan's investment options. This gives the employees the ability to manage their own retirement assets. The employer selects an array of available investment options that usually include stocks, bonds, and cash equivalents. Typical investment options include stock mutual funds, balanced stock-and-bond mutual funds, fixed-income funds, and shares of the company you work for. Contact your 401 (k) administrator for investment literature to help you decide in which funds you would like to invest. You tell your employer what percentage or dollar amount you would like to voluntarily contribute from your paycheck each pay period. If you are deducting a specific dollar amount versus a percentage, when you receive a raise, be certain to increase your dollar amount contribution to keep your retirement savings growing at the rate that your standard of living is increasing. Your earnings are tax-deferred until withdrawal, and your contributions reduce your current-year taxable income. 401 (k) plans are one of the best ways to save for retirement.

403 (b) plans are similar to 401 (k) plans; however, they are offered to employees of tax-exempt organizations such as educational institutions, churches, hospitals, and health-care facilities. 403 (b) funds can be funded with annuities with insurance companies or custodial accounts with mutual funds.

Keogh plans are intended for self-employed individuals and their employees. You usually need professional help to set up Keogh plans. There are several ways to set them

Retirement Funds

up and to fund them. Contributions to Keogh plans are tax deductible, up to certain limits—currently a maximum limit of $30,000/year. With a Profit-Sharing Keogh, you can save up to 15% each year and change the percentage amount that you save each year. With a Money Purchase Keogh, you can save 1% to 25% of your income per year up to the maximum limit. A Paired Keogh combines features of the Profit-Sharing Keogh with the Money Purchase Keogh—the money purchase part is fixed for the life of the Keogh while the percentage profit-sharing contribution can change each year with the 15% limitation. The combined maximum of a Paired Keogh is still 25% of your income or the maximum limit—whichever is less.

SEP or Simplified Employee Pension is a plan for self-employed individuals or small companies. SEPs allow employers to make tax-deductible contributions to employee individual retirement accounts (IRAs). The employee determines if the funds will be invested in stocks, mutual funds, or bonds. Your employer can contribute up to 15% of your adjusted net earned income (excluding income over a maximum ceiling—$6,000 in 1997). In any given year, you can have both a SEP and an IRA and contribute the maximum to both. SEPs are easy to set up and administer, and have little or no administrative expenses.

What options for your retirement fund do you have if you leave your employer? Avoid the temptation to take the money. If you ask your old employer to send you the retirement funds in a check made payable to you, the employer is required by law to withhold 20% of the taxable portion of your savings. The 20% withheld is sent by the employer to the IRS to be applied to federal income taxes. This 20% is taken out even if you plan on rolling your savings over into an IRA account within 60 days. For example, let's say you

Retirement Funds

are working for Employer #1 and decide to go to work for Employer #2. You have $100,000 saved in Employer #1's savings plan. You ask Employer #1 to send you a check payable to you—a big mistake. Employer #1 withholds 20% or $20,000 from your $100,000 savings, sends the $20,000 to the IRS, and sends you a check for $80,000 (made payable to you—another mistake). The IRS applies the $20,000 to the federal tax you might have to pay in the year of the distribution. You decide to roll your savings over to another savings plan. You are required to roll the total amount of the distribution, including the amount withheld, within 60 days to avoid negative tax consequences. Employer #1 will not return the $20,000 to you. You must come up with the $20,000 out of your own pocket to replace the funds in order to roll the entire $100,000 into a new savings plan. If you only roll over the $80,000, you subject the $20,000 withheld to taxation in the current year at your normal tax rate plus a 10% penalty for withdrawal before age 59½. Worse yet, if you do not roll any of the distribution over within 60 days, you subject the entire $100,000 to your current year's tax rate plus the 10% penalty for early withdrawal before age 59½.

Fortunately, the IRS gives you several ways to avoid the 20% withholding. One option is to initiate a direct rollover. When using a direct rollover, you transfer your retirement plan savings from your plan's trustee to a new IRA or another eligible retirement plan—your old employer sends the check to the new account, not directly to you. Your old employer may send the funds electronically. This allows your savings to continue to grow tax-deferred until withdrawal and avoids ordinary income taxes, tax penalties, and the 20% tax withholding withdrawal requirement imposed by the federal government. If your old employer requires that the check be sent to you, it should be made *payable to your*

Retirement Funds

new account *"For the Benefit of [Your Name]"*—check with your plan administrators to get the exact wording for the check. It is best to set up a new conduit IRA or other eligible retirement plan when completing the rollover. Do not mix the funding with existing retirement accounts or future savings. This preserves your right to roll the distribution savings over into a future employer's plan—if available. Serious tax consequences can arise at retirement time if the conduit IRA funds have been commingled with previous IRA contributions or money from other pension plans. Another option is to leave your money in your old employer's savings plan to avoid taxes and penalties. Usually, if your assets are greater than several thousand dollars, your old employer will allow you to leave your money in the plan. Another option is to transfer your savings plan from your old employer to the new employer's savings plan. Be certain to review the new employer's savings plan for costs and investment options. If your new employer has a one-time-per-year sign-up period for the savings plan enrollment, you may have to establish a conduit IRA to temporarily take your distribution until the new employer plan is available to receive the transfer. Another option is to keep your savings tax-deferred and begin receiving payments through either an installment program or an annuity—subject to the payments' receiving normal tax treatment plus any penalties. Annuities are investments whose earnings are tax deferred until withdrawn. Annuities may provide a guaranteed stream of income over your lifetime. Annuities have no limit on the amount you can invest.

Many financial advisors recommend saving enough for retirement so that no more than 4% to 6% of your total portfolio must be used in any given year for living expenses. The following retirement portfolio withdrawal table shows what percentage of your portfolio

Retirement Funds

can be withdrawn each year—it assumes you will deplete your principal during retirement. The percent shown for the first year of the period would be increased 4% per year to offset inflation.

Retirement Portfolio Withdrawal Table					
Percent of Portfolio That May Be Withdrawn Each Year (Taking Rising Withdrawals of 4%/Year to Offset Inflation)					
	Average Annual Investment Return				
Retirement Period	5%	6%	7%	8%	9%
10 years	10.4%	10.9%	11.3%	11.8%	12.2%
15 years	7.1%	7.6%	8.1%	8.6%	9.1%
20 years	5.5%	6.0%	6.5%	7.0%	7.5%
25 years	4.5%	5.0%	5.5%	6.1%	6.6%
30 years	3.8%	4.3%	4.9%	5.5%	6.1%

For example, assume you are 30 years from retirement and anticipate your portfolio earning 5%/year. You could withdraw 3.8% from your portfolio in your 30th year prior to your anticipated death. In year 29, you could withdraw 3.95% (3.8% x 1.04 = 3.95%), and so forth.

The Employee Benefits Security Administration, Division of Technical Assistance and Inquiries, U.S. Department of Labor, is the national guardian of the vast private retirement and welfare benefit system. They enforce the Employee Retirement Income Security Act (ERISA) of 1974, which protects retirement plans and their assets from misuse. If you detect possible mishandling of your retirement funds, contact the following:

U.S. Department Of Labor
Employee Benefits Security Administration 200 Constitution Avenue, NW
Washington, DC 20210
1-866-275-7922
http://askebsa.dol.gov/

Retirement Funds

For assistance in determining your retirement savings' future value projections, please complete the following steps:

1. Open the "SS18 Calculator-Investment Future Value.xls"; see Figures 10.1. and 10.2.
2. Click "Yes" to enable macros, if necessary.
3. Fill in your own personal information in each white cell (you may tab from one white cell to another).
4. After completing the information in all of the white cells, press "Tab" and then click on the "MMW Recalculation Button"—the spreadsheet will make the remaining calculations for you.

Figure 10.1 Calculator-Investment Future Value

Fill in the annual dollar amount you plan to save for retirement.

Fill in the "Total # Of Year End Deposits" you plan to make—e.g., the number of years you have before retirement.

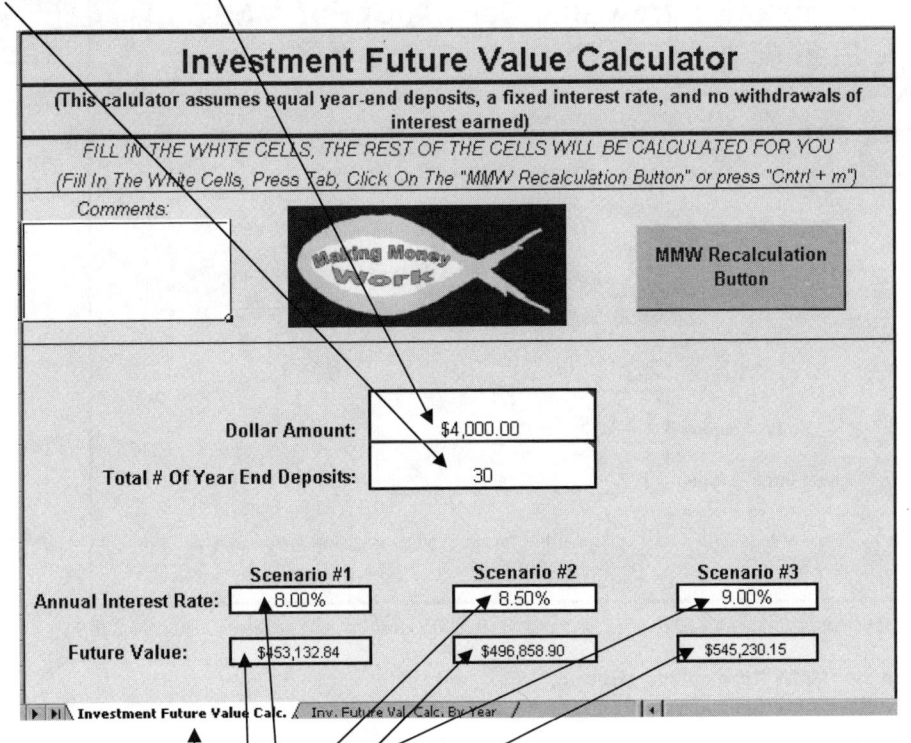

Investment Future Value Calculator

(This calulator assumes equal year-end deposits, a fixed interest rate, and no withdrawals of interest earned)

FILL IN THE WHITE CELLS, THE REST OF THE CELLS WILL BE CALCULATED FOR YOU
(Fill In The White Cells, Press Tab, Click On The "MMW Recalculation Button" or press "Cntrl + m")

Dollar Amount:	$4,000.00
Total # Of Year End Deposits:	30

	Scenario #1	Scenario #2	Scenario #3
Annual Interest Rate:	8.00%	8.50%	9.00%
Future Value:	$453,132.84	$496,858.90	$545,230.15

Open the "Investment Future Value Calc." Sheet.

Fill in the annual interest rate return you anticipate your portfolio to average—this calculator allows you to project 3 different scenarios at the same time.

The calculator projects the future value of your savings with the different interest rate projections.

The next sheet, "Inv. Future Val. Calc. By Year" (Investment Future Calculator by Year) calculates the value of your savings plan by year for up to 50 years using the same "Dollar Amount" and "Interest Rate Amounts."

Retirement Funds

Figure 10.2 Investment Future Value Calculator for a Savings Plan of a Series of Equal Deposits by Year

Click on the "Inv. Future Val. Calc. By Year" sheet tab.

Fill in the annual dollar amount you plan to save for retirement.

Fill in the annual interest rate you project you will average on your portfolio.

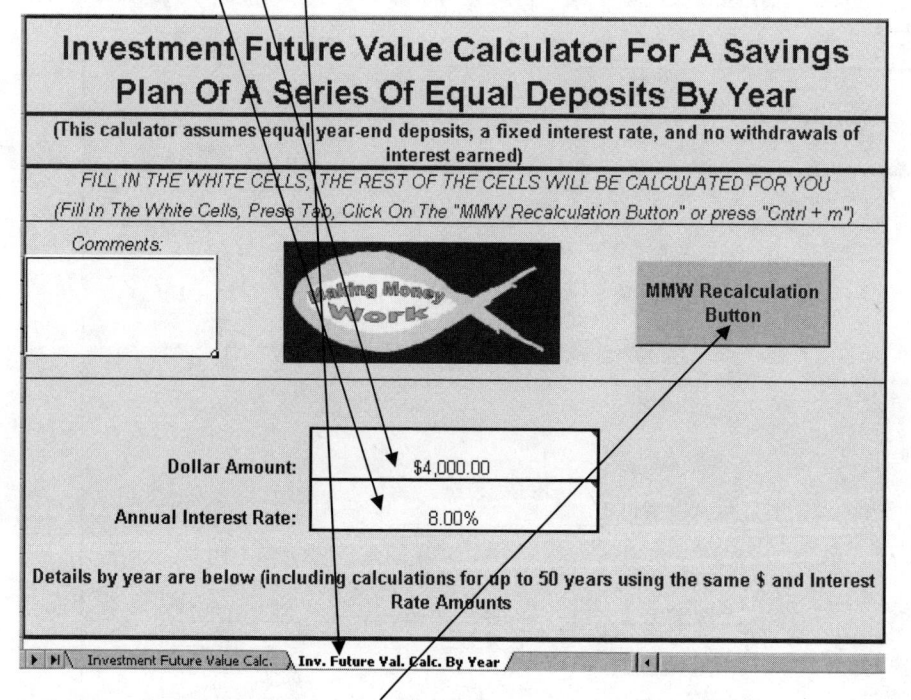

Click on the "MMW Recalculation Button."

126

Retirement Funds

Details by year are below (including calculations for up to 50 years using the same $ and Interest Rate Amounts

Year	Value At The Beginning Of Year	Interest Earned	Deposit At End Of Year	Ending Value
Year 1	$0.00	$0.00	$4,000.00	$4,000.00
Year 2	$4,000.00	$320.00	$4,000.00	$8,320.00
Year 3	$8,320.00	$665.60	$4,000.00	$12,985.60
Year 4	$12,985.60	$1,038.85	$4,000.00	$18,024.45
Year 5	$18,024.45	$1,441.96	$4,000.00	$23,466.40
Year 6	$23,466.40	$1,877.31	$4,000.00	$29,343.72
Year 7	$29,343.72	$2,347.50	$4,000.00	$35,691.21
Year 8	$35,691.21	$2,855.30	$4,000.00	$42,546.51
Year 9	$42,546.51	$3,403.72	$4,000.00	$49,950.23
Year 10	$49,950.23	$3,996.02	$4,000.00	$57,946.25
Year 11	$57,946.25	$4,635.70	$4,000.00	$66,581.95
Year 12	$66,581.95	$5,326.56	$4,000.00	$75,908.51
Year 13	$75,908.51	$6,072.68	$4,000.00	$85,981.19
Year 14	$85,981.19	$6,878.49	$4,000.00	$96,859.68
Year 15	$96,859.68	$7,748.77	$4,000.00	$108,608.46
Year 16	$108,608.46	$8,688.68	$4,000.00	$121,297.13
Year 17	$121,297.13	$9,703.77	$4,000.00	$135,000.90
Year 18	$135,000.90	$10,800.07	$4,000.00	$149,800.97
Year 19	$149,800.97	$11,984.08	$4,000.00	$165,785.05
Year 20	$165,785.05	$13,262.80	$4,000.00	$183,047.86

For example, suppose you plan to save $4,000 per year, anticipate earning an average of 8% on your portfolio, and plan to retire in 20 years; you would have saved $183,047.86 toward your savings goal.

- - -

Year 25	$267,059.04	$21,364.72	$4,000.00	$292,423.76
Year 26	$292,423.76	$23,393.90	$4,000.00	$319,817.66
Year 27	$319,817.66	$25,585.41	$4,000.00	$349,403.07
Year 28	$349,403.07	$27,952.25	$4,000.00	$381,355.32
Year 29	$381,355.32	$30,508.43	$4,000.00	$415,863.74
Year 30	$415,863.74	$33,269.10	$4,000.00	$453,132.84
Year 31	$453,132.84	$36,250.63	$4,000.00	$493,383.47
Year 32	$493,383.47	$39,470.68	$4,000.00	$536,854.15
Year 33	$536,854.15	$42,948.33	$4,000.00	$583,802.48
Year 34	$583,802.48	$46,704.20	$4,000.00	$634,506.68
Year 35	$634,506.68	$50,760.53	$4,000.00	$689,267.21
Year 36	$689,267.21	$55,141.38	$4,000.00	$748,408.59
Year 37	$748,408.59	$59,872.69	$4,000.00	$812,281.28
Year 38	$812,281.28	$64,982.50	$4,000.00	$881,263.78
Year 39	$881,263.78	$70,501.10	$4,000.00	$955,764.88
Year 40	$955,764.88	$76,461.19	$4,000.00	$1,036,226.07
Year 41	$1,036,226.07	$82,898.09	$4,000.00	$1,123,124.16
Year 42	$1,123,124.16	$89,849.93	$4,000.00	$1,216,974.09
Year 43	$1,216,974.09	$97,357.93	$4,000.00	$1,318,332.02
Year 44	$1,318,332.02	$105,466.56	$4,000.00	$1,427,798.58
Year 45	$1,427,798.58	$114,223.89	$4,000.00	$1,546,022.47
Year 46	$1,546,022.47	$123,681.80	$4,000.00	$1,673,704.27
Year 47	$1,673,704.27	$133,896.34	$4,000.00	$1,811,600.61
Year 48	$1,811,600.61	$144,928.05	$4,000.00	$1,960,528.66
Year 49	$1,960,528.66	$156,842.29	$4,000.00	$2,121,370.95
Year 50	$2,121,370.95	$169,709.68	$4,000.00	$2,295,080.63

This calculator assumes equal year-end deposits (your actual savings should be higher, especially if you are using payroll deduction to make contributions out of each paycheck throughout the year), a fixed interest rate (of course, in the real world, your average interest earned per year will fluctuate), and no withdrawals of interest earned.

Retirement Funds

Oppenheimer published a report stating that 80% of American households will retire with less than half the savings they need to live comfortably.[1] The most critical factor for retirees for a satisfying retirement is financial preparedness. Regardless of net worth, the retirees who save the longest are the most satisfied in retirement. Utilize the proper planning, retirement funds, tax deferral strategies, and steady savings habits to insure you have enough funds to provide for your needs during your retirement years. Of course, there are other needs besides financial ones in retirement such as socialization, enjoyment, accomplishment, and so on. A Gallup Organization poll of more than 1,000 nonretired American investors found the following:[2]

1. 68% of those polled would like to work in retirement as consultants in their field of expertise.
2. 67% of those polled would like to work for pleasure—not out of financial necessity.
3. 57% of those polled plan to work part-time.

"*There is treasure to be desired and oil in the dwelling of the wise; but a foolish man spendeth it up*"—Proverbs 21:20 (King James Version).

---

[1] Michael Penn, *Retirement Plans Used Too Little, Too Late,* Morning Star 5 Star Investor, November 1993, page 12.
[2] *Americans Rethink Retirement,* Solutions from Lincoln, Summer 2002, page 1.

Investments — Historical Returns

Chapter 11

Investments—Historical Returns

Historical returns are not necessarily indicative of the future because the future is a moving target. However, by studying historical returns, most people can get a better idea of what the future might hold. Annualized returns for different investments from December 31, 1950 through December 31, 2000 are as follows:

Type of Investment	50-Year Annualized Return (Through 12/31/2000)[1]	$1,000 Initial Investment at the End of 50 Years (Excluding Tax Calculations)
United States Small Company Stocks	14.1%	$731,614.36
Standard & Poor's 500 Stock Index	12.8%	$412,529.47
Dow Jones Industrial Average	8.3%[2]	$53,384.15
United States Intermediate Term Government Bonds	6.4%	$22,237.27
United States Long-Term Corporate Bonds	6.2%	$20,240.71
United States 30-Day Treasury Bills	5.2%	$12,237.27
United States Inflation Rate	**4.0%**	

Few people have a 50-year time frame to invest for retirement. If the above-annualized returns were used as an example for a 30-year investment time frame, the chart would look like this:

---

[1] Source: Ibbotson Associates.
[2] Source: Extrapolated from "The Financial Center" data (in 1950, the DJIA was at 201.80; in 2000, the DJIA was at 10,786.85).

Investments – Historical Returns

Type of Investment	50-Year Annualized Return (Through 12/31/2000)	$1,000 Initial Investment at the End of 30 Years (Excluding Tax Calculations)
United States Small Company Stocks	14.1%	$52,308.15
Standard & Poor's 500 Stock Index	12.8%	$37,091.38
Dow Jones Industrial Average	8.3%	$10,875.45
United States Intermediate Term Government Bonds	6.4%	$6,430.56
United States Long-Term Corporate Bonds	6.2%	$6,077.38
United States 30-Day Treasury Bills	5.2%	$4,575.85
United States Inflation Rate	**4.0%**	

You should start investing early to take advantage of compound interest. You should invest regularly. You should invest for the long term. You should diversify your portfolio holdings to lessen potential losses from any one investment or financial area. You should establish a well-balanced portfolio that will exceed the rate of inflation to protect your buying power. Use stock funds for growth—historically, stock markets have been up two-thirds of the time. Use fixed-income funds for preservation of capital. In general, the higher the investments risk, the higher the return. Everyone has different tolerance levels for risk; you have to decide what level of risk you are willing to accept for your investments.

Some basic characteristics of investments are as follows:

1. Safety of Principal—the ability to get back your original investment. Generally speaking, the safer the investment regarding safety of principal, the lower the return on the investment. For example, United States Treasury Bills assure that you cannot loose what you invest because they are backed by a government guarantee; hence, they usually offer a lower rate of return than stocks or mutual funds that cannot make the same promise for safety of principal.
2. Safety of Income—some investments guarantee certain periodic amounts of income. Some investments may guarantee safety of income but not guarantee safety of principal.
3. Current Income—the return on investment expected in the first year.
4. Growth of Principal—some investments increase the value of the principal over time. Stocks and real estate may produce growth of principal.

Investments — Historical Returns

5. Growth of Income—some investments increase the level of periodic income to help keep up with inflation.
6. Liquidity—refers to the ability to quickly and easily cash in an investment. The less liquid the investment, the higher its return should be. For example, real estate may appreciate in value well; however, property can be difficult to sell quickly if the money is needed quickly.
7. Tax Benefits—some investments such as municipal or federal bonds are exempt from federal or state income taxes or local taxes. Some investments allow your principal and future contributions to compound tax-free until withdrawal.

Review the following chart to help you decide your risk comfort level with the following investments:

Investment Type	Safety of Principal	Safety of Income	Current Income	Growth of Principal	Growth of Income	Liquidity	Tax Benefits
Stocks	Volatile	Low	Sometimes	Sometimes	Sometimes	High	None
Mutual Funds	Sometimes	Moderate	Sometimes	Sometimes	Sometimes	High	None
Corporate Bonds	Usually High	Usually High	Moderate to High	None	None	High	None
Government Bonds	High	High	Moderate	Sometimes	Sometimes	High	Yes
Fixed Annuities	Good to High	Good to High	Sometimes	Sometimes	None	Moderate	Yes
Variable Annuities	Good	Good	Sometimes	Sometimes	Sometimes	Moderate	Yes
Real Estate	Good	Moderate	Low to Moderate	Sometimes	Sometimes	Low	Yes
Treasury Bills	Highest	Highest	Low	None	None	High	Yes

Higher returns usually involve more volatile, higher risk investments. If you put all your savings into higher risk investments, you are in danger of loosing a substantial portion of your savings if the investments decline in value. There is also a risk involved with being too conservative in your investments—the risk of not accumulating enough money to adequately fund your retirement.

The investment portfolio challenge is determining the right mix of higher, moderate, and low risks investments that collectively will provide you with a high enough annualized return to help you reach your retirement objectives while providing diversification to protect you against substantial losses in any one investment area and to

Investments — Historical Returns

do so within your own personal risk tolerance comfort level. "*Forethought and diligence are sure of profit; the man in a hurry is sure of poverty*"—Proverbs 21:5.

Various financial investments will be reviewed in more detail in the following chapters. Remember, history is no guarantee of future investment performance. The only guarantee you can absolutely count on is God's unconditional love. Your personal conviction that God exists, confession of your sins, and conversion from your sins is the best "investment" you will ever make—it is an eternal investment in your soul and a free gift from God. Financial investments are unimportant in comparison to "the eternal investment." "*For what shall it profit a man, if he shall gain the whole world, and lose his own soul?*"—Mark 8:36 (King James Version).

Chapter 12

Abundance Thinking Versus a Scarcity Mentality

God's resources are infinitely abundant. It helps to develop "abundance thinking" versus a "scarcity mentality" when investing. Abundance thinking is a state of mind in which there is plenty for everyone and the more you share, the more you receive. "*He who is generous to the poor lends to the Lord; he will repay him in full measure*"—Proverbs 19:17. The antithesis of abundance thinking is the scarcity mentality. The scarcity mentality is that for every winner there must be a loser. One person wins while the other person looses. A scarcity mentality compels an investor to try to make an unreasonable amount of money quickly by assuming unnecessary risks. A scarcity mentality develops greed. Webster's dictionary defines greed as "an overwhelming desire to acquire or have, as wealth or power, in excess of what one requires or deserves." To paraphrase a thought from Mahatma Gandhi, there is more than enough for every man's need and never enough for a man's greed. "*Greed is a disgrace to a man; better be a poor man than a liar*"—Proverbs 19:22. Greedy people find their security in money as opposed to finding their security in God.

Some people consider the lottery an investment—it is not! Many people have bought lottery tickets with the hope of winning millions when in reality they have had less than a 1 in 13 million chance of winning—that's not investing; it is gambling. Gambling with those odds of success virtually assures that your money will be lost. Gambling with a 1 in 2 chance of winning gives you a 50% chance of loosing your money. It is a zero-sum

Abundance Thinking Versus a Scarcity Mentality

game—one-person wins, and the other looses. Smart investors do not gamble with their money. Intelligent investors avoid zero-sum games. In 1992, the World Lottery Almanac stated that 51% of lottery monies went to prizes, 37% went to government programs, and 12% went to overhead, including retailer's commissions. A wiser use of those funds would be if the individuals would donate 100% of the lottery monies directly to the government programs or schools for the benefit of all as opposed to a few lucky recipients of prizes and the recipients of the overhead expenses.

The *Atlanta Journal* conducted an analysis of Georgia's lottery shortly after it began and found that residents of low-income neighborhoods spend more per capita than more affluent neighborhoods:

Per Capita Income	Sales of Lottery Tickets per Resident[1]	% of Six-County Metro Atlanta Area Average
Less than $12,000	$22.06	126.5%
From $12,000 to $15,000	$21.66	124.2%
From $15,000 to $21,000	$16.18	92.8%
More than $21,000	$12.10	69.4%
Six-County Metro Area Average (portions of Clayton, Cobb, DeKalb, Fayette, Fulton, and Gwinnett Counties)	**$17.43**	**100%**

Lower-income families would be better off to save and invest their money versus playing the lottery.

The financial world has many investments that are much too risky for the average investor. Commodities are goods such as gold, metals, crude oil, gasoline, cotton, wheat, pork bellies, corn, lumber, sugar, coffee, and others that are used to make the products we

---

[1] Carrie Teegardin and Charles Walston, *The poorer the neighborhood, the higher the ticket sales,* Atlanta Journal-Constitution article, 1993.

Abundance Thinking Versus a Scarcity Mentality

buy. Commodities are traded to assure a supply of something at a specific price at a future point in time. For example, a jewelry company that is expecting the price of gold to rise might buy a contract guaranteeing a certain amount of gold at a set price. If the price of gold rises down the road, the jewelry company has locked in the prior agreed-upon price of the gold and the amount. Another reason commodities are traded is speculation. For example, if drought is expected during next summer, speculators might buy corn futures expecting the drought to produce less corn and thus higher corn prices. If the drought occurs, the speculators will likely make a profit; if the drought does not occur, the speculators could lose money. Commodity futures trading is very risky and is suited for only the most sophisticated investors. Also, most investors should avoid options and penny stocks—they are too risky for the average investor. Options and futures are contracts that expire on a fixed date—investors must decide to exercise the contact before the fixed date or allow the contract to expire. According to the *Wall Street Journal*, "Investing in commodities and financial futures is about as extreme as you can get on the risk scale."[2] In his book about penny stocks, Bruce G. McWilliams defines penny stocks as "securities, priced less than $5.00 (and many between 10 cents and $1)."[3] Penny stocks can be wildly volatile and should only be purchased by seasoned, knowledgeable investors.

Even if you are an expert investor, you should not invest more than 5% of your portfolio in commodities, options, or penny stocks due to the extra risky nature of those

---

[2] Tom and David Gardner, The Motley Fool, *Commodities' risk outweighs benefits,* Atlanta Journal-Constitution article, July 14, 2002.
[3] Bruce G. McWilliams, *Penny stocks: how the small investor can make large profits in the penny market,* Doubleday, Garden City, NY, 1982.

Abundance Thinking Versus a Scarcity Mentality

investments. To paraphrase the wisdom of the farm boy who became a stockbroker, pigs get fed but hogs get slaughtered!

You develop abundance thinking by realizing that you do not need to gamble with your money to reach your financial goals. Assuming reasonable risks and rates of return from your investments, making regular contributions to your savings, and doing so over the long term will enable you to achieve your goals. Buying a stock for only a few weeks, days, or hours is gambling, not investing. Avoid day trading. In the short term, anything can happen in the stock market, including crashes. It is impossible to predict short-term changes in the stock market with any degree of regularity. The longer your investment time frame, the more likely the stock market is to rise. There has never been a period in history when the stock market did not increase from a decline given enough time. In the long term, if you put money into good stocks year after year, you are virtually guaranteed to make a profit. The key to stock market success is time—the longer you are invested, the lower your risk and the more money you generally will make.

Funds needed within a year should be put into money market mutual funds or certificates of deposit that will mature before you actually need the money. Money market mutual funds and certificates of deposit are more stable than the stock market. For money that will not be needed until one to five years in the future, you might consider investments that offer slightly higher yields but are still conservative investments—for example, treasury bills or other government-backed securities, high-quality government bonds, or possibly low-risk mutual funds. For money that will not be needed for more than five years, consider investing in the stock market. While stocks are more volatile, they normally provide higher returns. The longer time frame allows you to wait out any

Abundance Thinking Versus a Scarcity Mentality

temporary market declines. A long-term perspective in the stock market is the best defense against temporary declines. Since 1926, over any five-year period, the odds have been 9 to 1 that the stock market will rise.

Select investments that match your time horizon, your risk tolerance, and your overall portfolio objectives. Everyone invested in the market with well-balanced portfolios who monitors his or her investments periodically and eliminates those investments that are loosing money will make a profit—even if their investment choices are average—over time. Not some winners and a lot of losers—everyone. That's abundance thinking.

Investment Risks and Suggested Asset Allocation

Chapter 13

Investment Risks and Suggested Asset Allocation

Risk is multifaceted. Some risks must be taken since the greatest hazard in life is to risk nothing. To risk nothing is to gain nothing. Investing always involves some risk. Stock investments can be very risky in the short run; however, in the long term, the risk of loss in stocks decreases dramatically, eventually disappearing. Stock prices will go up and down. Short-term speculating in the stock market is a formula for disaster. Extraneous factors and speculation greatly influence short-term results in the stock market; however, they have little impact in the stock market on long-term results. You achieve maximum total returns by investing for the long term in top-quality companies that are leaders in their fields, have excellent managers, and have excellent balance sheets. Since 1926, the Standard & Poor's 500-stock index's odds of increasing have been as follows

S&P Odds of Increasing	Over Period of Time
7 to 3	Any 12 month period
9 to 1	Any 5 year period
25 to 1	Any 10 year period

Stock market declines are unpredictable in timing, magnitude, and duration. Since 1953, the average market drop has lasted 8 months with 75% of the declines recovering within 7 months. Full recoveries on average were achieved in just over a year. Short-term movements in the stock market cannot be predicted with any great accuracy. Intermediate and long-term movements in the stock market can be predicted with more accuracy. In general, stocks lose money about one-third of the time and make money about two-thirds

Investment Risks and Suggested Asset Allocation

of the time. Investors must be financially and psychologically prepared for the ups and downs of the stock market. View temporary downturns as the price of investing and part of the process in achieving higher returns over the long term. Every portfolio will have winners and losers. All investors eventually select a security on which they lose money. In fact, even exceptional investors are only correct about 6 or 7 out of 10 investment choices. It is essential to obtain the proper mix of investments for your overall portfolio to achieve the right amount of diversification to protect against losses in any one investment area. This portfolio mix will change with each stage of life you go through—the younger you are, the more time you have to wait out market corrections and the riskier you can be with your investments. The older you are, the less time you have to wait out market corrections and the more conservative you need to become in your investments. The stock market provides investors' opportunities that are difficult to match with other investments regarding the risk-reward ratio—the amount of risk you must take to receive the reward or return. After 20 years, you are virtually assured of making money with stocks. Long-term investors can reasonably expect to earn about 10% from their stock investments versus around 5% on government bonds and 3.6% on treasury bills. A well-balanced portfolio includes stocks and their higher returns to offset the lower returns of safer investments such as bonds and treasury bills. Well-balanced portfolios contain the proper mix of stocks, bonds, and cash reserves to match your time horizon, risk tolerance, and personal financial situation. A well-diversified portfolio includes several asset classes and sectors designed to allow your portfolio not only to profit from advances in the market, but also to protect you against substantial losses

Investment Risks and Suggested Asset Allocation

during market corrections. Asset allocation is one of the most important decisions investors can make.

For assistance in reviewing your tolerance for risk and suggested asset allocation ranges, please complete the following steps:

1. Open the "SS19 Calculator-Risk Assessment & Suggested Asset Allocation.xls"; see Figures 13.1a and 13.1b.
2. Click "Yes" to enable macros, if necessary.
3. Fill in your own personal information—only one white cell for each statement! (You may tab from one white cell to another.)
4. After completing the information, press "Tab" and then click on the "MMW Recalculation Button"—the spreadsheet will make the remaining calculation for you.

Figure 13.1a Calculator-Risk Assessment and Suggested Asset Allocation

Fill in only one number for each of the 10 statements that represent the response that most closely relates to your personal preference (for "Strongly Agree," fill in 10; for "Agree," fill in 8; for "Neutral," fill in 6; for "Disagree," fill in 4; for "Strongly Disagree," fill in 2):

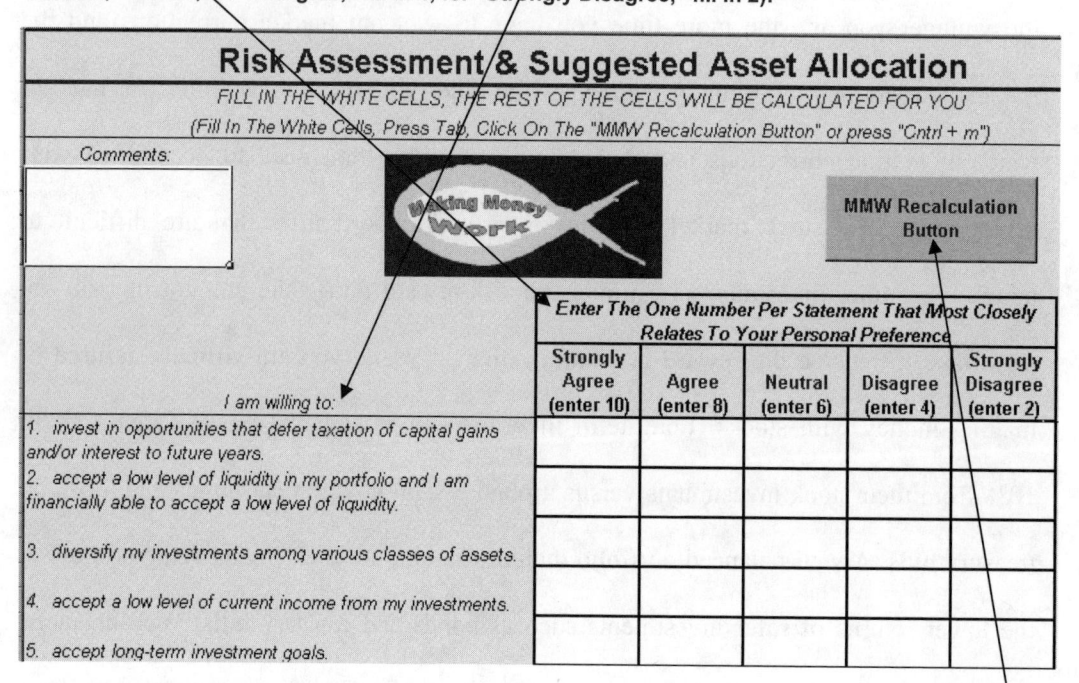

Risk Assessment & Suggested Asset Allocation

FILL IN THE WHITE CELLS, THE REST OF THE CELLS WILL BE CALCULATED FOR YOU
(Fill In The White Cells, Press Tab, Click On The "MMW Recalculation Button" or press "Cntrl + m")

Comments:

Enter The One Number Per Statement That Most Closely Relates To Your Personal Preference

I am willing to:	Strongly Agree (enter 10)	Agree (enter 8)	Neutral (enter 6)	Disagree (enter 4)	Strongly Disagree (enter 2)
1. invest in opportunities that defer taxation of capital gains and/or interest to future years.					
2. accept a low level of liquidity in my portfolio and I am financially able to accept a low level of liquidity.					
3. diversify my investments among various classes of assets.					
4. accept a low level of current income from my investments.					
5. accept long-term investment goals.					

After placing one response for each of the 10 statements, press "Tab" and then press the "MMW Recalculation Button."

Investment Risks and Suggested Asset Allocation

Figure 13.1b Calculator-Risk Assessment and Suggested Asset Allocation

	corrections.				
	9. be prepared for investment losses in my portfolio.				
	10. risk short-term losses in return for potential higher long-term rates of return.				

Your Total Risk Assessment Score: 0

The higher your score (100 maximum), the higher your level for risk.

Suggested Investment Allocations--Use The Score Range Below That Includes "Your Total Risk Assessment Score"

Score	High Risk	Aggressive Growth	Core Investments	Conservative Assets	Savings
85-100	0-5%	30-50%	30-40%	10-15%	10-
61-84	0-5%	10-20%	35-50%	25-45%	10-
38-60	0-5%	5-10%	30-40%	35-50%	10-
20-37	0-5%	0-5%	15-20%	55-65%	10-

High Risk Investments include: Commodities, Options, Penny Stocks, and other "Very High Risk" Investments.
Aggressive Growth Investments include: Aggressive Growth Stocks, Low Quality Bonds, Limited Partnerships, and other "High" Investments.
Core Investments include: Blue Chip Stocks, Quality Growth Stocks, Real Estate, and other "Average Risk" Investments.
Conservative Assets include: Government Bonds, Corporate Bonds, Tax-Free Bonds, Retirement Funds, Growth & Income Mutual and other "Low Risk" Investments.
Savings include: Bank Certificates Of Deposit, Savings Accounts, Credit Union, Insurance Policies, Guaranteed Money Market other "Guaranteed" Investments.

"Your Total Risk Assessment Score" will be calculated for you; 100 is the maximum score. The higher the score, the higher your level of risk tolerance. Make note of your score and find the score range into which it falls. For example, if your score were 78, your score range would be 61–84. Your "Suggested Investment Allocations" are listed to the right of the score range. Please note that this guide is based on a few risk-tolerance statements and responses—number of years from retirement is also an important consideration in asset allocation. The score range corresponds to age groups as follows:

Score	Age Group
85–100	20–35
61–84	36–50
38–60	51–65
20–37	66 and up

If you are 66 years old and scored 100 on the risk assessment statements, you will still realistically want to use the score range 20–37 because your investment time horizon is short. Since you scored high on the risk assessment, you may choose to allocate your assets on the high end of the "Suggested Guideline Asset Allocation" percent ranges for the higher risk investments—"High Risk," "Aggressive Growth," and "Core Investments." For example, in "Aggressive Growth," the guideline is "0–5%" for ages 66 and up; if you scored high on the risk assessment statements, you may feel comfortable investing the full 5% in aggressive growth investments.

You will have the opportunity to use % asset allocations by "Age Group" later in this book (Chapter 26) when you recap your portfolio.

The greatest risk, of course, is not having faith and belief in God because you lose life eternal in heaven. *"Be faithful until death, and I will give you the crown of life"*— Revelation 2:10 (Soul Care Bible).

Stocks

Chapter 14

Stocks

Common stock is a share of ownership in a corporation. Common stock receives the lowest priority for repayment in the event of a corporate liquidation. Stocks are sometimes called "equities." Stocks may increase in market value increasing investment profit. Of course, they may also decrease in value. The market value of a company is the share price times the number of shares outstanding.

Stocks may or may not pay dividends. Dividends are a portion of the company's profit paid to its shareholders in either cash or additional shares. Companies tend to increase dividends during good times. During bad times they tend to freeze, reduce, or eliminate dividend payouts. For example, if company XYZ makes a profit and decides to pay its shareholders a $0.50/share dividend on the current stock price of $16.65/share, the dividend yield is 3% (e.g., $0.50 annual dividend rate divided by $16.65/share present market price = 3% current yield). Historically, dividends have provided less than half of the total return from stocks. During the period 1926 through 1998, dividends accounted for 40% of the total return from stocks. During the 1926 through 1998 period, the average dividend yield was 4.5% of the 11.2% total return from stocks.[1]

Stocks are traded on stock markets. Stock markets are very similar to an auction—stock shares trade at prices buyers are willing to pay and at prices sellers are willing to accept. It is a matter of supply and demand. For example, if a company is experiencing

---

[1] Source: Ibbotsons Associates.

Stocks

amazing growth in sales and it anticipates future record earnings, there will be a surge in demand for the company stock. On the other hand, if the company announces that it has financial difficulty and plans to file for bankruptcy, then there will likely be many more sellers than buyers and the stock price will fall. This fluctuation in stock price can make stocks rather volatile—especially in the short term. Volatility is the tendency of an investment to experience price swings (either up or down) over periods of time. In the short term, stocks can be very volatile investments; however, in the history of the U.S. stock market, no investor with a <u>balanced portfolio</u> has ever lost money if he or she held investments for 10 years or more—even if the stocks were bought at the absolute worst time. Note that individual stocks are more volatile than a diversified portfolio. On average, stocks advance 72% of all five-year periods and 77% of all 10-year periods. After 20 years, there's a 100% probability of making a profit with stocks.

When you purchase stocks, you are buying either earnings or assets. Investors buying stocks of companies they expect to grow and prosper are buying future earnings. Investors buying stock in a company they expect to be acquired or broken up at a premium over its market price are buying assets. The book value of a company is the accounting net worth of the company calculated by adding the company's assets, subtracting its liabilities, and then dividing the resulting number by the number of shares outstanding. The price/book value ratio of a company is calculated by dividing the current stock price by the latest book value. For example, if the company stock is priced at $34.00/share and the book value is $17.00, its price/book value is 2.00 (e.g., $34.00/share divided by $17.00 = 2 price/book value ratio). The lower the price/book

Stocks

value ratio, the cheaper the stock. The higher the price/book value ratio, the higher the stock.

Over the long term, stock prices rise in direct proportion to a company's growth in earnings and dividends. A company adds up all of its sales and subtracts the direct cost of the goods it resells including expenses such as salaries, rent, insurance, utilities, interest payments, taxes, depreciation or amortization, and so on, to determine earnings. Depreciation is a way to account for the cost of something tangible such as a delivery truck or office equipment. Amortization is a way of accounting for something intangible such as a copyright. A company may also deduct an extra charge for severance packages, factory closings, or other deductions that reduce earnings. Sometimes a company may have a gain when they sell investments or assets at a higher price than the items are listed at on the company books—that would increase earnings. The Financial Accounting Standards Board sets the rules covering how companies calculate their earnings. Wise investors research the company before buying its stock to determine both current earnings and future earnings projections. Earnings measure how a company is performing. The more the company sells goods or services and the more profit the company makes, the better the earnings. Higher earnings drive stock prices higher. Lower earnings drive stock prices lower. Increased sales and earnings will result in increased stock prices. Companies report earnings during the months of January, April, July, and October. Investors typically look to pay around two times future growth rates. Growth rate estimates, company earnings, and future earnings estimates for company stocks can be found at the Thomson Investors Network, www.thomsoninvest.net or www.thomsonfn.com.

Stocks

Earnings per share are calculated by dividing the company's earnings by the number of shares of common stock outstanding. The price-to-earnings ratio is the current stock price divided by earnings per share (EPS)—usually the most recent 12 months before the company's last reporting period. The price-to-earnings ratio, or P/E, or sometimes called the "stock's multiple," is calculated as follows: if the current stock price is $34.00/share and the earnings per share is $2.00, the P/E is 17 ($34.00/share price divided by $2.00 earnings per share = 17 "multiple" or P/E). The P/E ratio reflects investor sentiment on the worth of the stock. A P/E of 17 means investors are willing to pay $17.00 for every $1.00 of profit that the company earns. Or, looked at another way, investors are willing to wait 17 years to recover their investment if the company continues to earn exactly the same amount of money. To calculate the earnings yield, just reverse the ratio by dividing the annual earnings per share by the current stock price—for example, $2.00 EPS divided by $34.00/share current stock price = 0.0588 or 5.88%. Compare the 5.88% return to risk-free treasury bills to assess your risk/reward returns.

Stocks trade on expectations, not history. Most investment professionals look at the "forward P/E." The forward P/E is calculated by dividing the current stock price by the estimate of next year's earnings. P/E ratios average about 16 times earnings over time; however, high multiples are not necessarily bad. Investors are willing to pay more for stocks in companies that are experiencing exceptional growth, and thus the stock may have a high P/E ratio. This works well as long as the company is meeting or exceeding security analyst estimates; however, if the company does not meet earnings expectations, the stock price will likely take a drastic fall—even if it misses earnings expectations for just one quarter. High multiples or P/E ratios beyond any expectation of future profit

Stocks

growth are dangerous because they make the stock vulnerable to a sell-off in a weak market or if the company misses earnings estimates. Compare the P/E ratio of the stock you are considering purchasing to other companies in the same market sector. For example, do not compare a technology stock with a P/E of 60 with high earnings estimates and growth potential to a more established automobile manufacturing company with a P/E of 10. The technology stock could still be a good investment if it delivers on growth and earnings; however, if other similar technology companies have a P/E of 30, your stock could take a huge dive during a correction or earnings disappointment. Overpriced stocks are always vulnerable to sudden stock price losses if the company's profit weakens. Stocks that trade with low P/E ratios usually have very low growth expectations. Sometimes a low P/E ratio can be a signal that investors are expecting bad news soon. Many stocks with low P/E ratios report losses in the next quarter's reports. A low P/E ratio does not mean that there is not risk of a further decline in the stock's price. P/Es change with trends in the stock market—P/Es are not stagnant. There is no single P/E standard for judging all stocks.

While earnings drive the stock price, consider more than just the stock's P/E ratio when evaluating a potential stock purchase. Some stock price drivers are financial such as earnings, cash flow, revenue, and dividends. Other stock price drivers include effective company management, new product development, market position, and cost management. Rivel Research Group polled 200 portfolio managers and asked them to

Stocks

rank the factors they considered to be the most critical in driving stock prices. The results of the Rivel Research Group poll were as follows:[2]

1. Earnings (124 votes)
2. Cash flow (70 votes)
3. Management (66 votes)
4. New product development (43 votes)
5. Offering the lowest product price in the industry group (30 votes)
6. The company's industry group (24 votes)
7. Dividends (20 votes)
8. Revenue (16 votes)
9. Efficient control of overhead cost (11 votes)

Total return of an investment takes into account any changes in share price plus dividends or interest over a specific period of time. Total return is often reported as an annualized rate of return. A stock's total return is its dividend payout plus its price appreciation. For example, let's assume you purchased a stock and originally invested $5,000 in it. The dividends were reinvested in the stock, and it also increased in value so that the total value of the stock is now $8,000. The total return would be calculated as follows: $8,000 minus $5,000 = $3,000 divided by $5,000 = 0.6 x 100 (to express as a percentage) = a 60% total return. Total return tells you the investment performance. When common stocks are overvalued on the basis of earnings and dividends, investors will take money out of stocks and put their money into bonds or money market securities, which in turn depresses stock prices.

"Preferred" stock is a share of a publicly held corporation and has priority over common stock in the payment of dividends and in the distribution of assets if the company fails. Most domestic preferred stock pays fixed dividend interest amounts. Most

---

[2] Tom Walker, *Profit seen as No. 1 force in movement of stock prices,* Atlanta Journal-Constitution, August 20, 1995.

Stocks

preferred stock is perpetual with no stated maturity date with the fixed dividends being paid indefinitely. Issuers may call or retire outstanding preferred stock at predetermined prices. As interest rates fall, issuers may call or retire preferred stock and replace it with lower-cost securities. Some types of preferred stock are the following:

1. Cumulative preferred—if a company has a poor quarter and skips paying a dividend, cumulative preferred stock holders would receive the skipped dividend at a future date.
2. Straight preferred—dividends are fixed for the life of the investment; skipped dividends are not paid at a future date.
3. Participating preferred—shareholders are entitled to any earnings in excess of the stated dividend.
4. Convertible preferred—these preferred stock shareholders may swap convertible preferred shares for a predetermined number of common stock shares.
5. Adjustable rate preferred stock—dividends are adjusted each quarter within minimum and maximum limits.

Stock options—not to be confused with futures options—give an executive or some other employee the chance to buy a certain number of company shares at some future point for the price of the shares on the day the option grant was made available. For example, if your company gives you a stock option of 100 shares at $25.00/share and in three years the stock climbs to $50.00/share, you exercise the option to buy the shares at $2,500 (100 shares x $25.00/share = $2,500), and you make a profit of $2,500 (100 shares x $50.00 = $5,000 - $2,500 cost = $2,500 profit). Normally the profit on exercised options is taxed as ordinary income and is paid in the current year with no tax deferral. Stock options normally take three to five years to become vested—meaning that they definitely belong to you. Stock options generally must be exercised within 10 years of the grant date. If the company stock goes down instead of up, you would not exercise your option, and the option would expire worthless. If you quit or retire from the company, you normally have three months to exercise your stock options.

Stocks

How much you invest and where you put your money depends on your age, investment goals, years to retirement, risk tolerance, and financial circumstances. How much of your portfolio should you invest in the stock market? A rule of thumb is to subtract your age from 100 to get a percentage of assets that might be acceptable for stock market investments. For example, if you are currently 60 years of age, take 100 minus 60 = 40—a rough estimate of stock market investments, as a total of your portfolio would be 40%. Never commit more than 10% of your portfolio to any one individual stock if you can avoid it. To diversify your portfolio, you should own at least 10 to 20 individual stocks. If you do not have a portfolio dollar amount large enough to achieve this level of diversification, consider buying mutual funds instead to achieve the diversification you need to protect your assets.

Enron Corporation started in the 1920s as a gas pipeline company. By the 1990s Enron was the largest energy trader in the United States with $65 billion on the stock market and 20,600 employees. Enron Corporation quickly collapsed under controversial accounting practices and filed the largest-ever U.S. bankruptcy. The company lost more than 99% of its value. The workers' retirement funds and the value of shareholder equity were decimated. Enron's collapse points out the vital importance of diversifying your portfolio to protect against sudden losses in any one investment area. Investing a lot of your retirement assets in your employer's stock is a risky proposition because your paycheck and much of your financial well-being is already linked to the company. Diversification is one of the most important investment principles. By maintaining a well-diversified portfolio, you have the advantage that declines in one asset class are generally offset by gains in another asset class. A good asset allocation strategy keeps a

Stocks

blend of stocks, bonds, and cash available in your portfolio. Let's say you have an under-diversified portfolio of $50,000 with $25,000 in Company A stock and $25,000 in Company B stock. If Company B's stock falls by half to $12,500, your portfolio is now worth $37,500—a 25% drop in value due to losses on one stock. That is exposing your portfolio to too much risk.

An overdiversified portfolio can be almost as bad as an underdiversified portfolio. For example, assume you own a $50,000 portfolio with 25 stocks at $2,000 each (or 4% of your portfolio). If one of the stocks triples to $6,000 (a 200% increase), your portfolio is now worth $54,000 (only an 8% increase). If you only own 10 stocks at $5,000 each (or 10% of your portfolio) and one of them triples to $15,000, your portfolio is now worth $60,000 (a 20% increase!). There is no best number of stocks to own; however, most investors can achieve proper diversification with 10 to 15 stocks as long as the stocks are in different industries with no more than 10% invested in any one individual stock. More than 20 stocks results in an unmanageable portfolio.

Earnings are the key driver of stock prices, and growing businesses are the primary means of generating wealth. Individual investors should find good companies to invest in that they feel comfortable with over the long term. Anything less than 2 years in the stock market is considered short-term thinking. Tales of instant wealth from new stock offerings may tempt any investor; however, history shows that wealth is more likely to come through investing in established companies that are well managed, safe, and profitable in the long term. An IPO is an "initial public offering" and a way to initially sell stock shares to the public to raise money to expand a company's business. IPOs are extremely risky. Investors are gambling on the company's future prospects. If the future

Stocks

earnings do not materialize, the company stock prices are likely to decline sharply. Most small investors should avoid investing in IPOs. Most IPOs are marginal performers over the long term. Five thousand IPOs were studied between 1970 and 1990, and they averaged an annual return of 5% in the five years after they were issued. If the stockholders had invested in more established public companies, they would have earned a 12% annual return.

When then is the best time to invest in a company? When it is making money—not during the research phase or the IPO phase, but when it is actually earning a profit. The average company that is operating efficiently earns 4 to 5 percent. Have realistic expectations of the company's earning potential. Invest in good companies with excellent growth and profitability. In 9 cases out of 10, the competitive company that is today's market leader will be tomorrow's market leader. On the other hand, today's laggard will typically be tomorrow's laggard. Over the long term, stock prices rise in close parallel to corporate earnings and dividends. Invest in companies you know and respect in real life that have managers with the highest integrity and ability. Ask yourself if the company has good products or services. Is the company a leader in its industry? Is it an established company? Is the company's industry growing? Are the company sales growing? Are the company's profits growing? Is the valuation of the company reasonable—is the P/E ratio in a similar range to its industry peers? Even the best companies can become overvalued and be poor investments for a long time, even though they have good growth in earnings and dividends. Do not buy stocks on tips. Buying stock without researching the company is foolhardy. Do not buy the most popular stocks at the time if they have extremely high P/E ratios. The most popular stocks are usually the ones whose earnings are currently

Stocks

growing the fastest. Fast growth attracts competition. Stiff competition can result in shrinkage of both earnings growth and profit margins. This shrinkage can then cause the stocks with high P/E ratios to plummet. Do not chase last quarter's stock winners. Just because they were hot last quarter does not mean they will repeat the same performance. Recent performance is irrelevant to what will occur in the future. Hot investments tend to cool off. Another word of caution: do not buy stock in companies who are weak competitors in their industries in hopes that they will get stronger. In the business world, the successful companies tend to become more successful, and the unsuccessful companies tend to become less successful. To paraphrase a thought from Warren Buffet—one of America's most successful investors—it is much better to buy a great company at a fair price than a fair company at a great price."

You can review a company's annual report to research many important financial aspects. Company reports are mailed to stockholders and may be obtained at libraries, or you may contact the U.S. Securities and Exchange Commission at http://www.sec.gov/cgi-bin/browse-edgar to research the latest reports issued by a company.

The company's balance sheet is a listing of all its assets and liabilities. The balance sheet tells if the company has enough money to continue to fund its own growth or whether it is going to have to take on debt, issue debt, or issue more stock in order to keep going. The balance sheet can let you know if the company has too much inventory and if the company is collecting money from customers in a reasonable amount of time.

Please review the hypothetical balance sheet in Figure 14.1.

Figure 14.1 Balance Sheet

Stocks

Hypothetical 1 Corporation Balance Sheet December 31, 2003	
Current Assets	
Cash and Equivalents	$100,000
Short-Term and Long-Term Investments	$100,000
Accounts Receivable	$5,000,000
Inventories	$3,000,000
Prepaid Expenses	$200,000
Total Current Assets	**$8,400,000**
Property and Equipment (Cost Minus Net of Accumulated Depreciation and Amortization)	**$3,000,000**
Goodwill	**$500,000**
Total	**$11,900,000**
Liabilities and Stockholders' Equity	
Current Liabilities	
Accounts Payable	$4,000,000
Accrued Expenses	$1,500,000
Short-Term Notes Payable	$600,000
Total Current Liabilities	**$6,100,000**
Long-Term Debt	**$2,000,000**
Total Liabilities	**$8,100,000**
Stockholders' Equity	
Common Stock	$200,000
Retained Earnings	$3,600,000
Total Stockholders' Equity	**$3,800,000**
Total	**$11,900,000**

Stocks

A balance sheet is a statement of the financial condition of a company at a specific point in time. The company's balance sheet shows what a company owns (its assets), what it owes (its liabilities), and what the shareholders have invested in the company (its equity).

"**Current Assets**" are the assets easily converted into cash within one operating cycle. The operating cycle is the time it takes to sell a product and collect cash from the sale—usually around 60 to 180 days. "Cash and Equivalents" is money in the bank, bearer bonds, or money market funds. "Short-Term and Long-Term Investments" are investments such as bonds with durations of less than one year—they earn more interest than cash accounts; however, they are not as liquid or as easily converted back into cash. "Accounts Receivable" are monies currently owed to the company by customers. "Inventories" are components and finished products in stockpile. "Prepaid Expenses" are expenditures already paid to suppliers in advance.

"**Property and Equipment**" is the original cost of the company's fixed assets such as plants minus their accumulated depreciation. Accounting does not usually use market prices—either selling prices or replacement costs—for fixed assets since the company normally does not plan on selling the assets. Market resale prices are not relevant because they fluctuate up and down. The original cost of the property and equipment minus depreciation and amortization is a better measuring stick of management's use of the resources for the stockholders.

"**Goodwill**" is an intangible asset that provides a competitive advantage such as a strong brand reputation or high employee morale. An acquiring company may list on its

Stocks

balance sheet as goodwill the difference between the purchase price and the net tangible assets of the acquired company.

"**Current Liabilities**" are the monies a company owes in short-term debts to its suppliers and creditors. "Accounts Payable" are monies owed to suppliers, partners, and employees—one company's accounts receivables are another company's accounts payable. "Accrued Expenses" are normally marketing and distribution expenses that are not due yet. "Short-Term Notes Payable" are monies drawn from lines of credit that need to be paid back within twelve months—this might include long-term debt that has become due within twelve months.

"**Long-Term Debt**" is debt that has a due date more than one year in the future.

"**Stockholders' Equity**" is the shareholders' proportional share of ownership in the company. "Common Stock" is a security representing partial ownership in either a public or private corporation. "Retained Earnings" is the income a company has earned minus dividends it has paid—the income has been "retained" or kept in the business rather than being distributed to stockholders in the form of a dividend.

"**Total Stockholder's Equity**" is assets minus liabilities.

Experts use ratios to determine the solvency and financial stability of a company:

Current ratio is the current assets divided by the current liabilities. It measures a company's ability to quickly pay its debts, usually in less than one year. In the Figure 14.1 balance sheet example, it would be $8,400,000 (current assets) divided by $6,100,000 (current liabilities) = 1.3 to 1 (current ratio). The larger the current ratio, the better a company can withstand a cash problem. As a general rule, a current ratio of 1.5 or more is normally sufficient to meet the near-term operating needs of a company in

Stocks

order for the company to comfortably pay its bills. Compare the company's current ratio to the industry norms.

Quick ratio is the current assets minus the inventory divided by the total current liabilities. The larger the ratio, the less vulnerable a company is to a sales slump. In the Figure 14.1 balance sheet example, it would be $8,400,000 (current assets) minus $3,000,000 (inventories) = $5,400,000 divided by $6,100,000 (total current liabilities) = 0.88 to 1 (quick ratio). The quick ratio takes inventories out of the equation to determine whether or not the company has enough liquid assets to meet short-term operating needs. A quick ratio in excess of 1.0 indicates enough cash on hand to pay the bills. Compare the company's quick ratio to industry peers.

Debt-to-equity ratio is the long-term debt divided by the total stockholder's equity. In the Figure 14.1 balance sheet example, it would be $2,000,000 (long-term debt) divided by $3,800,000 (total stockholder's equity) = .52 to 1. A ratio of more than one means the company has more debt than equity—in the event that the company liquidates, less would be available to shareholders than to creditors.

Debt ratio is the short-term debt plus the long-term debt divided by total assets. The debt ratio measures the percentage of assets financed through debt. The lower the debt ratio, the greater the chance the company will be able to endure hard times. In the Figure 14.1 balance sheet example, it would be $6,100,000 (total current liabilities) + $2,000,000 (long-term debt) divided by $11,900,000 (total assets) = 0.68 to 1. A 68% debt ratio means creditors have supplied about $0.68 of every $1.00 of company assets. A lower percentage is generally better than a higher one. Companies with high debt ratios

Stocks

may have trouble borrowing any more money, or they may have to pay higher interest rates for loans.

Working capital is current assets minus current liabilities. In the Figure 14.1 balance sheet example, it would be $8,400,000 (total current assets) - $6,100,000 (total current liabilities) = $2,300,000. Working capital is the lifeblood of a company. With all other things being equal, a company with a positive working capital will outperform a company with a negative working capital.

A company's income statement tells you how much money the company made from selling its products or services. An income statement is sometimes called an earnings statement or statement of operations. An income statement shows the company's earnings or profit.

Please review the hypothetical income statement in Figure 14.2.

Figure 14.2 Income Statement

Hypothetical 2 Corporation Income Statement (In Thousands) December 31, 2003		
	2003	**2002**
Sales Revenue		
Product Sales	$12,000	$10,000
Services	$7,000	$6,000
Total Sales Revenue	$19,000	$16,000
Sales Costs		
Product Sales	$6,000	$5,000

Stocks

Services	$3,000	$2,500
Total Sales Costs	$9,000	$7,500
Gross Profit	$10,000	$8,500
Gross Margin Percent	52.6%	53.1%
Operating Expenses		
Sales and Marketing	$4,000	$3,500
General and Administrative	$1,000	$900
Research and Development	$2,000	$1,800
Total Operating Expenses	$7,000	$6,200
Operating Income	$3,000	$2,300
Interest Payments to Bondholders	$100	$200
Earnings Before Income Taxes (EBIT)	$2,900	$2,100
Taxes on Income	$1,000	$700
Net Income (Earnings)	$1,900	$1,400
Dividends Paid to Shareholders	$10	$10
Earnings Available to Shareholders	$1,890	$1,390

"**Total Sales Revenue**" is the income from the sale of products and services. It is sometimes called sales, net sales, revenue, or net revenue.

"**Total Sales Costs**" are expenses directly related to making the products or services. The expenses would include the costs of raw materials, salaries, and depreciation.

"**Gross Profit**," or sales profit, is sales revenue minus sales costs.

"**Gross Margin Percent**" is gross profit divided by total sales revenue.

Stocks

"**Total Operating Expenses**" are expenses associated with but not directly applicable to the current products and services being sold. These expenses include costs for sales and marketing, general and administrative costs, and research and development costs.

"**Operating Income**" is gross profit minus total operating expenses. It is pretax and preinterest profit.

"**Net Income (Earnings)**" is total income minus total expenses. It is the after-tax profit before paying dividends. It is the number that goes to the top of the cash flow statement.

"**Earnings Available to Shareholders**" is the money left after paying dividends. It is used to calculate earnings per share and the price to earnings ratio.

In the Figure 14.2 Income Statement for Hypothetical 2 Corporation example, the "Earnings Available to Shareholders" grew from $1,390 to $1,890—a 36% increase. You need to refer to the company's cash flow statement to determine how the company is paying for this growth.

The cash flow statement shows how a company is paying for its operations and its future growth. Positive numbers on the cash flow statement represent cash flowing in to the company. Negative numbers on the cash flow statement represent cash flowing out of the company to the outside world.

Please review the hypothetical cash flow statement in Figure 14.3.

Figure 14.3 Cash Flow Statement

Stocks

<table>
<tr><th colspan="3">Hypothetical 3 Corporation
Cash Flow Statement (In Thousands)
December 31, 2003</th></tr>
<tr><th></th><th><u>2003</u></th><th><u>2002</u></th></tr>
<tr><td>Net Income (Earnings)</td><td>$1,900</td><td>$1,400</td></tr>
<tr><td>Noncash Adjustments</td><td></td><td></td></tr>
<tr><td> Depreciation</td><td>$1,000</td><td>$800</td></tr>
<tr><td> Other Adjustments to Earnings</td><td>$45</td><td>-$15</td></tr>
<tr><td>Net Cash Provided by (or Used in) Operating Activities</td><td>$2,945</td><td>$2,185</td></tr>
<tr><td>Proceeds From Issuing New Stock</td><td>$380</td><td>$250</td></tr>
<tr><td>Payments to Repurchase Stock</td><td>-$400</td><td>-$275</td></tr>
<tr><td>Stock Dividends Paid</td><td>-$10</td><td>-$10</td></tr>
<tr><td>Net Cash Provided by (or Used in) Financing Activities</td><td>-$30</td><td>-$35</td></tr>
<tr><td>Additions to Property, Plant, and Equipment</td><td>-$2,500</td><td>-$2,000</td></tr>
<tr><td>Net Cash Used in Investing Activities</td><td>-$2,500</td><td>-$2,000</td></tr>
<tr><td>Change in Cash and Equivalents During the Year</td><td>$400</td><td>$200</td></tr>
<tr><td>Cash and Equivalents (Beginning of Year)</td><td>$2,300</td><td>$2,100</td></tr>
<tr><td>Cash and Equivalents (End of Year)</td><td>$2,700</td><td>$2,300</td></tr>
</table>

A cash flow statement consists of three main components: 1. operating activities, 2. investing activities, and 3. financial activities. Cash flow measures money flowing into or out of a company's bank account. A cash flow statement is a great way to gain insight into a company's financial health.

Stocks

Operating activities are those activities that make money by selling products and services. Investing activities show how the money is being spent on future growth. Investors would like to see that the company is able to pay for investing activities from its operating activities. Financial activities involve raising money by issuing stocks and bonds. Investors would like to see that the company is able to fund investing activities from operating activities without having to use financial activities to raise money. If a company issues new stock to raise money, it dilutes the existing shareholders' holdings. If the company issues bonds, the future bond interest payments will punish future earnings.

"Net Cash Provided by (or Used in) Operating Activities" is net income, changes in working capital, and so on. It is the most important number in financial reports. It begins with the "Net Income (Earnings)" number from the income statement. It is then added to depreciation, not subtracted. Depreciation is added to make the adjustment for the paper expense that was taken out of net income (earnings) on the income statement. This is done because depreciation does not involve the flow of actual money from the company to an outside organization. By adding depreciation back in to operating activities, you remove its effect. Other components that do not entail the flow of actual money are added back to net income (earnings) as well. The more net cash that is being generated, the better. The company has more funds to generate more future growth. If the net cash is declining, the company has fewer funds to generate future growth. Declining net cash by operating activities can be an early warning signal that the stock is in for a fall—unless the company is using the money to fund future growth that results in higher net cash during subsequent reporting periods.

Stocks

"Net Cash Provided by (or Used in) Financing Activities" includes proceeds from issuing new stock, payments to repurchase stock, and paying dividends. Issuing new stock dilutes existing shareholder holdings. When a company repurchases its own stock or buys back its own debt, it increases existing shareholder holdings and value in the company.

"Net Cash Used in Investing Activities" includes capital expenditures for property, plant, and equipment. It also includes buying and selling stocks, bonds, and other companies. The "Additions to Property, Plant, and Equipment" affects the Net Cash Used in Investing Activities" section of the cash flow statement in the year the purchase was made and then gets expensed over many years on the income statement via depreciation.

Every company that files a report with the Securities and Exchange Commission (SEC) is required to include a cash flow statement in both its quarterly and annual reports. The SEC files the reports immediately in their EDGAR database.

Investors can research company filings with the SEC at www.sec.gov or www.freeedgar.com. As the name implies, FreeEDGAR is free and also contains a table of contents to help you locate the information you want to review. Be careful to search for the latest quarterly reports (10Q) and annual reports (10K). You may want to compare the financials from one report period to another period to spot trends. Reviewing reports can also help in projecting future financials.

Adequately research a stock before investing in it in order to minimize your chances of selecting a loser. Do not sell a stock simply because its price has not moved—stocks normally move in quick spurts. Do not sell a stock due to paper losses or paper profits—short-term fluctuations are normal. The original purchase price of the stock should have

Stocks

little to do with decisions on buying more of the stock or selling the stock. Do not sell a stock on temporary bad news. Focus on the company fundamentals. However, as an investor, you should be psychologically prepared to make mistakes. Not every investment will make money. Occasionally, you will have losses. To minimize losses, some investors set up stop-loss orders on their investments to minimize losses at 10% to 25% from the stock's most recent peak. Stop-loss orders are instructions investors give brokers to automatically sell shares when they fall to a specific price. If the reasons you purchased the shares initially no longer apply, it may be time to sell. If management does not keep its promises, if management personnel changes for the worse, if negative developments threaten the company, if growth of the company is slower than anticipated, if the industry sector the company competes in is declining, if the company has maximized its market potential, if profit margins shrink, if earnings decline for several quarters, if sales and earnings look good but company employee insiders are selling their stock, or if you simply discover a better investment that has more profit potential and less downside risk, it may be time to sell. Keep track of trends and changes. Read newspapers daily—especially the business sections.

If institutional investors have bought 60–65% of the company, be wary. While institutional investors can drive up the stock price, institutional investors' selling can cause a costly stampede. If your company is acquiring another company, you may wish to review the fundamentals. Acquiring companies normally take on additional debt, which may cause the company's stock to decline. When new developments surface, ask yourself if you would still buy the stock knowing what you know today—if the answer is yes, hold on to the stock; if the answer is no, sell the stock. Reevaluate your investments

Stocks

periodically to determine if you are still comfortable with them. If your stock has increased in value 30–40%, review the fundamentals. If the P/E ratio indicates that the stock is now extremely overvalued in regards to its earnings potential, it is time to sell. Few stocks do well in the future when they are at the pinnacle of their popularity.

The key to any sell decision should be fundamental changes in the company. A Northwestern University's Kellogg Graduate School of Management study found that the best time to sell a company stock is when its 12-month earnings declined. Eugene Lerner and William Breen—two Northwestern University professors—conducted a study on when to sell stocks and discovered three rules that have potential to boost returns. In their study over a 12-year period ending in 1985, if you sold stock when it jumped 15% within a month, you would have averaged a 15% annual gain compared to the Standard & Poor's 500 stock index 11% annual gain during the same time period. Selling if the P/E exceeded the growth rate resulted in a 17% annual return. The best result came from selling when the company reported earnings decline over any 12-month period—a 19% annual return.[3]

Buying and holding a stock is not always the best strategy. Be prepared to sell when your stock becomes overvalued.

---

[3] Robert Luke, *The pros tell when to sell a stock,* Atlant Journal-Constitution, August 2, 1993. Staff and News Services, *Deciding when to sell stock far harder than picking one,* Atlanta Journal-Constitution.

Stocks

The technique of putting the same amount of money into stocks or mutual funds at regular intervals is called dollar cost averaging. The regular intervals can be weekly, monthly, quarterly, or annually. The key is investing equal dollar amounts at each time period. By using dollar cost averaging, you buy fewer shares when the price is high and more shares when the price is low. Discipline makes dollar cost averaging effective by buying shares regardless of whether the market is up or down. It eliminates the almost impossible task of trying to time the market. You end up buying more shares when prices are low and fewer shares when prices are high. The cheaper shares purchased rise more rapidly in value when the market climbs. Dollar cost averaging forces good discipline through regular investing. To illustrate the advantage of dollar cost averaging, let's assume Investor A puts $10,000 into company stock at $10.00 per share—he now owns 1,000 shares. Let's assume Investor B uses dollar cost averaging to purchase his stock. Review figure 14.4.

Figure 14.4 Dollar Cost Averaging

$10,000 over 5 purchases:

Period	Dollar Amount of Equal Investments	Stock Price at Time of Purchase	# of Shares Purchased
Period 1	$2,000	$10.00	200
Period 2	$2,000	$12.00	166.66
Period 3	$2,000	$9.00	222.22
Period 4	$2,000	$9.00	222.22
Period 5	$2,000	$10.00	200
Totals:	$10,000	$50.00 divided by 5 = $10.00 average	1,011.1

Note that while both Investor A and Investor B spent $10,000, and both averaged their purchases at $10.00 per share, Investor B using dollar cost averaging owns 11.1 (1,011.1 for B minus 1,000 shares for A = 11.1) more shares than Investor A. Dollar cost

Stocks

averaging in equal periodic purchases rewards the investor with more shares, and typically, the shares are purchased at a lower price. A word of caution: over time, the amount of your periodic purchase needs to be increased to offset the effect of inflation. Without adjusting the purchase amount, the inflation adjusted value decreases over the years.

For assistance in tracking your stock purchases and sales, please complete the following steps:

1. Open the "SS20 Calculator-Stock Purchase, Sale, Split.xls"; see Figure 14.5.
2. Click "Yes" to enable macros, if necessary.
3. Fill in your own personal information in each white cell (you may tab from one white cell to another).
4. After completing the information in all of the white cells, press "Tab" and then click on the "MMW Recalculation Button"—the spreadsheet will make the remaining calculations for you.

Figure 14.5 SS20 Calculator-Stock Purchase, Sale, Split.xls

Click on the "Stock Recap" sheet.

Fill in your personal tax information.

Stock Purchase/Sale Recap (Tax Planning Estimator)

FILL IN THE WHITE CELLS, THE REST OF THE CELLS WILL BE CALCULATED FOR YOU

(Fill In The White Cells, Press Tab, Click On The "MMW Recalculation Button" or press "Cntrl + m")

	Federal Tax	State Tax	Total Estimated Tax Liability*
Enter Your Long Term Capital Gains Tax Rates (Investments Held More Than One Year):	20.00%	6.00%	26.00%
Enter Your Short Term Capital Gains Tax Rates (Investments Held Less Than One Year):	28.00%	6.00%	34.00%

* Estimated Tax Liability Only—check with your tax consultant for more accurate estimates—some investments are tax exempt from State taxes, etc. Your individual tax situation will affect these estimates. You may need to add additional taxes for early withdrawal penalties from tax deferred stock saving accounts, etc.

Suggestion: Place the planned tax amounts in a secure savings account so the funds will be available when your taxes are due.

Name of Stock	Trans-action Type	Trans-action Date	# Of Months Held	# Of Shares	Price Per Share	Extended Cost Of Shares	Broker Fees, et. al	Invested Balance/ Balance	Profit/Loss	Estim. Taxes
Home Depot (HD)	Bought	09/15/98		100	$41.6800	$4,168.00	$41.68	$4,209.68		
(Example)	Sold	12/29/99	15.44	100	$68.7500	$6,875.00	$18.00	$6,893.00	$2,683.32	$697
	Bought					$0.00		$0.00		
	Sold		0.00			$0.00		$0.00	$0.00	$0.0
	Bought					$0.00		$0.00		

Fill in your personal stock information.

The calculator accounts for long-term versus short-term tax rates using the transaction dates you input.

Stocks

The calculator will estimate your taxes due on the sale of stocks—check with your tax consultant for more accurate estimates since individual tax circumstances, tax-free investments, tax penalties, and so on, will affect the dollar amounts. Suggestion: put the tax due amount in a safe money market account or other liquid account so the money is available to you when your taxes become due. While taxes should not be your prime consideration in buying and selling stocks, some investors sell losing stocks along with stocks they've made money on to help offset tax liabilities. Your main consideration in buying and selling stocks should be what you can keep after you pay Uncle Sam—that necessitates focusing on buying stocks that will increase in value. Save a copy of the "Stock Purchase/Sale Recap (Tax Planning Estimator)" form along with supporting documents—it will help tremendously when completing your tax forms.

Technically speaking, when a company has a stock split, nothing changes. It is similar to getting two $10 bills for a $20 dollar bill—the amount of money does not change. No stockholder is either richer or poorer. Stock splits require no action on the part of the shareholder and have no tax implications regarding tax liabilities or tax savings. Stock splits do not affect the investment merits of the company. Stock splits in essence cut the ownership interests of the investors into smaller portions. For example, if a stock is selling for $100/share and the company implements a 2 for 1 stock split, the investor now owns 2 shares at $50.00 each versus the previous one share at $100.00 each. A 3 for 1 stock split would mean the investor now owns 3 shares at $33.333 each, and a 4 for 1 stock split means the investor now owns 4 shares at $25.00 each. The dollar amount of stock owned remains the same; the number of shares changes. Reverse stock splits are the opposite. For example, if a company's stock is selling for $10.00/share and they have a

Stocks

reverse 1 for 2 stock split, the stockholder now owns half as many shares at the new share price of $20.00 each. While stock splits add no value to shares, historically, stocks that have stock splits often rise in price faster than stocks that do not undergo stock splits. Stock splits are usually considered bullish events because they broaden the demand for the stock by lowering the cost, and that makes them more attractive to smaller shareholders.

Round lots are shares of stock purchased in 100-share increments or 200-share increments, and so forth. Investors normally like to purchase in round lots because the trading costs are lower than when you deal in odd lots of fewer than 100 shares. If a stock is selling at $100 per share, 100 round lots x $100 each = $10,000. If the stock has a 4 for 1 split, the shares now cost $25.00 each; 100 round lots x $25.00 each = $2,500. Many more investors are now able to afford to buy shares in the company. Companies like to have individual investors buy their company stock because individual investors tend to be more loyal than institutional investors. Loyalty cuts down on a stock's volatility. Thus, companies with high stock prices typically split their shares to make them more attractive to individual investors. While he was a professor at Rice University in Houston, David Ikenberry reviewed the performance of 1,275 companies that had stock splits from 1975 through 1990. He found that the stocks that split returned 8% more than their peers that did not split during the year after the stock splits were announced.[4] Stock splits should not be the determining factor in whether or not you buy a stock—consider all of the company's financial fundamentals when making a buying decision.

---

[4] *To combat sticker shock, companies split stock,* Knight Ridder Newspapers, February 16, 1999.

Stocks

For assistance in calculating stock splits, please complete the following steps:

1. Open the "SS20 Calculator-Stock Purchase, Sale, Split.xls"; see Figures 14.6a and 14.6b.
2. Click "Yes" to enable macros, if necessary.
3. Fill in your own personal information in each white cell (you may tab from one white cell to another).
4. After completing the information in all of the white cells, press "Tab" and then click on the "MMW Recalculation Button"—the spreadsheet will make the remaining calculations for you.

Figure 14.6a SS20 Calculator-Stock Purchase, Sale, Split.xls

Click on the "Stock Split" sheet.

Fill in the stock split information.

Finish completing the remaining white cells.

Click on the "MMW Recalculation Button."

- - -

Figure 14.6b SS20 Calculator-Stock Purchase, Sale, Split.xls

169

Stocks

Name of Stock*	Transaction Type	Transaction Date*	Stock Split Date	# Of Shares*	Price Per Share*	Extended Cost Of Shares	Broker Fees, et. al*	Invested Balance	
		Stock Split (i.e.)		2 3	For For		1 2		
Example: Home Depot	Original Purchase	9/15/98	Below	100	$41.6800	$4,168.00	$18.00	$4,186.00	Stock splits do not affect the total value of your holdings. To keep track of your cost basis, once you have completed your "After Stock Split Information," record the adjustment to your Stock Recap the following*: Name of Stock*, Transaction Date* (Original Purchase Date —not Stock Split Date**), # Shares*, Price Per Share*, and Broker Fees*.
After Stock Split Information: Home Depot	After Split	9/15/98	12/30/99	150	$27.7867	$4,168.00	$18.00	$4,186.00	
Before Stock Split Information: Hypothetical Corp.	Original Purchase	7/14/01	Below	200	$15.6800	$3,136.00	$18.00	$3,154.00	
After Stock Split Information: Hypothetical Corp.	After Split	7/14/01	8/14/02	400	$7.8400	$3,136.00	$18.00	$3,154.00	
After Stock Split Information to record on your Stock Recap:									
After Stock Split Information: Hypothetical Corp.	After Split	7/14/01		400	$7.8400		$36.00		

**Important: enter the Purchase Date on your Stock Recap instead of the Stock Split Date because it has long-term versus short term tax implications in calculations. Your cost basis is determined from the original purchase date.

Once the calculator has tabulated your "After Stock Split Information," record the adjustments to your "Stock Recap" form. Be certain to record your original purchase date versus the stock split date since it might have long-term versus short-term tax implications.

Attach your trade confirmation receipts to your stock purchase/sale recap and save the information for as long as you own the stock and at least three years (preferably seven years) after you close out your position in the stock. Your stock position is normally closed out when you sell the stock. You will need this information to prepare your tax returns and in case of a tax audit at a later date.

During the American colonial days, hogs roamed the grain fields of what is now lower Manhattan in New York City. The residents of Manhattan decided to limit the damage caused by these free-roaming hogs by erecting a wall on the northern edge of lower Manhattan. A street was developed alongside the wall—it was named Wall Street. Wall Street is now home to the New York Stock Exchange (NYSE). The NYSE is America's biggest, oldest, and most important securities exchange. Most of the nation's largest and

Stocks

best-established companies are listed on the NYSE. Originally founded on the streets of lower Manhattan, the American Stock Exchange (Amex) specializes in newer firms that do not qualify for the New York Stock Exchange's capital and other requirements. The National Association of Securities Dealers (NASD) is a self-regulatory organization that is responsible for the operation of the NASDAQ stock market and over-the-counter markets. The NASDAQ is a computerized system that facilitates broker/dealer trading of securities with current bid and ask price quotes on over-the-counter stocks and some listed stocks. An over-the-counter stock is a security that is not traded on an exchange—normally due to the security's inability to meet listing requirements.

Newsman Charles H. Dow—the founder of Dow Jones & Co.—created the world famous Dow in 1884. Charles Dow originally compiled a list of 11 stocks and published the average in a financial bulletin he established with his partner, Eddie Jones. In 1896, the Dow Jones Industrial Average (Dow or DJIA) index was comprised of 12 stocks: American Cotton Oil, American Sugar, American Tobacco, American Sugar, Chicago Gas, Distilling & Cattle Feeding, Laclede Gas, U.S. Leather, U.S. Rubber, National Lead, Tennessee Coal & Iron, and General Electric. Most of the companies merged with other companies or went completely out of business. Note that General Electric is the only remaining company that is part of today's Dow—proof that at some point in time, you may need to sell shares of your stock or face losses. The stock market is in a constant state of change, there are no investments that you can purchase and then forget. Since 1928, the Dow has been comprised of 30 blue-chip companies. The original Dow average was calculated by totaling the prices of the component stocks and then dividing by 30. Later, the Dow divided the sum of the component stocks by a "divisor." The divisor is

Stocks

used to account for stock splits, stock dividends, changes to the companies that make up the Dow average, spin-offs of companies, mergers of companies, and so on. The divisor frequently changes to maintain the historical continuity of the average. Today, the divisor is way under 1—less than 0.20. Proponents of the Dow say the component stocks are chosen as being representative of the broad market and American industry, are widely held by investors, and are major factors in their industries. Some critics of the Dow argue that the index is not representative enough of the market in total (component stocks can represent less than 15% of the market value of stocks traded on the New York Stock Exchange), that there are not enough companies represented in the Dow, and that the companies represented in the Dow are the wrong ones. Still, the DJIA is the oldest and most frequently quoted market index in the country. The Dow does not indicate activity on the American Stock Exchange or the NASDAQ over-the-counter market. The Dow can climb while other indexes fall.

Webster's dictionary describes an index as "something that serves as a pointer or indicator." Stock market indexes "indicate" how the market in general is doing.

The Standard & Poor's 500 (S&P 500) index represents around 70% of all U.S. publicly traded companies. The S&P 500 usually is considered the benchmark for U.S. equity performance. While most of the S&P 500 American companies are listed on the NYSE, it also includes companies listed on the NASDAQ stock market and the Amex.

The NASDAQ composite index is a market-value-weighted index of all common stocks listed on NASDAQ. The stocks are heavily weighted toward technology and small companies. A market value weighted index is a stock index in which each stock affects the index in proportion to its market value.

Stocks

The Wilshire 5000 index is composed of more than 6,500 companies from the NYSE, Amex, and the NASDAQ over-the-counter market. The Wilshire 5000 index provides a broad measure of trends in stock prices across the whole of the market.

The Russell 3000 index measures the performance of the 3,000 largest U.S. companies based on total market capitalization. The index represents approximately 98% of the investable U.S. equity market. The Russell 2000 index tracks mostly small company stocks.

Market declines can be triggered by any number of things. Some conditions that might be "bearish," or negative, for stocks is a tight Federal Reserve credit policy (from 1955–1990, on average, 12 months after the Fed increased rates, the Dow increased only 8%), interest rates that are high and/or climbing, falling or stagnant corporate profits, political instability or international conflict, rising unemployment, and high or rising inflation. If the market declines 5% or less, it is usually considered a minor correction. A 10% decline is usually considered a normal correction. A 15% to 19% decline is a nasty correction. Declines of 20% or more in a major stock index from its high are usually considered to be "bear markets." The Dow Jones Industrial Average is often used as the measuring stick for bear market declines. Bear markets have occurred in both weak and strong economies. Bear markets have occurred when inflation and interest rates were high and also when they were low. A recession is a significant economic decline spread across the economy that lasts more than a few months. A recession is visible in industrial production, employment, real income, and wholesale-retail sales. Recessions begin after the economy reaches a peak and end after the economy reaches its trough. Some economists define a recession as two consecutive quarters of economic decline.

Stocks

In between the economic trough and peak, the economy is in expansion. Some conditions that are "bullish," or positive, for stocks is an easy Federal Reserve credit policy (from 1955 to 1990, on average, 12 months after the Fed decreased rates, the Dow increased 18%), interest rates that are low or falling, rising corporate profits, political stability, growing employment, and low or declining inflation. A bull market is a prolonged period of rising prices over several months. A gain of 20% or more is considered a bull market. Bull markets usually last longer and rise higher on average than the comparable declines of bear markets. From 1900–1994, Wall Street suffered 22 bear markets with declines of more than 20%. Twelve bear markets had losses of more than 30%. Nine bear markets had losses greater than 40%. From 1900–1994, Wall Street advanced in 26 bull markets with increases of 30% or more. Twenty-one bull markets had gains of 50% or more. Thirteen bull markets had gains of 80% or more. Eight bull markets had gains of 100% or more.[5] The numbers indicate that you are more likely to make money in the stock market than to loose money. Over time, your likelihood of making money increases.

Generally speaking, emotions run contrary to making good investment decisions. When the stock market is high and you are feeling exhilarated and your other friends are feeling exhilarated with their economic growth, the market is probably overvalued and perhaps headed for a fall. On the other hand, when you are feeling depressed about portfolio losses and your friends are feeling depressed about economic losses, the stock market has probably reached a trough and is now headed for expansion. Do not sell out of

---

[5] Source: Ned Davis Research—based on the DJIA as the market barometer.

Stocks

fear. Do not buy out of greed. Keep investing over the long term and let the market proceed with its ups and downs. Use your mind, research the fundamentals, be willing to adjust to the changing business environment, and be willing to change your investment strategies to reflect your own changing economic goals.

Stock market investors who try to time the market by buying stocks at their peaks and purchasing them at their lows face a daunting challenge. Market timing rarely works. No one has consistently predicted turning points in the market. Economic activity reflects human behavior. Human behavior is much too complicated to predict with any degree of regularity. Besides, market turning points are usually determined by unpredictable events. The best market gains have historically come in very short bursts. H. Nejat Seyhun, chairman of the finance department of the University of Michigan School of Business Administration, conducted a study of the 7,802 trading days from 1963 through 1993. If investors had missed just 90 of the best trading days (or a mere 1.15 percent of the time period), they would have lost 95% of all the market's gains.[6] The odds of predicting the timing of those 90 days are virtually impossible. Market timing works only if you buy low and sell high. Market timers must not only be correct in picking the correct time to sell in anticipation of a decline, but they must be able to pick the correct time to get back into the market—it is virtually an impossible task. Trying to time the market is a fruitless exercise and will typically do more harm to the investor's portfolio than good. Even if you are correct in timing the market and sell at the beginning of a decline, you will be out of the market and miss some of the periods when stock prices rise. The better strategy is

---

[6] Jane Bryant Quinn, *Study suggests market timing hazardous to your returns,* Atlanta Journal-Constitution.

Stocks

to be invested in the market in order to take advantage of the stock price increase windfall when it occurs. Market timers, on average, do worse than the stock market over time. Peter Lynch, the Fidelity Magellan mutual fund manager guru, once said, "Far more money has been lost by investors preparing for corrections or trying to anticipate corrections than has been lost in corrections themselves."[7] History shows that the stock market moves higher more frequently than it moves lower—the real risks for investors is missing the opportunities to be invested when stocks increase in short bursts. There has never been a time when the stock market did not resume its upward climb. Even financial professionals who try to time the market have returns that are one-fourth less in total return than investors who buy quality stocks of companies with solid finances, good profit margins, and good prospects for sales and profit growth and who hold on to them through the markets ups and downs—occasionally weeding out the underachievers and replacing them with potentially better-performing stocks. Good companies usually overcome stock price declines by correcting their problems.

Dalbar research findings--a Boston investment research firm--found that between 1986 and 1995, people who bought stocks and held on to them during the markets ups and downs increased their portfolios 300%. Those who bought and sold stocks as they attempted to time the market increased their portfolios just 96%.

Stocks can sometimes be purchased from companies that permit direct initial stock purchases—check with the company to see if it has a direct purchase program. A growing number of companies allow investors to purchase shares directly from them, which

---

[7] Robert Luke, *Market timers face a daunting task,* Atlanta Journal-Constitution article, August 21, 1995.

Stocks

allows the investors to bypass brokers and their transaction fees. "Dividend reinvestment plans" (DRIPs) are great for investors who have limited resources but wish to get started purchasing company stocks. There are more than 1,300 DRIPs for domestic and foreign stocks. Typically, the investor must purchase a modest "one" share from a stockbroker to get started in a DRIP. This initial "one" share can be expensive since brokers might charge $25–$50 to have a stock certificate sent to you. Some companies might allow you to make the initial purchase through their DRIP program. Once you own the initial share registered in your name, you are then able to purchase additional stock shares with dividends and cash purchases as small as $10.00 each time directly through the DRIP. Companies have varying minimum initial investment amounts for their DRIP programs. The company typically charges moderate or no fees or broker commissions for the DRIP stock purchases. Call the company whose stock you would like to purchase. Ask them if they have a DRIP program. Get a prospectus that describes the plan and outlines any fees. Purchase one share to be registered in your name—from a stockbroker or from the DRIP if allowed. Complete the DRIP enrollment form. By making small but steady contributions to your DRIP program, your savings plan can grow substantially over time. Since DRIP plans pool investors' monies and make company stock purchases daily, weekly, monthly, or quarterly—depending on the individual plan—the investor has little control over the timing of the purchases or the price of the stock when it is purchased or the price of the stock when selling. However, the lack of control over the purchase price and selling price of the stock does not deter long-term investors since they are taking advantage of dollar cost averaging by making regular periodic investments in the company's stock. Fractional shares of stock are issued when contributions are insufficient

Stocks

to purchase a full share. Some DRIPs even offer investors the opportunity to purchase their stock at a discount from the market price. DRIP investors must keep great records for tax purposes—saving year-end account statements is a must. Some companies that have dividend reinvestment plans pay all the expenses of the plans. Usually the investor must pay the expenses when selling the shares. DRIPs are a great way for beginning investors to start saving.

Some people choose to conduct their own stock research and purchase the stocks themselves online to save money on trade fees and brokerage commissions. Discount brokers usually just execute investment buy and sell orders according to the investors' instructions—which saves the investor money on transaction costs. Discount brokers charge lower commission rates. Discount brokers' average fees may run around 0.85%. A full-service broker or traditional broker not only executes buy and sell orders but may also make investment recommendations, help with portfolio asset allocations, and manage your portfolio. Full-service brokers may charge around 3% to execute the same buy or sell order that you could have executed by yourself or with the help of a discount broker. Try not to spend more than 2% to 3% of an investment's value in fees—for example, a $1,000 equity investment should not cost you more than $20 to $30 in commissions and fees. Or viewed another way, your investment would have to grow by 2% to 3% just to break even. Studies indicate that broker recommendations rarely outperform the broader market averages. Actively participate in the management of your portfolio—even if you decide to use a full-service broker. Do not give a broker the authority to buy and sell investments in your portfolio without your prior approval. If you decide to use a broker, how do you go about choosing one? Ask your friends, work

Stocks

colleagues, lawyer, and accountant for broker recommendations. Develop a list of possible candidates. Check with the state securities agency in your state to see if the recommended brokers are properly licensed. Check to see if the brokers have any customer complaints, disciplinary actions, or any regulatory violations against them. Call the Better Business Bureau to investigate any complaints. Also, call the National Association of Securities Dealers (NASD) hotline at 1-800-289-9999 or visit its website at www.nasd.com. The NASD can provide information concerning criminal convictions, civil judgments, pending disciplinary proceedings, and criminal indictments. Ask the broker for their Central Registration Depository number (CRD) and check with the NASD Public Disclosure Program (PDP). NASD maintains regulatory information from registered persons, member firms, government agencies, and other sources in a database system and releases information to the investing public through their public disclosure program. You can go online at www.nasdr.com to check a firm's background by inputting its CRD number and can check individual brokers by inputting their names. Only deal with brokers and brokerage firms that are members of the NASD and the Securities Investors Protection Corporation (SIPC). The SIPC insurance provides limited customer protection (up to $500,000 in losses) caused by a brokerage firm's bankruptcy. It does not protect you against losses from bad advice, broker misconduct, or protect you against market losses. Ask the brokers for written information concerning their fee schedules.

Around 88% of investors fail to check out their brokers or brokerage firms before investing with them—it is a mistake. The Securities and Exchange Commission from 1995 through 2000 was only able to recover from 4.3% to 20.2% of the dollars from

Stocks

security law violators.[8] It is wise to conduct a background check on brokers or investment advisors before investing any money with them.

Once you have selected a broker or financial advisor, if you are dissatisfied with his or her performance, contact him or her to see if you can get the issue resolved. If that does not work, contact his or her supervisor to see if you can resolve the issue (make sure your complaint is in writing). If that does not work, contact the compliance department at your broker's main office. If that does not work, contact the Securities and Exchange Commission's Office of Investor Education and Assistance—www.sec.gov (Investor Information/File a Tip or Complaint). You may also contact the NASD—www.nasdr.com/2100.asp (NASD Complaint Program, online complaint form). Some reasons for arbitration might include the broker pushing you into buying investments that do not match your wealth, understanding, or financial goals; churning (the broker executes an excessive number of transactions on your account; there is little chance of you making any money after paying all the commissions); or if the broker misrepresents his statements to you (such as guaranteeing a 25% no-risk return). You may also wish to consider legal action in order to get your issues resolved.

---

[8] Source: *USA Today* analysis of Securities and Exchange Commission data. Kevin McCoy, *Conned investors may never see refunds,* USA Today article, January 9, 2001.

Stocks

A word on the economy in general: gross domestic product (GDP) is the total amount of goods and services produced in the United States during the year. GDP is calculated by adding together the market values of all of the final goods and services produced in a year. According to the U.S. Department of Commerce Bureau of Economic Analysis (www.bea.doc.gov/), in 2001, the United States GDP was $10,082,200,000,000. During the 72 years from 1930 through 2001, the GDP averaged a +3.5458% increase per year.[9] Consumer spending represents about two-thirds of the U.S. economy. The rest of the U.S. economy depends on corporate spending and government spending.

Investing is indeed a journey. Think in terms of the destination, not the level of today's Dow or the value of your portfolio. The stock markets ups and downs are just interim stops during your journey's travels to your destination. Successful investing in equities is a result of time "in," not timing "of," the stock market. Of course, for the Christian, the ultimate destination is life eternal with God. "*If, then, you have not proved trustworthy with the wealth of this world, who will trust you with the wealth that is real?*"—Luke 16:11.

---

[9] Extrapolated from the U.S. Dept. of Commerce Bureau of Economics data.

Mutual Funds

Chapter 15

Mutual Funds

Mutual fund companies bring together money from many people and invest it in stocks, bonds, or money market instruments. Mutual funds originated in Europe in the early 1800s. The first American mutual fund started in 1924. The mutual fund's portfolio is the combined holdings of stocks, bonds, or other assets the fund owns. Investors own shares in the mutual fund, which represent a part of the holdings comprising the fund's portfolio. The shareholders share in the income, profits, and losses of their mutual fund's investments. The financial company offering the mutual fund provides a professional manager to select the investment securities. Professional management is particularly an advantage to those investors who are uncomfortable selecting their own stocks or bonds. Since monies are pooled from many investors and invested in a myriad of assets, mutual funds usually offer a degree of diversification individuals could not achieve by purchasing individual investments on their own—that is a real advantage. Because the investor is not tied to the fortunes of only one company, diversification among numerous companies cuts down on the investor's risks. Mutual funds are liquid—they are quickly bought and sold.

Mutual funds can be purchased from banks, brokers, financial planners, or directly from the mutual fund companies themselves. Also, to buy stocks and mutual funds online through direct investing plans, look at the following websites: www.moneypaper.com (includes information on Dividend Reinvestment Plans or DRIPs) and www.netstockdirect.com (be certain to check out fees before investing). Mutual fund

Mutual Funds

shares may also be purchased through your retirement savings account at work. Mutual funds are not federally insured—even if purchased through your bank. Some funds have relatively small initial investment requirements such as $250, and some have high initial investment requirements such as $10,000 or more.

Mutual funds can be divided into three categories depending on the market value, or capitalization, of the companies whose shares the funds buy:

1. Small-cap funds—up to $1 billion in total market value (tend to be more volatile, hence riskier).
2. Mid-cap funds—between $1 billion and $5 billion in market value (average volatility, moderate risk).
3. Large-cap funds—more than $5 billion in market value (lower volatility, more stable, lower risk because they invest in the biggest American companies).

These groups can be further categorized according to how the fund managers choose the stocks in which they invest:

    A. Growth funds—look primarily at corporate sales and earnings and the likelihood that they will increase faster than the overall market (they invest primarily in common stock that has potential for long-term capital growth).

    B. Value funds—look primarily at companies whose share prices are undervalued versus the companies' underlying strengths; the fund manager believes they will appreciate more than the market in general.

    C. Blend funds—include both growth and value characteristics.

In general order of declining risks, some investment objectives or types of fund investments are as follows:

1. International funds invest in stocks outside the U.S.
2. Global funds invest in both foreign and U.S. stocks.
3. Small-company funds invest in the stocks of small, young companies that have the potential for rapid growth.

Mutual Funds

4. Aggressive funds seek appreciation in price versus growth in dividends—they are higher risk investments.

5. Growth funds invest in stocks with the potential for rapid appreciation and usually reflect high risk.

6. Growth-and-income funds offer the potential for growth in share price and regular income from stock dividends and usually reflect moderate risk.

7. Equity-income funds invest in dividend-paying stocks—usually of well-established companies.

8. Balanced funds invest in common stocks, preferred stocks, and bonds in an effort to obtain the highest return but a lower risk—they are generally less risky than funds that invest solely in stocks but are less lucrative during stock market booms. Balanced funds attempt to provide consistent returns under varying market conditions while minimizing risk associated with investing in only stocks or only bonds.

9. Income funds generate current income rather than appreciation in price and usually reflect lower risk—they invest primarily in bonds that provide long-term income.

10. Money market funds invest in short-term money market instruments to provide high current yields, stability, and liquidity—they normally are lower risk funds.

Index funds mirror the holdings of a broader-based market index such as the S&P 500. For example, let's say you invest $1,000 in an S&P 500 index fund—the weighting of your investments will be as follows: add up the market value of all 500 stocks and divide by the individual market value of each stock. If IBM = 1.6% of the total 500 market value, you would have $16.00 invested in IBM (i.e., $1,000 x 1.6% = $16.00). Your investment in the other 499 companies would be calculated the same way. Index funds offer an "almost market" return—the index's performance less a fraction for the cost of running the fund. For example, if an index jumps 20%, the fund investors get about 19.75%. Index funds are passively managed, which keeps cost low. The minimal portfolio turnover helps to keep index funds tax efficient. Index funds work best as part of a larger investment plan as a core holding. Over time, index funds beat most funds that

Mutual Funds

are actively managed. With index funds, you will not receive the highest possible returns; however, you will not suffer the worst losses either. For more information about index funds, visit www.indexfunds.com. According to John Bogle (founder of the Vanguard Group, now one of the two largest mutual fund organizations in the world), index funds are the best way for a new investor to get started with a mutual fund program because they "give highly predictable relative performance, low cost, the broadest diversification available, and it will let [the investor] . . . get familiar with stock investing over a period of several years."[1]

Sector funds invest their assets in stocks of a single industry, which does not in itself provide adequate diversification.

Funds are broadly classified as open-end funds or closed-end funds. Open-end funds allow investors to buy new shares or sell (redeem) shares at any time back to the fund for the net asset value (NAV). The net asset value of a fund is determined on any given day by totaling the sum of each company's market value in the fund's portfolio and then dividing that sum by the number of fund shares outstanding. Closed-end funds are funds that have made public sales of their shares but then close their doors to new investors and existing investors. Closed-end funds are then traded on stock exchanges or in the over-the-counter market. Investors buy and sell these closed-end funds at whatever price the market determines—at, above, or below the net asset value.

You make money with mutual funds through dividends and interest earned by investments, gains realized by the fund from selling its investments at a profit, and gains

---

[1] John Bogle, interview, Mutual Funds magazine, March 1996, page 66.

Mutual Funds

realized when you sell shares of the fund at a profit because of share price or net asset value (NAV) increases. The fund subtracts its expenses from income and then distributes the remainder to investors as dividends. The fund may issue distributions in cash or reinvest them in additional shares—either way, these distributions are normally taxable. The dividends and short-term capital gains (investments held less than one year) are taxed as ordinary income. Long-term capital gains (investments held more than one year) are taxed at the lower long-term capital gains rate. A capital gain occurs if the sale price is greater than your purchase price. A capital loss occurs if the sale price is less than your purchase price. Capital gains and losses are reported to the IRS when you complete your taxes. Funds that have had hefty distributions will often post slight NAV increases. Funds that have made few distributions will often have large increases in their NAV. NAV changes reflect only the price movement of the securities held by the fund. Remember, the fund's total return is composed of three parts:

1. Share price (or NAV)
2. Capital-gains distributions
3. Income distributions

Therefore, different funds with matching total returns can arrive at those gains in different ways.

A mix of small-cap, mid-cap, and large-cap growth, value, and blend funds offer diversification. A properly diversified portfolio includes funds that have different objectives, styles, and market areas that do not highly correlate. You may also wish to keep a small portion of your portfolio in international funds to help offset the effects of a U.S. stock market reversal. Select funds based on your personal objectives. Consider the rate of return you need and how much risk you are willing to accept. Conservative

Mutual Funds

investors might use more balanced funds versus aggressive investors who might use more small-cap funds. Select funds to achieve the proper balance that will help you obtain your objectives. If you are a small investor, you can have a well-diversified portfolio with 4 or 5 mutual funds—as long as they are invested in different market areas. Five to ten mutual funds should properly diversify the portfolio of an investor with $50,000 or more in assets. Probably no more than one-third of your fund portfolio should be committed to a single mutual fund. Since mutual funds by themselves provide diversification, owning dozens of them is unnecessary and probably results in overlap of investment areas. Ten funds that range across investment objectives from aggressive growth to income should provide enough diversification for most investors. One of any given index fund should suffice. Two or three treasury or corporate bond funds should be sufficient for more conservative portfolios. With money market funds, most people just choose a single fund as a repository for their cash reserves and an all purpose savings vehicle; however, for some people, 3 or 4 money funds might make sense as well.

Mutual funds typically charge investors for the following fees:

1. Transaction costs—the fund must pay brokerage commissions as it buys and sells securities. Since the mutual fund buys and sells in large quantities, these fees are normally much lower than the costs bore by purchases from individual investors.
2. Operating expenses—the fund incurs day-to-day operating costs such as salaries, telephone expenses, lease or rental expenses, printing charges for annual reports and prospectuses, and so on.
3. Portfolio management fees—these fees pay the portfolio management team for making the investment decisions. These management fees (or advisor fees) are the primary way mutual fund companies make their money.

Mutual fund management expenses can range as follows:

Mutual Funds

Mutual Fund Expenses	% Range
Very Low	0% to 0.77%
Low	0.78% to 1.53%
Average	1.54%
High	1.55% to 2.55%
Very High	2.56% and up

Usually, the larger the fund, the lower the management fee. Many funds have management fees of less than 1%—while that may sound small, the dollar amounts can be huge. For example, if you were invested as part of a $30 billion fund that has an annual 0.30% management fee, the fund company would collect $9,000,000 per year in management fees. Annually recurring asset-based fees are combined into a single cost measure referred to as an expense ratio. The expense ratio is disclosed in shareholders' reports. The average annual expense ratio for all stock funds is around 1.40%. Morningstar recommends that expense ratios should be as follows:[2]

Type of Fund	Expense Ratio Should Be
Bond Funds	Under 0.80%
Stock Funds	Under 1.25%

Lower expense funds will have higher long-term returns versus comparable investments by their peers that have higher expenses.

---

[2] Christine Benz, Peter Di Teresa, Russel Kimel, Morningstar *"Guide To Mutual Funds 5-Star Strategies For Success"*, New York: Wiley, 2003, page 50.

Mutual Funds

In addition, many mutual fund companies charge "loads" which are mostly sales fees. Roughly 60% of mutual funds charge a sales load. Load fees can range up to 8.5%. "Low-load" funds charge reduced sales fees. "No-load" funds do not charge sales fees.

Sales Commissions	Fees	Normally Purchased From:
High-Load Funds	4% to 8.5%	Stockbrokers, Independent Fund Salesmen
Low-Load Funds	Up to 4%	The Fund Company
No-Load Funds	0%	The Fund Company

A front-end load or sales charge of 8.5% is deducted from your investment immediately. For example, if you invest $1,000 in the mutual fund, $85 ($1,000 x 8.5% = $85.00) is deducted by the salesman or sales organization, and only $915 of your money goes toward purchasing fund shares. If all other things are equivalent, no-load funds will outperform low-load and high-load funds because more of your investment is working for you immediately. Loads negatively impact your total return.

Most funds do not charge redemption fees; however, some funds charge a back-end load or redemption fee. When an investor redeems or sells shares back to a fund, some funds charge up to a 5.3% charge on the amount of the sale. The fees might be set at high levels for short holding periods such as a 5% redemption fee if sold during the 1st year, 4% during the 2nd year, 3% during the 3rd year, 2% during the 4th year, 1% during the 5th year, and 0% in year 6 and after. Redemption fees discourage investors from frequent trading.

Most funds allow investors to automatically reinvest all capital gain and income distributions in new shares with no sales charges. However, some funds charge a

Mutual Funds

"reloading charge" on reinvestments of capital gains distributions. The maximum reloading charge is 7.25%. For example, let's assume you own shares in a fund. The fund makes a $100 capital gains distribution. If the fund charges a 7.25% reload charge, they will keep $7.25 ($100 x 7.25% = $7.25) and reinvest the other $92.75 in new fund shares for you.

12b-1 fees are named after a provision in the Securities and Exchange Commission rules that govern mutual funds. 12b-1 fees allow fund companies to charge investors up to 0.75% per year for marketing expenses and distribution costs. These fees can only be used to advertise and promote the fund to prospective investors.

Sales loads may be worth it to you if the broker's advice results in a total return from a fund that is acceptable to you after deducting the load fees. However, load fees, redemption fees, reload charges, and 12b-1 fees can be a serious drag on your fund's performance—avoid them if you can by selecting comparable funds that do not charge the same fees, or comparable funds that charge lower fees. Load fees, redemption fees, and 12b-1 fees are not necessary to the mutual fund's operation—they merely pay for transactions—they do not positively impact the fund's performance. There is no appreciable difference between the investment performance of load funds versus comparable no-load funds. There is no connection between how good a mutual fund is and how much it charges—in fact, the more the fund charges, the lower the total return.

The following shows the comparison of some of the above-mentioned fees and their effect on a $10,000 investment earning 10% per year over a 20-year time frame:

Mutual Funds

Type of Fee	Calculation of Fee	Ending $ Amount of $10,000 @ 10%/Year Over 20 Years[3]
No-Load	$10,000 @ 10% over 20 years	$67,275.00
5% Front-End Load (one-time fee)	$10,000 - $500 ($10,000 x .05) = $9,500 @ 10% over 20 years	$63,911.25
5% Back-End Load (one-time fee)	$10,000 @ 10% over 20 years = $67,275 - $3,363.75 ($67,275 x .05)	$63,911.25
12b-1 Fee of 0.75% (annually)	$10,000 @ 10% over 20 years minus 0.75% of the yearly balance each of the 20 years (- $4,336.09 in total costs)	$58,304.38

The no-load fund produced a total return of $67,275.00—the highest return in this example because all of your money was working for you from the start. The 5% front-end load fund and the 5% back-end load fund both produced $63,911.25 at 10% over 20 years. The annual reoccurring 0.75% 12b-1 fee was the biggest drag on investment performance costing $4,336.09 over the 20-year period and resulting in the worst total return of $58,304.38. Unlike load fees that are charged only once, 12b-1 fees cost shareholders year after year for as long as they own shares in the fund. While the percentages of annual fees can appear to be small, they have a huge effect on your fund's performance over time. Avoid 12b-1 fees if at all possible and choose funds with the smallest annual costs whenever possible—if all other considerations are equal. Benjamin Franklin said, "Beware of little expenses. A small leak will sink a great ship."[4]

---

[3] For illustration purposes—this amount does not include the fund's management fees.
[4] Benjamin Franklin, www.llywelyn.net, Quotes and Quotes, *Benjamin Franklin Quotes*.

Mutual Funds

Other miscellaneous fund fees might include exchange fees, which pay a fund family's transfer agent to redeem shares from one fund and purchase shares of another fund. A wire-redemption charge compensates the agent to transmit cash from redeemed mutual fund shares to a bank/savings account. Some funds charge an account closeout fee. Some funds charge a systematic-withdrawal-plan fee—a charge for withdrawing fund assets over regular time periods. Some funds charge an automatic-investment-plan fee for setting up a periodic share-purchase plan. Some funds charge small investors an account minimum fee that can offset any likelihood of the investor breaking even when combined with other charges and then subtracted from the funds return. "Caveat emptor" is a term meaning "let the buyer beware." Regarding fund fees, the investor must assume responsibility to diligently review the fund's prospectus prior to purchasing to become familiar with any fees that might apply. Investors' ultimate concern should not be the fund's annual percentage of return, but the amount of money they end up with after deducting for all the costs involved.

Mutual fund corporations must be registered with the U.S. Securities and Exchange Commission. Under the Investment Company Act of 1940, mutual funds must provide a prospectus (updated at least once per year) for all new and prospective investors. In addition, funds must disseminate reports, which include the fund's portfolio investments to shareholders, at least twice a year. When reviewing the prospectus, you should pay close attention to five basic considerations:

1. The fund's investment objective
2. The fund's portfolio strategy or investment risks
3. The fund's fees and expenses

Mutual Funds

4. The fund's management—will list the professional experience of the fund managers and whether they were responsible for the fund's past performance

5. The fund's performance—usually the prospectus will list the fund's performance over 1-, 3-, 5-, and maybe 10-year periods and compare the performance to a market index

Expenses are an important consideration because they reduce your overall return. However, more important is the actual overall return you receive after deducting taxes, commissions, fees, or other transaction costs.

When you request the prospectus, ask the fund to send you its latest annual, or interim, stockholder report so you can review the fund's investment holdings.

Fund companies send to shareholders at the end of the calendar year a summary (known as Form 1099) of all distributions made during the year. The fund company also sends a copy of the Form 1099 to the IRS. In fund parlance, a distribution is a dividend. Fund companies make two types of distributions:

1. Long-term capital gains
2. Income—interest and/or dividends earned on investments, and short-term capital gains

Most funds give shareholders the choice of taking distributions in cash or reinvesting them in new fund shares. The choice of receiving cash or reinvesting the shares makes no difference to the shareholder on tax consequences; however, if you reinvest the shares, your portfolio grows quicker. Mutual fund companies usually distribute in December any capital gains they've made during the course of the year. Do not invest in the fund late in the year and just before the dividend date—you'll end up paying taxes on the capital gains for price share increases in which you did not participate. The immediate distribution may seem like an immediate payback, but it is really a tax liability. For

Mutual Funds

example, let's say you purchase shares in a fund with a $40.00 NAV. The next day, the fund distributes a $4.00/share accumulated net capital gain. As soon as the $4.00 is distributed to the shareholders, the NAV drops to $36.00/share, and you have to pay taxes on the $4.00 distribution received. It is better to purchase fund shares after the distribution, participate in the NAV share price increase, and then pay taxes on your gain. Call the fund's shareholder telephone number and ask them when the "ex-dividend" date will be; then, invest in the fund after that date. The ex-dividend value reflects what the share price will be after distributions are paid.

Fund companies are among the most highly regulated corporations in America. The overall risk associated with a mutual fund depends on what the fund buys for investments. There are mutual funds that invest in almost every type of security imaginable—blue chip stocks, growth stocks, over-the-counter stocks, small company stocks, preferred stocks, foreign stocks, corporate bonds, government bonds, mortgage investments, U.S. Treasury bills, gold, bank certificates of deposit, commercial paper, convertible securities, and so on. More than likely, there will be a mutual fund that serves the investment objective you seek.

Mutual funds offer the small investor numerous advantages. Since mutual funds consist of portfolios that may contain many securities, most of them provide a greater level of diversification than individuals might achieve on their own. Mutual funds provide professional portfolio supervision. Mutual funds provide liquidity—the ability to sell an investment at a moment's notice. Mutual funds buy and sell securities in larger blocks, which results in lower trading costs than typical investors could achieve on their own. Most of the paperwork for investing in mutual funds is done by the mutual fund

Mutual Funds

company for its shareholders. Mutual fund investors do not have to concern themselves with purchases in round-lot increments like individual stock investors. Mutual fund investors simply purchase or sell in whatever dollar amounts they like—subject to the minimum guidelines established by the mutual fund company. Since mutual funds can be purchased in small amounts at periodic intervals steadily over time, they are ideally suited to reap the benefits of dollar cost averaging. Dollar cost averaging guarantees the investor's average cost of fund shares will be less than the average prices paid when the funds were purchased—as long as you've selected a fund that increases in value over time. Dollar cost averaging works because you purchase more in fund shares when the market declines and fewer shares when the market is rising—that lowers the average cost of shares you purchase over time.

A fund's volatility should be a consideration before purchasing fund shares. Choose funds that are acceptable from a volatility standpoint with your own risk tolerance levels. Beta is a measure of a mutual fund's volatility. Beta is normally compared to the Standard & Poor's 500 index. A fund with a beta of 1 is exactly as volatile as the S&P 500. A fund with a beta of 0.75 is 25% less volatile than the S&P 500. A fund with a beta of 1.25 is 25% more volatile than the S&P 500. Low beta funds tend to lag behind other funds when the market is increasing. Low beta funds tend to fall less quickly when the market is decreasing. High beta funds tend to rise more quickly when the market is increasing. High beta funds tend to decline more quickly when the market is decreasing.

As with other investments, the earliest steps in investing in mutual funds are basic—figure out how much money you have to invest, your investment time horizon, and the amount of risk you want to assume and then begin selecting securities that will provide

Mutual Funds

you with a well-diversified portfolio. Know what your fund invests in—successful funds can have as few as a couple of dozen holdings and as many as 1,000. Research the fund's prospectus and other financial reports. Utilize independent research information such as fund newsletters and Morningstar reports. Chicago-based Morningstar is the leading supplier of mutual fund information to consumers. Morningstar is famous for its 1-, 2-, 3-, 4-, or 5-star rating system. A 4-star or 5-star rating from Morningstar is the equivalent of being in the top third of the fund's peer group. One of the best ways to evaluate a fund's performance is to look at its long-term performance compared with its peer group—be careful to look at a fund's performance year by year because one outstanding year can skew the results. Funds that have produced returns in the top of their peer group for 1 year can easily drop dramatically the following year. Funds that have consistently produced returns in the top of their peer group over a 3- to 5- or 10-year period tend to stay in the top of their peer group. Funds that lag behind their peer group over a 3- to 5- or 10-year period tend to continue to lag behend their peer group. Funds with great long-term track records can turn mediocre; however, funds with poor long-term records almost never get better. Investment advisor Sheldon Jacobs (publisher of the *No-Load Fund Investor* newsletter) conducted a study on the performance of hundreds of new funds over a 20-year period and found that more than half of them underachieved first-year results compared to the average of their peers. Favor more-established funds. Of course, history is no guarantee of future returns. Morningstar's ratings (based on history) are only a starting point, not a decision point. Morningstar's star system tells you which funds were good, not necessarily which funds will be good. For example, if there's been a management change in the fund, it's the fund manager's previous record that's more

Mutual Funds

important than the fund's record. The ratings do not predict future performance, and they are not buy/sell recommendations. Morningstar ratings describe how well a fund has balanced risk and return in the past and compares that performance to similar funds. Past performance does not necessarily make for great forecasting without including other variables—the fund's management style, how it operates, expenses, objectives, volatility, portfolio fit, and so on. Fund newsletters and Morningstar reports might be available at your local library. You can view information from Morningstar at www.morningstar.com (some fees may apply). Another good source for independent research is Value Line. Value Line provides investment research on stocks, mutual funds, and options and offers a family of no-load mutual funds. Value Line reports can be viewed at www.valueline.com. Major libraries will also have the Value Line reports.

Most mutual funds have toll-free telephone numbers your may call to get a new account application form to buy shares—be sure to ask if the fund is available for sale in your state; not all funds are available for sale in every state. Simply mail the application form back to the fund along with your check or other payment to begin investing. Funds may be purchased through your stockbroker or other investment analyst. In addition, many employers allow you to purchase mutual funds through payroll deductions at work. Over one-third of the assets in mutual funds are from IRAs, 401 k plan's, and defined contribution accounts. Most funds allow free or low-cost transfers of investments from one fund to another via mail, telephone, or electronic instruction.

Both load and no-load funds can be sold directly back to the fund itself. You may also sell the fund shares back to your broker, investment analyst, or possibly through your company's benefit administrator's program. You may wish to sell fund shares due to poor

Mutual Funds

performance, due to a change in management or management style, because the fund no longer fits with your investment portfolio objectives, to realize a loss and get a tax refund, because annual expenses are too high, or because you just need the money for a house, college tuition, medical expenses, or other expenses. It is best to compare a fund's performance to its peers' performance versus comparing to an index when considering selling. Performance is not just returns; it is also volatility and risk. If the fund has trailed its peers for more than 18 months, consider selling.

As with trying to time the market by buying and selling individual stocks, timing the market by buying and selling mutual funds is virtually impossible. Markets often rise sharply after their biggest falls. Jumping in and out of funds might lock in the downturns and miss out on market rebounds. Wise investors save and invest during all market conditions. Usually, when the general investor sentiment is bearish, it is bullish for the market. When the general investor sentiment is bullish, it is bearish for the market.

The *Wall Street Journal* and most daily newspapers give price quotations for mutual funds with more than 1,000 shareholders or more than $25 million in assets. If the fund is not listed in your newspaper, you may call the fund directly to get price quotations. Newspapers normally quote fund shares with one or two prices. The first price or the only one showing is normally under the heading NAV (net asset value). Some newspapers use the term "bid" for NAV. The bid price is the actual value of the fund shares and the actual price at which shareholders were able to sell their shares the previous day. The second price, called the "offer price" or "asked" price represents the price paid by investors the previous day. The offer price is always higher than the bid price because it includes the maximum sales charge paid by the new investors. Newspapers may rank

Mutual Funds

funds on performance versus similar funds with the same objective. For example, a newspaper may rank a fund as "A" if it is in the top 20% of its peers performance wise, "B" if in the next 20%, "C" if in the middle 20%, "D" if in the next 20%, and "E" if in the bottom 20%. Limit your investments to the top A- and B-ranked funds.

What are some of the common mistakes or "deadly sins" that mutual fund investors make? Overrating historical performance is one of the most common mistakes—especially short-term performance of one year or less. Do not chase "hot funds." Last year's hot fund will likely turn cold the following year. Another mistake is paying too much for your investment. Do not invest based solely on numbers—especially historical numbers. Another mistake is misunderstanding risk or giving inadequate weight to risk. Understand your risk-tolerance levels and your investment time horizon and select a broad range of investments that will help you achieve your goal within acceptable risk limitations. Another mistake is trading too often. Investors should do their fund research before buying for the long term and then be patient during the market's ups and downs. Investors should be willing to hold on to their investments as long as the fundamentals of the investments remain constant. Trading too often can result in selling at lows and missing out on gains. Trading too often can also have negative tax implications for you. Short-term market traders who try to time the market are in a very speculative business and are likely headed for a fall. A "sister sin" to trading too often is "buying and forgetting." A successful investor is willing to sell a fund when its fundamentals change—if after 18 months the fund is no longer producing in the top third of its peer group, its management changes for the worse, its investment objectives change and it is experiencing style drift, the investor's goals change and the fund no longer fits the

Mutual Funds

portfolio objectives, and so on. Investors should adjust their portfolios every 12 to 18 months to rebalance their mix of assets. If possible, the rebalancing should be accomplished with new investment money to lessen taxes. Be certain your portfolio does not become overweighted in any one kind of investment option. Rebalance your portfolio to minimize your risk and to maintain a complementary allocation of assets.

Another common mistake fund investors make is neglecting the effect of tax consequences. High portfolio turnover can lead to big tax liabilities. Taxes should not be your most important consideration when investing in mutual funds, but they should be considered as one of the variables. Investors can choose to receive capital gains and dividends in the form of a check from the fund or have the gains and dividends automatically reinvested in the fund—either way triggers a taxable event in the current year. Automatic reinvestment of capital gains and dividends often creates tax obligations unanticipated by some shareholders. Keeping thorough records is essential to knowing the tax basis of your funds. Save your annual mutual fund statements—if the annual statement recaps your year's transactions, you may discard the quarterly statements. Knowing your cost basis is necessary for determining your capital gain or loss. With a no-load fund, your tax basis is what you paid per share for the fund. For example, if you buy shares of a fund this month with an $18.53/share net asset value, your tax basis for those shares is $18.53. Next month, you buy more shares of the same fund at $18.83/share NAV; your tax basis on those shares is $18.83. If you buy a load fund, you should include the sales commission in the calculation of your tax basis. For example, if you invest $10,000 in a load fund with a $25.00/share NAV that charges a 2% sales load, only $9,800 is invested in the fund ($10,000 x .02% sales load = $200; $10,000 - $200 =

Mutual Funds

$9,800). $9,800 divided by $25.00/share NAV = 392 actual shares bought. To calculate your actual tax basis, include the sales fee: $10,000 divided by 392 shares = $25.51 tax cost basis—note that this prorates the sales charges over the number of shares bought in the transaction. Since your mutual fund company sends you a tax form that reports all of the dividends you reinvest during the year, and you have to report these dividends on Schedule B of your income tax return, you are paying taxes annually. Reinvested dividends increase your cost basis. Your cost basis is the total of the following:

1. Your original investment plus sales commissions
2. Any additional purchases plus sales commissions
3. Reinvested dividends

Anything that causes your cost basis to decrease will increase the taxes you owe. For example, if the mutual fund company makes a tax-free return of your investment capital or principal, you must reduce your cost basis in the fund by the value of the return. Anything that causes your cost basis to increase will decrease the taxes you owe. Keeping meticulous records will help you avoid overpaying taxes based on your cost. Remember, if you used automatic reinvestment of dividends, you already had to pay taxes on those distributions each year, even though the money was reinvested in the fund. It is up to you to know the tax basis of your funds—keep track of every initial purchase and every reinvestment.

Legislation has been proposed to simplify the calculation of the basis for mutual fund shares. Until such legislation is passed, the IRS gives you four options for figuring the basis of the fund shares you sell or redeem:

1. Average cost per share—the easiest and most commonly used method. It is the average price of all the shares you have purchased.

Mutual Funds

Review the following chart to see how you compute your average cost per share for your mutual fund:

Transaction Date	Bought or Sold	Dollar Amount (Including Sales Commissions)	Number of Shares	Average Cost per Share (Dollar Amount Divided by Number of Shares)
02/14/02 (initial purchase)	Bought	$2,000.00	100	$20.00
05/13/02 (additional purchase)	Bought	$2,326.00	100	$23.26
12/31/02 (reinvested dividend)	Bought	$250.00	10	$25.00
Totals as of 12/31/02		$4,576.00	210	$21.79

Note that the dollar amount invested is $4,576.00 ($2,000.00 + $2,326.00 + $250.00 = $4,576.00). The number of shares in the fund is 210 (100 + 100 + 10 = 210). The average cost per share is $21.79 ($4,576.00 divided by 210 = $21.79). If you sell 100 shares at $25.00 per share for $2,500, then, using the average cost per share method, your gain per share would be $25.00 minus $21.79 = $3.21 x 100 shares = $321.00 in taxable gains. This is the method of choice for most mutual fund investors.

2. Average cost per share, double categories—this accounts for both short-term and long-term holdings by separating shares into those you have held for more than one year and those that you have held for less than one year. You then find the average cost of each group like you did in the average cost per share method in method #1. You can then decide whether you want to choose the shares to sell that are long-term or short-term gains or losses.

3. First in, first out (FIFO)—using this method, the first shares purchased are considered the first sold. Your tax basis is the actual price of the shares you sold. For funds that have steadily increased in value, this method may result in the largest amount of taxable gain and will usually produce the biggest tax bill. Using the example in method #1, if you sold 100 shares at $25.00/share using FIFO, your taxable gain would be computed as follows: 100 x $25.00 = $2,500.00. 100 x $20.00 (original purchase price) = $2,000. $2,500 - $2,000.00 = $500.00 taxable gain. (In comparison, if the average cost per share method had been used, your taxable gain would have been calculated as follows: 100 x $25.00 = $2,500.00. 100 x $21.79 = $2,179.00. $2,500 - $2,179.00 = $321.00 taxable gain).

4. Specific shares—using this method, you identify the specific shares you are selling. It is the most flexible method because you can choose shares with the highest or lowest basis depending on which suit your tax need. With the specific

Mutual Funds

share basis, you tell your fund or broker in writing exactly what shares to sell. Using the example in methord #1, if you sold 10 shares at $25.00/share = $250.00, you could designate the following:

a. 02/14/02 initial purchase, 10 shares x $20.00 = $200.00 cost. $250.00 - $200.00 = $50.00 taxable gain.

b. 05/13/02 additional purchase, 10 shares x $23.26 = $232.60 cost. $250.00 - $232.60 = $17.40 taxable gain.

c. 12/31/02 reinvested dividend, 10 shares x $25.00 = $250.00 cost. $250.00 – 250.00 = $0.00 taxable gain.

If you want to avoid paying taxes, specifying the shares in example 4c will be your best choice. If you've sold other shares in your portfolio that had a loss of $50.00, you will probably want to designate the shares in 4a to offset your losses to minimize your tax payments. If you've sold other shares in your portfolio that had a loss of $17.40, you may want to designate 4b as the specific shares to sell, which will offset your reportable loss. Designating specific shares allows you to maximize your reported losses, maximize your reported gains, or choose somewhere in between—whichever situation best benefits your current year tax situation. Before the redemption, tell the fund which shares to sell and identify the shares by the purchase price and the date purchased.

You may choose different methods of calculating your cost basis for different funds. Choose the most tax-efficient method of reporting gains or losses. Once you use a method for a particular fund, you need the Internal Revenue Service's permission to change it. If you switch money among funds, a taxable event occurs—even if you switch money within the same fund family. If you write a check against a mutual fund, it is considered a sale of shares. If you write several checks, the record keeping can become very difficult. To avoid the hassle of extra accounting procedures, it's best to avoid writing checks on your mutual funds if possible. If the mutual fund sale is sizable, consider talking to your employer payroll department about adjusting your withholding to accommodate the extra taxes that will be due. Or you could make an estimated tax payment to the IRS to cover the additional taxes. If you withhold less than necessary, you

Mutual Funds

could owe not only taxes on your mutual fund sale, but you also might owe the IRS a penalty. If in doubt, consult your tax advisor. All capital gains distributions are subject to federal income taxes, and they might be subject to state income taxes as well. Fund companies are required to send tax-related information to shareholders by January 28 of each year.

When you inherit mutual fund shares, your basis is generally the value of the mutual fund shares on the day the previous owner died. This means that any appreciation on shares during the decedent's life is passed on to the inheritor tax-free. The inheritor will owe tax only on the appreciation after the shares are inherited. If the shares drop in value, then the inheritor can deduct the loss when they sell. This can be an enormous tax advantage. If someone you know who has mutual fund investments dies, consider getting the family a copy of the *Wall Street Journal* on the day of the death—it could be an excellent reference resource when the inheritors get around to dealing with the deceased person's financial matters. If you do not have access to the basis of the inherited shares, you might call the mutual fund company and ask for the net asset value on the day the previous owner died. You might also check with libraries for back issues of newspapers that carry fund prices to get the information you need. If you and your spouse jointly own mutual fund shares and your spouse dies, you automatically become sole owner of the funds. You are treated as if you inherited one-half of the shares. The basis of that one-half is stepped up to the date of death value. Failing to make the date of death adjustments in your mutual fund share's basis will result in your overpaying your taxes when you ultimately sell your shares.

Mutual Funds

If someone gives you mutual fund shares, your basis depends on whether you redeem the shares for a gain or a loss. If you sell the shares for a gain, your basis is the same as the person who gave you the shares. If you sell the shares for a loss, your basis is either the donor's basis or, if lower, the value of the shares on the date of the gift. This means that while the donor can give you the tax bill that goes along with the shares' appreciation while they owned them, the donor cannot pass on the tax-saving power of any capital losses. To calculate your gain/loss on shares that are given to you, you need to know both the shares' value on the date of the gift and the donor's basis in the shares. If you receive mutual fund shares as part of a divorce settlement, your basis is the same as your ex-spouse's basis.

For assistance in keeping track of your mutual fund purchases and redemptions for non-IRA accounts only, please complete the following steps:

1. Open the "SS21 Calculator-Mutual Fund Purchases & Sales.xls"; see Figures 15.1a, 15.1b, and 15.1c.
2. Click "Yes" to enable macros, if necessary.
3. Fill in your own personal information in each white cell (you may tab from one white cell to another).
4. After completing the information in all of the white cells, press "Tab" and then click on the "MMW Recalculation Button"—the spreadsheet will make the remaining calculations for you.

Figure 15.1a SS21 Calculator-Mutual Fund Purchases & Sales.xls

Mutual Funds

Mutual Fund Purchases & Sales Recap (Non-IRA Accounts)

FILL IN THE WHITE CELLS, THE REST OF THE CELLS WILL BE CALCULATED FOR YOU

(Fill In The White Cells—Row 25 Must Be Completed, Press Tab, Click On The "MMW Recalculation Button" or press "Cntrl + m")

MMW Recalculation Button

Name of Mutual Fund:

Mutual Fund Ticker Symbol:

Mini-Calculator To Determine The Number Of Shares (Input The Dollar Amount--excluding commissions--and the NAV Of Your Fund Shares On The Purchase Date)

Dollar Amount (Actually Spent On Fund Shares)	Net Asset Value	Number Of Shares
		#DIV/0!

Transaction Date	Bought Or Sold	Dollar Amount (Including Sales Fees--This Transaction)	Number Of Shares (This Transaction)	Average Cost Per Share (This Transaction)	Total Cost Basis (All Transactions)	Total Shares Owned (All Transactions)	"Average Basis" Per Share (All Transactions)	"Average Basis" Of Sold Shares (This Transaction)
7/31/02	Bought	$10,300.00	541.1255	$19.03	$10,300.00	541.1255	$19.03	Not Sold

- - -

Fill in the name of your mutual fund and the mutual fund ticker symbol.

Use the "Mini-Calculator" if you only know the "Dollar Amount" spent on fund shares—this amount does not include sales commissions, only the amount of money actually used to buy fund shares—and the "Net Asset Value" of the funds when you purchased them. The Mini-Calculator will then tell you the "Number Of Shares" you purchased. You may then input the "Number Of Shares" into the main body of the calculator.

Mutual Funds

Figure 15.1b SS21 Calculator-Mutual Fund Purchases & Sales.xls

	Name of Mutual Fund:			
	Mutual Fund Ticker Symbol:			

Mini-Calculator To Determine The Number Of Shares (Input The Dollar Amount--excluding commissions--and the NAV Of Your Fund Shares On The Purchase Date)	Dollar Amount (Actually Spent On Fund Shares)	Net Asset Value	Number Of Shares
			#DIV/0!

Transaction Date	Bought Or Sold	Dollar Amount (Including Sales Fees--This Transaction)	Number Of Shares (This Transaction)	Average Cost Per Share (This Transaction)	Total Cost Basis (All Transactions)	Total Shares Owned (All Transactions)	"Average Basis" Per Share (All Transactions)	"Average Basis" Of Sold Shares (This Transaction)
7/31/02 (e.g.Bought)	Bought (example)	$10,300.00	541.1255	$19.03	$10,300.00	541.1255	$19.03	Not Sold
8/30/02 (e.g. Sold)	Sold (example)	-$2,000.00	-122.9256	$16.27	$7,960.18	418.1999	$19.03	$2,339.82
12/30/2002 (e.g. Div. Reinv.)	Bought (example)	$163.70	10.0000	$16.37	$8,123.88	428.1999	$18.97	Not Sold
				#DIV/0!	$0.00	0.0000	Sold	Not Sold
				#DIV/0!	$0.00	0.0000	Sold	Not Sold

- - -

Record the transaction date (it will help you determine short-term gains from long-term gains). Be certain to begin recording with your first purchase on the very first row so formulas operate correctly.

Record whether the transaction is for a buy or sell.

Record the "Dollar Amount"—special note: this amount should include any sales commissions or loads. If the amount is for a "sold" order, be certain to enter the amount as a negative number with a minus in front of it (e.g., sold $2,000 is recorded as "-$2,000.00").

Record the number of shares—special note: if the amount is for a "sold" order, be certain to enter the amount as a negative number with a minus in front of it (e.g., sold 122.9256 shares is recorded as "-122.9256.").

<u>Without the negative signs ("-") for sold orders, the calculator does not compute the "Total Cost Basis," "Total Shares Owned," the "Average Basis Per Share,", or the "Average Basis Of Sold Shares" correctly.</u>

This recap of mutual fund purchases and sales should provide you and your tax advisor with enough information to be able to quickly compare the results of using different accounting methods and thus help you decide which accounting method best suits your needs. Note: for "Average Cost Per Share—Double Categories" you would need to separate short-term from long-term transactions using two of the additional worksheets.

Figure 15.1c SS21 Calculator-Mutual Fund Purchases & Sales.xls

Mutual Funds

Transaction Date	Bought Or Sold	Dollar Amount (Including Sales Fees--This Transaction)	Number Of Shares (This Transaction)	Average Cost Per Share (This Transaction)	Total Cost Basis (All Transactions)	Total Shares Owned (All Transactions)	"Average Basis" Per Share (All Transactions)	"Average Basis" Of Sold Shares (This Transaction)
7/31/02 (e.g.Bought)	Bought (example)	$10,300.00	541.1255	$19.03	$10,300.00	541.1255	$19.03	Not Sold
8/30/02 (e.g. Sold)	Sold (example)	-$2,000.00	-122.9256	$16.27	$7,960.18	418.1999	$19.03	$2,339.82
12/30/2002 (e.g. Div. Reinv.)	Bought (example)	$163.70	10.0000	$16.37	$8,123.88	428.1999	$18.97	Not Sold
				#DIV/0!	$0.00	0.0000	Sold	Not Sold
				#DIV/0!	$0.00	0.0000	Sold	Not Sold

Fund (1) / Fund (2) / Fund (3) / Fund (4) / Fund (5) / Fund (6) / Fund (7) / F

This worksheet already has 20 different tabs for Fund #1 through Fund #20 to help you keep track of your funds.

This workbook is unprotected so you can change the "Fund #" names if you like. Follow these steps:
1. Right click on the "Fund #" tab you would like to rename.
2. Click on "Rename."
3. Type in the fund name or the fund ticker symbol.
4. Click on "Save."

Also, if you would like to make more copies of the existing 20 different funds recap forms, follow these steps:
1. Click on "Edit."
2. Click on "Move or Copy Sheet."
3. Under "Before Sheet," arrow down and highlight "(Move to end)."
4. Put a check mark in " √ Create a Copy."
5. Click on "OK." The additional sheet tab will appear at the end of the Fund #20 tab.

Mutual funds are the public's most popular investment vehicle. Congratulations on your completion of Chapter 15 on mutual funds. This chapter exposes you to more mutual fund information than is known by more than 90% of existing mutual fund shareholders. Use these strategies/knowledge to make better decisions regarding your mutual fund investments. "*If any of you lacks wisdom, he should ask God, who gives generously to all without finding fault, and it will be given to him*"—James 1:5 (New International Version).

As with stocks, it might benefit you from a tax perspective to transfer shares of mutual funds directly to a nonprofit, tax deductible, charitable 501 (c) (3) not-for-profit organization.

Bonds

Chapter 16

Bonds

Investing in bonds or bond funds is in essence loaning money to corporations, governments, municipalities, federal agencies, or other entities known as the issuer of the bonds. The issuer may borrow money and repay it over time to finance projects by selling bonds. Bonds are essentially IOUs. Income from bond investments is called "fixed income" because the bond issuers promise to repay the amount of the loan—that is, the principal or face value—on a set maturity date and to make periodic fixed interest payments over the life of the loan. The total return from a bond is the interest payment plus the gain or loss in its market value. Bonds typically have a predictable stream of payments and repayment of principal. People might invest in bonds to preserve and increase their capital or to receive dependable interest income. Investing in bonds can help you achieve a number of financial goals. Lower-risk investments are especially important the closer you get to retirement. The length of time until the face value of the bond is repaid is referred to as the "maturity." The following chart outlines some bond maturities:

	Maturity	**Typical Investment Returns**	**Vulnerability to Interest Rate Fluctuations**
Short-Term Bonds:	1–3 years	Lower	Lower
Intermediate-Term Bonds:	4–9 years	Medium	Between
Long-Term Bonds:	10–30 years[1]	Higher	Higher

---

[1] Some bonds mature in terms as long as 100 years.

Bonds

The price or value of the bond is not fixed and is closely tied to interest rates. Interest rates and bond prices are related in an inverse fashion. When interest rates fall, bond prices of existing bonds increase. When interest rates rise, bond prices of existing bonds decrease. Why is there an inverse relationship between bond prices and yields? Let's say you have a bond that yields 5%. If interest rates rise and new bonds are issued yielding 5.25%, you will have to sell your now less attractive 5% bond at a discount to compensate for the lower yield. This correlation exists so that existing bonds and new bonds offer potential buyers similar returns. For the same reason, if newly issued bonds decline in yields, existing bonds will rise in price. If you purchase a bond and must sell it before the maturity date and if interest rates have risen, you will usually get a lower price than you originally paid for the bond. In fact, if interest rates rise far enough, bond prices will drop so far that they can offset the fund's yield, which produces a negative return on your investment. Conversely, if interest rates have fallen, you will usually get a higher price than you originally paid for the bond. A 5-year duration bond fund will respond with roughly a 5% price change following a 1% interest rate change. A 5-year duration bond fund will respond with roughly a 10% price change following a 2% interest rate change.

Not only do interest rates affect the price you pay for bonds, but other variables such as supply and demand, credit quality, tax status, and maturity affect the price as well. The longer the maturity of a bond, the greater the risk of price fluctuations the bond will have. Also, the longer the maturity, the greater risk of price fluctuations in larger amounts the bond will have. Investors expect to be compensated for taking that extra risk. The longer the investor's money is at risk, the more an investor should expect to earn.

Bonds

There are two basic choices for bond investing:

1. Purchasing individual bonds
2. Investing in bond mutual funds

Individual bonds assure a fixed return on your investment if held until maturity. In addition, the issuer promises to return your entire face-value investment upon the bond's maturity. However, some bonds are "callable"—they can be redeemed by the bond issuer before the agreed-upon maturity at a specified date—this happens most often during periods of declining interest rates. The bond issuer cannot redeem noncallable bonds prematurely. The opposite of "call provisions" is "puts." Bonds that have puts allow the investor the option of requiring the issuer to repurchase the bonds at specific times prior to the bond's maturity.

Most bonds are issued at a $1,000 face value or "par." The stated interest rate, or "coupon rate," is normally fixed—although, some bonds carry floating rates. A floating-rate bond's interest rate is reset periodically according to changes in some interest rate index such as the interest rate on treasury bills. Usually, bond interest is calculated on an annual basis and paid out twice per year. For example, a $1,000 bond with a stated interest rate of 5% would provide $50 in interest income annually, paid out twice per year at $25.

Zero-coupon bonds pay one payment at maturity that is equal to the purchase price (principal) plus the total interest rate. The following is an example of a zero-coupon bond that is sold at a substantial discount from its face value:

Bonds

Bond Face Amount:	$20,000	Maturing in 20 years then paid to investor.
Discount From Face Value:	$5,050	Original purchase price to the investor.
7% Interest Compounding Automatically:	$14,950	If it is a taxable bond, the interest is taxed as it occurs.

"Yield" is the rate of return or "profit received" that you actually realize from the bond investment. Yield includes the bond-trading prices, which fluctuate resulting in both prices above, or at a "premium," to par and also below, or at a "discount," to par. For example, let's say you pay a premium of $1,100 for a $1,000 face-value bond that pays 5% interest. Interest is only calculated on face value—for example, $1,000 x 5% annually = $50.00. $50.00 divided by the $1,100 "premium to par" = a 4.5% current yield. Let's say you pay a "discount" of $900 for a $1,000 face value bond that pays 5% interest. $1,000 x 5% = $50.00. That $50.00 divided by the $900 "discount to par" = a 5.5% "current yield" or "annual return." Even more meaningful than current yield is "yield to maturity" and "yield to call" because they tell you the total return you receive by holding the bond until maturity or when it is called. Yield to maturity equals all the interest you receive from the bond purchase date until maturity, which includes the interest on the interest. Yield to maturity also includes any gain (bond purchase below par) or less (bond purchase above par). Yield to call is calculated the same way as yield to maturity but assumes the bond will be called and the investor will receive the face value back on the call date. Ask your investor advisor for the yield to maturity and the yield to call on any bond you are considering buying. Yield to maturity and yield to call allow you to compare bonds with different maturities and coupons.

Bonds

Bonds can be almost as volatile as stocks; however, bond prices might hold up well when stock prices falter. If the economy slows, the rate of business profits might slow and stock prices might decline. Bond prices during the same period might be going up. Bond prices tend to rise and fall at different times from equity (stock) prices. Owning both stocks and bonds provides you with a more stable portfolio than owning only one of those assets. While money tends to grow much faster in stocks than bonds over the long term, owning bonds or bond funds can help to buffer your portfolio against the inevitable downturns that occur in even the strongest stock market. Bonds generally provide more stable and higher interest returns compared to investments such as money market funds, certificates of deposit, or bank passbook accounts. Know the purpose bonds serve in your portfolio whether it's income generation or risk reduction through broad diversification. If you need your money to grow, you would not want to put all of it in bonds. While U.S. Government bonds are considered to be the safest investment in the world, they typically do not offer the rate of return that many other investments offer. Sometimes, bonds do not exceed the rate of inflation—if not, that turns your investment into a money eater. Steep rises in economic growth can lead to inflation. Inflation raises the costs of goods and services, which leads to higher interest rates. Higher interest rates erode a bond's value. That is why bond markets tend to react negatively to reports about strong economic growth. However, a portion of your assets probably should be allocated to bonds to ensure that you always have some money on hand—especially money that you will need for near-term purchases and for emergencies. Remember, proper diversification considers risk-reward ratios and involves owning several classes of investments: some

Bonds

cash equivalents (such as checking accounts, savings accounts, certificates of deposit), some fixed-income investments (such as bonds), and some growth assets (such as stock).

It makes good sense to diversify your portfolio. You can use "laddering" as a diversification strategy for bonds. Laddering is purchasing securities that have various maturity dates. A portfolio of bonds with various maturities distributed over time reduces your portfolio's sensitivity to interest rate risk. For example, you might invest in equal amounts in securities maturing in 2, 4, 6, 8, and 10 years. When the first bonds mature in 2 years, you would reinvest the money into 10-year bonds, thus maintaining the ladder sequence. Laddering provides a higher return than if you bought only short-term bonds. Also, your risk would be less than if you had purchased only long-term bonds, which are more sensitive to changes in interest rates than short-term bonds. Laddering provides better protection against interest rate changes than purchasing bonds with only one maturity date.

Most individual bonds are bought and sold in the over-the-counter market (OTC) in $5,000 denominations. Some bonds are listed on the NYSE. You can also buy and sell bonds that have already been issued in the secondary market. In the secondary markets, bond prices are quoted as if they were traded in $100 increments. For example: a bond quoted at 98 refers to a bond priced at $98 per $100 face value or a 2% discount. Bond prices normally include a markup for the dealer's cost and profit. Sometimes a commission is added as well. Each firm establishes its own prices. Recent and historical price data on municipal bonds can be viewed at www.investinginbonds.com. Also, you can compare prices for specific securities by contacting several dealers to obtain bids.

Bonds

Bond mutual funds pool the money of a large number of investors to buy many different individual bonds. Bond mutual funds provide professional managers to monitor the bond portfolio and provide greater diversification versus purchasing individual bonds. The professional manager selects bonds according to the criteria set forth in the fund's prospectus. As the professional manager buys and sells bonds continuously, the interest paid on your investment, as well as the share price of the fund, changes almost daily. You can add to or withdraw funds from your bond fund in amounts and at times you choose. Bond <u>funds</u> do not have a specified maturity date. "Open-end" funds allow you to buy or sell your shares in the fund whenever you choose. "Closed-end" bond funds have a specific number of shares traded on a stock exchange. After the initial offering, existing shares can only be bought from existing shareholders. Bond mutual funds are liquid—an important advantage. The fund must buy back your shares whenever you want to sell them; however, the bond fund share prices fluctuate and may be more or less than your original purchase price. The maturity for a bond fund is the average number of years until the bonds in the fund come due. The longer the maturity, the more interest a bond will normally pay and the more sensitive the bond is likely to be to interest rate changes. Higher interest rates for longer maturities is meant to compensate investors for tying up their money over longer periods of time. Bond funds typically have low minimum investment requirements that range from around $250 to $500. Investors can arrange for fund earnings to be reinvested automatically so that interest as well as principal earn interest and the investment grows more quickly. The net asset value (NAV) is the price you pay for a fund. The NAV is the total value of the fund, less expenses, divided by the number of outstanding shares.

Bonds

A bond issuer provides details as to its financial soundness and creditworthiness in a document called an "offering document," "prospectus," or in an "official statement."

Several bond-rating services grade bonds using their own various bond-rating designations. The following chart lists some bond-rating designations based on credit risk:

	Credit Ratings		Credit Risk
Moody's	**Standard & Poor's**	**Fitch Ratings**	**Investment-Grade**
Aaa	AAA	AAA	Highest quality bonds—issuers are considered to be extremely dependable and stable. High grade and relatively low risk.
Aa	AA	AA	High quality bonds—the long-term investment risks are slightly higher than the "highest quality bonds." Very strong credit rating. High grade and relatively low risk.
A	A	A	Upper medium grade—bonds with many favorable investment attributes.
Baa	BBB	BBB	Medium grade bonds—the quality of the bonds is adequate at present; however, the long-term stability may be doubtful. These bonds pay higher yields but carry greater risk than the "A" bonds.
			Not Investment-Grade (High Yield Bonds or Junk Bonds)
Ba	BB	BB	Somewhat speculative—security of payments is not well safeguarded.
B	B	B	Speculative—security of payments is not well safeguarded.
Caa	CCC	CCC	Highly speculative—extremely speculative; the danger of default is high.
Ca	CC	CC	Most speculative—extremely speculative; the danger of default is high.
C	C	C	Imminent default—the danger of default is extremely high.
C	D	D	Default—the bonds are in default.

Bonds

The lower the risk for bonds, usually the lower the interest rate earned. The higher the interest rates, the higher the risks. You can check bond credit ratings at the following websites:

Credit Rating Service	Website
Moody's Investor Service	www.moodys.com
Standard & Poor's Corporation	www.standardandpoors.com
Fitch Ratings	www.fitchratings.com

In addition, many local libraries have these services' published reports and ratings. Security firms and banks also have research staffs who monitor bond issuers' ability and willingness to make interest and principal payments when due. The bond issuer or your investment advisor can provide you with current research on the specific bond you are considering purchasing.

An investor might buy bond insurance from specialized insurance firms serving the fixed-income market. Bond insurance guarantees the timely payment of principal and interest on insured bonds. Credit ratings can change over the life of a bond—check the rating regularly to ascertain whether it still fits your risk tolerance comfort level.

The following are some different types of bond funds:

1. Bond unit investment trusts—a fixed portfolio of investments in government, municipal, corporate, or mortgage-backed bonds that are professionally selected and remain constant throughout the life of the trust. Units in the trust are sold to investors. Until all the bonds in the portfolio are called or mature, payments are

Bonds

made to investors periodically. Investors know exactly how much they'll earn because the portfolio remains stable. There is usually no management fee. There is a sales charge that is frequently higher than those for mutual funds, and so these investments should therefore be considered long term. They have a small annual fee for supervision, evaluation expenses, and trustee fees. Initial investments are usually between $1,000 and $5,000. Investors earn interest during the life of the trust and recover principals as securities in the trust are redeemed. Most do not allow you to reinvest earnings. Bond unit investment trusts (UITs) typically end when the last investment matures. Shares in UITs can be sold on the secondary market—investors may realize more or less than they originally paid for the shares since their value moves inversely to market interest rates.

2. Mortgage pass-through securities—are shares in mortgages pooled by banks and other lenders. Usually the pools are 30-year fixed-rate loans and mortgages on single-family homes. Payments made by homeowners are "passed through" to the investor minus a small service fee. Most are backed by agencies of the U.S. Government such as the Government National Mortgage Association (GNMA). GNMA securities are referred to as Ginnie Maes. Mortgage pass-through securities have the following features:

   a. Payments are monthly and include interest and return of principal.
   b. Payments vary because some homeowners might pay the loans off early.
   c. They have no fixed maturity date since loan payments cannot be predicted.
   d. They have a minimum investment of $25,000.

Bonds

3. U.S. Government securities—buy and sell debt securities of the U.S. Treasury or other federally sanctioned bond-issuing agencies. The U.S. Government backs treasury securities with its "full faith and credit" making them one of the safest types of investments available. The U.S. Treasury market offers securities of every maturity and where all issues bear the same top credit quality. Government bond funds have a low risk of default and generally pay lower interest rates than other funds. There are 3 types of treasuries:

   a. <u>Treasury bills</u> (TBills) are short-term obligations of 1 year or less. They are highly liquid with maturities in 3, 6, or 12 months. The minimum face value is $10,000. They are sold at a discount and return the full face value at maturity. For example: a $10,000 TBill selling at a discount of 5.25% costs you $9,475 to buy. At maturity, you receive $10,000 or $525 more than your cost. $525 divided by the $9,475 = a 5.54% yield—note that the yield is always higher than the quoted discount rate.

   b. <u>Notes</u> have terms of one year through 10 years. The minimum investments are $5,000 for fewer than 5 years or $1,000 for 5 years or more. Notes pay a fixed rate of interest semiannually and return the face value at maturity.

   c. <u>Bonds</u> are long-term obligations of more than 10 years. The minimum investment is $1,000. U.S. Treasury bonds offer special tax advantages—no state or local income tax on the interest earned. Bonds pay a fixed rate of interest semiannually and return the face value at maturity.

Bonds

Treasury securities can be purchased through brokerage firms, government security dealers, some banks, or directly through the Federal Reserve. Securities purchased directly through the Federal Reserve cannot be sold on the secondary market. The investor must hold them to maturity. An advantage is that there is no transaction fee when you buy directly from the Federal Reserve. For information on purchasing commission-free treasury securities directly from the government, visit www.treasurydirect.gov. Also, I-Bond information can be found at www.publicdebt.treas.gov. These are U.S. savings bonds that are inflation protected. While government bond funds are a favorite among conservative investors, they are not guaranteed against loss. The interest payments of government bond funds are certain; however, the funds' share prices will fluctuate due to interest rate moves just as with other types of bond funds.

4. Municipal bond funds buy bonds issued by state and local governments and their agencies. The interest paid on municipal bond funds is not normally subject to federal income tax. Some may be free from state or local taxes as well. "Triple tax-free" funds are exempt from federal, state, and local taxes. Your real rate of return on a municipal bond fund depends on your tax rate—refer back to Chapter 9, Figure 9.1 ("Taxable Equivalent Yield") to compute comparisons against non-tax-free investments. As with other tax-free accounts, municipal bonds are not an appropriate investment for tax-sheltered accounts such as Individual Retirement Accounts or Keogh plans. Money you withdraw during retirement from IRA, Keogh plans, and other tax-sheltered accounts will be considered taxable income regardless of what the money was invested in. You are better off investing your

Bonds

retirement savings in higher yielding—although taxable—investments since they compound tax-free in IRAs or Keogh plans until you begin withdrawing the money during retirement. Municipal bond funds usually pay less interest than corporate bond funds.

5. <u>National municipal bond funds</u> invest in a mixed portfolio of debt obligations of states, cities, highway authorities, school districts, and local public agencies. These funds are referred to as "munis." The returns you earn are exempt from federal income tax. Munis usually offer investors a lower interest rate than government and general bond funds.

6. <u>General bond funds</u> invest in bonds of the most creditworthy U.S. companies.

7. <u>Corporate bond funds</u> invest in bonds issued by companies. Convertible bonds are corporate bonds that can be exchanged for the issuing companies' stock.

8. <u>High-yield corporate bond funds</u> invest in speculative companies. While they offer high returns, the risks of default on the loans is also high. These funds are sometimes called junk bond funds. Junk bond funds are very risky and are a gamble similar to investing in a speculative stock fund.

9. <u>International bond funds</u> invest in the debt of governments and corporations outside the United States.

10. <u>Flexible bond funds</u> invest in a wide range of bonds from all categories.

Since bond funds may provide slimmer investment returns than equity (stock) investments, it is important to pay close attention to the bond fund's expenses. Investors can control expenses by choosing funds with costs that are acceptable to them. Many financial advisors say any expenses per year over 1% for bond funds are too high. The

Bonds

average annual expense ratio for all bond funds is around 1.02%. With all other things being equal, it is also best to avoid 12b-1 fees that can take up to 0.75% each year from your investment to cover marketing costs. It is also best to avoid bond funds that charge loads. Seek out bond funds that have high quality designations by credit rating services, are top-performers, and have below-average expenses. As with stock equity funds, it is best to invest in bond funds using dollar cost averaging. A program of regular, systematic investments each week, month, or quarter allows you to purchase more shares when they are low and fewer shares when they are high. That gives you a below average cost for the total number of shares you buy.

When you invest, you are giving up use of your money today in exchange for an expected future return on your investment. In the case of bonds, the return is based on the bond's yield and capital return, which is the change in price of the bond. A financial formula called "present value" allows you to calculate the value today of that future return. The formula for the present value of a dollar is

$$PV = 1/(1+R)^T$$

Where
PV = Present Value
R = Rate (interest rate earned)
T = Time (the length of time of the investment)

For example: if you would like to know the present value of $1.00 at 5% interest in 10 years, the formula would work like this—

$$PV = 1/(1+0.05)^{10} = \$0.6139$$

So, 61.39 cents today invested at 5% interest over 10 years will be worth $1.00 in the future.

Bonds

For assistance in determining the present value of an investment, please complete the following steps:

1. Open the "SS22 Calculator-Present Value-Bond.xls"; see Figure 16.1a.
2. Click "Yes" to enable macros, if necessary.
3. Click on the sheet tab titled "Present Value."
4. Fill in your own personal information in each white cell (you may tab from one white cell to another).
5. After completing the information in all of the white cells, press "Tab" and then click on the "MMW Recalculation Button"—the spreadsheet will make the remaining calculations for you.

Figure 16.1a SS22 Calculator-Present Value-Bond.xls (Present Value Sheet Tab)

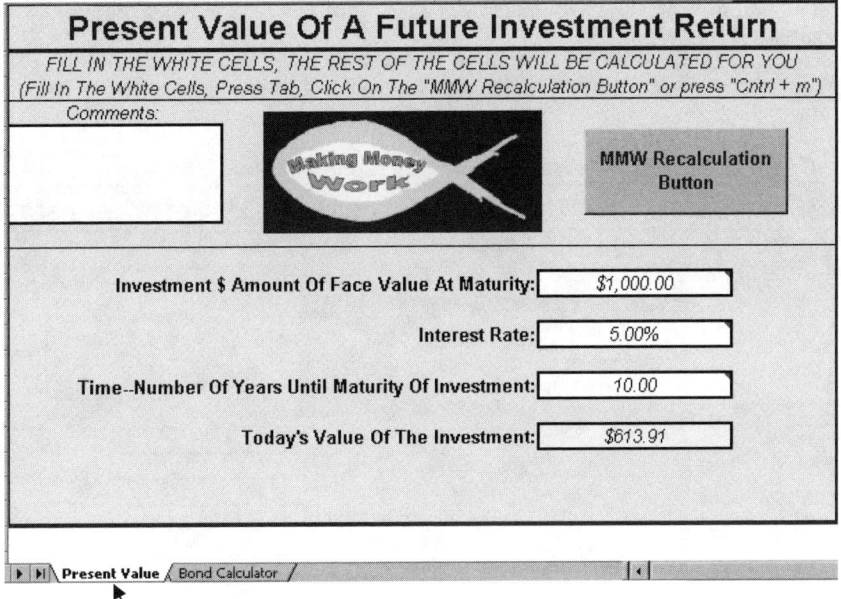

Present Value Of A Future Investment Return

FILL IN THE WHITE CELLS, THE REST OF THE CELLS WILL BE CALCULATED FOR YOU
(Fill In The White Cells, Press Tab, Click On The "MMW Recalculation Button" or press "Cntrl + m")

Comments:

MMW Recalculation Button

Investment $ Amount Of Face Value At Maturity:	$1,000.00
Interest Rate:	5.00%
Time--Number Of Years Until Maturity Of Investment:	10.00
Today's Value Of The Investment:	$613.91

Present Value / Bond Calculator

Click on the "Present Value" sheet tab.

A bond investor is buying an income stream and the right to receive the face value of the bond at maturity. A bond investor needs to know what the face value will be when the bond matures and how to value the coupon payments. Fortunately, there is a formula to help with the calculations:

Price = Coupon payment x Present value of future coupon payments + Face value of bond x The present value of the bond principal

Where
Coupon payment = the $ amount of interest paid each payment period.

Bonds

Present value of future coupon payments = $1/(1+\text{Interest Rate})^1 + 1/(1+\text{Interest Rate})^2 + 1/(1+\text{Interest Rate})^3 + \ldots 1/(1+\text{Interest Rate})^{\text{Through end of coupon payment periods}}$

Present value of bond principal = $1/(1+\text{Interest Rate})^{\text{Number of Coupon Payment Periods}}$

These financial calculations are rather complicated. To help make the calculations easier, please open the **SS22 Calculator-Present Value-Bond.xls**.

For assistance in making bond calculations, please complete the following steps:

1. Open the "SS22 Calculator-Present Value-Bond.xls"; see Figures 16.1b, 16.1c, and 16.1d.
2. Click "Yes" to enable macros, if necessary.
3. Click on the sheet tab titled "Bond Calculator."
4. Fill in your own personal information in each white cell (you may tab from one white cell to another).
5. After completing the information in all of the white cells, press "Tab" and then click on the "MMW Recalculation Button"—the spreadsheet will make the remaining calculations for you.

Figure 16.1b SS22 Calculator-Present Value-Bond.xls (Bond Calculator Sheet Tab)

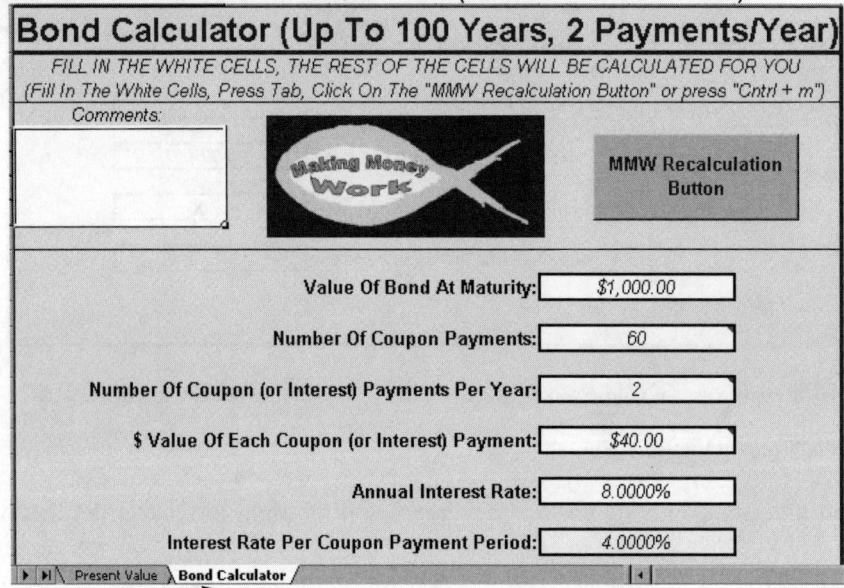

Bond Calculator (Up To 100 Years, 2 Payments/Year)

FILL IN THE WHITE CELLS, THE REST OF THE CELLS WILL BE CALCULATED FOR YOU
(Fill In The White Cells, Press Tab, Click On The "MMW Recalculation Button" or press "Cntrl + m")

Comments:

Value Of Bond At Maturity:	$1,000.00
Number Of Coupon Payments:	60
Number Of Coupon (or Interest) Payments Per Year:	2
$ Value Of Each Coupon (or Interest) Payment:	$40.00
Annual Interest Rate:	8.0000%
Interest Rate Per Coupon Payment Period:	4.0000%

Present Value | **Bond Calculator**

Click on the "Bond Calculator" sheet tab.

- - -

224

Bonds

Value Of Bond At Maturity:	$1,000.00
Number Of Coupon Payments:	60
Number Of Coupon (or Interest) Payments Per Year:	2
$ Value Of Each Coupon (or Interest) Payment:	$40.00
Annual Interest Rate:	8.0000%
Interest Rate Per Coupon Payment Period:	4.0000%
Present Value Of Future Coupon Payments:	$904.94
Present Value Of The Bond Principal:	$95.06
Value Of The Bond:	$1,000.00

Note in the example above that a $1,000 bond maturing in 30 years with semiannual coupon payments (30 x 2 = 60) at 8% interest has the following:
Present Value of Future Coupon Payments: $904.94
Present Value of the Bond Principal: $95.06
Value of the Bond: $1,000.00

In the same example, note what happens to the bond if interest rates climb to 10%:

Figure 16.1c

Value Of Bond At Maturity:	$1,000.00
Number Of Coupon Payments:	60
Number Of Coupon (or Interest) Payments Per Year:	2
$ Value Of Each Coupon (or Interest) Payment:	$40.00
Annual Interest Rate:	10.0000%
Interest Rate Per Coupon Payment Period:	5.0000%
Present Value Of Future Coupon Payments:	$757.17
Present Value Of The Bond Principal:	$53.54
Value Of The Bond:	$810.71

Present Value of Future Coupon Payments: $757.17
Present Value of the Bond Principal: $53.54
Value of the Bond: $810.71

In the same example, note what happens to the bond if interest rates fall to 6%:
Figure 16.1d

Bonds

Value Of Bond At Maturity:	$1,000.00
Number Of Coupon Payments:	60
Number Of Coupon (or Interest) Payments Per Year:	2
$ Value Of Each Coupon (or Interest) Payment:	$40.00
Annual Interest Rate:	6.0000%
Interest Rate Per Coupon Payment Period:	3.0000%
Present Value Of Future Coupon Payments:	$1,107.02
Present Value Of The Bond Principal:	$169.73
Value Of The Bond:	$1,276.76

Present Value of Future Coupon Payments: $1,107.02
Present Value of the Bond Principal: $169.73
Value of the Bond: $1,276.76

As mentioned earlier, when interest rates rise, bond prices fall. When interest rates fall, bond prices rise. The bond calculator helps you determine the prices. For more information concerning bonds, bond funds, or purchasing bonds visit the following websites: www.bondsonline.com or www.investinginbonds.com.

While bond total returns traditionally are lower than stock total returns, bonds can give your portfolio stable income and offset some of the inevitable fluctuations in the stock market.

Get rich quick schemes in finances are recipes for disaster. Consistency and perseverance are keys to lasting financial success. "*He who tills his land will have plenty of bread, but he who follows frivolity will have poverty enough!*"—Proverbs 28:19 (The Soul Care Bible).

Money Market Funds

Chapter 17

Money Market Funds

A money market account (MMA) is an interest earning savings account offered by a Federal Deposit Insurance Corporation (FDIC)—insured financial institution with limited transaction privileges stipulated by Regulation D, Reserve Requirements of Depository Institutions. Generally, you are limited to 6 transfers or withdrawals per month with no more than 3 transactions as checks written against the account. MMAs have minimum balance requirements. MMAs normally pay higher interest rates than the same financial institution pays on passbook savings.

In contrast to money market accounts, money market mutual funds (money funds) are not insured by the Federal Deposit Insurance Corporation (FDIC) or guaranteed by the U.S. government. Money market mutual funds are pooled investments in short-term, highly liquid securities such as U.S. treasuries, certificates of deposit issued by major commercial banks, municipal bonds, and commercial paper issued by established corporations. When you own shares in a mutual fund, you actually own fractional interest in the mutual fund's investments. Money market funds usually maintain a stable dollar value for their invested principal, although income varies daily. The value of a share in a money fund should always be $1.00. The interest rate may fluctuate, but the share price usually remains constant. However, it is possible to lose money by investing in money funds because there is no assurance that they will be able to maintain a stable net value of $1.00 a share. The Securities Exchange Commission requires the average maturity of money fund investments to be less than 90 days. Most money funds allow investors to

Money Market Funds

withdraw their money at any time. Money market mutual funds usually have a minimum initial investment between $1,000 and $10,000. The type of debt they purchase can classify money funds. Government money funds buy U.S. government and agency securities. Some government funds only invest in treasuries. Some government funds buy a myriad of government and agency securities. Nongovernment corporate money funds invest in securities issued by businesses. Tax-free money funds invest in municipality securities.

You can compare money market rates, annual percentage yield, and minimum deposits at www.bankrate.com. The annual percentage yield (APY) is the actual percentage increase over a 1-year period, and it provides a means for comparing differing compound interest rates (refer to Chapter 5, "The Magic of Compound Interest"). The formula for APY is:

$APY = (1 + R/N) \wedge (N) - 1$

Where
APY = annual percentage yield
R = interest rate expressed as a decimal (e.g., 2.5% = 0.025)
N = number of compounding periods per year

Annual percentage yield gives you the rate of return on an investment for a 1-year period. Please note the following annual percentage yields on an investment returning a 2.37% interest rate at various compounding periods:

Money Market Funds

Period	Number of Compounding Periods per Year	Annual Percentage Yield (APY)
Annual	1	APY = (1+ .0237/1) ^ (1) - 1 = .023700 = 2.3700%
Semiannual	2	APY = (1+ .0237/2) ^ (2) - 1 = .023840 = 2.3840%
Quarterly	4	APY = (1 + .0237/4) ^ (4) - 1 = .023911 = 2.3911%
Monthly	12	APY = (1 + .0237/12) ^ (12) - 1 = .023959 = 2.3959%
Daily	365	APY = (1 + .0237/365) ^ (365) - 1 = .023982 = 2.3982%

Note that an investment with a 2.37% interest rate compounding 1 time per year (annually) has an annual percentage yield of 2.37%. An investment with a 2.37% interest rate compounding 365 times per year (daily) has an annual percentage yield of 2.3982%. Annual percentage yield is a better comparison for your investments than merely comparing interest rates alone.

For assistance in determining the annual percentage yield of your investment, please complete the following steps:

1. Open the "SS23 Calculator-Annual Percentage Yield.xls"; see Figure 17.1.
2. Click "Yes" to enable macros, if necessary.
3. Fill in your own personal information in each white cell (you may tab from one white cell to another).
4. After completing the information in all of the white cells, press "Tab" and then click on the "MMW Recalculation Button"—the spreadsheet will make the remaining calculations for you.

Figure 17.1 SS23 Calculator-Annual Percentage Yield

Money Market Funds

Annual Percentage Yield
(This calulator gives you the rate of return on an investment for a one-year period)
FILL IN THE WHITE CELLS, THE REST OF THE CELLS WILL BE CALCULATED FOR YOU
(Fill In The White Cells, Press Tab, Click On The "MMW Recalculation Button" or press "Cntrl + m")

Interest Rate (e.g. 2.37% = 2.37%):	2.3700%
# Times/year interest is compounded:	365
Annual Percentage Yield (APY):	2.3982%

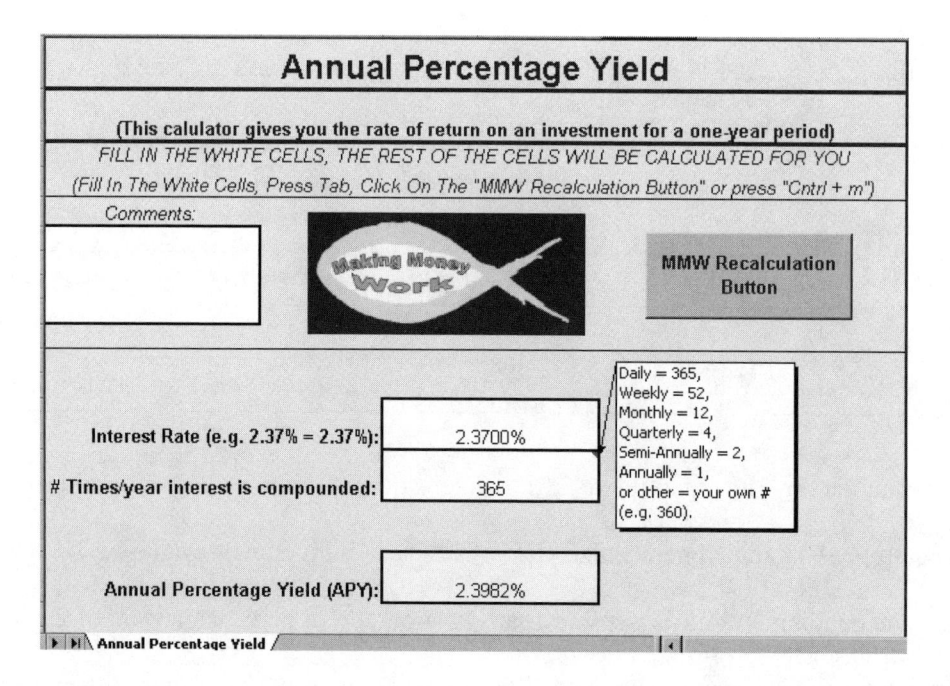

Daily = 365, Weekly = 52, Monthly = 12, Quarterly = 4, Semi-Annually = 2, Annually = 1, or other = your own # (e.g. 360).

Money can make a good servant, but it always makes a terrible master. "*No servant can serve two masters. Either he will hate the one and love the other, or he will be devoted to the one and despise the other. You cannot serve both God and Money*"—Luke 16:13 (New International Version).

Certificates of Deposit

Chapter 18

Certificates of Deposit

Certificates of deposit (CDs) are deposit accounts with a bank or thrift institution. CDs usually pay higher interest rates than regular savings accounts. When you purchase a CD, you are in essence lending money to the financial institution in return for interest. CDs offer investment opportunities in fixed sums of money for fixed periods of time—3 months, 6 months, 1 year, 5 years, or more. Interest is typically paid at regular intervals. When you redeem your CD, you receive your original investment plus any accrued interest. However, if you redeem your CD before it reaches maturity, early withdrawal penalties and/or reductions in interest income might apply. CDs are federally insured for up to $100,000 per depositor per institution. If you have more than $100,000 invested, be certain to open different accounts in different institutions to get the $100,000 Federal Deposit Insurance Corporation (FDIC) protection.

There are variable-rate CDs, long-term CDs, and CDs with other special features. Some long-term CDs have "call features." Only the financial institution may call, or terminate, the CD after a set period of time. If interest rates fall, the bank could call the CD. The investor then might have to shop for another investment at a lower rate of return.

The investor should find out when the CD matures and request to see the maturity date in writing. Also, the investor should understand the difference between call features and maturity. For example, a "federally insured one-year noncallable CD" means the bank cannot redeem the CD in one year—it may still have a maturity date of 15 or 20 years in the future. Long-term CDs might make sense for younger investors with longer

Certificates of Deposit

investment horizons, and they may make less sense for older investors with shorter investment horizons.

Investors can purchase CDs through banks, brokerage firms, and independent salespeople known as deposit brokers. Before purchasing CDs from a deposit broker, check to see if the broker has any history of complaints or fraud by calling your state securities regulator or calling the National Association of Securities Dealers' Central Registration Depository at 1-800-289-9999. Find out how the CD is held. Unrelated investors with each owning a piece sometimes jointly hold brokered CDs. Ask for a copy of the exact title of the CD. The deposit broker may not list each person's name in the title; however, the investor should make sure the broker is merely acting as an agent for the owners. For example, "ABC Brokerage as Custodian for Customers" ensures that your portion of the CD qualifies for up to $100,000 in FDIC coverage.

Check the CD disclosure document to determine the interest rate and whether the rate is fixed or variable. If it is a variable rate, make sure you understand how and when the rate can change. Some variable rate CDs increase or decrease interest rates over time according to a preset schedule. Some variable rate CDs pay interest rates that track the performance of a specified market index such as the S&P 500 or Dow Jones Industrial Average. Ask how often the CD pays interest—for example, does it pay monthly or semiannually? Find out how the interest is paid—for example, is it paid by check or by electronic transfer of funds? Before buying a CD, find out the cost of early withdrawal penalties and ask if you risk losing any portion of your principal.

Call your financial institutions to check CD rates, compounding methods, annual percentage yields, and minimum deposits. With the interest rate and the number of

Certificates of Deposit

times/year compounded, you can use the SS23 Calculator-Annual Percentage Yield.xls to calculate the annual percentage yield (APY). You can also compare various CDs at www.bankrate.com.

Laddering CDs works well. Buy CDs in small amounts with varying maturity dates. That way, if you need to cash some in for quick cash, you avoid having to pay early withdrawal penalties on your entire investment. Another rule of thumb is to buy short-term CDs when interest rates are going up and long-term CDs when interest rates are falling.

"*Plans fail for the lack of counsel, but with many advisers they succeed*"—Proverbs 15:22 (New International Version).

Individual Retirement Accounts (IRAs)

Chapter 19

Individual Retirement Arrangements

Individual retirement arrangements—IRAs—are popular retirement savings vehicles that give you tax advantages for setting aside money for retirement. An IRA is a trust or custodial account set up for the exclusive benefit of you or your beneficiaries. The custodian or trustee of the IRA can be a bank, a federally insured credit union, a savings and loan association, or an entity approved by the IRS such as a mutual fund company, stockbroker, or insurance company. IRAs must meet Internal Revenue Code requirements. Generally, you may make contributions to your IRA from earned compensation from working. For IRA compensation purposes, earned income includes wages, salaries, tips, bonuses, professional fees, commissions, self-employment income, alimony, and separate maintenance. For IRA compensation purposes, earned income does not include profits from property such as rental income, interest income, dividend income, pension or annuity income, compensation payments postponed from a past year, income from a partnership for which you did not provide services that are a material income-producing factor, and any amounts you exclude from income such as foreign earned income and housing costs. Earned income may be invested in virtually any kind of investment vehicle you can imagine for your IRA. For example, a mutual fund company may offer numerous investment vehicles—you simply designate the account as an IRA when you set it up as opposed to a normal investment account. Normal investment account monies may not be comingled with IRA account dollars. Both you and your spouse may have IRAs if both have income; however, you cannot participate in the same

Individual Retirement Accounts (IRAs)

IRA. You may make contributions to an IRA regardless of whether you are covered by another retirement plan; however, you may not be able to deduct all of your contributions. In IRAs, contributions (both deductible and nondeductible) and the earnings and gains from those contributions accumulate untaxed until withdrawn—a benefit that allows your retirement savings to grow at a much greater pace than a taxable savings plan could accomplish. For example, if you invest $3,000 in an IRA this year and it achieves a 10% return, you have earned $300 tax deferred. If you are in the 28% tax bracket and invest $3,000 in a taxable savings account this year and it achieves a 10% return, you have earned $300 - $84 ($300 x 28% taxes = $84) = $216.00. Furthermore, the IRA $3,300 grows tax deferred faster than the $3,216.00 after tax amount. For example:

$3,300 @ 10% over 20 years = $22,200.75

$3,216 @ 10% over 20 years = $12,918.51[1]

Of course, eventually you must pay taxes on your withdrawals—except the nondeductible contributions you have made to your traditional IRA. Dividends and capital gains accumulate tax deferred until you ultimately withdraw your money. Most individuals move into a lower tax bracket when they retire, so when they do pay taxes on their IRA accounts, it is at a lower tax rate.

Original IRAs are sometimes referred to as "ordinary IRAs," "regular IRAs," or "traditional IRAs"—a traditional IRA is <u>not</u> a Roth IRA or a SIMPLE IRA. Traditional IRAs can be an individual retirement account or an annuity. The traditional IRA can be

---

[1] The example takes out 28% federal tax each year.

Individual Retirement Accounts (IRAs)

part of a simplified employee pension (SEP) or an employer or employee association trust account. If you are at least 18 years of age and under age 70½, you can contribute up to the maximum annual IRA contribution limit, or 100% of your taxable compensation, whichever is less, to your IRA each year. You cannot make IRA contributions during the calendar year in which you turn age 70½ or any of the following years after age 70½. During any year in which you did not work, you cannot make contributions to an IRA unless you received alimony or you file a joint return with a spouse who had compensation. You do not have to contribute to your IRA every tax year. For most people, you can contribute for the prior year up until April 15 (the deadline for filing your prior year's taxes) of the current year—be certain to denote to your financial institution to which calendar year you wish to have the contribution applied. Limits for immediate tax deductions apply if either spouse is covered by an-on-the-job retirement plan for any part of the year. Check your W-2 form—Box 15 will be checked if you have a retirement plan. You may also ask your employer or plan administrator. The government is constantly changing the rules for IRA contributions. To get the latest IRA rules and regulations, call the Internal Revenue Service (IRS) at 800-829-3676 and ask for Publication 590 or go to www.irs.gov and download a copy of the booklet. As of the writing of this book, the following are IRA contribution limits:

Figure 19.1 Contribution Limits

Individual Retirement Accounts (IRAs)

For Tax Year	IRA Contribution Limit	Annual IRA Catch-Up[2] Contribution for Investors Age 50 or Older
2002–2004	$3,000	$500
2005	$4,000	$500
2006–2007	$4,000	$1,000
2008	$5,000	$1,000
2009 and future years	$5,000 increased by cost of living adjustments in $500 increments	$1,000

The earlier you begin your IRA investments, the more savings you will accumulate.

Figure 19.2 Example of IRA Investment Beginning at Different Ages

$3,000 per Year IRA Investment		
Calculated Using an 8% Growth Rate		
Assumes an Age 65 Retirement Date		
Beginning IRA Investing Age	**# of Years of Investing $3,000/Year**	**IRA $ Amount at 65 Years of Age**
25	40	$887,047.61
35	30	$339,849.63
45	20	$137,285.89
55	10	$43,459.69

---

[2] Individuals age 50 and over may make special additional "catch-up" IRA contributions.

Individual Retirement Accounts (IRAs)

You may even be able to take a tax deduction for your contributions.

Your adjusted gross income (AGI) is your gross income minus deductions that are available to all taxpayers, whether or not they itemize. Your income tax Form 1040 or 1040 A provide instructions on calculating your AGI. If you are not an active participant in any employer-sponsored retirement plan, your entire contribution to your traditional IRA is tax deductible. If you do participate in an employer-sponsored retirement plan, your traditional IRA contribution may be completely, partly, or not deductible on your tax return depending on your filing status and AGI. If your AGI is up to the lower limit, your contribution is deductible. If your AGI falls between the lower limit and the upper limit, the contribution is partly deductible.[3] If your AGI falls above the upper limit, then your contribution is not tax deductible. The government adjusts the upper and lower limits each year. As of the writing of this book, the following were the upper and lower limits of IRA contributions for tax deductions:

Figure 19.3 Traditional IRA Lower and Upper Limits

	Single Tax Payer		Married Tax Payer Filing Jointly	
Tax Year	Lower Limit	Upper Limit	Lower Limit	Upper Limit
2003	$40,000	$50,000	$60,000	$70,000
2004	$45,000	$55,000	$65,000	$75,000
2005	$50,000	$60,000	$70,000	$80,000

---

[3] You must be at least 18 years of age, less than 70½ years of age, and cannot be a student or individual claimed as a personal exemption on someone else's tax return.

Individual Retirement Accounts (IRAs)

2006	$50,000	$60,000	$75,000	$85,000
2007	$50,000	$60,000	$80,000	$100,000

Even if you cannot take a full deduction or partial deduction for your IRA contribution, you can still contribute up to the maximum annual IRA contribution limit or 100% of compensation, whichever is less.

To determine your partly deductible IRA tax deduction, use the following steps:

Figure 19.4 Determining Partly Deductible Traditional IRA Tax Deductions[4]

Step	Example[5]	Worksheet for Your Specific Numbers
1. Determine the amount by which your AGI exceeds the lower limit.	2003 tax year; $3,000 contribution; age 50; active participant in an employer retirement plan; married (filing jointly); AGI is $65,555. $65,555 (AGI) - $60,000 (Lower Limit) = $5,555	
2. Divide by $10,000	$5,555/$10,000 = .5555	
3. Multiply this divisor by the IRA contribution limit for the year.	$3,000 x .5555 = $1,666.50	
4. Subtract this number from the IRA contribution limit.	$3,000 (contribution limit) - $1,666.50 = $1,333.50	
5. Round down to the nearest $10.00	$1,330.00	
6. Your deductible contribution is the greater of the amount in #5 or $200.	$1,330.00	

You should keep track of your basis on nondeductible contributions to your IRA so you will be able to determine the taxable amount once distributions from the IRA begin.

---

[4] Based on the 2002 IRS IRA Publication 590 worksheet tables.
[5] Reminder—check IRS Publication 590 for yearly changes —the example uses information from 2003.

Individual Retirement Accounts (IRAs)

Even if your AGI exceeds the upper limits and does not qualify for any current year tax deduction, IRAs are usually a great investment because of the tax-deferred growth opportunities.

Traditional IRA distributions are usually taxable in the year you receive them. IRA withdrawals before age 59½ may be subject to an early 10% tax penalty in addition to regular income taxes. Early distributions of taxable amounts from your traditional IRA must be included in your current-year gross income. The 10% tax penalty for early withdrawal may not apply if you die or become disabled; you use the money to pay certain higher education expenses for yourself, your spouse, child, or grandchild; the withdrawal is used to pay for eligible first-time home buyer expenses; the distribution is one of a scheduled series of substantially equal periodic payments over your life expectancy for at least 5 years or until you reach age 59½; the distribution does not exceed the amount of your deductible medical expenses for the year; if you were unemployed and certain distributions were used to pay for health insurance coverage; and certain distributions were used to pay overdue taxes.

You must start taking IRA withdrawals by April 1—the required beginning date—following the year in which you turn age 70½ to avoid penalty taxes. Minimum withdrawals are determined by dividing the IRA(s) balance(s) as of the close of business on December 31 of the preceding year by your life expectancy or applicable distribution period—life expectancy tables are provided in IRA Publication 590. The excise tax penalty is 50% of the difference between the minimum withdrawal amount required and your actual withdrawals during the year. Considering the 50% penalty, it is wise to

Individual Retirement Accounts (IRAs)

consult your tax advisor and or financial institution for assistance with your withdrawals to make certain they are correct.

An individual retirement annuity is an annuity contract or endowment contract purchased from a life insurance company. The following are requirements for individual retirement annuities:

1. All of your interest in the contract must be nonforfeitable.
2. The contract stipulates that you cannot transfer any portion to anyone other than the issuer.
3. There must be flexible premiums so that as your compensation changes, your annuity payment can also change.
4. Contributions per year are limited (see IRA annual limits), and any refunded premiums must be used to pay for future premiums or to purchase more benefits before the end of the calendar year in which you receive the refund.
5. After you reach age 70½, distributions must begin by April 1 of the following year.

A Roth IRA is an individual retirement plan invested as an account or an annuity. When you set up the account or annuity, you must designate it as a Roth IRA. With Roth IRAs, you invest posttax money and eventually withdraw the posttax dollars tax-free. While you do not claim losses or pay taxes on gains from year to year, you will eventually have to pay taxes on your Roth IRA gains upon withdrawal. Unlike a traditional IRA, you cannot claim deductions for any contributions to a Roth IRA; however, qualified distributions are tax-free. Also, unlike traditional IRAs, you may continue to make contributions to your Roth IRA after age 70½ and as long as you live. Regardless of your age, you may be able to make nondeductible contributions to a Roth IRA. There are no age restrictions for making contributions to Roth IRAs. You can generally make contributions to a Roth IRA if you have taxable compensation, which

Individual Retirement Accounts (IRAs)

includes wages, salaries, tips, professional fees, bonuses, personal service fees, commissions, self-employment income, taxable alimony, and separate maintenance payments. In addition to taxable compensation, your modified AGI must be less than the amounts listed in Figure 19.5.

Figure 19.5 Roth IRA Modified AGI Limits

Tax Filing Status	Modified AGI Must Be Less Than[6]
Married filing jointly or qualifying widow(er)	$160,000
Married filing separately and you lived with your spouse at any time during the tax year	$10,000
Single, head of household, or married filing separately and you did not live with your spouse at any time during the tax year	$110,000

Contributions to Roth IRAs can be made at any time during the year or before the due date of your tax return for the year. Generally, you can contribute up to the same dollar amounts to your Roth IRA as the traditional IRA contribution limits will allow or your taxable compensation—whichever is less. If your modified AGI is above a certain amount, your Roth IRA contribution may be reduced. If you contribute to both Roth IRAs and traditional IRAs, your contribution limit is the lesser of the following:

1. The allowable IRA contribution limit (see Figure 19.1 or IRS Publication 590) minus all contributions (except employer contributions under a SEP or SIMPLE IRA plan) for the year to all IRAs other than Roth IRAs

2. Your taxable compensation minus all contributions (except employer contributions under a SEP or SIMPLE IRA plan) for the year to all IRAs other than Roth IRAs

---

[6] As of 2002; check IRS Publication 590 for changes during your current tax-filing year.

Individual Retirement Accounts (IRAs)

In other words, if the annual traditional IRA contribution limit is $3,000, you may put $3,000 into a Roth IRA, or you can put up to a total of $3,000 into a combination of a Roth IRA (e.g., $1,000) and a traditional IRA (e.g., $2,000). You cannot put $3,000 in a Roth IRA and an additional $3,000 in a traditional IRA. If you contribute too much during any tax year to your Roth IRA, you will have to pay a 6% excise tax on any excess contribution. Any excess contribution that is withdrawn prior to the due date for filing your tax return for the year is considered an amount not contributed.

The following chart shows the effect of your modified AGI (if you have taxable compensation) on your Roth IRA contribution:

Figure 19.6 Effect of Modified AGI on Roth IRA Contributions[7]

Tax Filing Status	Modified AGI[8]	Comments[9]
Married filing jointly or qualifying widow(er)	Under $150,000	You can contribute up to the maximum allowable IRA contribution limits (see Figure 19.1).
	At least $150,000 but less than $160,000	The amount you can contribute is reduced (see Figure 19.8).
	$160,000 or more	You are not allowed to contribute to a Roth IRA.
Married filing separately and you lived with your spouse at any time during the year	$0.00 (no earned income)	You can contribute up to the maximum allowable IRA contribution limits (see Figure 19.1).

---

[7] Based on the 2002 IRS IRA Publication 590 worksheet tables.
[8] Information is as of 2002 tax returns—check IRS Publication 590 for updated regulations for your current tax year.
[9] As of 2002, check IRS Publication 590 for changes during your current tax-filing year.

Individual Retirement Accounts (IRAs)

	More than $0.00 but less than $10,000	The amount you can contribute is reduced (see Figure 19.8).
	$10,000 or more	You are not allowed to contribute to a Roth IRA.
Single, head of household, or married filing separately and you did not live with your spouse at any time during the year	Less than $95,000	You can contribute up to the maximum allowable IRA contribution limits (see Figure 19.1).
	At Least $95,000 but less than $110,000	The amount you can contribute is reduced (see Figure 19.8).
	$110,000 or more	You are not allowed to contribute to a Roth IRA.

Use the following worksheet to determine your modified AGI for Roth IRA purposes:

Figure 19.7 Determining Your AGI for Roth IRA Purposes[10]

Step[11]	Amount
1. Enter your adjusted gross income (AGI) from your IRS Tax Form 1040 or 1040A:	
2. Enter any income from the conversion of an IRA (other than a Roth IRA) to a Roth IRA:	
3. Subtract the amount in Step 2 from the amount in Step 1:	
4. Enter any traditional IRA deduction from your IRS Tax Form 1040 or 1040A:	
5. Enter any student loan interest deduction from your IRS Tax Form 1040 or 1040A:	
6. Enter any tuition and fees deduction from your IRS Tax Form 1040 or 1040A:	
7. Enter any foreign earned income and/or housing exclusion from your IRS Tax Form 2555 or IRS Tax Form 2555-EZ:	
8. Enter any foreign housing deduction from your IRS Tax Form 2555:	
9. Enter any bond interest that is excluded from your IRS Tax Form 8815:	

---

[10] Based on the 2002 IRS IRA Publication 590 worksheet tables.
[11] Information is as of 2002 tax returns—check IRS Publication 590 for updated regulations for your current tax year.

Individual Retirement Accounts (IRAs)

10. Enter any employer-paid adoption expenses that are excluded on your IRS Tax Form 8839:	
11. Add the amounts listed in Step 3 through Step 10:	
12. Enter one of the following— ♦ $160,000 if married and filing jointly or qualifying widow(er) ♦ $10,000 if married filing separately and you lived with your spouse at any time during the year ♦ $110,000 for all others	
13. If the amount in Step 11 is less than the amount in Step 12, then your modified AGI is the amount in Step 11. If the amount in Step 11 is more than the amount in Step 12 and you have other income or loss items such as Social Security income or passive activity losses that are subject to AGI-based phaseouts, you may use worksheet 1 in appendix B of the IRS Publication 590 to refigure your AGI.	

If your Roth IRA contribution limit is reduced, use the following worksheet to determine how much it is reduced:

Figure 19.8 Determining Your Reduced Roth IRA Contribution Limit[12]

Step	Example[13]	Worksheet for Your Specific Numbers
1. Enter your modified AGI for Roth IRA purposes	$100,000	
2. Enter— ♦ $150,000 if filing a joint return or qualifying widow(er) ♦ $0 if married, filing a separate return, and you lived with your spouse at any time during the year ♦ $95,000 for all others	$95,000	
3. Subtract Step 2 from Step 1	$5,000	

---

[12] Based on the 2002 IRS IRA Publication 590 worksheet tables.
[13] Reminder—check IRS Publication 590 for changes that occur yearly; the example uses information from 2003.

Individual Retirement Accounts (IRAs)

4. Enter— ♦ $10,000 if filing a joint return or qualifying widow(er) or married filing a separate return ♦ $15,000 for all others	$15,000
5. Divide the amount in Step 3 by the amount in Step 4—enter the result as a decimal carried to three places. If the result is 1.000 or more, then enter 1.00 (i.e., $5,000 divided by $15,000 = 0.333)	0.333
6. Enter the lesser of ♦ Your contribution limit (Figure 19.1) ♦ Your taxable compensation	$3,000
7. Multiply the number in Step 5 by the amount in Step 6 (i.e., 0.333 x $3,000 = $999)	$999
8. Subtract the amount in Step 7 from the amount in Step 6 (i.e., $3,000 - $999 = $2,010)—if the result is less than $200, then enter $200	$2,001
9. Enter any contributions made in the year to other IRAs	$0.00
10. Subtract the amount in Step 9 from the amount in Step 6 (i.e., $3,000 - $0.00 = $3,000)	$3,000
11. Enter the lesser of ♦ The amount in Step 8 ♦ The amount in Step 10 This equals your reduced Roth IRA contribution limit.	$2,001

Qualified distributions, or distributions that are a return of your regular contributions from Roth IRA(s), are not included in your gross income. Qualified distributions from your Roth IRA meet both of the following requirements:

Individual Retirement Accounts (IRAs)

1. The distribution was made after the 5-year period beginning with the first taxable year during which a contribution was made to your Roth IRA.

2. The distribution or payment was

    A. made on or after the day you reached age 59½;

    B. made because you became disabled;

    C. made because of your death and went to a beneficiary or to your estate; or

    D. made under the requirements listed for first home.

A simplified employee pension (SEP) plan allows employers to make contributions to employees' retirement without the complexities of more complex retirement plans. If employers are self-employed, they can make contributions to their own retirement. These SEP contributions for participating employees are deductible for the employer and made to individual retirement arrangements set up for the participants in the plan. The employer can contribute the lesser amount of the following:

1. 25% of the employee's compensation
2. $40,000[14]

You may set up a salary reduction arrangement to have your employer contribute part of your pay to your SEP IRA. That way, only the remaining portion of your pay is taxable in the current year. Tax on the current contribution is deferred and referred to as an "elective deferral."

---

[14] For the 2002 tax year.

Individual Retirement Accounts (IRAs)

"Savings Incentive Match Plans for Employees" (SIMPLE IRAs) are tax-favored retirement plans that certain small employers and self-employed individuals can set up to benefit their employees for retirement. Under this salary reduction agreement between you and your employer, you may reduce your compensation via salary reduction contributions or elective deferrals by a certain percentage each pay period and have your employer contribute the salary reductions to your SIMPLE IRA. The SIMPLE IRA can be either an individual retirement account or an annuity. In addition to salary reduction contribution, your employer must make either matching contributions or nonelective contributions. Usually your employer must make matching contributions to your SIMPLE IRA up to 3% of your compensation for the calendar year. Generally, the same distribution or withdrawal rules that apply to traditional IRAs apply to your SIMPLE IRA. Once you start your SIMPLE IRA, you must leave your funds in the account for a 2-year period before they can be rolled over tax free to an IRA other than a SIMPLE IRA, a qualified plan, a tax-sheltered annuity, or a deferred compensation plan of a state or local government. If the SIMPLE IRA early distribution falls within the 2-year period following the first date you participated in the employer's SIMPLE plan, the additional tax is increased from 10% to 25%.

You can roll over both the taxable and the nontaxable portion from qualified plans into a traditional IRA. A rollover is a tax-free distribution of cash or other assets from one retirement plan that you contribute to another retirement plan. The second retirement plan receives the rollover contribution. The amount is then taxed when the new plan distributes that amount to you, your beneficiary, or your estate. Usually, you must complete the rollover by the 60th day after you receive the distribution or face early

Individual Retirement Accounts (IRAs)

withdrawal penalties.[15] If you are leaving one employer and wish to roll your qualified plan monies over to another IRA account, it is usually best to have the financial institutions handle the rollover directly between themselves so you avoid the possibility of missing the 60-day time limit for the transfer. In other words, you can complete a rollover form asking your first financial institution to send a rollover contribution directly to the second financial institution without them sending the money to you. Traditional IRA rules allow the following types of transfers:

- transfers from one trustee to another trustee;
- rollovers;
- transfers due to a divorce.

You should keep track of your basis (separate deductible and nondeductible IRA contributions) for your IRA accounts in order to determine the taxable amount once distributions from your IRA accounts begin. Traditional IRA distributions may be fully or partially taxable, depending on whether or not your IRA includes any nondeductible contributions. Deductible contributions will be taxed when the IRA distributions are made (normally at retirement age) as opposed to the current tax year—a benefit that allows your IRA fund to grow faster. Deductible contributions to your traditional IRA result in "no basis" in your IRA accounts. Nondeductible contributions to traditional IRAs result in a cost basis or investment in the contract equal to the nondeductible contribution amounts.

---

[15] The IRS may make some hardship exceptions to the 60-day rollover rule; if not, you will have to pay taxes during the year the money was distributed, and you may have to pay a 10% early distribution tax.

Individual Retirement Accounts (IRAs)

Nondeductible contributions are not taxed when you receive normal IRA distributions because you already paid taxes on the money (i.e., "after tax dollars invested") during the year you made the contribution. Nondeductible contributions are a return of your investment dollars in your IRA. Until all of your cost basis, nondeductible contributions have been distributed, each distribution is partly nontaxable and partly taxable.

When you file your federal taxes, you are required to update your cumulative total cost basis or nondeductible contributions for your traditional IRA(s). Some states may also require that you keep track of your deductible contributions. If you would like assistance in keeping track of your traditional IRA deductible contributions and nondeductible contributions, then please open "SS24 Calculator—Traditional IRA Cost Basis.xls."

1. Open the "SS24 Calculator-Traditional IRA Cost Basis.xls."
2. Click "Yes" to enable macros, if necessary.
3. Fill in your own personal information in each white cell (you may tab from one white cell to another).
4. After completing the information in all of the white cells, press "Tab" and then click on the "MMW Recalculation Button"—the spreadsheet will make the remaining calculations for you.

Figure 19.9 SS24 Calculator—Traditional IRA Cost Basis.xls

Individual Retirement Accounts (IRAs)

Traditional IRA Cost Basis (do not include Roth IRA)
FILL IN THE WHITE CELLS, THE YELLOW CELLS WILL BE CALCULATED FOR YOU
(Fill In The White Cells, Press Tab, Click On The "MMW Recalculation Button" or press "Cntrl + m")

Comments:

MMW Recalculation Button

Enter the year you first made a Traditional IRA contribution: 0

Independent Retirement Account(s) (IRA's) For:

Year	Deductible Contribution	Nondeductible Contribution
0		
1		
2		
3		
4		
5		

When you fill in the year (e.g., 1996), press "Tab," and press the MMW Recalculate Button, all of the subsequent years will be filled in for you.

Enter the name of the owner of the IRA.

Each year, enter the "Deductible Contribution" and the "Nondeductible Contribution" you made to your traditional IRA. These dollar amounts are the cumulative totals for the year of all your traditional IRA contributions for the year (excluding any Roth IRA contributions).

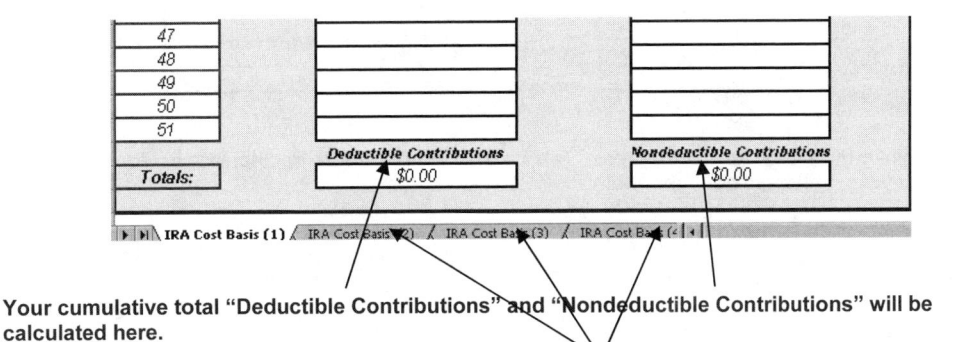

- - -

	Deductible Contributions	Nondeductible Contributions
47		
48		
49		
50		
51		
Totals:	$0.00	$0.00

IRA Cost Basis (1) / IRA Cost Basis (2) / IRA Cost Basis (3) / IRA Cost Basis (4)

Your cumulative total "Deductible Contributions" and "Nondeductible Contributions" will be calculated here.

Additional calculators—IRA Cost Basis (2)-(5)—are located here for use with your spousal account and any additional IRAs.

If you would like assistance in keeping track of your Roth IRA(s) nondeductible contributions, then please open "SS25 Calculator—Roth IRA Nondeductible Contributions.xls."

Individual Retirement Accounts (IRAs)

1. Open the "SS24 Calculator-Roth IRA Cost Nondeductible Contributions.xls."
2. Click "Yes" to enable macros, if necessary.
3. Fill in your own personal information in each white cell (you may tab from one white cell to another).
4. After completing the information in all of the white cells, press "Tab" and then click on the "MMW Recalculation Button"—the spreadsheet will make the remaining calculations for you.

Figure 19.10 SS24 Calculator—Roth IRA Nondeductible Contributions.xls

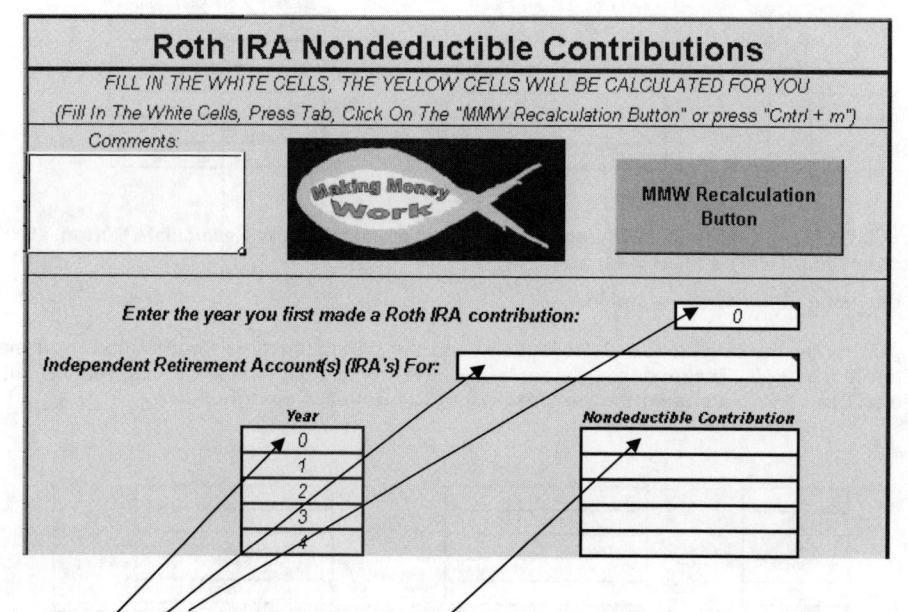

Roth IRA Nondeductible Contributions
FILL IN THE WHITE CELLS, THE YELLOW CELLS WILL BE CALCULATED FOR YOU
(Fill In The White Cells, Press Tab, Click On The "MMW Recalculation Button" or press "Cntrl + m")

Comments:

MMW Recalculation Button

Enter the year you first made a Roth IRA contribution: 0

Independent Retirement Account(s) (IRA's) For:

Year	Nondeductible Contribution
0	
1	
2	
3	
4	

When you fill in the year (e.g., 1998), press "Tab," and press the MMW Recalculate Button, all of the subsequent years will be filled in for you.

Enter the name of the owner of the IRA.

Each year, enter the "Nondeductible Contribution" you made to your Roth IRA (Roth IRAs are not deductible). These dollar amounts are the cumulative totals for the year of all your Roth IRA contributions for the year (excluding any traditional IRA contributions).

- - -

Individual Retirement Accounts (IRAs)

Your cumulative total nondeductible contributions will be calculated here.

Additional calculators—Roth IRA Contributions (2)-(5)—are located here for use with your spousal account and any additional Roth IRAs.

Roth IRA contributions are returned tax-free; however, earnings and gains are taxable when distributions are made.

IRAs can be one of the most important vehicles for helping individual investors achieve their retirement savings goals. The combination of possible current year tax deductions (for traditional IRAs), tax-deferred growth on earnings and gains, and the magic of compound interest make IRAs a powerful ally in accumulating savings.

Future value is the amount your present value will grow to when compounded at a given rate. The formula for future value is

$$FV = PV(1+R)^N$$

Where
FV = Future Value;
PV = Present Value;
R = Rate (interest rate earned);
N = Number of compounding periods.

For example, a one-time $5,000 investment that earns 8% over 30 years would calculate as follows:

$FV = \$5,000(1+.08)^{30} = \$50,313.28$. To calculate equal year-end deposits in addition to the future value of just one lump sum deposit, you add in the annual amount of the year-end investment each year.

Individual Retirement Accounts (IRAs)

For assistance in projecting the investment future value of equal year-end deposits over the life of your investment, please open the SS26 Calculator—Investment Future Value Calculator; See Figures 19.11 and 19.12. This calculator is very similar to the one you used in Chapter 11 (SS18 Calculator—Investment Future Value.xls) except a few small changes for IRA illustrative purposes have been made.

1. Open the "SS24 Calculator—Investment Future Value Calculator.xls."
2. Click "Yes" to enable macros, if necessary.
3. Fill in your own personal information in each white cell (you may tab from one white cell to another).
4. After completing the information in all of the white cells, press "Tab" and then click on the "MMW Recalculation Button"—the spreadsheet will make the remaining calculations for you.

Figure 19.11 SS24 Calculator—Investment Future Value Calculator.xls

Investment Future Value Calculator

(This calulator assumes equal year-end deposits, a fixed interest rate, and no withdrawals of interest earned)

FILL IN THE WHITE CELLS, THE REST OF THE CELLS WILL BE CALCULATED FOR YOU
(Fill In The White Cells, Press Tab, Click On The "MMW Recalculation Button" or press "Cntrl + m")

Comments:

MMW Recalculation Button

Dollar Amount: $5,000.00
Total # Of Year End Deposits: 30

	Scenario #1	Scenario #2	Scenario #3
Annual Interest Rate:	7.50%	8.00%	8.50%
Future Value:	$516,997.01	$566,416.06	$621,073.63

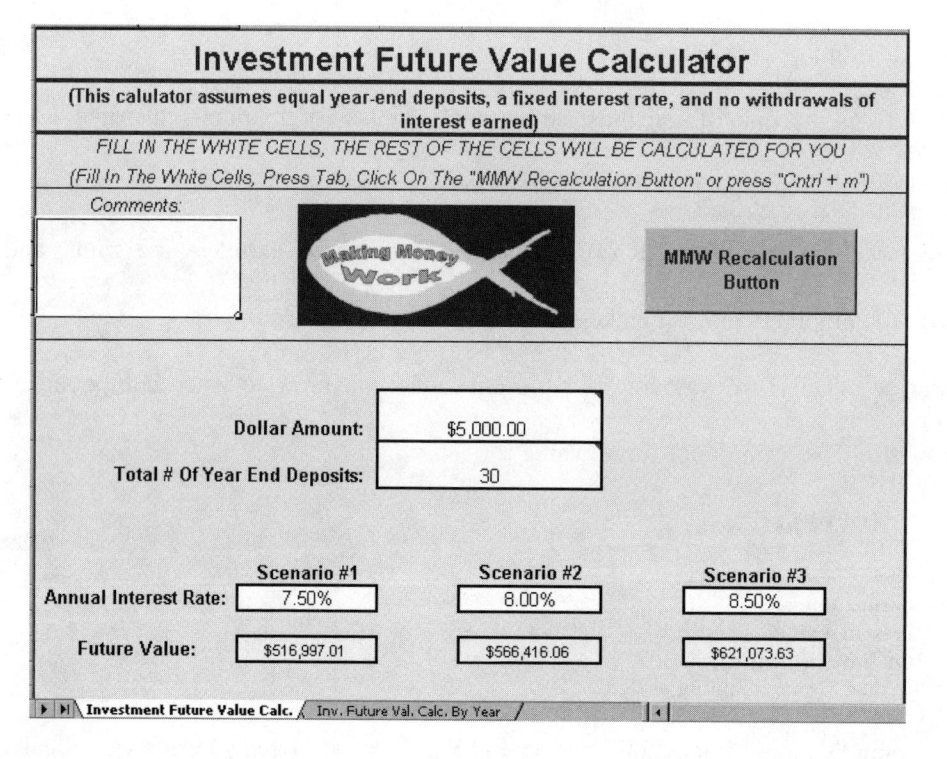

Let's assume it is year 2008 (the first year you can put $5,000 into your IRA account), and you plan to make maximum year-end contributions every year for 30 years. You would enter $5,000 under the dollar amount and 30 under the "Total # Of Year End Deposits." Scenario #1, Scenario #2, and Scenario #3 allow you to put in 3 different

Individual Retirement Accounts (IRAs)

anticipated interest rate returns to compare different investments and their future value dollar amounts.

Figure 19.12 SS24 Calculator—Investment Future Value Calculator.xls

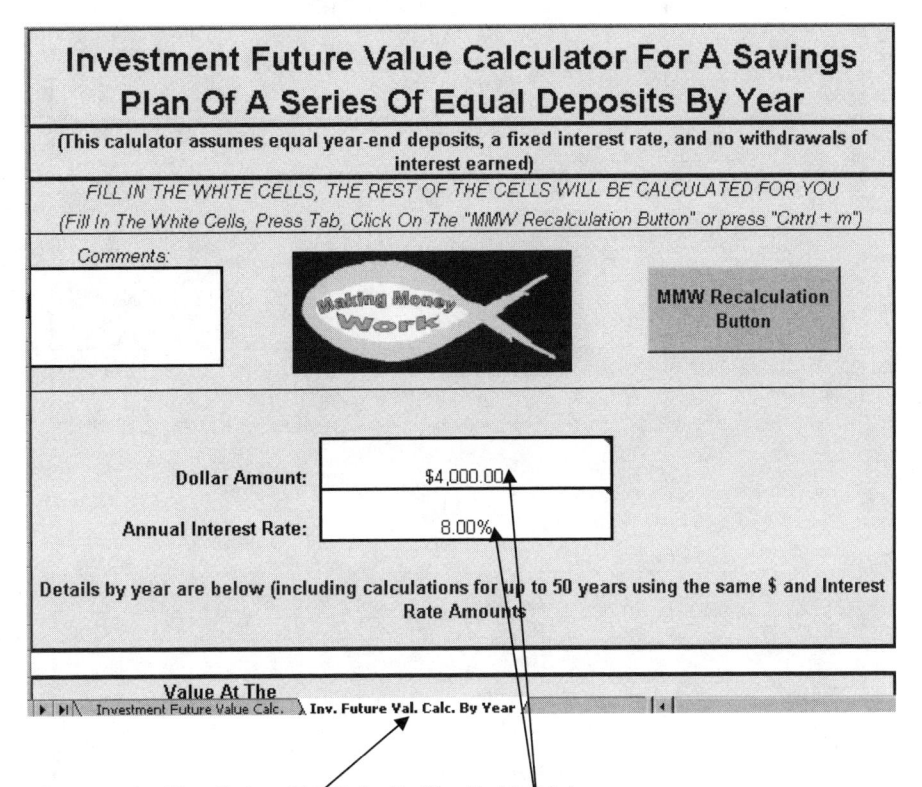

1. Click on the "Inv. Future Val. Calc. By Year" sheet tab.
2. Fill in your own personal information in each white cell (you may tab from one white cell to another).
3. After completing the information in all of the white cells, press "Tab" and then click on the "MMW Recalculation Button"—the spreadsheet will make the remaining calculations for you.

- - -

Individual Retirement Accounts (IRAs)

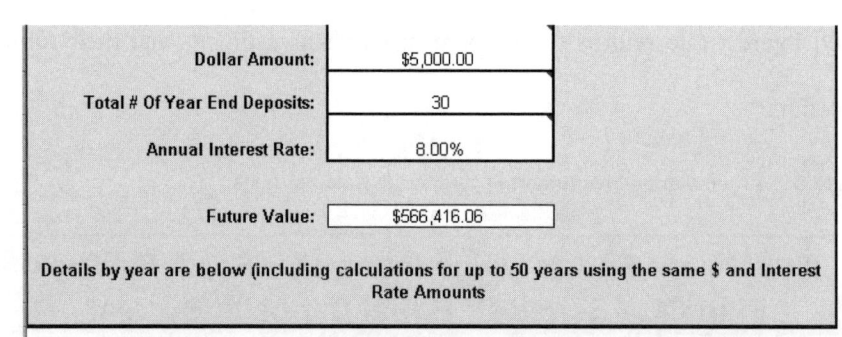

Dollar Amount:	$5,000.00
Total # Of Year End Deposits:	30
Annual Interest Rate:	8.00%
Future Value:	$566,416.06

Details by year are below (including calculations for up to 50 years using the same $ and Interest Rate Amounts

Year	Value At The Beginning Of Year	Interest Earned	Deposit At End Of Year	Ending Value
Year 1	$0.00	$0.00	$5,000.00	$5,000.00
Year 2	$5,000.00	$400.00	$5,000.00	$10,400.00
Year 3	$10,400.00	$832.00	$5,000.00	$16,232.00
Year 4	$16,232.00	$1,298.56	$5,000.00	$22,530.56
Year 5	$22,530.56	$1,802.44	$5,000.00	$29,333.00
Year 6	$29,333.00	$2,346.64	$5,000.00	$36,679.65
Year 7	$36,679.65	$2,934.37	$5,000.00	$44,614.02
Year 8	$44,614.02	$3,569.12	$5,000.00	$53,183.14
Year 9	$53,183.14	$4,254.65	$5,000.00	$62,437.79
Year 10	$62,437.79	$4,995.02	$5,000.00	$72,432.81

- - -

Year 30	$519,829.68	$41,586.37	$5,000.00	$566,416.06
Year 31	$566,416.06	$45,313.28	$5,000.00	$616,729.34
Year 32	$616,729.34	$49,338.35	$5,000.00	$671,067.69
Year 33	$671,067.69	$53,685.41	$5,000.00	$729,753.10
Year 34	$729,753.10	$58,380.25	$5,000.00	$793,133.35
Year 35	$793,133.35	$63,450.67	$5,000.00	$861,584.02
Year 36	$861,584.02	$68,926.72	$5,000.00	$935,510.74
Year 37	$935,510.74	$74,840.86	$5,000.00	$1,015,351.60
Year 38	$1,015,351.60	$81,228.13	$5,000.00	$1,101,579.73
Year 39	$1,101,579.73	$88,126.38	$5,000.00	$1,194,706.11
Year 40	$1,194,706.11	$95,576.49	$5,000.00	$1,295,282.59
Year 41	$1,295,282.59	$103,622.61	$5,000.00	$1,403,905.20
Year 42	$1,403,905.20	$112,312.42	$5,000.00	$1,521,217.62
Year 43	$1,521,217.62	$121,697.41	$5,000.00	$1,647,915.03
Year 44	$1,647,915.03	$131,833.20	$5,000.00	$1,784,748.23
Year 45	$1,784,748.23	$142,779.86	$5,000.00	$1,932,528.09
Year 46	$1,932,528.09	$154,602.25	$5,000.00	$2,092,130.33
Year 47	$2,092,130.33	$167,370.43	$5,000.00	$2,264,500.76
Year 48	$2,264,500.76	$181,160.06	$5,000.00	$2,450,660.82
Year 49	$2,450,660.82	$196,052.87	$5,000.00	$2,651,713.69
Year 50	$2,651,713.69	$212,137.09	$5,000.00	$2,868,850.78

Note that this calculator gives you the future value for a savings plan of a series of equal deposits by year (up to 50 years maximum).

Individual Retirement Accounts (IRAs)

So, while one lump sum $5,000 IRA deposit in 2008 at an 8% return over thirty years grows to only $50,313.28, a series of deposits of $5,000/year over 30 years in an IRA at 8% grows to $566,416.06!

The following are suggestions concerning maximizing investment results from IRA accounts:

1. Start investing in your IRA(s) as soon as you meet the IRS regulations for doing so (e.g., 18 years of age with earned income).
2. Contribute to your IRA(s) every year that you have earned income (and before age 70½ for traditional IRAs).
3. Contribute the full amount allowable by the IRS every year (if you cannot contribute the full amount, then contribute as much as possible toward the full amount during any year).

If you have tax questions concerning IRA regulations, you may call the IRS at 1-800-829-1040 (federal customer service number for everyone). If you need to order forms, instructions, and publications, call 1-800-829-3676. You can also access the IRS on the Internet at www.irs.gov (1-800-876-1715, help desk number for website only). This website has frequently asked tax questions, detailed rules and regulations on IRAs, IRA worksheets (e.g., to figure IRA current year deductions, taxable portions of distributions, additional taxes from contributing too much or early withdrawals, required minimum distributions, etc.), life expectancy tables for use with calculating IRA information, forms and publications, forms that can be filled in electronically, a search for regulations and the Internal Revenue Code, local IRS office numbers, and many other features. Also, many libraries, post offices, and IRS local offices have certain forms, instructions, and publications. The regulations change constantly; make sure you check the current tax year regulations so you are working within the proper guidelines.

Individual Retirement Accounts (IRAs)

"*And it is he* [God] *who will supply all your needs from his riches in glory because of what Christ Jesus has done for us*"—Philippians 4:19 (The Living Bible).

Annuities

Chapter 20

Annuities

Webster's New World College Dictionary defines an annuity as "an investment yielding periodic payments during the annuitant's lifetime, for a stated number of years, or in perpetuity." An annuity is an insurance company product sold in the form of a contract that guarantees a fixed or variable payment at a future date to the individual (annuitant) purchasing the annuity. The annuitant (or investor) puts money into the annuity for retirement and does not have to pay taxes on the earnings until the funds are withdrawn—typically at retirement age starting at 59½. Annuities may be purchased as a single investment with a lump sum payment or as a series of investments over a period of time. Annuities set no top limit on the amount you can invest.

There are 2 phases to annuities:

1. Accumulation phase—the period during which the annuitant makes contributions to the account. It might be a single payment or a series of payments.
2. Annuitization phase—the period during which the annuitant receives the value of the annuity in payments. There might also be a death benefit, which pays your beneficiary in case you die before the insurer makes any payments to you.

Unlike with IRAs, federal law does not limit the amount or frequency of contributions to your annuity. You usually can "annuitize" your withdrawals by converting them to a guaranteed lifetime income, take the withdrawal in one lump sum, or take the funds in withdrawal increments as you need them. Annuitizing the withdrawal usually results in a lower tax bite versus lump sum or incremental withdrawals. However, by choosing the annuitizing withdrawal method, in most (not all) cases the insurance company gets any remaining funds after your death versus your beneficiary's receiving them. You give up

Annuities

access to the money in your account when you annuitize. If you choose this method, make sure you have funds elsewhere to access in case of an emergency when extra funds would be needed beyond the annuity withdrawals.

There are 2 basic types of annuities:

1. Fixed annuities
2. Variable annuities (VAs)

If you have purchased a fixed annuity, the insurance company commingles your assets with those of its general accounts and later pays you fixed payments for a particular number of years or for the rest of your life. The insurance company chooses the fixed annuity investments. Fixed annuities are usually conservative and provide guaranteed interest rates for a period of years after which a new interest rate is established. While fixed annuities are similar to certificates of deposit, sometimes the guaranteed rate of interest on a fixed annuity is higher than that of a CD. Unlike CDs, fixed annuities are not federally insured by FDIC. With a fixed annuity your savings are locked up with the insurance company in exchange for a lifetime stream of income payments.

Variable annuities are usually held in separate accounts from the insurance company's general accounts. With variable annuities, the annuitant selects from a variety of professionally managed investment vehicles such as stocks, bonds, or money market instruments. Variable annuities pool money to buy securities, post gains and losses, and charge annual expenses. Variable annuities offer greater potential return than fixed annuities; however, they also involve more risk. Variable annuities fluctuate in value. The amount paid to you depends on the investment vehicles chosen and their performance—hence, the reason they are called "variable." In the event of your death

Annuities

before the investment payouts begin, variable annuities offer insurance guarantees that protect your heirs from capital losses on the original investment amount—the "death benefit" is usually increased 5% to 7% each year. Your heirs get the amount you invested or the current market value of your investment or a stepped-up benefit based on the value of the account on a certain date—whichever is greater. The insurance portion of the variable annuity is called an "account" or "policy" while the mutual fund investments are called "sub-accounts." Investment returns on both income and gains are tax deferred until you withdraw your money or begin receiving payments. Investments can be moved from one sub-account to another without triggering tax consequences. In essence, a variable annuity is a mutual fund wrapped in a life insurance contract.

Annuities can be poor investments because of the costs (the level of fees and commissions) involved. Request a prospectus from the insurance company on the annuity you are considering—it will outline the costs involved. The insurance company may charge an "insurance charge," which typically ranges from 0.5% to 2.0% per year in addition to the management fees charged on each of the mutual fund sub-accounts, which average 0.9% per year (can be more than 3%) of assets. The sales commission on the annuity might be as high as 7% of the amount of the annuity—as a rule of thumb, the higher the commission, the worse the product. Annuities typically have 7-year surrender charges, which means if you terminate the contract in the 1st year you incur a 7% penalty; the 2nd year, a 6% penalty; the 3rd year a 5% penalty; and so on, until the surrender charge disappears after the seventh year is completed. Extra cost lowers your net return. Also, under most circumstances, any withdrawals before age 59½ will incur an additional 10% IRS penalty. The illiquidity of variable annuities cannot be

Annuities

overemphasized—investors will suffer stiff penalties for early withdrawal and should view their money as not being available for years. Variable annuities usually make sense only for investors willing to invest for 10 years or longer.

Most investors should put as much money as possibleinto other retirement plans that have tax advantages before putting money into annuities. For example, once you have put the maximum into your company retirement plan with matching funds, 401(k), 403(b), and/or IRA(s), and you still have discretionary funds to invest, then consider annuities. Check to see if the annuity meets your financial needs—tax-deferred growth is great; however, there may be cheaper and more flexible alternatives such as purchasing U.S. Treasury bonds. Depending on the cost involved in the annuity, it might even be better to purchase non-tax-deferred mutual funds directly as opposed to purchasing them through a variable annuity product—your net return might be better in the long run. Laddering CDs that are non-tax-deferred might also provide a greater net return once you compare them to an annuity with high costs. Annuity payments are taxed as ordinary income—a rate that is typically higher than the capital gains rate on mutual funds. In general, the lower your tax rates, the lower your investment earnings rates, the shorter the accumulation phase time frame, and the higher the annual insurance fees, the *less advantageous* variable annuities will be for your portfolio. In general, the higher your tax rates, the higher your investment earnings rates, the longer the accumulation phase time frame, and the lower the annual insurance fees, the *more advantageous* variable annuities will be for your portfolio. Once you weigh the cost factors, if you decide that variable annuities are right for your portfolio, make sure the plan has the right mix of funds from which you

Annuities

would like to choose. Variable annuities can be a good investment if you live beyond your life expectancy and take payouts in the form of income for life.

If you buy an annuity at one company, the same type of annuity might be different at the next company. When you buy an annuity, you are counting on the financial stability of the insurance company—if the company does not survive, you could lose a portion of your money. Check the following websites to make certain your annuity company has 1 of the highest 2 insurance ratings:

Insurance Rating Firm	Website	Highest 2 Insurance Ratings
Moody's Investors Service	www.moodys.com	Aaa to Aa
A. M. Best	www.ambest.com	A++ to A-

Annuity contracts can be laden with complicated legal jargon. It is wise to consult your financial advisor or tax advisor to determine if an annuity is right for you.

To learn more about variable annuities visit the following websites: www.sec.gov/investor/pubs/varannty.htm or the National Association of Insurance Commissioners at www.naic.org.

Some people who retire have pension plans or a retirement benefit programs, which allow investors to make numerous choices on how they will receive the accumulated funds. One choice might be to take the money in one lump sum to invest as you choose. Another choice might include purchasing annuity products that might give you several options such as the following:

Annuities

1. Straight life annuity with the same monthly benefit payment until you die (Social Security payments, once you are eligible to begin receiving them, would be in addition to the annuity product benefit payment)—once you die, annuity monthly benefit payments cease.

2. Straight life annuity with a survivor's benefit—for example, when you die, your spouse or possibly another beneficiary would receive a portion of your monthly benefits (e.g., 50% or 70%)—survivor's benefits result in lower monthly benefit payments.

3. Straight life annuity with constant total income or leveling of benefits—the annuity product would provide higher benefit payments initially and then decrease close to the amount of your Social Security benefit payments once you begin to receive them—thus your total monthly benefit receipts remain about the same.

4. Straight life annuity with constant total income or leveling of benefits with a survivor's benefit (e.g., 50%).

Comparing the alternatives can be confusing. It helps to project or estimate the amount of future benefit payments over your life expectancy before making the one-time decision at retirement concerning what to do with your money.

Open the SS32 Cal-Annuity Comparison Estimator SS Vs SS Leveling.xls.

1. Open the "SS32 Cal-Annuity Comparison Estimator SS Vs SS Leveling.xls"; see Figure 20.1.
2. Click "Yes" to enable macros, if necessary.

Figure 20.1

Annuities

Annuity Comparison Estimator For Social Security Versus Social Security Leveling Benefits

FILL IN THE WHITE CELLS, THE REST OF THE CELLS WILL BE CALCULATED FOR YOU
(Fill In The White Cells, Press Tab, Click On The "MMW Recalculation Button" or press "Cntrl + m)

Comments:

	Amount/or Number
Annuity Monthly Benefit Excluding Social Security:	$2,458.59
Social Security Monthly Benefit Amount:	$950.00
Annuity Monthly Benefit With Social Security Leveling:	$2,996.13
Age At Retirement:	55
Retirement Year:	2003
Age To Begin Receiving Social Security Payments:	62
Number Of Months In First Year For Retirement Benefits:	5

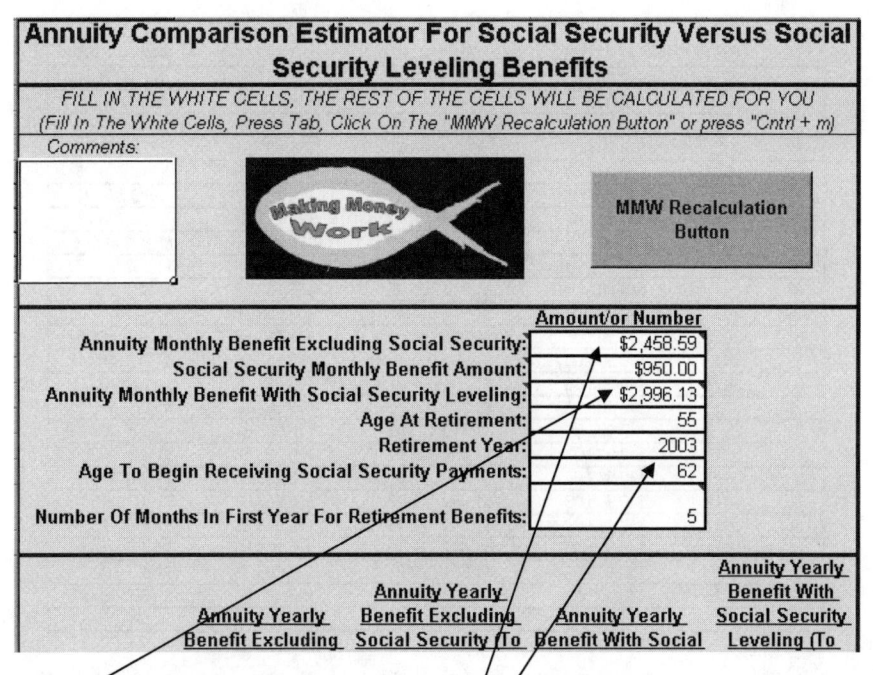

Note: in this example, the retiree would receive $2,458.59 per month from the annuity with Social Security being an additional benefit starting at age 62. Or the retiree might select the "Annuity Monthly Benefit With Social Security Leveling," which pays a higher dollar amount initially of $2,996.13 but then declines once Social Security benefits begin to be paid, thus keeping the total monthly benefits approximately the same.

Age	Year	Annuity Yearly Benefit Excluding Social Security	Annuity Yearly Benefit Excluding Social Security (To Date $)	Annuity Yearly Benefit With Social Security Leveling	Annuity Yearly Benefit With Social Security Leveling (To Date $)
55	2003	$12,292.95	$12,292.95	$14,980.65	$14,980.65
56	2004	$29,503.08	$41,796.03	$35,953.56	$50,934.21
57	2005	$29,503.08	$71,299.11	$35,953.56	$86,887.77
58	2006	$29,503.08	$100,802.19	$35,953.56	$122,841.33
59	2007	$29,503.08	$130,305.27	$35,953.56	$158,794.89
60	2008	$29,503.08	$159,808.35	$35,953.56	$194,748.45
61	2009	$29,503.08	$189,311.43	$35,953.56	$230,702.01
62	2010	$40,903.08	$230,214.51	$35,953.56	$266,655.57
63	2011	$40,903.08	$271,117.59	$35,953.56	$302,609.13
64	2012	$40,903.08	$312,020.67	$35,953.56	$338,562.69
65	2013	$40,903.08	$352,923.75	$35,953.56	$374,516.25
66	2014	$40,903.08	$393,826.83	$35,953.56	$410,469.81
67	2015	$40,903.08	$434,729.91	$35,953.56	$446,423.37
68	2016	$40,903.08	$475,632.99	$35,953.56	$482,376.93
69	2017	$40,903.08	$516,536.07	$35,953.56	$518,330.49
70	2018	$40,903.08	$557,439.15	$35,953.56	$554,284.05
71	2019	$40,903.08	$598,342.23	$35,953.56	$590,237.61
72	2020	$40,903.08	$639,245.31	$35,953.56	$626,191.17

Note: once Social Security benefits begin to be paid with the "Annuity Yearly Benefit Excluding Social Security," the total of the Social Security benefit payment plus the annuity benefit payment totals more per year than the "Annuity Yearly Benefit With Social Security Leveling."

Annuities

75	2023	$40,903.08	$761,954.55	$35,953.56	$734,051.85
76	2024	$40,903.08	$802,857.63	$35,953.56	$770,005.41
77	2025	$40,903.08	$843,760.71	$35,953.56	$805,958.97
78	2026	$40,903.08	$884,663.79	$35,953.56	$841,912.53
79	2027	$40,903.08	$925,566.87	$35,953.56	$877,866.09
80	2028	$40,903.08	$966,469.95	$35,953.56	$913,819.65
81	2029	$40,903.08	$1,007,373.03	$35,953.56	$949,773.21
82	2030	$40,903.08	$1,048,276.11	$35,953.56	$985,726.77
83	2031	$40,903.08	$1,089,179.19	$35,953.56	$1,021,680.33
84	2032	$40,903.08	$1,130,082.27	$35,953.56	$1,057,633.89
85	2033	$40,903.08	$1,170,985.35	$35,953.56	$1,093,587.45
86	2034	$40,903.08	$1,211,888.43	$35,953.56	$1,129,541.01
87	2035	$40,903.08	$1,252,791.51	$35,953.56	$1,165,494.57
88	2036	$40,903.08	$1,293,694.59	$35,953.56	$1,201,448.13
89	2037	$40,903.08	$1,334,597.67	$35,953.56	$1,237,401.69
90	2038	$40,903.08	$1,375,500.75	$35,953.56	$1,273,355.25
91	2039	$40,903.08	$1,416,403.83	$35,953.56	$1,309,308.81
92	2040	$40,903.08	$1,457,306.91	$35,953.56	$1,345,262.37
93	2041	$40,903.08	$1,498,209.99	$35,953.56	$1,381,215.93
94	2042	$40,903.08	$1,539,113.07	$35,953.56	$1,417,169.49
95	2043	$40,903.08	$1,580,016.15	$35,953.56	$1,453,123.05
96	2044	$40,903.08	$1,620,919.23	$35,953.56	$1,489,076.61
97	2045	$40,903.08	$1,661,822.31	$35,953.56	$1,525,030.17
98	2046	$40,903.08	$1,702,725.39	$35,953.56	$1,560,983.73
99	2047	$40,903.08	$1,743,628.47	$35,953.56	$1,596,937.29

A retiree who dies at age 78 in this example would have received approximately these dollar amounts in total benefits paid on the two options in this example. Also, it is a good idea to review life expectancy tables (as noted previously in this book) to determine the age at which you are likely to die and then compare the "To Date $" numbers between your available choices. For example, a female with a life expectancy of age 78 in this example would receive an accumulated total of $884,663.79 taking the annuity product that excludes Social Security payments after Social Security is factored in versus taking the annuity product with Social Security leveling feature, which would pay $841,912.53—a potential difference of $42,751.26. Of course, potential money is just one factor in the decision process in addition to your current state of health, your anticipated state of health, your personal desires regarding survivorship benefits, and other variables.

Type over the numbers in the example to calculate your own information:
3. Fill in your own personal information in each white cell (you may tab from one white cell to another).
4. After completing the information in all of the white cells, press "Tab" and then click on the "MMW Recalculation Button"—the spreadsheet will make the remaining calculations for you.

"*For wisdom is protection just as money is protection. But the advantage of knowledge is that wisdom preserves the lives of its possessors*"—Ecclesiastes 7:12 (New American Standard Bible).

Housing

Chapter 21

Housing

Housing costs should be less than 30% of your income. Some people choose to rent their housing as opposed to buying their own homes. Some renters may not like the yard work, lawn work, and maintenance associated with owning their own houses. Renting versus buying might make economic sense if the renter expects to relocate soon and will not be living in the area long enough to recoup the costs of buying a house. Some renters may not need as much space as a typical house might provide. Some renters believe they can get a better return on their money by investing it elsewhere as opposed to tying it up in the equity of a house. Renting might allow the renter to get in a better location for a lower monthly payment versus purchasing a house. Renting might also make sense if you do not like worrying about the unpredictability of the real estate market. Of course, when you pay rent, the rental money goes to the landlord and you do not build up any equity in your home. Also, renters do not get the tax breaks that homeowners enjoy. Renters do not get to deduct their monthly rent on their tax returns. One of the most important considerations when deciding to rent or buy is the amount of time you are planning to live in the accommodations. If you plan to move within a few years, from an economic viewpoint you are probably better off renting versus buying.

In the early years of a home loan or amortization schedule, most of the monthly payment is interest versus principal payment (or the building up of equity in the home). Amortization is the process of gradually paying off the principal part (the outstanding

Housing

loan balance) of a mortgage with each payment. Equity is the amount of real estate that the homebuyer actually owns—it is computed by subtracting the mortgage balance from the sales price. For example, let's assume you borrow $100,000 on a home loan at 8% interest over 30 years for a $733.77 per month mortgage bill—note the following amounts paid to principal and interest during payment #1 versus the last payment #360 in the 30th year:

Monthly Payment	Principal Paid	Interest Paid
#1 (the very first payment)	$67.10	$666.67
#2	$67.55	$666.22
Etc. (from payment #3 thru #358)	Increasing	Decreasing
#359	$724.08	$9.69
#360 (the last payment in the 30th year of the home loan)	$728.91	$4.86

Note that from the $733.77 monthly payment, most of the payment goes to interest ($666.67 in the first payment) at first, and then interest payment declines over the life of the loan until most of the $733.77 monthly payment goes to the principal payment ($728.91 in the 360th payment). Mortgage interest payments are deductible on your tax return. Since interest payments decline over the life of the home loan, more interest monies are tax deductible early in the loan repayment process versus later on. During the first five years of our $100,000 loan at 8% over 30-year example, the homeowner is able to deduct $39,095.73 from their income on their tax return versus $7,837.77 during the last five years. During the first five years, of course, the homeowner is not building up much equity—only $4,930.14 versus $36,188.13 during the last five years of the loan.

Housing

Unless you can pay cash for a home, one of the first steps should be getting prequalified for a loan with an experienced mortgage lender. This will help to establish a maximum purchase price for your home and a monthly payment with which you will be comfortable. Prequalification for a mortgage loan enables you to negotiate the purchase of your new home from a position of strength. Shop for the lowest interest rates by calling your local banks or thrifts, checking local newspapers to compare local mortgage rates, and comparing mortgage-lending rates at www.bankrate.com. To approximate the size mortgage for which you might be able to qualify, open the SS27 Calculator—Mortgage Loan Estimate.xls.

1. Open the "SS227 Calculator-Mortgage Loan Estimate.xls"; see Figure 21.1.
2. Click "Yes" to enable macros, if necessary.
3. Fill in your own personal information in each white cell (you may tab from one white cell to another).
4. After completing the information in all of the white cells, press "Tab" and then click on the "MMW Recalculation Button"—the spreadsheet will make the remaining calculations for you.

Figure 21.1

Housing

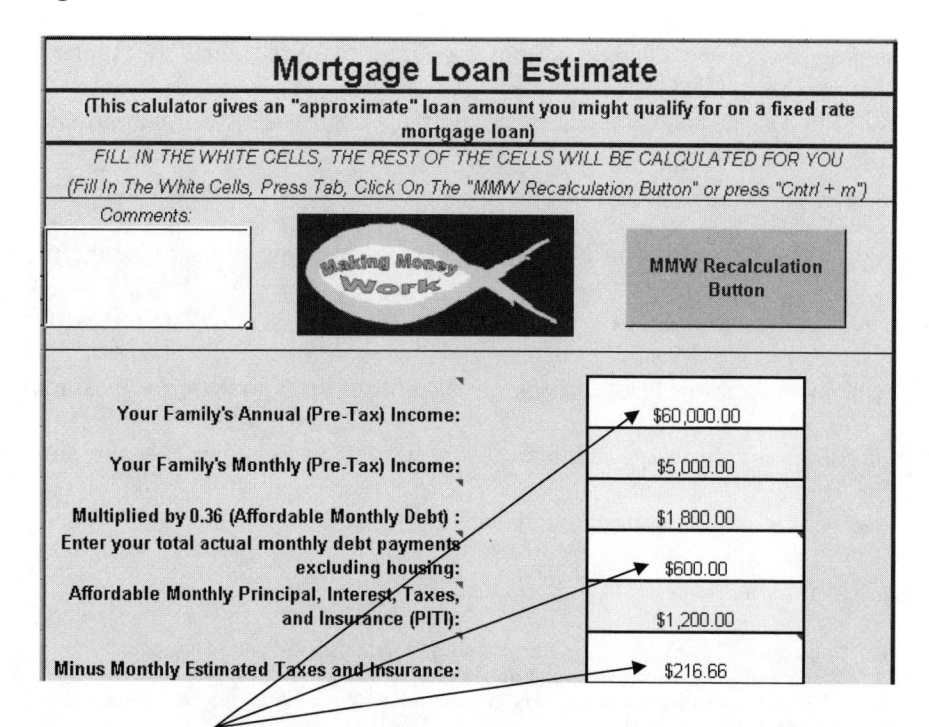

Mortgage Loan Estimate

(This calulator gives an "approximate" loan amount you might qualify for on a fixed rate mortgage loan)

FILL IN THE WHITE CELLS, THE REST OF THE CELLS WILL BE CALCULATED FOR YOU

(Fill In The White Cells, Press Tab, Click On The "MMW Recalculation Button" or press "Cntrl + m")

Comments:

MMW Recalculation Button

Your Family's Annual (Pre-Tax) Income:	$60,000.00
Your Family's Monthly (Pre-Tax) Income:	$5,000.00
Multiplied by 0.36 (Affordable Monthly Debt):	$1,800.00
Enter your total actual monthly debt payments excluding housing:	$600.00
Affordable Monthly Principal, Interest, Taxes, and Insurance (PITI):	$1,200.00
Minus Monthly Estimated Taxes and Insurance:	$216.66

Fill in your own personal information in each of the white cells by typing over the example information already entered.

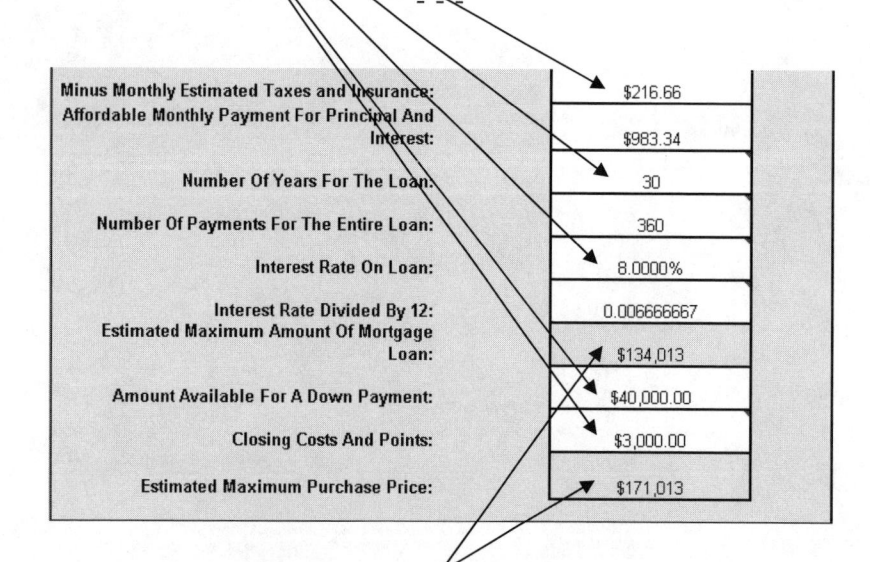

Minus Monthly Estimated Taxes and Insurance:	$216.66
Affordable Monthly Payment For Principal And Interest:	$983.34
Number Of Years For The Loan:	30
Number Of Payments For The Entire Loan:	360
Interest Rate On Loan:	8.0000%
Interest Rate Divided By 12:	0.006666667
Estimated Maximum Amount Of Mortgage Loan:	$134,013
Amount Available For A Down Payment:	$40,000.00
Closing Costs And Points:	$3,000.00
Estimated Maximum Purchase Price:	$171,013

The calculator computes the "Estimated Maximum Amount of Mortgage Loan" for you in addition to the "Estimated Maximum Purchase Price" for your home.

Housing

The "Estimated Maximum Amount of Mortgage Loan" or loan amount formula is

$$LA = MP * (1 - (1 + i)^{-N}) / i$$

Where:
LA = Loan Amount
MP = Monthly Payment
i = Interest Rate divided by 12 (12 monthly payments per year)
N = Total # of Monthly Payments (e.g., 12 monthly payments for 30 years is 12 x 30 = 360).

The SS27 Calculator—Mortgage Loan Estimate.xls calculates the math for you.

Your annual property taxes may be obtained from the seller of the home, your county courthouse (you'll need the location of the property and the current title holder's name), or perhaps your real estate agent. If you are purchasing a new home, comparable property taxes to homes in your purchasing area should be close to the amount you will have to pay. Your homeowner's insurance cost can be obtained from your insurance agent. Refer to Chapter 4 for the budget you prepared to determine the amount available for a down payment. The information for closing costs and points can be obtained from your mortgage finance lender of choice. Closing costs charges such as fees for title searching and property tax adjusting are paid when the paperwork is completed at your house closing. Closing is the moment title and property is transferred from the seller to the buyer. Closing cost charges are negotiable and might be paid either by the seller of the home or the buyer of the home—the sales contract should stipulate who is paying what. A point is 1% of the loan amount. For example, if you borrow $100,000, 1 point would equal $100,000 x 1% = $1,000. There might be "origination points" and "discount points." Origination points might be charged for originating or launching your mortgage. Paying discount points serves to lower your interest rate and thus lower your payments and is optional. By paying more money up front at the beginning of your loan—that is,

Housing

paying discount points—you pay less over time. The more discount points you pay up front, the lower interest rate you get. The longer you plan to stay in your house, the more worthwhile it can be to pay discount points. You can figure your break-even point on paying discount points. For example, if you plan to borrow $100,000 and pay 2 discount points, you have to pay $2,000 up front to get a lower interest rate. If the lower interest rate saves you $25.00 per month versus not paying the discount points, it would take you 80 months ($2,000 divided by the $25.00/month mortgage payment savings) to break even. Some borrowers get "negative points" that lower the borrower's cash requirement at closing. Some borrowers finance the closing costs by adding them to the mortgage loan amount.

Fixed rate mortgages might make the most sense for you if you plan to live in your home for more than five years—for example, a fixed rate mortgage might be at 8% interest throughout each year of the loan for 30 years. Adjustable rate mortgages (ARMs) are mortgages with a variable interest rate. ARMs can have an initial interest rate that is much lower than that of fixed rate loans; however, after a certain period, the rate adjusts with inflation. The mortgage might be a 1-year ARM, 3-year ARM, 5-year ARM, 7-year ARM, or 10-year ARM (ARMs can run from 1 month to 10 years). For example, a 5-year ARM on a 30-year mortgage would have a fixed rate for the first 5 years of the loan and then adjust annually for the next 25 years based on a change in a preselected index plus a fixed margin. Some common indexes are 1-year treasury securities, the prime rate, 6-month certificates of deposit, and so on. For example, let's say you have an ARM currently at 4.5%; the prime rate moves to 5%, and you have a margin of 2%—the fully indexed rate once the adjustment is made will be 5% prime + 2% margin = 7%. As a rule,

Housing

the shorter the time frame before the loan makes its first adjustment, the lower the start interest rate. With ARMs, monthly payments most likely will increase in some years and decrease in others. Fixed rate mortgages might be better for you if knowing your mortgage payment could rise in coming years as is likely with ARMs causes you stress and anxiety. Fixed rate mortgages might be better for you if you have limited or fixed income and could not afford the increased mortgage payments should inflation rise dramatically. If you are planning on living in your house a long time, you are better off having a fixed rate mortgage. However, most people do not live in their home for 30 years. If you know you will be moving before the initial ARM period is over, there is no risk, and you would save money by getting a lower interest rate. ARMs usually offer the borrowers some protection against rapidly rising rates, which might include yearly and lifetime caps on increases.

Balloon mortgages have fixed rates for so many years at the end of which you have to pay a lump sum, which includes the entire unpaid principal balance. For example, a 7-year balloon mortgage will have a fixed rate of interest for 7 years at which time the borrower must pay back the unpaid principal balance. The borrower might be able make this payment by refinancing at the current rates available at the end of the 7 years. There are many types of mortgage loan products—be sure the one you select matches your individual needs. Fixed rate loans are the most common.

To help get an approximate idea of the cost of your fixed rate loan, open the SS28 Calculator-Amortization.

1. Open the "SS28 Calculator-Amortization.xls"; see Figure 21.2.
2. Click "Yes" to enable macros, if necessary.
3. Fill in your own personal information in each white cell (you may tab from one white cell to another).

Housing

4. After completing the information in all of the white cells, press "Tab" and then click on the "MMW Recalculation Button"—the spreadsheet will make the remaining calculations for you.

Figure 21.2

Click on the "Amortization Schedule" tab.

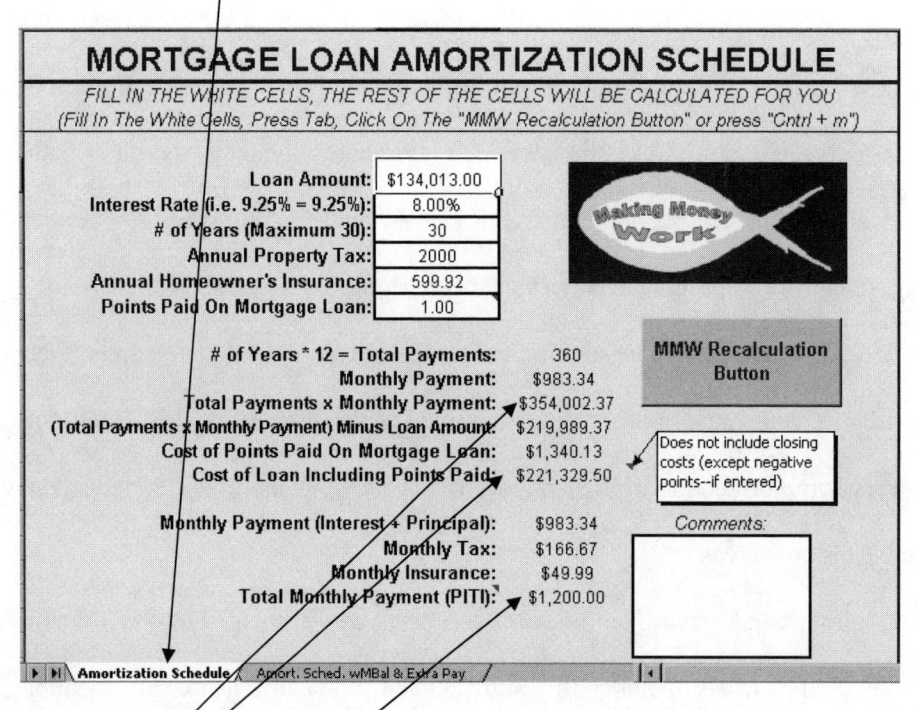

MORTGAGE LOAN AMORTIZATION SCHEDULE
FILL IN THE WHITE CELLS, THE REST OF THE CELLS WILL BE CALCULATED FOR YOU
(Fill In The White Cells, Press Tab, Click On The "MMW Recalculation Button" or press "Cntrl + m")

Loan Amount:	$134,013.00
Interest Rate (i.e. 9.25% = 9.25%):	8.00%
# of Years (Maximum 30):	30
Annual Property Tax:	2000
Annual Homeowner's Insurance:	599.92
Points Paid On Mortgage Loan:	1.00
# of Years * 12 = Total Payments:	360
Monthly Payment:	$983.34
Total Payments x Monthly Payment:	$354,002.37
(Total Payments x Monthly Payment) Minus Loan Amount:	$219,989.37
Cost of Points Paid On Mortgage Loan:	$1,340.13
Cost of Loan Including Points Paid:	$221,329.50
Monthly Payment (Interest + Principal):	$983.34
Monthly Tax:	$166.67
Monthly Insurance:	$49.99
Total Monthly Payment (PITI):	$1,200.00

MMW Recalculation Button

Does not include closing costs (except negative points--if entered)

Comments:

Amortization Schedule / Amort. Sched. wMBal & Extra Pay

This calculator will give some valuable information such as the following:

"Total Payments x Monthly Payment," or the amount of principal and interest paid over the life of the loan.

The "Cost of Loan" including points but excluding closing costs.

Your "Total Monthly Payment (PITI)," which includes principal, interest, taxes, and insurance.

If you were to keep the loan in this example for the full 30 years (360 monthly payments) x $1,200/month (PITI), the total cost for your home would be $432,000! Amortization loans are costly. When you have extra cash to invest, one of the safest investments you can make is prepaying principal on your home loan. Most mortgage loans permit prepayments without penalty charges; however, just to make sure, check

Housing

with your lender first. Prepayment is not difficult. Most mortgage payment coupons have a space noted with a label that reads something like "additional principal" where you would denote the amount you are paying. Be certain to inform your lender that the amount goes toward principal prepayment; otherwise, the lender might apply the prepayment to your escrow account, and you will not be receiving the effects of the prepayment on principal until the correction is made—that mistake can cost you thousands of dollars. Prepaying principal on your home loan is virtually risk-free and can easily compare favorably to the stock market even during periods of high returns. To help get an idea of the savings you can generate by prepaying principal on your fixed rate home loan, open the "SS28 Calculator-Amortization.xls," and this time click on the "Amort. Sched. wMBal & Extra Pay" sheet tab.

1. Open the "SS28 Calculator-Amortization.xls"—Note: Figure 21.3
2. Click "Yes" to enable macros, if necessary.

Figure 21.3 Click on the "Amort. Sched. wMBal & Extra Pay" sheet tab.

MORTGAGE LOAN AMORTIZATION SCHEDULE
(With Monthly Balance Information)

FILL IN THE WHITE CELLS, THE REST OF THE CELLS WILL BE CALCULATED FOR YOU
(After Filling In The White Cells, Press Tab, Then Click On The "MMW Recalculation Button")

Loan Amount:	$134,013.00
Interest Rate (i.e. 9.25% = 9.25%):	8.00%
# of Years (Maximum 30):	30
Annual Property Tax:	2000
Annual Homeowner's Insurance:	599.92
# of Years * 12 = Total Payments:	360
Monthly Payment:	$983.34
Total Payments x Monthly Payment:	$354,002.37
Monthly Payment (Interest + Principal):	$983.34
Monthly Tax:	$166.67
Monthly Insurance:	$49.99
Total Monthly Payment (PITI):	$1,200.00

MMW Recalculation Button

Comments:

Extra Payment

Housing

	Total Monthly Payment (PITI):	$1,200.00			

Payment Number	Monthly Principal Paid	Monthly Interest Paid	Loan Balance	Extra Payment Applied On Principal (Alert Mortgage Company To Apply To The Principal)	Loan Amount Minus Extra Payment	New Balance Due On Loan Amount (Includes Extra Payment & Principal Paid)
1	$89.92	$893.42	$353,019.03	$0.00	$134,013.00	$133,923.08
2	$90.52	$892.82	$352,035.69	$0.00	$133,923.08	$133,832.56
3	$91.12	$892.22	$351,052.35	$0.00	$133,832.56	$133,741.44
4	$91.73	$891.61	$350,069.01	$0.00	$133,741.44	$133,649.71
5	$92.34	$891.00	$349,085.67	$0.00	$133,649.71	$133,557.37
6	$92.96	$890.38	$348,102.33	$0.00	$133,557.37	$133,464.41
7	$93.58	$889.76	$347,118.99	$0.00	$133,464.41	$133,370.83
8	$94.20	$889.14	$346,135.65	$0.00	$133,370.83	$133,276.63
9	$94.83	$888.51	$345,152.31	$0.00	$133,276.63	$133,181.80
10	$95.46	$887.88	$344,168.97	$0.00	$133,181.80	$133,086.34
11	$96.10	$887.24	$343,185.63	$0.00	$133,086.34	$132,990.24
12	$96.74	$886.60	$342,202.29	$0.00	$132,990.24	$132,893.50
Year 1:	$1,119.50	$10,680.58	$342,202.29	$0.00	$132,990.24	$132,893.50
13	$97.38	$885.96	$341,218.95	$0.00	$132,893.50	$132,796.12
14	$98.03	$885.31	$340,235.61	$0.00	$132,796.12	$132,698.09

- - -

337	$838.39	$144.95	$22,616.82	$0.00	$21,742.18	$20,903.79
338	$843.98	$139.36	$21,633.48	$0.00	$20,903.79	$20,059.81
339	$849.61	$133.73	$20,650.14	$0.00	$20,059.81	$19,210.20
340	$855.27	$128.07	$19,666.80	$0.00	$19,210.20	$18,354.93
341	$860.97	$122.37	$18,683.46	$0.00	$18,354.93	$17,493.95
342	$866.71	$116.63	$17,700.12	$0.00	$17,493.95	$16,627.24
343	$872.49	$110.85	$16,716.78	$0.00	$16,627.24	$15,754.75
344	$878.31	$105.03	$15,733.44	$0.00	$15,754.75	$14,876.44
345	$884.16	$99.18	$14,750.10	$0.00	$14,876.44	$13,992.28
346	$890.06	$93.28	$13,766.76	$0.00	$13,992.28	$13,102.22
347	$895.99	$87.35	$12,783.42	$0.00	$13,102.22	$12,206.23
348	$901.97	$81.37	$11,800.08	$0.00	$12,206.23	$11,304.26
Year 29:	$10,437.92	$1,362.16	$11,800.08	$0.00	$12,206.23	$11,304.26
349	$907.98	$75.36	$10,816.74	$0.00	$11,304.26	$10,396.28
350	$914.03	$69.31	$9,833.40	$0.00	$10,396.28	$9,482.25
351	$920.12	$63.22	$8,850.06	$0.00	$9,482.25	$8,562.13
352	$926.26	$57.08	$7,866.72	$0.00	$8,562.13	$7,635.87
353	$932.43	$50.91	$6,883.38	$0.00	$7,635.87	$6,703.43
354	$938.65	$44.69	$5,900.04	$0.00	$6,703.43	$5,764.78
355	$944.91	$38.43	$4,916.70	$0.00	$5,764.78	$4,819.88
356	$951.21	$32.13	$3,933.36	$0.00	$4,819.88	$3,868.67
357	$957.55	$25.79	$2,950.02	$0.00	$3,868.67	$2,911.12
358	$963.93	$19.41	$1,966.68	$0.00	$2,911.12	$1,947.19
359	$970.36	$12.98	$983.34	$0.00	$1,947.19	$976.83
360	$976.83	$6.51	$0.00	$0.00	$976.83	($0.00)
Year 30:	$11,304.26	$495.82	$0.00	$0.00	$976.83	($0.00)

Note that in this example of a 30-year loan, with no early payments or prepayments of principal, the loan is paid off in year 30 with payment number 360.

Housing

Now, let's assume that you receive $1,000 in unexpected income, and you would like to see what effect the money would have if you prepaid principal on your loan in the 11th year with payment # 121.

Payment Number	Monthly Principal Paid	Monthly Interest Paid	Loan Balance	Extra Payment Applied On Principal (Alert Mortgage Company To Apply To The Principal)	Loan Amount Minus Extra Payment	New Balance Due On Loan Amount (Includes Extra Payment & Principal Paid)
120	$198.27	$785.07	$236,001.58	$0.00	$117,760.78	$117,562.51
Year 10:	$2,294.44	$9,505.64	$236,001.58	$0.00	$117,760.78	$117,562.51
121	$199.59	$783.75	$235,018.24	$1,000.00	$116,562.51	$115,362.92
122	$214.25	$769.09	$234,034.90	$0.00	$115,362.92	$115,148.66
123	$215.68	$767.66	$233,051.56	$0.00	$115,148.66	$114,932.98
124	$217.12	$766.22	$232,068.22	$0.00	$114,932.98	$114,715.86
125	$218.57	$764.77	$231,084.88	$0.00	$114,715.86	$114,497.29
126	$220.02	$763.32	$230,101.54	$0.00	$114,497.29	$114,277.27
127	$221.49	$761.85	$229,118.20	$0.00	$114,277.27	$114,055.78
128	$222.97	$760.37	$228,134.86	$0.00	$114,055.78	$113,832.81
129	$224.45	$758.89	$227,151.52	$0.00	$113,832.81	$113,608.36
130	$225.95	$757.39	$226,168.18	$0.00	$113,608.36	$113,382.40
131	$227.46	$755.88	$225,184.84	$0.00	$113,382.40	$113,154.95
132	$228.97	$754.37	$224,201.50	$0.00	$113,154.95	$112,925.97
Year 11:	$2,636.53	$9,163.55	$224,201.50	$1,000.00	$113,154.95	$112,925.97
133	$230.50	$752.84	$223,218.16	$0.00	$112,925.97	$112,695.47

Enter the extra principal payment here, tab, and then hit the recalculate button.

- - -

342	$924.23	$59.11	$17,700.12	$0.00	$8,866.52	$7,942.29
343	$930.39	$52.95	$16,716.78	$0.00	$7,942.29	$7,011.90
344	$936.59	$46.75	$15,733.44	$0.00	$7,011.90	$6,075.31
345	$942.84	$40.50	$14,750.10	$0.00	$6,075.31	$5,132.47
346	$949.12	$34.22	$13,766.76	$0.00	$5,132.47	$4,183.35
347	$955.45	$27.89	$12,783.42	$0.00	$4,183.35	$3,227.90
348	$961.82	$21.52	$11,800.08	$0.00	$3,227.90	$2,266.08
Year 29:	$11,130.59	$669.49	$11,800.08	$0.00	$3,227.90	$2,266.08
349	$968.23	$15.11	$10,816.74	$0.00	$2,266.08	$1,297.84
350	$974.69	$8.65	$9,833.40	$0.00	$1,297.84	$323.16
351	$981.19	$2.15	$8,850.06	$0.00	$323.16	($658.03)
352	$987.73	-$4.39	$7,866.72	$0.00	($658.03)	($1,645.76)
353	$994.31	-$10.97	$6,883.38	$0.00	($1,645.76)	($2,640.07)
354	$1,000.94	-$17.60	$5,900.04	$0.00	($2,640.07)	($3,641.01)
355	$1,007.61	-$24.27	$4,916.70	$0.00	($3,641.01)	($4,648.62)
356	$1,014.33	-$30.99	$3,933.36	$0.00	($4,648.62)	($5,662.95)
357	$1,021.09	-$37.75	$2,950.02	$0.00	($5,662.95)	($6,684.05)
358	$1,027.90	-$44.56	$1,966.68	$0.00	($6,684.05)	($7,711.95)
359	$1,034.75	-$51.41	$983.34	$0.00	($7,711.95)	($8,746.70)
360	$1,041.65	-$58.31	$0.00	$0.00	($8,746.70)	($9,788.35)
Year 30:	$12,054.43	-$254.35	$0.00	$0.00	($8,746.70)	($9,788.35)

Note that now the entire loan is paid off in year 30 during payment #351 for making just the one $1,000 prepayment against principal. Here are your savings: $983.34 monthly payment - $323.16 remaining loan amount in payment #351 = $660.18. Also, 9 payments saved (payment numbers 352

Housing

through 360) x $983.34/month = $8,850.06. $660.18 + $8,850.06 = $9,510.24 saved! If you had taken the $1,000 and invested it in the stock market making 10% over the same 20-year period (using the SS15 Calculator-Compound Interest.xls), your money would be worth $6,727.50. In this case, you would be $2,782.74 better off prepaying principal on your amortization loan versus a stock market investment over 20 years at 10% growth—and without the risk of stock market fluctuations.

Now that you understand the example, type in your personal information into all the white cells, tab, and then hit the MMW Recalculate Button to calculate your own numbers.

The shorter the time frame of the loan, the less you will pay (e.g., a 20-year loan will cost less over the life of the loan versus a 30-year loan, a 15-year loan costs less than a 20-year loan, and a 10-year loan costs less than a 30-year loan. Get the shortest loan you can that gives you affordable monthly payments.

There is an old real estate adage that asks, "What are the three most important considerations in buying a home?" The answer is "location, location, location!" Determine the area in which you would like to live and the one that has housing within your budget guidelines. The prices of the homes will depend on comparable resale values in your immediate area. Less expensive homes in the area usually appreciate faster than the more expensive homes in the area. The quality of the schools in the area has a profound effect on real estate values. School quality can be a major factor for buyers that have school-age children. One way to quickly compare schools in your area is to type in the name of the school system you are researching and the words "school test results" in the search engine on your computer. Most state and county school systems have various test results by school listed on their websites. Some newspapers will occasionally post the same information. Families tend to gravitate toward the better schools, which increases demand for housing, and that drives up real estate prices. If you want to make an investment in the future value of your home in addition to improving the quality of

Housing

education for students, during local elections vote for school referendums that raise money to improve the quality of education.

Once you locate the home you would like to purchase, it is a good idea to get a professional appraisal done. An appraisal is an expert opinion on the value and quality of the real estate on a given date in time. You typically sign a sales contract with an offer to buy the home. Usually, the sales agent will require earnest money, which is a deposit that buyers pay upon signing the sales contract to show they are serious about the purchase. The deposit is then deducted from the down payment or refunded if the contract offer is not finalized. A title is a document delineating ownership rights and possession of a property. It is a good idea to get a title search on the property. A title search is a check of title records to make sure the purchaser is buying from the property's legal owner and that no liens, pending lawsuits, or unpaid assessments exist on the property. It is also a good idea to get title insurance. Title insurance protects lenders and owners against loss of interest in a property if the title has legal defects. Mortgage title insurance protects the lender and is usually required to get a mortgage. Owner's title insurance protects the buyer. It is also recommended to get a professional inspection completed on the home—on either a resale home or a new home.

Check with your county tax office to see if they have "homestead exemption" and if you qualify to receive the tax break. Homestead exemption is an amount subtracted from the value of your home before your county tax office calculates your property taxes. Homestead exemption can save you several hundred dollars in property taxes. Millage rates are the rates at which taxes are assessed. Millage rates are set annually by county commissions and county school boards in order to raise funds for government and school

Housing

expenses. If you owned and lived in your home on January 1 of the current year, you usually can claim homestead exemption. Once you are approved for homestead exemption, you usually do not have to file again to receive the tax break as long as you live in your home. A word of caution: if you make any deed changes to your title or if you refinance, it is best to check to make sure you are still receiving the homestead exemption. Often, tax offices remove the exemptions when any changes occur. Always check your property tax bill—it will show whether or not you are receiving homestead exemption and the dollar amount. If you find any errors on your tax bill, contact your county tax commissioner's office to correct them.

For most people, a substantial part of their wealth is in the home in which they live. If you invest in other real estate, make sure it is not near your home. Your home price fluctuations impose considerable risk—do not increase that risk by purchasing additional real estate in the same neighborhood. By purchasing real estate in a different location, you help to spread your risk out better. If you are considering purchasing a second home for vacation purposes, add up all the costs involved including mortgage interest, taxes, insurance, utilities, maintenance fees, and so on, and compare that to the costs you would normally spend on a hotel or just renting a home. Often, buying is not the cheaper alternative. Other considerations might include how much time you will use the home, whether you are willing to vacation in the same spot every year, and location. Location for vacation homes can be even more crucial than for principal residences. Homes near the vacation area's main attractions tend to have the best rental and resale potential. Research the rental potential of the home—most buyers grossly overestimate the potential rental income and the number of weeks they will have renters.

Housing

When you purchase appliances for your home, most retailers want to sell you extended warranties, which are a great deal for the retailers and usually not a very good deal for the purchaser. Extended warranties can carry gross-profit margins of 40% and more. Fewer than 20% of products covered by extended warranties are ever brought in for repair. In most cases, you are better off taking the money you would have spent on an extended warranty and putting it aside in an emergency fund in case something does happen. In other words, set up a small fund as insurance against something going wrong with an appliance—it makes more economic sense. People who purchase extended warranties are gambling that the appliance will break after the manufacturer's warranty has expired but before the extended warranty expires and that the cost of the repairs will exceed the cost of the extended warranty—a very unlikely proposition. The following chart shows the age at which products are typically replaced:

Appliance	Range of Years Products Are Typically Replaced[1]
Gas Ranges	11–24 Years
Refrigerators	9–19 Years
Electric Ranges	10–20 Years
Dishwashers	7–14 Years
Color TV Sets	5–11 Years
Electric Dryers	10–16 Years
Microwave Ovens	7–12 Years
Gas Dryers	12–15 Years
Washing Machines	13–14 Years

[1] Source: *Appliance* magazine.

Housing

If you are considering home improvements, it is important to ascertain what the improvements will add to the resale value of your home. It is possible to overspend on remodeling costs versus the comparable value of homes in your area so that you cannot recoup your expenses. If you decide that the remodeling costs are a wise spend but need to borrow money, then you will have to check on possible financing. It might be possible to get a home equity loan. Home equity loans normally have low interest rates. Most interest you pay on a home equity loan is tax deductible. Home equity loans might be obtained through banks, credit unions, home finance companies, some brokers, and so on. Be certain to comparison shop for loans—interest rates can vary dramatically. Home equity "lines of credit" differ in that they usually allow a homeowner to draw upon their available equity whenever it's needed. It may be as simple as writing a check—the interest charges vary depending on the prevailing interest rates at the time the credit is tapped. As you pay off borrowed money, the credit line is replenished. An annual fee might be charged to keep the line of credit open, although most financial institutions do not charge a fee. Cash-out refinancing allows you to close out your existing mortgage with a new larger mortgage. You may be able to just get a larger first mortgage. Sometimes, there are Fannie Mae or Freddie Mac home improvement loans or second mortgages, rehabilitation mortgage loans, or special bank home improvement loans or second mortgages available—ask your financial institution about special loans. Keep good records on home improvements. Money you spend on improving your home (excluding normal maintenance expenditures) adds to the cost of your home and reduces the capital gains tax that might be due when you sell. Keep documentation on file for the tax year during which you sell your home. It is easier to keep the documentation as you

Housing

go versus attempting to reconstruct the expenditures years later when you sell. For assistance in keeping a recap of your property improvement expenditures open the SS29 Calculator-Home-Property Improvement.xls.

1. Open the "SS29 Calculator-Home-Property Improvement.xls"; see Figure 21.4.
2. Click "Yes" to enable macros, if necessary.
3. Fill in your own personal information in each white cell (you may tab from one white cell to another).
4. After completing the information in all of the white cells, press "Tab" and then click on the "MMW Recalculation Button"—the spreadsheet will make the remaining calculations for you.

Figure 21.4

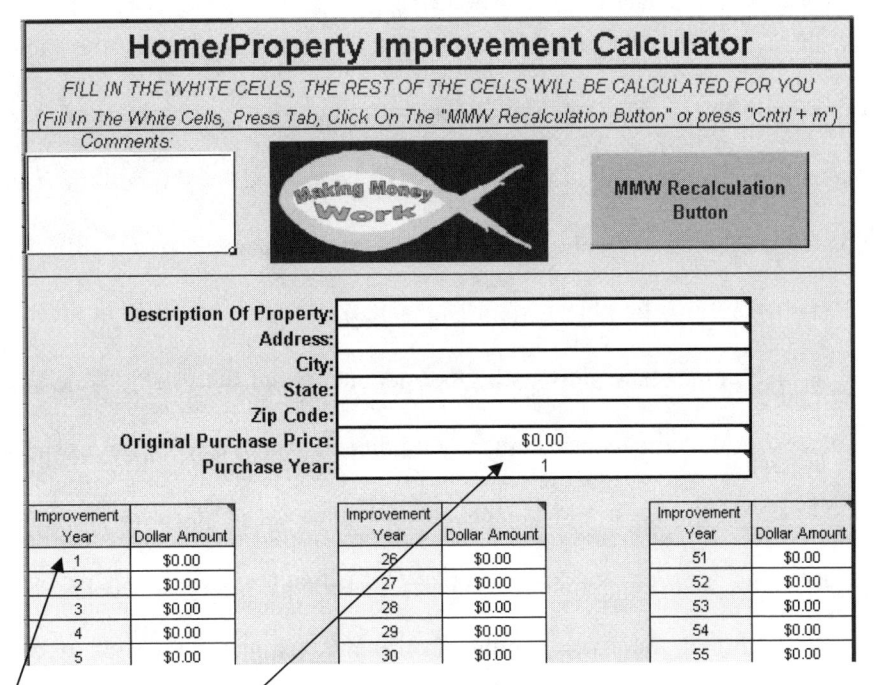

When you type in the "Purchase Year," tab and then click on the "MMW Recalculation Button"; all of the "Improvement Year" dates will automatically be typed in for you.

- - -

Housing

18	$0.00		43	$0.00		68	$0.00
19	$0.00		44	$0.00		69	$0.00
20	$0.00		45	$0.00		70	$0.00
21	$0.00		46	$0.00		71	$0.00
22	$0.00		47	$0.00		72	$0.00
23	$0.00		48	$0.00		73	$0.00
24	$0.00		49	$0.00		74	$0.00
25	$0.00		50	$0.00		75	$0.00

Original Purchase Price:	$0.00
Total Property Improvements:	$0.00
Purchase Price Plus Improvements In Property:	$0.00

Home-Property Improvement (1) / Home-Property Improvement (2) / Home-

Note: The "Purchase Price Plus Improvements in Property" will be calculated for you—be certain to keep receipts as documentation for tax purposes in the year you sell.
There are 10 sheets to keep track of different properties.

A time-share is the right to use a vacation property at a particular time each year—typically in one-week increments. The buyer pays a purchase price plus a prorated share of the maintenance costs for the individual unit or condo and for the building's common areas. Some time-shares sell you a specified week each year while others offer a floating time slot. You may also be able to join (for a fee) time-share exchange networks that allow you to trade time-share slots with other people around the world. Time-shares can be very expensive. The time-share company might sell you one week out of the year for $15,000; $15,000 x 52 weeks = $780,000 in total sales for the time-share company for the individual unit. Adjacent condos or property units that are not time-shares can sell for less than half of that, and you would own the entire year. Of course time-share salespeople state that for $15,000 you get a vacation week versus having to pay $300,000 to own a condo or unit nearby. Still, time-shares are extremely expensive. Add the cost of the time-share, maintenance fees, cleaning fees, membership in exchange networks, and other miscellaneous charges and compare that to the cost of just renting a unit in the area—often, just renting is less expensive, and you do not have a long-term obligation. There is almost no secondary market for time-shares. If you do decide to sell, most likely

Housing

you'll be competing with the time-share company who is still selling units in your program. Resort Properties Association ran a survey of time-share owners: 58% of them had tried to sell for 4.4 years with only 3% succeeding. Time-share owners who want to get out of their time-share units will likely have to resign themselves to the loss of their investments—and they may still be liable for the yearly maintenance fees. So, do not consider time-shares as an investment; consider them as the purchase of future vacations. If you are interested in buying a time-share, consider buying a resale unit from an individual owner. Resales are often less than half the cost of new time-shares. In some cases, you might even be able to negotiate getting the time-share for no cost and assuming the yearly maintenance fees. Private sellers might be found in newsletters, local newspapers, bulletin boards, or by talking with current owners at the property.

Jesus told this parable concerning the spiritual importance of keeping God's word first in your life: "*What then of the man who hears these words of mine and acts upon them? He is like a man who had the sense to build his house on rock. The rain came down, the floods rose, the wind blew, and beat upon that house; but it did not fall, because its foundations were on rock. But what of the man who hears these words of mine and does not act upon them? He is like a man who was foolish enough to build his house on sand. The rain came down, the floods rose, the wind blew, and beat upon that house; down it fell with a great crash*"—Matthew 7:24–27.

Chapter 22

Real Estate Investment Trusts

A real estate investment trust (REIT) is a corporation or business trust that invests in real estate, mortgages, or real estate securities. Legislation requires that REITs pay investors 90% of their earnings in the form of dividends—the REIT avoids having to pay federal taxes on its income. REITs are available on the public stock exchanges or privately. Most investors buy REITs because of their high dividend yields and stable cash flow.

Real estate investment trusts (REITs) usually specialize in owning and operating either apartment complexes, office buildings, self-storage units, hotels, warehouses, shopping centers, regional malls, discount malls, mobile-home parks, or other real estate properties. Buying stock in a REIT is an affordable way to invest in numerous properties. Investing in numerous properties provides some diversification and a hedge against inflation. As prices go up, rents and often the underlying property values increase as well. The typical REIT owns 20 to 100 pieces of income-producing real estate. Of course, the real estate market has ups and downs—you can loose money with REITs. When considering REITs as investments, you should look for REIT management that has been around for a while. You can get a better idea of the quality of the REIT if you inspect the property in person—is the property in a strategic location? Check the balance sheet and financial documents of the REIT.

Real Estate Investment Trusts

If you decide to invest in REITs via mutual funds, look for no-load funds with low expense ratios and good professional management.

The consequences of our sins are the dividends from investments in poor choices.

Futures Markets

Chapter 23

Futures Markets

Virtually everything trades in the U.S. futures markets, everything from beef, corn, cotton, soybeans, and gas to currencies, bonds, gold, and stock market indexes. A <u>futures</u> contract is an obligation to either buy or sell a security (e.g., a stock) or commodity (e.g., corn or soybeans) on a specific future date at a specific price. An <u>options</u> contract is a right to buy or sell a security or commodity in the future at a specific price. The <u>futures</u> contract may necessitate the futures trader having to take possession of the security or commodity unless the contract has been traded before it expires. The <u>options</u> contract may allow the options trader to walk away from the contract when it expires—although possibly at a huge loss. Future contracts and options contracts are derivatives. The value of derivatives depends on the value of some underlying assets. A futures contract is an investor's prediction of which way the price of a stock or commodity will move in the future. A futures contract is a hedge against a loss—either in escalating prices or decreasing prices. For example, a wheat farmer might sell a futures contract on his crop to protect against price declines that might occur 3 months in the future at harvest time—this will guarantee that he will receive at least the current price levels when he sells his crop. A baking company might be predicting a price increase on wheat and buy the futures contract to protect itself against the anticipated higher price levels. The futures markets are important in helping to run our economy; however, they are very risky. Futures markets offer potential for great gains; however, they also offer potential for

Futures Markets

great losses. For your prediction to be right, another person's prediction has to be wrong—you have a 50% chance of losing money, and that is too much risk for most investors. Futures markets are very speculative in nature and are generally too risky for the average investor. The futures markets are complex. **Unless you are a professional investor with in-depth knowledge of the futures markets, you should avoid these risky derivative investments.**

"*A fool thinks that he is always right; wise is the man that listens to advice*"—Proverbs 12:15. "*The fool talks on and on; but no man knows what is coming.*"—Ecclesiastes 10:14.

Household Records

Chapter 24

Household Records

You should have a filing system to keep track of your receipts/paperwork. It might include the following folders:

Appliances	Hobbies	Pets
Automobile Records	Home Improvement	Postage
Bonds	Household Inventory	Property
Budget	Insurance-Automobile	Retirement Plans & Benefits
Business Expenses	Insurance-Homeowners	Safe Deposit Box
Casualty or Theft Losses	Insurance-Life	Savings Account Info.
Checking Account Info.	Insurance-Medical	Sports
Children	Insurance-Miscellaneous	Stocks
Church	IRA's	Taxes
Clothing Receipts	Jewelry	T-Bills
Club Receipts	Lawn & Garden	Telephone Bills
Coupons	Licenses	Television
Credit Cards	Loans	Tools
Credit Union	Medical Receipts	Utility Bills
Donations	Miscellaneous	Vacations
Electronic Equipment	Money Market Funds	Veterinarian
Extra Income, Interest	Mortgage Payments	Voter Registration
Furniture	Moving Expenses	Wage Statements
Garbage Disposal	Mutual Funds	Warranties
Gifts	Newspaper Receipts	Water Bills
Heat Bills	Office Supplies	Will Information

Open "File Folders.doc"—Figure 23.1

Figure 23.1

290

Household Records

Appliances		Automobile Records	
Bonds		Budget	
Business Expenses		Casualty or Theft Losses	
Checking Account Info.		Children	
Church		Clothing Receipts	
Club Receipts		Coupons	
Credit Cards		Credit Union	

- - -

Vacations		Veterinarian	
Voter Registration		Wage Statements	
Warranties		Water Bills	

Warranties		Water Bills	
Will Information			

You can print these file folder tabs using "Avery Standard 5066-File Folder" sheets available at most office supply stores. If you prefer, you can print file folder tabs using your own favorite labels.

Open the "File Folders.xls—Figure 23.2.

Figure 23.2

Household Records

Number	Tab
1	Appliances
2	Automobile Records
3	Bonds
4	Budget
5	Business Expenses
6	Casualty or Theft Losses
7	Checking Account Info.
8	Children
9	Church
10	Clothing Receipts
11	Club Receipts
12	Coupons
13	Credit Cards
14	Credit Union
15	Donations
16	Electronic Equipment
17	Extra Income, Interest
18	Furniture
19	Garbage Disposal
20	Gifts
21	Heat Bills
22	Hobbies
23	Home Improvement

Change this worksheet to suit your needs and then use Microsoft's "Mail Merge" feature to design your own file folder tabs.

Federal tax returns can be audited for up to three years after the filing date or up to six years after the filing date if underreported income is involved. For tax purposes, most accountants recommend the following retention periods to keep your paperwork:

Type of Records	Retention Period
IRAs (nondeductible contributions)	Until all funds are withdrawn from your IRA[1]
Investments	Until after the assets are sold[2]
Real estate records	Permanent
Home improvement records	Ownership period plus 7 years (or until capital gains taxes are paid plus 7 years)[3]
Investment records	Ownership period plus 7 years
Bank statements, bank deposit slips, cancelled checks	7 years
Expense reports/entertainment records	7 years
Tax records	6 years minimum (no statute of limitations for filing fraudulent income)

---

[1] Save 1040 tax forms for each contribution year: Forms 8606, 1099-R, and 5498.
[2] Brokerage statements and other records will be needed to figure your capital gain.
[3] If you are able to defer capital gain taxes on the sale of your home by purchasing a new home at a higher price, you will need to save the home improvement records from the sale of your old home indefinitely because the gain of the sale affects the cost basis of your new home.

Household Records

It is a good idea to complete a household inventory form in case of a burglary or fire. In case of a burglary, you must show proof to your law enforcement department of ownership of recovered stolen items in order to claim them. You can positively identify an item by providing a serial number or a unique number you may have engraved on the item (such as your driver's license number). You should take photographs of valuables such as jewelry, silver, antiques, or art objects and make a record of any marks, blemishes, or other features that make the items identifiable. A household inventory helps to determine what items might be missing. A household inventory helps with your insurance adjustments. In the event of your death, a household inventory can be of enormous assistance to your executor when distributing your belongings. A household inventory also gives you a good indication of whether your insurance coverage is adequate.

Open the "SS31 Calculator-Household Inventory Form.xls—Figure 23.3.

1. Open the "SS31 Calculator-Household Inventory Form.xls"; see Figure 23.3.
2. Click "Yes" to enable macros, if necessary.
3. Fill in your own personal information in each white cell (you may tab from one white cell to another).
4. After completing the information in all of the white cells, press "Tab" and then click on the "MMW Recalculation Button"—the spreadsheet will make the remaining calculation for you.

Figure 23.3

Household Records

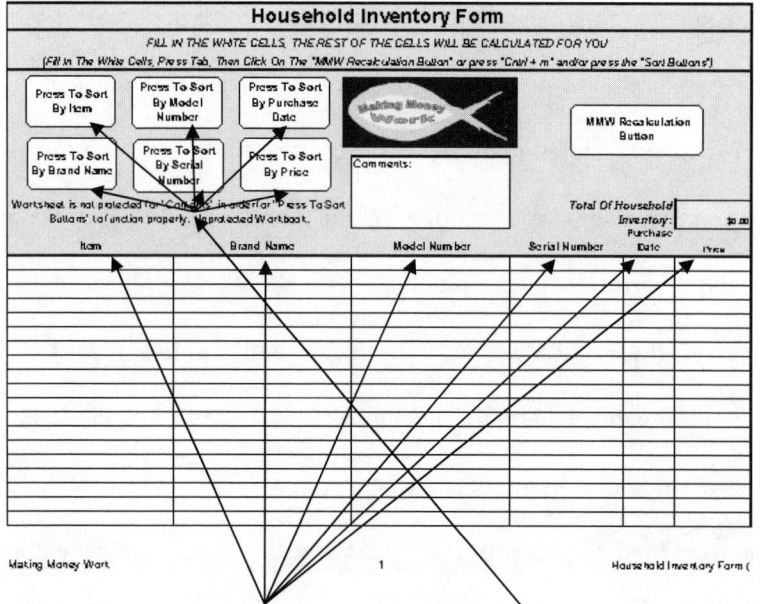

Once you have filled in your personal information, the "Press to Sort" buttons allow you to sort in ascending order by "Item," "Brand Name," "Model Number," "Serial Number," purchase "Date," or "Price." Each worksheet allows you to track 484 items, and there are 5 worksheets available for household inventories.

The calculator computes the "Total of Household Inventory" for you—this dollar amount is useful to make certain you have enough renter's insurance to cover losses without wasting money by purchasing too much insurance coverage. It is also useful when determining your homeowner's insurance needs (when combined with the value of your home). In addition to having a "written" household inventory form, it is also a good idea to have a video camera recording or photographs of each room, closet, and drawer in your house to identify your belongings.

You should consider where to keep your important documents. The following are some items you may want to store in a fireproof box at home:

Household Records

Items to Keep in a Fireproof Box at Home	
Birth Certificates	Medical Directives Regarding Care (Original Copy)
Cemetery Deeds and Requests (Original Copies)	Military Discharge Papers
Death Certificates	Passports
Financial Records	Powers of Attorney (Original Copies)
Funeral Arrangement Requests (Original Copies)	Property Tax Receipts
Income Tax Returns (Last 6 Years)	Warranties
Insurance Policies (Original Copies)	Wills (Original Copies)
Marriage Certificates	Wills—Living (Original Copy)

The following are some items you may wish to leave with your executor, a relative, attorney, or friend:

Items to Leave With Your Executor, Relative, Attorney, or Friend	
Address List of People Listed in Wills, Trusts, or Powers of Attorney	Powers of Attorney (Copies)
Burial Instructions (Copy)	Trusts (Copies)
Cemetery Deeds and Requests (Copies)	Wills (Copies)
Instructions on Administering Your Estate	Wills—Living (Copy)

Note that some of the above listed items should not be kept in your safe-deposit box in a financial institution because in the event of your death, your executor will not have the necessary paperwork to get in the safe-deposit box or begin the process of implementing your requests. The following are some items you may wish to keep in a safe-deposit box in your bank:

Items to Keep in a Safe-Deposit Box	
Adoption Papers	Legal Agreements
Appraisals of Property	Marriage Certificates
Assets (Lists of Savings Accounts, etc.)	Military Discharge Papers
Bills of Sale for Major Items	MMW Diskette With Your Pertinent Information
Birth Certificates	Mortgage Papers
Bonds	Naturalization Papers
Certificates of Deposit	Patents
Citizenship Papers	Pension Certificates
Contracts and Agreements	Precious Metals
Copyrights	Promissory Notes
Court Decrees	Savings Certificates

Household Records

Credit Card List (Phone Numbers/Addresses)	Securities
Death Certificates	Stock Certificates
Deeds	Titles (Vehicles and Property)
Employment Contracts	Trust Agreements
Insurance—Disability (Amounts, Insurers, Account Numbers; Not Policies)	Video Tapes of Property Or Photo Negatives
Insurance—Life (Amounts, Insurers, Account Numbers; Not Policies)	Will (Copy)
Insurance—Property and Casualty Policies	Will—Living (Copy)
IRA Records	

Safe-deposit boxes come in various sizes and are rented for varying annual fees (depending on the size of the box you rent) at most banks. It takes two keys to open the safe-deposit box—one that you keep and one that the bank keeps. Be careful not to loose your key, the bank does not keep a copy. If it is lost, you will have to pay to have the box lock drilled and replaced. Joint rentership of a safe-deposit box is recommended. If one renter dies, the other renter will still have access to the items in the box—however, in some states, the safe-deposit box may be sealed after the death of one renter until an inventory of the box can be made for tax purposes. If the box is rented by only one individual and he or she dies, the bank might not allow the box to be opened until the probate court issues a court order mandating that the box be opened. That's the reason it is important to keep some documents at home in a fireproof box—your will, insurance policies, and so on. Without them, it is difficult for your survivors to proceed with the handling of your affairs after your death. Banks might freeze the safe-deposit box after hearing about the renter's death from family, executors, and the Social Security Administration. The Social Security Administration might ask the bank to return a Social Security direct deposit check because of death.

"*You shall all rejoice, . . . for all the good things which the Lord your God has given to you and your family*"—Deuteronomy 26:11.

Checking Accounts

Chapter 25

Checking Accounts

Typically, checking accounts that pay higher interest rates cost more in monthly fees than those that pay lower rates. Some banks will waive the fees if your average daily or monthly balance is above a certain level—for example, $300 to $2,500. If the balance drops below the minimum level, you normally get charged another fee. Some banks allow you to write a certain number of checks free each month—for example, up to 25—and then charge additional per check fees for anything over that number. Other fees some banks might charge include fees for bouncing checks, making deposits, making withdrawals, getting copies of old checks, ordering stop payments on checks, making transactions with live tellers, using another bank's teller machine, using your own bank's teller machine, and on and on. Fees can easily vary by $40 or more per month between the lowest and highest cost accounts. Since fees and rules on checking and savings accounts can vary so dramatically from bank to bank, it is important to comparison shop at least 3 to 4 different institutions to get accounts that best suit your needs. First, you will need to determine your prior check-writing habits—how many checks per month do you normally write? What minimum balance can you maintain? Do you require that canceled checks be returned to you? If not, you will likely save fees on checks and processing. Do you prefer an account that pays interest but charges higher fees or do you prefer an account that pays lower interest but charges lower fees? Do you prefer having access to a local bank, on-line bank, or possibly a bank in another Federal Reserve district?

Checking Accounts

In the book *Megatrends—Ten New Directions Transforming Our Lives*, author John Naisbitt discusses the "information float" and how technology is shortening the time it takes to disseminate information to people. He uses the analogy of how the world changed from trading goods and services via a barter system to the process of switching to standardized currencies. Using money versus a barter system greatly speeded up transactions. John Naisbitt said, "Now, with the use of electrons to send money around the world at the speed of light, we have almost completely collapsed the money information float. The shift from money to electronics is as basic as when we went from barter to money."[1] Technology is rapidly eliminating the money float. For example, let's say you write a paper check today to pay for some goods or services. In the time it takes for the check to clear your account, you still have the funds in the account earning interest (assuming the account pays some interest). The longer it takes for the check to clear your account, the more time your money has to earn interest and the more money you make. It would make sense then to have a checking account in a Federal Reserve district outside the Federal Reserve district in which you live —thereby adding more time to the process for checks clearing your account. There are 12 Federal Reserve districts in the United States—each one serves geographical areas in up to 7 different states. The following are the 12 Federal Reserve districts:

---

[1] John Naisbitt, *Megatrends: ten new directions transforming our lives,* Warner Books, New York, NY, 1982.

Checking Accounts

Federal Reserve Districts		
Atlanta	Dallas	Philadelphia
Boston	Kansas City	Richmond
Chicago	Minneapolis	San Francisco
Cleveland	New York	St. Louis

The www.federalreserve.gov website has a map of the geographical areas covered by each district. So, as a consumer, you want to try to extend the time "float" of your interest-earning money account by paying bills when they are due—not before—and by possibly using an account outside your own Federal Reserve district to add time to the payment processing. On the other hand, you want to get money into your account as quickly as possible. Electronic deposit of your pay check or Social Security check cuts down on the time float and gets the money into your account so it can begin earning interest more quickly. Direct deposit is also safer and more convenient than receiving paper checks.

Of course, banks are doing everything they can to get the float on their side so that they are making the money instead of you. Debit cards are used like credit cards except they immediately take the money out of your checking account within a day or two of when you make a purchase—thereby eliminating most of the time float you might have been able to take advantage of when writing a paper check or paying by credit card, which can delay payment up to 45 days. Incidentally, there is no law that requires you to purchase your paper checks from the bank that holds your account. Checks from third-party check suppliers can be about half the price of bank checks. Compare the cost of bank checks by

Checking Accounts

asking for prices at your current bank and researching third-party check manufacturers by typing in "bank checks" in your Internet computer connection search engine or even by checking prices in your local newspaper ads.

Online banking accounts might suit your needs. The convenience of online bill paying services is hard to beat. Most utility, mortgage, and credit card companies are set up to receive electronic payments free of charge. If the billing company does not accept electronic payments, the bank will issue and mail a check to the company. You usually can set up automatically recurring payments for companies that maintain consistent bills such as mortgage or insurance premium payments. With online bill paying, you can usually set up the payment today to be executed at some date in the future—for example, let's say you get your property tax bill today, you might set up 1 payment due in 2 months and another payment due in 4 months, thus leaving the money in your own interest-earning account until the payments are actually due. With online banking accounts, you can conduct your banking as you travel via a laptop computer. Make sure your online bank is using secure socket layer (SSL) encryption technology, which protects your data against fraudulent activity. Check with your online bank to see if they have error and fraud protection guarantees similar to the $50.00 loss limit on credit cards.

Once you have determined your banking habits, you will be able to match an account to your behavior and cash flow. Ask several banks for a copy of their fee-disclosure schedules and also ask them to suggest a checking account based on your prior banking habits and current needs. You can compare different checking and savings accounts online at www.bankrate.com. After comparing the different banks, select the account with which you feel most comfortable. You should keep as little money as possible in

Checking Accounts

your checking account since interest rates (if available at all) are typically meager. As discussed earlier, you should keep enough money for 3 to 6 months' worth of expenses on hand in the event of an emergency or job loss. One month's worth of emergency funds in a checking account should be sufficient. You should have 2 to 5 months' worth of emergency funds in a money fund or savings account that earns a competitive interest rate. The rest of your funds should be invested in higher earning investment vehicles.

It is important to understand the health of your banking institution—banks and thrifts can and do fail. Some signs of trouble that might lead to bank failures are excessive growth that strains bank underwriting and risk standards, economic deterioration, insufficient capital to cover lower earnings and/or increased loan losses, too many loans in economic sectors that are in decline, managerial problems, liquidity problems, excessive salaries relative to the size of the bank, and so on. It is prudent to research the financial status of your checking/savings account institution similar to the research you would perform before purchasing a stock. Many checking/savings account institutions have some customer insurance protection through the Federal Deposit Insurance Corporation (FDIC). If your financial institution goes bankrupt, each account you have with it may be insured up to $100,000.[2] FDIC was created on Jan. 1, 1934, during the financial chaos of the Great Depression (after the stock market crash of October 1929 and the crash of March 1933). The FDIC is a U.S. Government federally backed corporation that provides stability and reassurance to depositors. The FDIC is not funded with taxpayer monies. The FDIC charges its financial institution members insurance

---

[2] FDIC insurance coverage as of the writing of this book.

Checking Accounts

premiums. Different ownership accounts such as single or joint accounts may be separately insured. Since the FDIC's inception in 1934, no depositor has lost a single cent of insured funds as a result of a participating financial institution's failure. To learn more about the FDIC insurance coverage visit its website at http://www.fdic.gov/. Ask your financial institution if it is a member of FDIC. If you have more than the maximum amount insured by FDIC, consider setting up separate accounts and putting monies over the maximum insured amount into a different financial institution to protect all of your assets.

Our U.S. currency has the term "In God We Trust" on it; however, sometimes we put more trust in money than we do in God. When you look at U.S. currency, let the "In God We Trust" slogan serve as a reminder to keep God as your number one priority in life.

Keeping Track of Your Portfolio

Chapter 26

Keeping Track of Your Portfolio

Review the following chart concerning historical results (the numbers were derived from a study conducted by the Vanguard Group) of various portfolio investments:

Portfolio Type	Average Annual Return for the Years 1926–1999	# of Years the Portfolio Would Have Lost Money From 1926–1999 (74 Years)	% of Time That the Portfolio Would Have Lost Money	Average Loss in Down Years
100% Stock	11.3%	20 years	27%	-12.3%
50% Stock, 50% Bonds	8.9%	16 years	21.6%	-6.6%
80% Stock, 10% Bonds, 10% Cash Equivalents	6.1%	10 years	13.5%	-3.3%

Several messages can be gleaned from this chart. While stock investments return higher average yields over the long term, they also result in greater average losses during down years. The younger you are and the longer your investment time horizon, the greater the percentage of your portfolio that you can invest in stocks. The older you become and the shorter your investment time horizon, the lower the allocation should be to stocks. Using the rule of subtracting your age from 100, a 50-year-old investor should have no more than 50% of his or her portfolio invested in stocks. This protects you against a potential downturn in stocks. No one can predict the timing of those downturns with any significant degree of accuracy. For older investors, investments in bonds and cash (or cash equivalents such as money market funds) are more likely to provide the income you will need versus the potential price appreciation of riskier stock investments. A 20-year-old investor should have about 80% of his or her portfolio invested in stocks to maximize

Keeping Track of Your Portfolio

the potential higher long-term returns. The investor's portfolio then is dynamic—it is constantly changing. It not only changes with age, it also changes with asset allocation, and it changes with investment choices. Poor investment choices are sold and replaced with more promising possibilities. Mark Twain advised, "We should be careful to get out of an experience only the wisdom that is in it—and stop there; lest we be like the cat that sits down on a hot stove lid. She will never sit down on a hot stove lid again—and that is well; but also she will never sit down on a cold one anymore."[1] For those investments that have declined in value, do not continue to hold them in an attempt to regain the value they once held if the criteria you initially used to buy them has changed. In other words, rather than holding on to a poor investment to regain what you have lost, accept the loss, sell the investment, and purchase an investment that does suit your current needs. The key question is not "How much has the investment lost?" The key question is "Would I purchase the investment today?" If you have allowed the investment sufficient time to produce for you and it has fallen to the lower 60% performancewise of its peer group, then it is likely you should replace it.

The portfolio is constantly adjusted to reflect the investor's age and investment time horizon. The portfolio is adjusted to achieve the proper diversification to suit the investor's risk tolerance. Adequate diversification includes the proper mix of stocks, bonds, and cash or cash equivalents such as money market funds. An examination of your portfolio on a quarterly, semiannual, or annual basis will alert you to whether or not price changes have lead to overconcentration in any particular areas. Proper diversification is

---

[1] *Lessons From The Bear Market Are Painful Yet Valuable,* In The Vanguard, Voyager Edition, Winter 2003.

Keeping Track of Your Portfolio

just as important to maintain when the portfolio has lower dollar amounts as it is when the portfolio is at its peak. A properly diversified portfolio allows you to maintain the right mix to maximize potential upside earnings while not overexposing yourself to the potential downside losses. Diversification and balance are the keys to preparing for the inevitable ups and downs of the market.

The following are the *Making Money Work* suggested guidelines for portfolio asset allocation management:

Investment Categories:	Speculative Investments	Aggressive Growth Investments	Core Investments	Conservative Investments	Savings
Risk Categories:	Very High Risk	High Risk	Average Risk	Low Risk	Guaranteed
Types of Investments:	Options, Penny Stock, Commodities, etc.	Aggressive Growth Stocks, Low Quality Bonds, Limited Partnerships, etc.	Blue Chip Stocks, Quality Growth Stocks, Real Estate, etc.	Government Bonds, Corporate Bonds, Tax-Free Bonds, Retirement Funds, Growth & Income Mutual Funds, etc.	Bank CDs, Savings Accounts, Credit Union, Insurance Policies, Guaranteed Money Market Funds, etc.
Ages 18 to 35 (or 30–45 years to retirement):	0% to 5%	30% to 50%	30% to 40%	10% to 15%	10% to 15%
Ages 36 to 50 (or 15–29 years to retirement):	0% to 5%	10% to 20%	35% to 50%	25% to 40%	10% to 15%
Ages 51 to 65 (or 0–15 years to retirement):	0% to 5%	5% to 10%	30% to 40%	35% to 50%	10% to 15%
Age 66 and up (or 0 years to retirement):	0% to 5%	0% to 5%	15% to 20%	55% to 65%	10% to 15%

The *Making Money Work* recommendation is that if you feel you must invest in speculative investments (very high risk), you should limit your investments to no more

Keeping Track of Your Portfolio

than 0% to 5% of your total dollar amounts invested in your portfolio at any age point in your life. Exceeding this limit exposes you to too much downside risk. Also, it is recommended that you keep 10% to 15% in guaranteed savings accounts throughout your life. The other investment categories would change as you age or get closer to retirement —the farther from retirement, the more risk you can assume, and the closer to retirement, the more conservative your investments should become.

To assist in keeping track of your portfolio and to help in reviewing your asset allocations by investment category, open the SS33 Calculator-Portfolio Allocation.xls.

1. Open the "SS233 Calculator-Portfolio Allocation.xls"; see Figure 25.1.
2. Click "Yes" to enable macros, if necessary.
3. Fill in your own personal information in each white cell (you may tab from one white cell to another).
4. After completing the information in all of the white cells, press "Tab" and then click on the "MMW Recalculation Button"—the spreadsheet will make the remaining calculations for you.

Figure 25.1

Ages 18-35 Portfolio Allocation (Or 30-45 Years To Retirement), INVESTMENT CATEGORIES:	SPECULATIVE INVESTMENTS	AGGRESSIVE GROWTH INVESTMENTS	CORE INVESTMENTS	CONSERVATIVE INVESTMENTS	SAVINGS
RISK CATEGORIES:	VERY HIGH RISK	HIGH RISK	AVERAGE RISK	LOW RISK	GUARANTEED
TYPES OF INVESTMENTS:	OPTIONS, PENNY STOCKS, COMMODITIES, ETC.	AGGRESSIVE STOCKS, LOW QUALITY BONDS, LIMITED PARTNERSHIPS, ETC.	BLUE CHIP STOCKS, QUALITY GROWTH STOCKS, REAL ESTATE, ETC.	GOVERNMENT BONDS, CORPORATE BONDS, TAX FREE BONDS, RETIREMENT FUNDS, GROWTH & INCOME MUTUAL FUNDS, ETC.	BANK CD'S, SAVINGS ACCOUNTS, CREDIT UNION, INSURANCE POLICIES, GUARANTEED MONEY MARKET FUNDS, ETC.
THE MAKING MONEY WORK SUGGESTED % ALLOCATION GUIDELINES:	0% To 5%	30% To 50%	30% To 40%	10% To 15%	10% To 15%

Investor's Name:
Date Of Portfolio Recap:

INVESTMENT CATEGORIES
SPECULATIVE INVESTMENTS

TOTAL (Speculative Investments): $0.00

AGGRESSIVE GROWTH INVESTMENTS

Portfolio For Ages 18-35 / Portfolio For Ages 36-50 / Portfolio For Ages 51-65

MMW Recalculation Button

Be certain to choose the correct sheet tab for your current age group (or years from retirement) since allocation guidelines vary from group to group. There are 4 different age group sheets. You may copy and paste your information from one sheet to another as you progress from one age

Keeping Track of Your Portfolio

group to another. Fill in your own personal information in each column for each investment type. Also, you may record your savings for college expenses at the bottom of the calculator to keep track of your progress—although the numbers are not calculated as part of your portfolio.

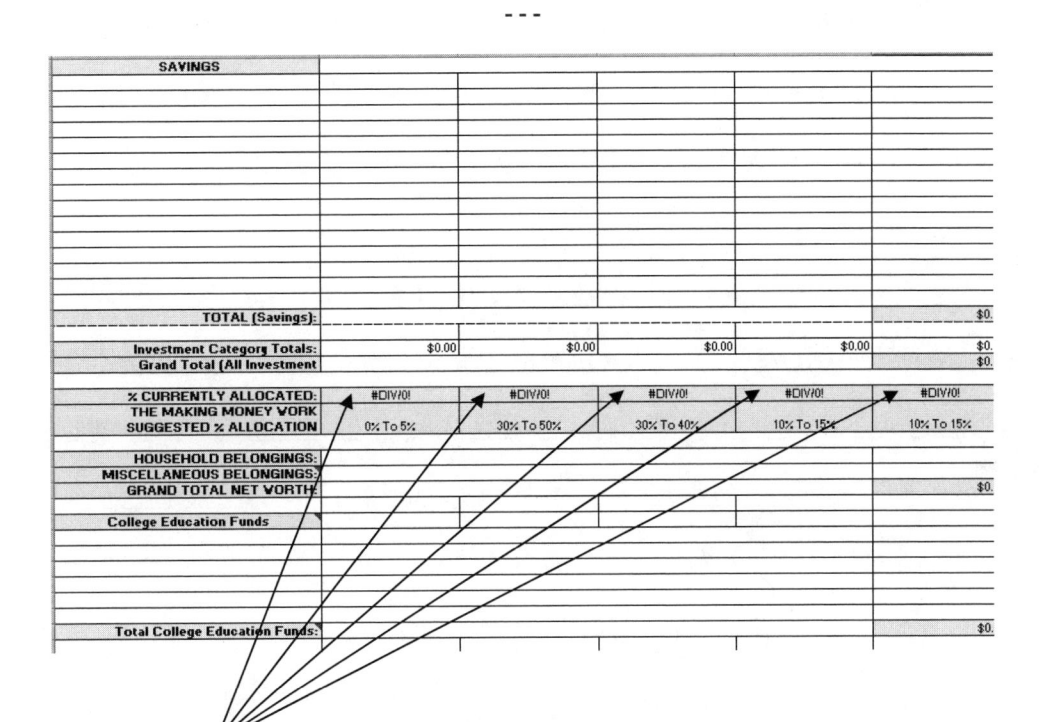

- - -

The "% Currently Allocated" will turn red to alert you that you are either under or over the "% Allocation Guideline." If this entry is red, then you may want to reallocate your investments to give your portfolio better diversification. Also, as noted earlier, review each investment either quarterly, semiannually, or at least annually. If the investment has fallen to be in the bottom 60% of its peer group and the reasons you initially selected it are no longer in place, sell the investment and replace it with a more promising possibility.

If you feel you would benefit from having the assistance of a financial adviser when managing your portfolio, you can locate local certified financial planners and other financial advisers at www.cfp-board.org. As with stockbrokers, check financial planners' backgrounds and any disciplinary actions taken against them before utilizing their services.

Do not obsess about retirement and your portfolio—if you do, you will not be able to enjoy each day as God intends. If you make earnings, savings, and wise investments a

Keeping Track of Your Portfolio

normal part of your activities during your working years, you will not have to worry about finances during your retirement, and you will enjoy life better. The key is keeping God first in your life and maintaining balance and moderation with your daily activities. *"The man who loves money can never have enough, and the man who is in love with great wealth enjoys no return from it. This too is emptiness. When riches multiply, so do those who live off them; and what advantage has the owner, except to look at them? Sweet is the sleep of the labourer whether he eats little or much; but the rich man owns too much and cannot sleep. There is a singular evil here under the sun which I have seen: a man hoards wealth to his own hurt, and then that wealth is lost through an unlucky venture, and the owner's son left with nothing. As he came from the womb of mother earth, so must he return, naked as he came; all his toil produces nothing which he can take away with him. This too is a singular evil: exactly as he came, so shall he go, and what profit does he get when his labour is all for the wind? What is more, all his days are overshadowed; gnawing anxiety and great vexation are his lot, sickness and resentment. What I have seen is this: that it is good and proper for a man to eat and drink and enjoy himself in return for his labours here under the sun, throughout the brief span of life which God has allotted him. Moreover, it is a gift of God that every man to whom he has granted wealth and riches and the power to enjoy them should accept his lot and rejoice in his labour. He will not dwell overmuch upon the passing years; for God fills his time with joy of heart"*—Ecclesiastes 5:10–20.

Credit Cards

Chapter 27

Credit Cards

Credit card companies collect from 2% to 4% on each purchase from <u>merchants</u>. In addition, credit card companies may charge the <u>credit card holder</u> interest, cash advance charges, yearly fees, and a myriad of other fees. MasterCard and Visa are two major credit card brand names that account for more than 85% of all U.S. charges. Visa is the card most widely accepted by merchants. There are more than 9,000 bank card issuers. The bank card issuer determines the interest rates and fees charged to the cardholder. Offers can vary dramatically between the various credit card issuers—it pays to shop for good rates or lower fees when looking for a credit card.

When choosing a credit card, read the fine print carefully on both the initial offer and later agreements. Some credit card companies will tout low annual percentage rates (APRs) at 6% to 8% interest and after a few months raise the rates to around 18%. Crucial details of the credit card agreement may even be omitted in the initial mailing and come in subsequent literature that could go unread. Read all of the credit card agreements. Credit card companies might charge a fixed interest rate or a variable interest rate. By federal law, fixed rates can change at any time. Variable rates are tied to some interest rate in the economy—typically the prime rate; for example, the credit card company might charge 3% + the current prime rate, say it's currently at 6%, = 9%. The prime rate is the rate at which banks will lend money to their most favored customers. The prime rate fluctuates up and down with changes made by the Federal Reserve Board. Variable rates can fluctuate monthly, quarterly, or semiannually. From a consumer

Credit Cards

standpoint, it behooves you to shop for the lowest rate you can get. Of course, if you pay off your entire monthly balance before the due date each month—as you should try to do, the APR does not mean much since you will avoid the interest charges.

Some credit card companies offer their cards for "no annual fee." Others charge annual fees. Some might charge no annual fee for the first year only and then begin charging annual fees. Read the fine print in the credit card agreement to determine your annual fees. From a consumer standpoint, the lower the annual fees, the better. Avoid cards with annual fees if possible. If you pay off your balance each month in order to avoid interest charges, the annual fee will likely be your next largest credit card expense.

The grace period is the number of days between the end of the credit card company's billing cycle and when you must make payments in full in order to avoid interest charges. If the purchases are not paid off in full, you loose the grace period on new purchases. Some credit card companies offer no grace periods—interest charges begin accruing immediately when you make a purchase. Most credit card companies offer grace periods, which can range from 20 to 26 days. A grace period of 25 days is typical. Grace periods are a great consumer ally—you can have your money in your own interest-earning account until the due date of the credit card loan. For the credit card holder, the longer the grace period the better.

Few credit card companies offer grace periods on cash advances. That means interest starts accruing immediately—even if you pay your balance in full when due. The credit card institution might even charge a higher interest rate for cash advances—read the fine print in the agreement. Cash advances can add substantially to the cost of your credit card loan.

Credit Cards

The credit card institution might charge late fees if your payment arrives to them one day past the due date. Late fees might also accrue interest charges.

The credit line is the minimum and maximum dollar amounts of credit available. You might also be charged with over-the-limit fees. Credit card issuers will typically set a maximum card limit for your purchases. If you exceed the limit, the credit card institution might assess a fee for each transaction you make when you exceed your credit card limit. Over-the-limit fees may also accrue interest.

Sometimes credit card companies use "two-cycle billing" to increase the amount of interest payments their credit card holders pay. Two-cycle billing works like this: even if you pay your prior month's bill in full, the credit card company assesses new interest charges on what you once owed, which can boost the interest you owe by 25%! Avoid two-cycle billing credit cards when possible.

Some issuers might charge fees to transfer balances to another lower rate credit card.

The "balance calculation method" is the way the credit card institution calculates the balance on which interest will be charged for credit card holders who do not pay their balances in full.

Balance Calculation Method Listed in Order of Best (#1) to Worst (#4) for Credit Card Holders Who Carry Balances
1. Average daily balance (excluding new purchases)
2. Two-cycle average daily balance (excluding new purchases)
3. Average daily balance (including new purchases)
4. Two-cycle average daily balance (including new purchases)

Credit Cards

You might be able to negotiate the terms of your card to get a lower interest rate, to have your annual fee waived, or to obtain a higher credit limit—it could be as simple as making a telephone call to your credit card issuer.

Some credit card issuers may include special perks—such as contributing points for each purchase to your frequent flyer program.

You can help to protect yourself against credit card theft. Only carry the credit cards you need. Leave other cards in a safe at home when you are not using them. Get your credit card back as soon as you've finished using it. Do not leave your credit card sitting on restaurant tables, sales counters, or hotel registration desks where thieves could memorize the account number. Properly handle all receipts—do not leave your account number on any piece of paper that could be stolen. Do not allow merchants to copy your credit card number when you are paying by check—if they require a credit card when making check purchases, let them note only the type of card and expiration date. Memorize personal identification numbers (PINs)—do not write them down and leave them in places such as your wallet, which could be lost or stolen. Do not give your credit card number to someone calling you on the phone—if you wish to make a purchase from him or her, telephone him or her back after verifying the legitimacy of the company. The Federal Trade Commission states that your liability for unauthorized credit card charges is limited to $50—that makes purchasing credit card liability insurance unnecessary. However, credit card theft is everyone's concern because credit card companies often raise interest rates or annual fees to compensate for credit card losses.

If you only pay the minimum balance, many credit cards will not be paid off for 20 years or more. Credit card abuse can lead to enormous financial difficulty. The wisest use

Credit Cards

of credit cards is to pay off your debt balance every month and to avoid the high interest rate charges. If you do have credit card debt, paying off the debt or reducing it should be your top priority—refer back to the example of eliminating cards and reducing debt by going to a credit card with a lower interest rate as noted in Chapter 4, "Debt Management." Once again, a good place to compare credit cards is at www.bankrate.com.

When used wisely, credit cards are a convenient way to make purchases and the grace period can be a powerful financial ally.

Stop buying to "be." "Be" for God.

"*Do not be a man who strikes hands in pledge or puts up security for debt*"—Proverbs 22:26 (New Internatinal Version).

Vehicles

Chapter 28

Vehicles

Next to housing, transportation costs are typically the second highest family expense. The average cost of owning and operating a standard-size vehicle during the average person's lifetime is more than twice the median sales price of a single-family home—excluding taxes, interest, and maintenance. However, unlike homes, which tend to appreciate, or grow, in value, vehicles generally depreciate, or decrease, in value. Vehicle depreciation is a primary expense.

Time Frame or Mileage	Depreciation Amount for Time Frame or Mileage	To Date Approximate Depreciation Amounts	Remarks
Year 1	15% to 30%	15% to 30%	1st year typical depreciation.
Year 2 to 3	20% to 35%	35% to 50%	Warranty typically expires at the end of year 3 or 36,000 miles (whichever comes first).
60,000 miles	5% to 10%	40% to 60%	Timing belt may have to be replaced.
80,000 miles	5% to 10%	65% to 70%	Drivetrain and parts wear out.
100,000 miles	Slower depreciation	Slower depreciation	The vehicle continues to depreciate but at a much slower rate.

In other words, at the end of year 1, a new vehicle typically is now worth only 70% to 85% of its original value. At the end of year 3, the typical vehicle is now worth only 65% to 80% of its original value. The early years of a vehicle's life expectancy decrease in value at the most rapid pace. Vehicle depreciation amounts vary significantly depending on the make, model, and year—for example, American-made vehicles tend to depreciate more rapidly than Japanese models. The average age of vehicles that are currently

Vehicles

operating on highways today is around 8 to 10 years. Purchasing used vehicles versus new vehicles can result in tremendous transportation savings.

Typical Medium-Priced New Car[1]	
Average Cost	**Typical 1st Year Expenses**
$20,000	$3,194.50 (15.97% of cost) for fuel, routine maintenance, taxes, insurance, et. al.
	$3,194.50 (15.97% of cost) for depreciation
Total 1st Year Expenses:	$6,389

Not only do you avoid the steepest depreciation in the early years by buying used cars, but older cars are also less expensive to insure—premiums are lower for collision and theft insurance. Because of depreciation, the older the vehicle, the lower the taxes. If your car is 4 years old or older, you might drop costly comprehensive and collision coverage. Purchasing a used vehicle versus leasing a vehicle usually saves you money also.

When shopping for a used vehicle, the first thing you should do is to analyze your own driving habits and needs. Decide on the size vehicle you need. Consider the number of family members you typically transport, the amount of miles you usually drive per year, the gas mileage you would like to get, the type of equipment you would like to have in your vehicle, and the price range that suits your finances. After you have determined the type and style of vehicle you would like to purchase, narrow the selections down to at least 2 or 3 makes and models within your price range. You cannot make your best car deal if you limit your choice to only one specific model.

---

[1] Based on Runzeimer International travel consulting group 1997 research.

Vehicles

Do some research on the reliability of the vehicles—*Consumer Reports* runs periodic articles on used cars that include a list of reliable vehicles as well as ones to avoid. *Consumer Reports* annual auto issue provides very valuable information for anyone purchasing either a used vehicle or new vehicle. The reports can also give you some idea of the maintenance costs you might expect in the future. Next, you will need to do some research to determine the market value of the vehicles of your choice. A good starting point is your local newspaper—look in the want ads for the make/model/year of your choice and note the asking price and mileage for the vehicles. Compare that to other references on used car prices. For a small fee, *Consumer Reports* New and Used Car Price Service will help to evaluate the value of veteran vehicles—call 800-258-0327 or visit their website at www.ConsumerReports.org.

Free pricing information is available at the Kelly Blue Book website, www.kbb.com. Kelly Blue Book has "used car retail value" if you plan to buy from a dealer and also "private party" value if you plan to buy from another consumer—this is typically much lower because the price does not include a dealer markup. Also, check Intellichoice at www.intellichoice.com for information concerning equipment, the original list price of the vehicle, the wholesale value, and the retail value. Another resource is Edmunds at www.edmunds.com, which provides consumer ratings of used cars, both used and new car pricing guides, and even helps to locate used vehicles in your area. Your local library and bookstore will provide publications and books that give information on used and new vehicles—ask for books such as *Edmunds' Used Cars & Trucks Buyer's Guide* and *Edmunds' New Cars & Trucks Buyer's Guide*. Another website that contains consumer-

Vehicles

based ratings and awards for autos, boats, homes, finance, travel, telecom, and more is www.jdpower.com (J.D. Power and Associates).

Once you have completed your research, you are ready to seek out vehicles that suit your needs. Individual sellers will often give you the best deal on vehicles since there is not a dealer markup and overhead figured into the price. Of course, normally there is no guarantee on the vehicle from an individual seller—purchase only from individuals you trust. Franchised new car dealers might sell used vehicles—usually, they will retain only the best trade-ins for resale and might have a used car warranty. If you use an independent dealer, select one that has been in business for some time. Check the Better Business Bureau for the complaint record if purchasing through a dealer. Check local newspapers and use the Internet to begin locating vehicles to look at in person. Numerous online services can help you locate vehicles to purchase (or sell) such as www.Autobytel.com, www.autos.msn.com, www.Autosite.com, www.AutoTrader.com, www.Autoweb.com, www.Carprices.com, www.Cars.com, www.CarsDirect.com, www.edmunds.com, and www.iMotors.com. Vehicle auctions advertised in your local newspaper might also be an option.

Very few states have effective "lemon laws" to protect consumers from dealers who sell faulty used vehicles. "Caveat emptor"—let the buyer beware—is especially important when purchasing a vehicle. Information is the best defense against purchasing defective products. After researching the vehicle, a thorough inspection by yourself and then a professional mechanic is critical before you make an offer to buy the vehicle. Take a friend with you on the initial inspection of the vehicle. Visually sight along each side of the vehicle and look for any misaligned body panels, waves in the paneling, or

Vehicles

differences in paint shades—all of which can indicate that the vehicle has been in an accident. If you suspect bodywork has been done on the vehicle, use a small magnet to detect bondo or putty work, which can hide repairs. Ask the owner if the vehicle has ever been in an accident. Dealers who represent the manufacturer of the vehicle can run a copy of the repair history for warranty work completed on a used vehicle and might be willing to share a copy of it with you. Uneven tread wear on the tires could be a result of poor alignment or more serious suspension problems. Shake the top of each tire—if there is play or a clunking sound, it might indicate loose or worn bearings or suspension joints. Push down on each corner of the vehicle and then let go—the vehicle should rise and then settle back to its original position. If it bounces, the struts or shock absorbers need replacing. Check the vehicle for rust—especially around the doors and wheel openings. While the vehicle is turned off on level ground, with the automatic transmission in park (or the straight gear in first or reverse gear), the emergency brake on, and the wheels chocked with blocks to prevent rolling, check under the vehicle—make sure the chassis is straight; if it is not, look elsewhere for a vehicle. Chassis rust is also a major concern. Fresh undercoating can be a sign that the seller is hiding some serious problems. Oil and coolant leaks or stains on the vehicle or ground underneath indicate serious problems. Check the radiator coolant while the engine is cold—it should not be rusty. Check the engine oil. People driving new cars off the lot that did not contain the proper fluid levels destroyed engines. Check all engine belts. Check the safety belts. Unlock the steering wheel before turning on the engine and turn the wheel to check to see that it does not have much free play. Turn on the engine and check to make sure the "check engine light" comes on—if it does not, the seller might have disconnected it to hide an emissions

Vehicles

control problem. To check leaks in the brake system, pump the breaks a few times and then press firmly on the brake pedal for 30 seconds—the pedal should not sink to the floor. Warm the engine and check the transmission fluid—it should be cherry red in color without any metal particles and should not smell burned. In addition, the transmission fluid should not have bubbles on it—indicating that the transmission is burning fluid. Turn on every control and display to make sure they are working properly. Your friend can help you check headlights, taillights, turn signals, and brake lights while you operate the controls from inside the vehicle. Inspect the interior of the vehicle and the trunk (if available) for carpeting stains and moldy smells that likely will indicate a difficult-to-repair water leak.

If you are still interested in the vehicle, take it for a road test. Engine pings or knocks could either indicate the vehicle needs a higher octane fuel, or it could signal the need for costly repairs. While driving on a level, straight road, the vehicle should track straight without constant steering correction. A vehicle that constantly pulls to one side could indicate a body that is twisted from an accident or a wrapped chassis—a major problem. Have your friend stand behind the vehicle as you drive straight ahead, the front and rear wheels should line up. If the vehicle veers to one side, it could just require an alignment; however, if it scuttles sideways, it likely has a bent chassis and should not be purchased. The automatic transmission should shift smoothly and not slip while you are driving. On a vehicle with a manual transmission (i.e., one for which you must shift the gears manually), the transmission should not grind, and the clutch should engage smoothly. On a quiet street with no traffic or another secluded driving area, accelerate in low gear to 15 miles per hour, release the accelerator, allow the speed to drop to 5 miles per hour, and

Vehicles

then floor the accelerator. Have your friend look behind the vehicle to see if smoke comes from the tailpipe. Blue smoke indicates the engine is burning oil—a very serious problem. White smoke may also indicate serious engine problems and could indicate that water is entering the combustion chamber. Black smoke normally indicates that the fuel system needs adjusting. It is normal for an engine to have a few puffs of smoke when starting on a cool damp day. In a safe area, at 45 miles per hour, step on the brakes sharply—the car should stop quickly in a straight line without pulling to one side or the other. You should road test the vehicle at all normal driving speeds. If you are still interested in purchasing the vehicle, check the model's safety recalls (or report safety concerns) at the U.S. Department of Transportation's DLT Auto Safety Hot Line at 800-424-9393 or visit the National Highway Traffic Safety Administration website at www.nhtsa.dot.gov. You can obtain other safety-related information at the Center for Auto Safety website at www.autosafety.org or Phil Edmonston's Lemon-Aid Car Guide at www.lemonaidcars.com. For a small fee of around $15 to $20, CARFAX Vehicle History Reports will check a vehicle's history for hidden problems such as odometer rollback, salvage damage, and so on. The website for CARFAX is www.carfax.com—you will need the vehicle's identification number (VIN), which is normally located on the dash on the driver's side of the vehicle and the driver's side door frame.

If you are still interested in purchasing the vehicle, it's time to take the vehicle to your own professional mechanic for examination. Word of mouth is a good way to get a reliable independent mechanic. You can check the name of independent shops against a list of AAA-approved facilities at www.aaa.com. Also, call your local Better Business Bureau to check complaints. Your mechanic should double-check all of the items you've

Vehicles

previously inspected plus conduct diagnostic tests to determine if there are any problems with the vehicle such as engine compression. Get a list of any needed repairs and an estimate to fix them. The older the car, the more important it is to conduct thorough inspections. Doing your research and inspections not only gives you peace of mind, but also can save you thousands of dollars in costly repairs.

Obviously, you want to negotiate the lowest sales price for the vehicle that you can get—having several acceptable alternative vehicles available gives you leverage when negotiating. It's a good idea to take a friend along who is skilled in negotiations when making an offer on a vehicle—sometimes the buyer becomes too emotional during the process to objectively negotiate the best deal possible. If possible, pay cash for the vehicle to avoid interest charges—automobile interest charges are not deductible for tax purposes. If you cannot pay cash for the vehicle, put as much money down as possible and then finance the remainder. Borrow as little money as possible, at the lowest interest rate possible, and for as short a term as possible. The longer you take to pay off the loan, the more it is going to cost you. Used car interest rates typically run higher than new car loans. Usually, your bank, thrift, or credit union will give you a lower interest rate than an auto dealer—although not usually lower than the special rates some carmakers might sometimes offer. Some financial institutions may be willing to negotiate on their interest rates—you won't know unless you ask. Check www.bankrate.com to compare auto loan interest rates in your area. Use the SS14 Calculator-Loan Payment.xls to compare your different loan options. Select the loan that costs the least in "Total Interest on the Loan" amount.

Vehicles

How much can you realistically save by purchasing used vehicles versus new vehicles? Review the hypothetical example in Figure 28.1.

Figure 28.1

Vehicle Price	10% Down Payment	Amount Financed	36 Months (3 years) @ 7% Interest =	Total Cost (Down Payment + Finance Payments) =	If Repeated Every 3 years for 30 years (10 x) =
Used Vehicle Cost					
$10,000.00	$1,000.00	$9,000.00	$10,004.18	$11,004.18	$110,041.80
New Vehicle Cost					
$20,000.00	$2,000.00	$18,000.00	$20,008.36	$22,008.36	$220,083.60
				Amount Saved:	$110,041.80

In this example, there is $110,041.80 that could be saved and invested in your portfolio in potential appreciating assets such as stocks and bonds versus depreciating assets such as vehicles.

If you can afford it and you prefer to purchase new vehicles as opposed to the potential cost savings of purchasing used vehicles, the following are some suggestions that might help with your new vehicle purchases. Complete the same steps you would go through if you were purchasing a used vehicle. Decide on your needs. Then research 3 or 4 new vehicles that would suit those needs. Use an auto pricing service to determine what the dealer paid for the vehicle plus the cost of each option you would like to include on the vehicle. It is usually cheaper to purchase a package for extras versus buying options individually. Note—you may use the same tools listed in the previous section on used vehicles to conduct your research. Once you have added up the total cost of what the dealer paid for the vehicle and options, you might plan to offer around 5% to 10% above

Vehicles

that cost—of course, vehicles in great demand may command higher markups. Include any current rebates, factory-to-dealer incentives, or holdbacks in your cost basis—use reference sources such as the free vehicle and pricing information on the www.nadaguides.com website at www.nadaguides.com (special offers, incentives, and rebates) to determine if the manufacturer is giving the dealer any extra incentives to sell the vehicle. You can check new car reviews, incentives, and rebates at www.edmunds.com. For a small fee, *Consumer Reports* will fax or mail a report to you that includes manufacturer-to-dealer rebates—you'll need the make, model, trim line, and options of the vehicle—call 1-800-933-5555. Having 3 or 4 choices of different vehicles in mind helps to give you lower price alternatives.

Always negotiate from the dealer's cost up—not the dealer's sticker price down. The invoice price is the manufacturer's initial charge to the dealer—it is usually higher than the dealer's final cost since dealers often receive allowances, rebates, or incentive rewards from the manufacturer for selling the vehicles. The invoice price includes destination and delivery charges. The base price is the manufacturer's suggested price of the car that does not include options. The base price includes standard equipment, factory warranty, destination, and delivery charges. The base price almost always includes dealer preparation. The Monroney sticker price includes the base price, manufacturer installed options, destination, and delivery charges. Federal law requires that this sticker along with the vehicle's fuel economy be affixed to the vehicle's window. There may also be a supplemental sticker for the dealer sticker price that includes the Monroney sticker price plus the suggested price of any options installed by the dealer such as rust proofing, pin stripping, or upgraded options.

Vehicles

Dealers often try to increase their profit margins by charging for added extras or "packs" such as a "protection package"—rust proofing, undercoating, paint sealant, fabric finish, windshield etching, and so on—items that may add little or no value for the purchaser and generally are overpriced but are very profitable for the dealer. Sticker prices may even include charges for ADP, ADM, or AMV—abbreviations that stand for additional dealer profit, additional dealer markup, and additional market value—a charge added so the dealer can make even more profit. Some dealers even try to add an advertising surcharge. Other additional charges the dealer may try to get you to pay are document fees for processing the paperwork involved in selling and registering the vehicle and gas tank fill-up fees. Negotiating up from the dealer's cost plus options helps to avoid many of these nuisance fees.

Some dealers are now promoting "one price" or "no haggle prices"—the price on their vehicles is not negotiable. If you are considering using such a dealer, make certain you comparison shop their "no haggle" price with at least 3 or 4 competitors—you might find a better price elsewhere. For dealers that do negotiate on price—which is the majority of them—take a friend along to help keep emotions in check for the negotiation process. It helps to have an acceptable price range in mind that pays the dealer a reasonable profit without costing you unnecessary dollars. You must be prepared to walk out of the dealership if they are not willing to negotiate a "win for you" and a "win for them" sales

Vehicles

price. Dealer profit margins typically run from 4% to more than 16%. The following is a general guideline for beginning price negotiations[2]:

MSRP (Manufacturer's Suggested Retail Price)	A Fair Offer Price Over the Invoice Amount
Up to $25,000	$300 to $500 over invoice
$25,000 to $40,000	$500 to $1,000 over invoice
> $40,000	$2,000 to $3,000 over invoice

Remember, there are numerous dealers with whom you can negotiate a reasonable price. Once you have reached a sales price agreement, then and only then should you discuss a trade-in of your old vehicle or financing. Often, a dealer might trim his profit margin on the new vehicle and increase his profit margin on a trade-in to close a deal—in which case your homework and preparation for the sales price goes for naught. If you make a trade-in deal with the dealer, keep the transaction totally separate from the new vehicle purchase. In fact, in most cases, you are probably better off selling the trade-in vehicle yourself versus selling it to a dealer. Research the value of your trade-in using the same research resources mentioned earlier regarding used vehicles. Decide on a reasonable sales price and leave some room for negotiations. Put a "for sale" sign with the price and contact information on the vehicle—it's great free advertising while driving around your local area. When you do not need to use the vehicle, park it on the side of a safe, highly traveled roadway (or possibly a parking lot) where potential buyers will see it. You might consider advertising the vehicle in your local newspaper. Use the proceeds

---

[2] Of course, vehicles vary significantly in supply and demand—the shorter the supply and the higher the demand, the more you will have to pay.

Vehicles

from the sale of your old vehicle toward the cost of your new vehicle—it helps to cut down on interest charges. Or better yet, if you can afford to, pay cash for your new vehicle to avoid interest charges altogether. If you must finance the vehicle, never accept the dealer's financing without comparison shopping interest rates with your own bank, thrift, credit union, or even some auto insurance companies that might offer more favorable terms. Some lenders might attempt to sell you credit insurance that pays off the loan if you die or become disabled—the insurance is not mandatory for getting a loan. Carefully read any sales contract before signing it. The sales contract should have a provision that states that you get your deposit money back in case the dealer does not perform some part of the agreement—such as delivering the vehicle on a specific date. Have an officer of the dealership sign the contract—the signature of a salesman may not be binding.

Often, the dealership will try to sell you an extended warranty—sometimes referred to as a service contract or mechanical breakdown insurance. Typically, extended warranties are not worth the money unless the model has had an unreliable repair history—if that's the case, you should have eliminated the model from your consideration during your research phase. Most new cars have a 3- to 7-year warranty included in the purchase price anyway. An extended warranty might make sense if you would like the extra peace of mind and plan to keep the vehicle beyond the original warranty expiration date. If you get an extended warranty, try to get one from the manufacturer versus an independent insurance company. Manufacturer extended warranties are typically better, easier to understand in their limitations, and easier to make claims against. Ask the following questions before getting an extended warranty:

Vehicles

1. What is covered by the original warranty and what is covered by the extended warranty?
2. What are the time limitations of coverage of both warranties and/or any mileage restrictions?
3. Are there deductibles?
4. What repairs are covered?
5. Does the contract cover parts, labor, or both parts and labor?
6. Are you limited to making repairs at the dealership, or can you use an independent mechanic?
7. Does the extended warranty have a cancellation or refund policy?
8. Is the extended warranty transferable to someone else to whom you might choose to sell your?

Of course, as long as your vehicle is under warranty, take the vehicle to your dealer for any needed warranty repairs. If the repair is not covered under warranty, you might choose to get estimates from the dealer and independent mechanics (independent mechanics are normally less expensive)—routine maintenance costs can vary significantly. Maintain the manufacturer's suggested service schedule on your vehicle to avoid costly problems later on. Check the owner's manual and use the manufacturer's recommended oil, coolant, and gasoline octane levels—to buy more expensive products is unnecessary and a waste of money.

Leasing a vehicle is another option. If you are able to claim tax deductions for the business use of a vehicle, then leasing might provide larger financial tax advantages versus buying. Most people who lease enjoy driving the vehicle during the first few years of the vehicle's life—which is usually the most trouble- and repair-free period—and then turning the vehicle back in to the dealer and leasing another new vehicle. It is a nice advantage; however, it is an expensive one over the long term. Ask yourself if you are willing to always have a car payment in return for driving a new vehicle every 2 to 3

Vehicles

years. If you plan to keep the vehicle more than 3 years, you usually are better off buying it from the start.

Leasing normally makes less sense from a long-term financial perspective than either buying a used vehicle or purchasing a new one. However, if you prefer driving new vehicles and lack a substantial down payment, leasing usually provides lower monthly payments than you could afford by purchasing a new vehicle. While the monthly payment might be less than if you bought the vehicle outright since the leasing company will get the vehicle back upon lease termination (or possibly give you the opportunity to buy the vehicle), the automobile dealer might compute the monthly cost basis on the manufacturer's suggested retail price (MSRP), resulting in your paying top dollar for the lease—read the fine print in the lease carefully. Leasing therefore might be considered a short-term solution that actually costs you more in the long term. As a consumer, you should approach shopping for leases just like you would if you were purchasing a new vehicle—research the vehicles manufacturer's invoice price plus options less rebates and incentives. Negotiate your lease from that price upward, not from the sticker price down. Most automobile dealers deal with at least 4 different leasing companies, and the leasing agreements can vary dramatically. Negotiating the sales price of the vehicle is your most important consideration in the overall lease cost. Conduct all the other research you would use when purchasing a new vehicle—such as anticipated repairs—because you might want to purchase the vehicle at lease end. Leasing contracts vary widely in their requirements—the cost of leasing the same vehicle might vary by thousands of dollars from one lease company to another—reading the lease carefully and comparison shopping for lease terms is a must. Lease contracts might include charges for "excessive

Vehicles

wear and tear"—be certain the lease clearly defines what is included in excessive wear and tear—per mile charges for anything over a specified mileage allowance (e.g., typically $0.15 to $0.25/mile extra for any miles driven over 10,000 to 15,000 miles/year), and early termination fees that can sometimes cost thousands of dollars. Do not sign a lease for longer than you plan to keep the vehicle. Most lease agreements have terms of 24, 36, or 48 months—although sometimes you'll see leases with different terms such as 30, 39, or 42 months. Some leases might even require high down payments. Automobile manufacturer leases are usually cheaper than the ones offered by independent leasing companies.

Lease candidates should analyze their own driving habits first—how many miles per year do you typically drive? Choose a lease that closely matches your driving habits in terms of mileage. The more miles you drive over the lease agreement terms, the less likely you are to be a good lease candidate. Calculate the anticipated extra cost you might incur for extra miles driven over your lease agreement terms. Most lease companies allow you to boost your mileage limits at inception of the lease to lower charges per mile (e.g., $0.08 to $0.16). If you drive less than the lease terms, the under mileage amount will amount to an extra windfall to the leasing company when you turn your vehicle in because its resale value will be higher. Are you usually hard on vehicles—do you typically get a lot of dents, dings, scratches, and so on? If so, the extra repair cost will likely make you a poor lease candidate. If you typically keep your vehicle in mint condition, you are a more likely candidate for a lease. The lower the down payment you have available, the more likely you are to be a lease candidate.

Vehicles

Lease acquisition fees or assignment fees are charges for processing the lease agreement and are probably not negotiable. The acquisition fee might not be explicitly mentioned in your lease contract; however, it is included in your capitalization cost when calculating monthly payments. The fee is typically in the range of $250 to $800—if it is charged. Obviously, for the lessee, the lower the fee the better as high acquisition fees only add to the dealer's and leasing company's profit margin. If you do not see it in your lease contract, ask about it.

Disposition fees are sometimes charged at the end of the lease. Disposition fees are designed to compensate the leasing company for disposing of the vehicle—they might try to charge them even if you purchase the vehicle; in which case you should try to negotiate. If disposition fees are charged, they typically run in the $250 to $450 range.

The lease may give you the option to purchase the vehicle at the end of the lease. Pay close attention to what the lease sets as the residual value, or what the vehicle would be expected to sell for used. Equity is the end-of-lease value after depreciation has been subtracted from the vehicle's original value—it is the vehicle's resale value. Keep in mind that the lower the residual value, the higher the monthly payments; and, the higher the residual value, the lower the monthly payments. The leasing company sets the residual value of the lease vehicle at the beginning of the lease as their estimate of its worth at lease end—it is normally not negotiable; however, you can shop around for better residual values. In addition to the make, model, and year depreciation, the leasing company sets the residual value according to the term and mileage limits in the lease.

Insist that your lease specify a purchase-option price in the event you wish to purchase it at lease end. Keep in mind that leasing to buy is almost always more costly that just

Vehicles

buying outright. If you decide you're interested in purchasing the vehicle, conduct the same research you would use when purchasing a used vehicle as outlined earlier. Determine the wholesale and retail values of the vehicle and compare that to your end-of-lease purchase option price. Comparison shop other places for prices on the same make and model—you might find a more competitive price elsewhere. Most lease agreements are closed-ended, which means you have no obligation to purchase the vehicle at the end of the lease or to make up any shortfall in residual value. Avoid open-ended leases, which require the lessee to make up any depreciation difference between the worth of the vehicle at lease end and the residual value.

Avoid leases that require substantial security deposits or up-front monies. Avoid leases that have short mileage terms that are below your typical yearly driving habits. Avoid leases that require mandatory insurance or costly low deductibles on your own insurance. Typical lease insurance requirements are as follows:

- Bodily injury—not less than $100,000 single person injuries/$300,000 multiple people injuries
- Property damage—not less than $50,000
- Combined bodily injury/property damage—not less than $500,000/accident
- Deductibles—not more than $1000 for either comprehensive or collision insurance

Gap insurance covers additional losses beyond your normal automobile insurance coverage—for example, your normal auto insurance might cover the actual cash value of the vehicle if it is totaled or destroyed in an accident; gap insurance would cover what is owed on the lease including possible termination fees. In other words, gap insurance covers the difference or gap between the cash value of the vehicle and what is owed on the lease. Some lease companies include gap insurance for free; others might charge a

Vehicles

couple of hundred dollars for the insurance for the duration of the lease. Gap insurance could be critical for you in the event the vehicle is totaled early in the lease. It is usually best to refuse the leasing company's disability insurance that covers payments in case you become disabled—it is typically overpriced and difficult to collect on. Normally you can get a better deal by purchasing your own disability insurance.

Try to avoid leases with end-of-lease termination fees. Some leases require consumers who terminate their lease agreement early to make up any difference between the vehicle's current value and the amount paid to that point. Some leases might require the consumer to pay all of the remaining payments when terminating a lease early. Avoid leases that are longer than the vehicle's warranty time frame—otherwise, you could end up paying hefty out-of-warranty repair bills on a vehicle you do not even own.

At least 2 months before financing or leasing a vehicle—which allows time for taking corrective action—check your credit rating with the 3 major credit-reporting agencies (Equifax, Experian, and TransUnion); note instructions in Chapter 4, "Debt Management." Fix errors and correct outstanding issues before applying for a loan. Lease finance companies typically run credit checks on their customers and save their best terms for those with unblemished credit records. Leasing companies often charge security deposits. Security deposits are returned to the lessee at lease end less any disposition or damage charges. Security deposits are normally about the same amount or sometimes a little more than a monthly payment. If you have a spotless credit rating, the leasing company might waive the security deposit.

The MSRP is the manufacturer's suggested retail price of the vehicle. The capitalized cost or cap cost is in essence the purchase price of the vehicle. When you lease a vehicle,

Vehicles

the dealer sells that vehicle to the leasing company for the cap cost, and the leasing company in turn leases the vehicle to the lessee. The capitalized cost reduction or cap cost reduction is the money you pay up front that is applied to the final purchase price—for example, a cash down payment or trade-in. Dealers and manufacturers might offer a rebate that reduces the cap cost—which lowers your total out-of-pocket dollars. The adjusted cap cost is the cap cost plus costs added to the lease minus the capitalized cost reduction.

Ask leasing companies what their lease rate or "money factor" is—the money factor is a number that is calculated into the monthly payments of the lease vehicle to include finance charges. The money factor is the cost of money similar to an interest rate. Money factors are used almost exclusively in vehicle leases. You can convert the money factor into the equivalent interest rate by multiplying it by 2,400—for example, a money factor of .003 x 2,400 = a 7.2% interest rate; a money factor of .004 x 2,400 = 9.6% interest. Conversely, if you do not know the money factor but you know the interest rate, you can divide 7.2% by 2,400 = a .003 money factor. Sometimes dealers will quote money factors as .3 or .4 to make them seem larger—if they do, you simply multiply them by 24 instead of 2,400 to get the interest rate—e.g., .3 x 24 = 7.2% and .4 x 24 = 9.6%. As you can see, seemingly small differences in the money factor number can have significant differences in the amount of finance charges. The money factor is not usually spelled out in the lease agreement. The lease agreement must disclose the total finance charge—called the "rent charge" or "lease charge." Do not deal with dealers who are unwilling to tell you their money factor—it has a huge impact on how much your lease will cost. The leasing company that deals with your auto dealer typically sets the money factor, down payment,

Vehicles

residual value, security deposit, and acquisition fees—the auto dealer acts only as an agent. These items typically are not as negotiable as the sales price of the vehicle, although sometimes the auto dealer can influence the leasing company to negotiate on some items. The money factor formula is as follows:

Money Factor = (Rent Charge / # of months in lease) / (Sum of Adjusted Cap Cost + Residual Value)

For example:
($2,613 Rent Charge / 36 months) = 72.58333
($11,796 Adj. Cap Cost + $10,000 Residual Value) = $21,796
72.58333 / $21,796 = .003330122 Money Factor
Further, .003330122 x 2400 = 7.99% Interest Rate

Check rates from your bank, credit union, www.bankrate.com, and subvented lease offers, which are special deals from auto manufacturers typically offered through their subsidiary financial operations (they might include lower finance charges and manufacturer rebates). Lease agreements are available from numerous sources in addition to the ones available at your auto dealer. Just as you do not have to arrange your financing through an auto dealer for a car purchase, you do not have to arrange your lease agreement through the dealer. Talk to at least 3 different dealers to compare lease options.

The finance charges on lease payments are calculated differently than other loan payments. The lease companies want to include depreciation as part of the monthly payments, finance charges, and normal local sales taxes. The formula for lease payments is as follows:

Lease Payment per Month = Depreciation Fee + Finance Fee + Sales Tax as follows:

  Depreciation Fee per Month = (Adj. Cap Cost – Residual Value) / # of Months in Lease
  For example:
  Depreciation Fee per Month = ($11,796 Adj. Cap Cost - $10,000 Residual Value) = $1,796 / 36 months = $49.89/month.

Vehicles

Finance Fee per Month = (Adj. Cap Cost + Residual Value) x Money Factor
For example:
Finance Fee per Month = ($11, 796 Adj. Cap Cost + $10,000 Residual Value) = $21,796 x .003330122 Money Factor = $72.58
Note: this formula results in your paying finance charges on both the depreciation and the residual value by adding them together. The monthly finance fee will not show in your lease agreement—it will only show the "Finance (Rent) Charge." The Monthly Finance Fee = Rent Charge / # of Months in Lease. For example: $2,613 Rent Charge / 36 months in Lease = $72.58.

$49.89 Depreciation Fee per Month + $72.58 Finance Fee per Month = $122.47 Lease Payment per Month + Sales Tax

The most common method to calculate sales tax is as follows[3]:
Sales Tax = (Lease Payment per Month x (Local Sales Tax)) + Lease Payment per Month
For example:
($122.47 Lease Payment per Month x (6% Local Sales Tax) = $7.3482) + $122.47 = $129.82

Lease Payment per Month = $49.89 Depreciation Fee + $72.58 Finance Fee + $7.3482 Sales Tax = $129.82.

These calculations are computed for you in the SS34 Calculator-Lease Agreement.xls discussed later.

With a lease, monthly payments are made at the beginning of the month in which they are due—unlike other traditional loan payments, which are usually due at the end of the month. You will make your first lease payment when you sign the lease agreement.

The following websites should be useful to you when shopping for a lease:

1. www.alg.com—The Automotive Lease Guide contains insights on money factors, residual values, and more.
2. www.checkbook.org—The Consumer Checkbook website is a nonprofit consumer information and service resource that for several hundred dollars will research lease options for you.
3. www.intellichoice.com—The IntelliChoice website has information under their finance section on manufacturer's leases, a glossary of leasing terms, and other information.

---

[3] Sales tax methods of calculation can vary from state to state or region to region. Usually, sales taxes are taxed at the local sales tax rate. If you make a down payment on your lease vehicle, you will be charged state and local sales tax payable at the time you sign your lease agreement. The rest of the sales tax is charged on a month-by-month basis. Since sales tax is calculated monthly in this way, you pay less in taxes versus purchasing the vehicle outright.

Vehicles

4. www.leaseguide.com—The LeaseGuide has a list of leasing resources and is the "Consumer Car Leasing Guide."
5. www.leasecompare.com—The LeaseCompare website allows you to compare real lease payments from multiple lenders instantly.
6. www.leasesource.com—The LeaseSource is an online leasing resource.
7. www.leasewizard.com—This site helps you to prepare to negotiate your lease.

You can save money on end-of-lease repairs by having your vehicle inspected by your lease company one month or so prior to the lease expiration date, noting necessary repairs, going to several independent garages or body shops for estimates, and then completing the repairs with an acceptable bidder versus using the dealer that sold you the lease. At the end of your lease, if you turn your vehicle back in, get a signed, written vehicle inspection condition report to avoid having to pay for repairs on damages that might occur after you've returned the vehicle. Also, be certain to get any security deposit back. If you decide to purchase the vehicle, the auto dealer or leasing company might negotiate a price below the purchase-option price quoted in your lease. About 30% of new cars on the road today are lease vehicles, and the number is increasing.

You should verify the calculations of your lease agreement to detect any errors, which might result in overcharges to you. Open the SS34 Calculator-Lease Agreement.xls.

1. Open the "SS34 Calculator-Lease Agreement.xls"; see Figure 28.1.
2. Click "Yes" to enable macros, if necessary.

Figure 28.1

Vehicles

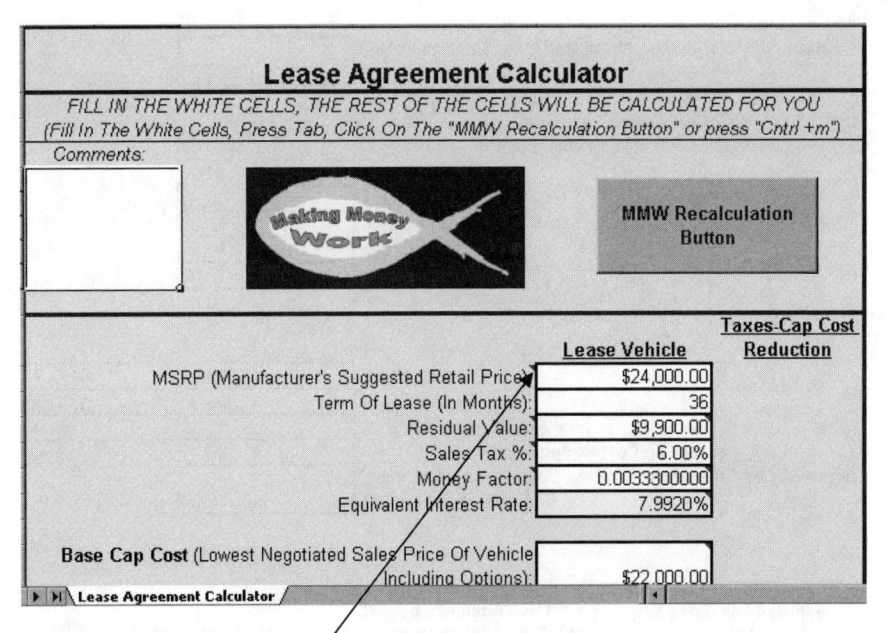

Lease Agreement Calculator

FILL IN THE WHITE CELLS, THE REST OF THE CELLS WILL BE CALCULATED FOR YOU
(Fill In The White Cells, Press Tab, Click On The "MMW Recalculation Button" or press "Cntrl +m")

Comments:

MMW Recalculation Button

	Lease Vehicle	Taxes-Cap Cost Reduction
MSRP (Manufacturer's Suggested Retail Price):	$24,000.00	
Term Of Lease (In Months):	36	
Residual Value:	$9,900.00	
Sales Tax %:	6.00%	
Money Factor:	0.0033300000	
Equivalent Interest Rate:	7.9920%	

Base Cap Cost (Lowest Negotiated Sales Price Of Vehicle Including Options): $22,000.00

\Lease Agreement Calculator/

Note: Important—place your mouse cursor on each of these comment boxes indicated by a small red triangle in the upper right corner of the cell for information about the calculator and numbers to be inputted.

- - -

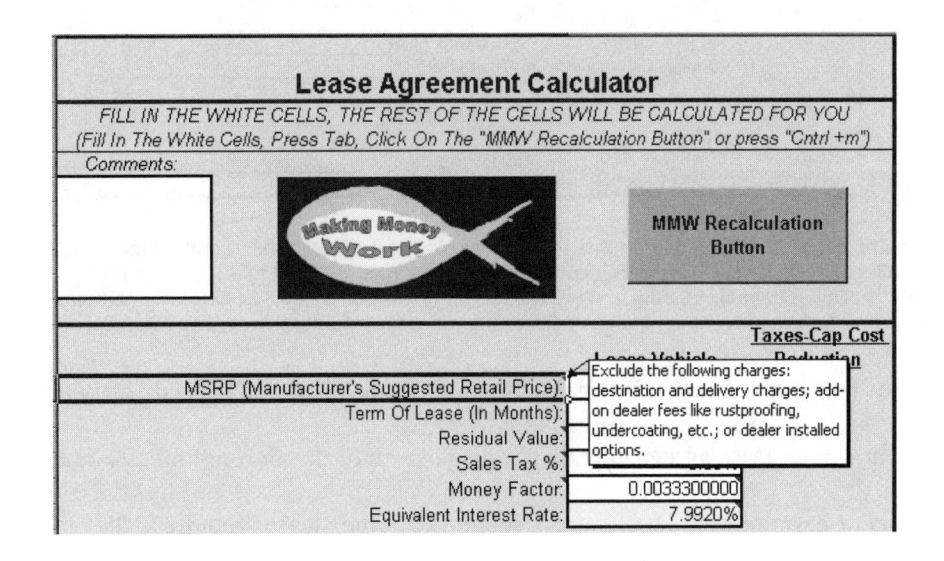

Lease Agreement Calculator

FILL IN THE WHITE CELLS, THE REST OF THE CELLS WILL BE CALCULATED FOR YOU
(Fill In The White Cells, Press Tab, Click On The "MMW Recalculation Button" or press "Cntrl +m")

Comments:

MMW Recalculation Button

	Lease Vehicle	Taxes-Cap Cost Reduction
MSRP (Manufacturer's Suggested Retail Price):	*Exclude the following charges: destination and delivery charges; add-on dealer fees like rustproofing, undercoating, etc.; or dealer installed options.*	
Term Of Lease (In Months):		
Residual Value:		
Sales Tax %:		
Money Factor:	0.0033300000	
Equivalent Interest Rate:	7.9920%	

- - -

Vehicles

Base Cap Cost (Lowest Negotiated Sales Price Of Vehicle Including Options):	$22,000.00	
Cost Added To Lease--		
"Acquisition Fees" or "Bank Fees":	$450.00	
Insurance:	$0.00	
Extended Warranty:	$0.00	
Outstanding Loan On Trade-In Or Lease:	$0.00	
Up-Front Tax Fees:	$0.00	
Other:	$0.00	
Total Costs Added To Lease:	$450.00	
Cap Cost Reductions--		
Down Payment:	$2,200.00	$132.00
Trade-In Value:	$5,000.00	$300.00
Other (Manufacturer Rebate, Incentive, etc.):	$0.00	$0.00
Total Cap Cost Reductions:	$7,200.00	
Adjusted Cap Cost ("Base Cap" + "Costs Added To Lease" - "Total Cap Cost Reductions"):	$15,250.00	

- - -

Adjusted Cap Cost ("Base Cap" + "Costs Added To Lease" - "Total Cap Cost Reductions"):	$15,250.00
Monthly Depreciation Fee:	$148.61
Monthly "Finance Fee" or "Rent Charge":	$83.75
Monthly Lease Payment (Depreciation Fee + Finance Fee):	$232.36
Monthly Sales Tax:	$13.94
Monthly Lease Payment (Depreciation Fee + Finance Fee + Sales Tax):	$246.30
Total Lease Depreciaiton Fee:	$5,350.00
Total Lease "Finance Fee" or "Rent Charge":	$3,014.98
Total Sales Tax:	$333.90
Total Of All Payments:	$8,866.88
Total Lease Cost:	$15,898.88

Note: The "Total of All Payments" in this lease example is $8,866.88. The "Total Lease Cost" is $15,898.88. (As noted in the comment box: "Total Lease Cost" = "Total Of All Payments" + "Down Payment" + "Down Payment Sales Tax" + "Trade-In" - "Trade-In Sales Tax Credit" + "Other (Manufacturer Rebate, Incentive, etc.)" + "Other (Manufacturer Rebate, Incentive, etc.) Sales Tax.")

Compare the numbers in this calculator with the ones disclosed in your lease agreement—note: lease agreements do not disclose all of the above numbers. The Federal Consumer Leasing Act Disclosures section of the lease requires the following information to be included in your lease:

- ✓ Residual Value
- ✓ Capitalized Cost (or Base Cap Cost)

Vehicles

- ✓ Lease Charges (or Total Costs Added to Lease)
- ✓ Capitalized Cost Reduction (or Total Cap Cost Reductions)
- ✓ Monthly Payments (or Monthly Lease Payment)
- ✓ Total of Payments (or Total of All Payments)

Compare each of these lease numbers to the ones you've calculated—if any do not match up, get an explanation from the dealer and **correct any errors before signing the lease**. Once you have signed the lease, it is too late. A word of caution: many lease contracts have errors in them.

In addition, the Federal Consumer Leasing Act Disclosures requires the following information to be included in your lease:

Amount due at signing
Other charges
How monthly payment is determined
Early termination statement
Wear and tear explanation

If there is a discrepancy with any numbers, get with your dealer for an explanation of what input numbers they used and how they calculated them. Correcting discrepancies or errors can save you a lot of money.

3. Now that you have reviewed the example, fill in your own personal information in each white cell (you may tab from one white cell to another).
4. After completing the information in all of the white cells, press "Tab" and then click on the "MMW Recalculation Button"—the spreadsheet will make the remaining calculations for you.

To summarize this section on vehicles, in essence, when considering transportation costs you are faced with several decisions—use public transportation and avoid a vehicle expense altogether, keep your old vehicle, buy a used or new vehicle, or possibly lease a vehicle. After filling in your personal information in the SS34 Calculator-Lease Agreement.xls, open the SS35 Calculator-Vehicle Keep, Buy, or Lease Comparison.xls.

1. Open the "SS35 Calculator-Vehicle Keep, Buy, or Lease Comparison.xls"; see Figure 28.2.
2. Click "Yes" to enable macros, if necessary.

Vehicles

Note: Important—place your mouse cursor on each comment box indicated by a small red triangle in the upper right corner of the cell for information about the calculator and numbers to be inputted.
Figure 28.2

Vehicle Keep, Buy, or Lease Comparison

FILL IN THE WHITE CELLS, THE REST OF THE CELLS WILL BE CALCULATED FOR YOU
(Fill In The White Cells, Press Tab, Click On The "MMW Recalculation Button" or press "Cntrl + m")

Comments:

MMW Recalculation Button

	Keep Old Vehicle	Buy A Used Or New Vehicle	Lease A Vehicle
Lowest Negotiated Sales Price Of Vehicle Including Options:		$22,000.00	$22,000.00
Sales Tax %:		6.00%	
Sales Tax:		$1,320.00	$333.90
Total Price With Sales Tax:		$23,320.00	$22,333.90
Plus Upfront Costs			
Processing Fees:		$80.00	
Other Fees:		$0.00	
Lease "Total Costs Added To Lease:			$450.00
"Total Gross Purchase Price":		$23,400.00	$22,783.90
Current Market Value Of Old Vehicle:	$5,000.00		

- - -

Current Market Value Of Old Vehicle:	$5,000.00		
Amount **Owed On** Old **Vehicle**:	$1,000.00		
Less Other Fees Owed On Old Vehicle:	$0.00		
Net Equity In Old Vehicle Available For Trade-In:	$4,000.00		
Minus Down Payment & Trade-In Value			
Down Payment:		$2,200.00	$2,200.00
Net Equity In Old Vehicle Available For Trade-In:		$4,000.00	$4,000.00
"Owed On Old Vehicle" And "Net Purchase Price On Buy Or Lease":	$1,000.00	$17,200.00	$16,583.90
Plus Finance Charges			
Amount Borrowed (Or Owned On Loan):	$1,000.00	$17,200.00	
Interest Rate Of Loan:	8.00%	8.00%	
Term (# Of Months) Of Loan:	12	60	36
Per Month Payment:	$86.99	$348.75	$246.30
Total Payments:	$1,043.86	$20,925.24	
Total Finance Charges, Or For A Lease--The Total "Rent Charge":	$43.86	$3,725.24	$3,014.98
Amounts Owed On Vehicles Plus Finance Charges Plus Sales Tax:	$1,043.86	$20,925.24	
Plus Other Costs Owed (Like Lease Termination Fees):	$0.00	$0.00	$0.00

Vehicles

Lease companies like to stress the lower monthly payment of leasing versus buying; however, you should be aware of all expenses before making a decision.

- - -

Plus Other costs owed (like lease termination fees):	$0.00	$0.00	$0.00
Minus Residual Value Of Vehicle At Term Of Deal			
Residual Value:	$900.00	$9,900.00	$9,900.00
Total Cost:	$143.86	$11,025.24	$9,698.88
Your Real Monthly Payment Excluding Operating Expenses:	$11.99	$183.75	$269.41
Plus Operating Expenses:			
Estimated Yearly Expense For--			
Yearly Vehicle Inspection Fees:	$30.00	$30.00	$30.00
Yearly Tag Fee:	$20.00	$20.00	$20.00
Yearly Ad Valorem Tax or Property	$80.00	$300.00	$300.00
Yearly Estimated Maintenance	$1,600.00	$800.00	$800.00
Yearly Insurance Costs:	$800.00	$1,800.00	$1,800.00
Other Yearly Estimated Expenses:	$0.00	$0.00	$0.00
Total Yearly Estimated Operating	$2,530.00	$2,950.00	$2,950.00
Per Month Estimated Operating Expenses:	$210.83	$245.83	$245.83
Your Real Monthly Payment Including Operating Expenses:	$222.82	$429.59	$515.25

Vehicle Keep, Buy, or Lease Cal

At the term of the considerations, these numbers are likely to be much closer to your real payments.

This worksheet is designed to help you become aware of some of the financial considerations when deciding whether to keep your existing vehicle, buy a used or new vehicle, or lease a vehicle. The calculator does not consider all financial implications—for example, if you must put down a security deposit in a lease, you could add the cost of the potential lost income from having that amount of money in your own investment account. In addition, if you have the discipline to take the difference between the monthly payment of buying your own vehicle (in this example: $348.75) and leasing (in this example: $246.30) and investing the money, the result increase in your net worth could

Vehicles

be factored into a lower total lease cost. For example: $348.75 - $246.30 = $102.45 x 12 months = $1,229.40; the future value of $1,229.40 invested at the end of the year each year for 3 years = $3,991.12.

3. After reviewing the example, fill in your own personal information in each white cell (you may tab from one white cell to another).
4. After completing the information in all of the white cells, press "Tab" and then click on the "MMW Recalculation Button"—the spreadsheet will make the remaining calculations for you.

In addition to the financial considerations, the decision depends on your own desires. If you are comfortable with your old vehicle and the maintenance costs are not more than the vehicle is worth, it may be better to keep driving it. If you can afford a new vehicle and prefer driving a new car, buying or leasing might suit your needs better. If you want to be able to pay off your vehicle and be payment free for a period of time and have lower long-term costs versus leasing, buying is probably better for you. If you prefer lower monthly payments in the short term, prefer driving a new vehicle that is always under warranty every 2 to 3 years, and do not mind paying more over the long term, then leasing might suit your needs.

We buy or lease vehicles for transportation. Jesus Christ never traveled more than 150 miles from home, and He walked almost everywhere He went. Yet Christ through the miracle of the resurrection prepared us for the longest journey of our lives by sacrificing His life as ransom for our sins so that those who choose to believe can travel through eternity with God. "*Jesus did many other miraculous signs in the presence of his disciples, which are not recorded in this book* [the Bible]. *But these are written that you may believe that Jesus is the Christ, the Son of God, and that by believing you may have life in his name*"—John 20:30–31 (New International Version).

College Expenses

Chapter 29

College Expenses

Investments in education typically pay back huge dividends. Benjamin Franklin once said, "An investment in knowledge always pays the best interest."[1]

Figure 29.1

Educational Level Attained	Lifetime Earnings[2]	% More Earned Over a Lifetime Versus the Average High School Nongraduate
High School 9th Grade to 12th Grade Nongraduate:	$608,810	—
High School Graduate:	$820,870	+ 134%
Bachelor's Degree From College:	$1,420,850	+ 233%
Master's Degree From College:	$1,618,970	+ 265%
Doctorate Degree From College:	$2,142,440	+ 351%
Professional Degree From College:	$3,012,530	+ 494%

In other words, investing in a law degree or some other professional degree from college will on average result in almost 5 times the lifetime earnings of someone who does not graduate from high school.

Figure 29.2

Educational Level Attained	Per Year Median Earnings[3]
Less Than 9th Grade:	$15,801
High School 9th Grade to 12th Grade Dropout:	$18,445
High School Graduate:	$24,656
Some College (but no degree):	$29,295
Associate Degree:	$31,536
Bachelor's Degree From College:	$40,939
Master's Degree From College:	$50,399
Doctorate Degree From College:	$66,002
Professional Degree From College:	$76,356

---

[1] Benjamin Franklin, www.llywelyn.net, Quotes and Quotes, *Benjamin Franklin Quotes*.
[2] Source: US Census Bureau information from 1997.
[3] Source: US Census Bureau 2001 information (www.census.gov).

College Expenses

The gap between educational attainment levels and earning power continues to widen every year. Obviously, over the long term, for most people it pays to stay in school and get as much education as possible.

Figure 29.3 What are the typical college costs?

Type of Educational Institution	Average Annual Tuition and Fees (2002 Through 2003 School Year)	Average Annual Room and Board (2002 Through 2003 School Year)[4]	Total Undergraduate Costs (2002 Through 2003 School Year)
4-Year Public School:	$3,900	$5,235	$9,135
4-Year Private School:	$15,639	$6,039	$21,678

Of course, these numbers are a snapshot in time and are constantly changing with year-to-year increases in college costs. An excellent website to search for a college that suits your needs is www.collegeboard.com. This website also gives you valuable information concerning specific colleges including entrance administrative contact information; annual college costs for living on campus, living at home, and commuting but not living at home; in-state tuition and fees; out-of-state tuition and fees; room and board costs; books and supplies costs; estimated personal expenses; transportation expenses; total costs for in-state students; total costs for out-of-state students; and more. It is also a great website to compare costs at different colleges.

---

[4] Source: Annual Survey of Colleges, the College Board, New York, NY.

College Expenses

Figure 29.4 How much have typical college costs been increasing?

Type of Educational Institution	10 Year % Increase (1987–1988 School Year Through the 2002–2003 School Year)[5]	Average Annual % Increase
4-Year Public School—		
Tuition and Fees:	37%	3.7%
Room and Board:	39%	3.9%
4-Year Private School—		
Tuition and Fees:	22%	2.2%
Room and Board:	19%	1.9%

You will need to make an educated guess of what your child's education costs will be when he or she enrolls in college. Open the SS36 Calculator-College Costs And Savings.xls.

1. Open the "SS36 Calculator-College Costs And Savings.xls"; see Figure 29.5.
2. Click "Yes" to enable macros, if necessary.

Figure 29.5 SS36 Calculator-College Costs and Savings Estimate

---

[5] Source: Annual Survey of Colleges, The College Board, New York, NY.

College Expenses

College Costs And Savings Estimate

FILL IN THE WHITE CELLS, THE REST OF THE CELLS WILL BE CALCULATED FOR YOU
(Fill In The White Cells, Press Tab, Click On The "MMW Recalculation Button" or press "Cntrl + m")

Comments:

MMW Recalculation Button

	Current Annual College Costs:	$10,000.00
	% Projected Increase In College Costs:	5.00%
	Number Of Years Before Student Begins College:	5.00
	Projected Number Of Years Attending College:	4.00
1	1st Year Projected Annual Costs Of College:	$12,762.82
2	2nd Year Projected Annual Costs Of College:	$13,400.96
3	3rd Year Projected Annual Costs Of College:	$14,071.00
4	4th Year Projected Annual Costs Of College:	$14,774.55
5	5th Year Projected Annual Costs Of College:	$0.00

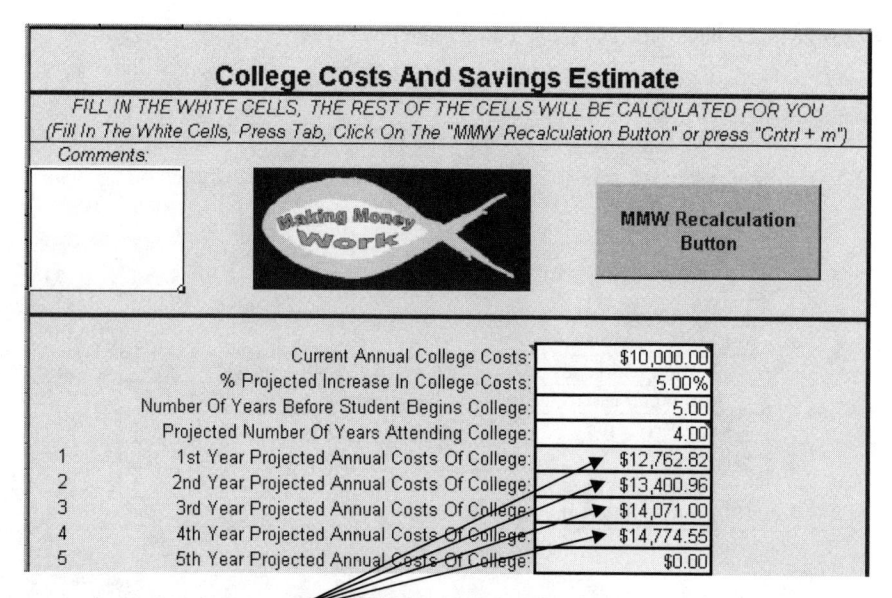

Note: The calculator estimates by year what your college costs will be.

- - -

6	6th Year Projected Annual Costs Of College:	$0.00
7	7th Year Projected Annual Costs Of College:	$0.00
8	8th Year Projected Annual Costs Of College:	$0.00
9	9th Year Projected Annual Costs Of College:	$0.00
10	10th Year Projected Annual Costs Of College:	$0.00
	Projected Future Total Costs Of College:	$55,009.33
	Current College Savings:	$10,000.00
	Estimated % Return On Investments For College Savings:	8.00%
	Projected College Savings Upon Entering College:	$14,693.28
	Projected Additional Amount Needed For College Costs:	$40,316.05
	Amount Needed To Be Saved Per Month To Cover Shortfall:	$817.46

Note: The calculator estimates the "Total Costs of College" and the "Projected Additional Amount Needed for College Costs."

3. After reviewing the example, fill in your own personal information in each white cell (you may tab from one white cell to another).
4. After completing the information in all of the white cells, press "Tab" and then click on the "MMW Recalculation Button"—the spreadsheet will make the remaining calculations for you.

Do not be dismayed at the amount needed to pay for college costs. Everyone willing to make the effort can afford an education. Regardless of your financial situation, there is financial aid assistance available for those experiencing funding shortfalls. Most families

College Expenses

pay the costs of college bills with a combination of savings, current income, loans, grants, scholarships, work-study jobs, and employer assistance where companies pay the costs of courses for employees. Around 66% of public college students receive financial aid, and around 80% of students at private colleges receive financial aid. About 60% of the financial aid comes in the form of loans, which graduates must repay. About 40% of financial aid comes in the form of grants, which do not have to be repaid. There is more than $90 billion available in aid—most federal aid is based on financial need and does not take grade point averages into consideration.

Ideally, parents should begin college savings accounts for their children as soon as they are born. You should plan to pay at least 50% to 66% of the student's education expenses through a combination of savings, current income, and loans. When you set up a taxable savings account in your child's name, the investment income is taxed at the child's rate (e.g., 15%) versus the usually higher parent's rate (e.g., 28%). Another advantage is that you may choose any type of investment vehicle you would like—such as stocks, bonds, mutual funds, CDs, and so on. While the lower tax rate is an advantage, putting your children's college funds in their names has some disadvantages. Once children turn legal age at 18, 19, or 21 (depending on the state in which you live), they have access to the funds and could spend the money on anything they want other than education—such as a vacation to Europe. Another disadvantage might come if you apply for financial aid from your educational institution. The aid eligibility formulas require students to use as much as 35% of their assets each year to pay college expenses versus 6% for parents. By keeping college savings accounts in the parents' names, you may qualify for more financial assistance.

College Expenses

The government has several college savings programs in place to encourage educational savings with tax advantages. The Coverdell Education Savings Account (CESA) allows annual nondeductible contributions to a specially designated investment trust account—somewhat similar to the way Roth IRAs work. The account grows free of federal income taxes, and if rules are met, the withdrawals are also tax-free. In addition, most states follow federal tax treatment of Coverdell education savings accounts. The Coverdell Education Savings Account allows up to $2,000 per year to be placed into each child's Coverdell account (the beneficiary must be under age 18 at the time of contribution). Contributions that exceed per-year limits are subject to a 6% excise penalty tax. There are some income restrictions on people making the contributions.

Figure 29.6 Coverdell Education Savings Account Contribution Limitations (CESA)[6]

Allowable Contribution	CESA Single Tax Filers	Joint (Married) Tax Filers
Full Contribution at AGI	$95,000	$190,000
Partial Contribution Phaseout Begins at	$95,001	$190,001
No Contribution at AGI of	$110,000	$220,000

Your contribution goes into an account with a financial institution and will eventually be given to your child if it is not <u>used for elementary, secondary, or after high school education expenses</u>—the assets in the account are considered to belong to the student. The account owner may choose whether the student or account owner has control of the account once the student becomes legal age (e.g., 18 years of age in most states). Any bank, mutual fund company, or any other financial institution can serve as custodian of Coverdell ESAs if it serves as custodian of IRAs.

---

[6] As of 2003. TIAA-Cref Funds, Coverdell Education Savings Account Disclosure Statement and Custodial Account Agreement, page 3, www.tiaa-cref.org/prospectuses/coverdell, 2004.

College Expenses

In a Coverdell ESA, you can pick any investments you wish. The account must be fully withdrawn by the time the beneficiary reaches age 30, or there are taxes and penalties. Part of the Coverdell education savings account withdrawal can become taxable—it is reduced by tuition you use to claim the "Hope" or "Lifetime Learning" credit. For more information concerning Coverdell ESAs, visit www.Savingforcollege.com.

Every state now has a version of 529 College Savings Plans, or qualified tuition programs—they are named for a section of the federal tax law making them possible. There are 2 types of plans (all states currently offer one plan or the other or both plans):

1. Prepaid tuition plans pay future tuition and fees at today's dollars. Parents, grandparents, or a family friend can establish a plan in a student's name to lock in future course units at today's prices and fund the plan with periodic investments or a lump sum. These plans guarantee that the money you save for college expenses will keep pace with all the tuition increases at the state's public colleges and universities until your child is ready to enroll. There are 2 main types of prepaid tuition plans:

    a. Prepaid units sell units of coursework representing a fixed percentage of tuition.

    b. A contract plan is an agreement on a specific number of years of tuition, mandatory fees, and/or room and board expenses.

    The purchase price depends on the future student's age, number of units or years purchased, and the payment plan—periodic payments or lump sum. Most of these plans greatly limit the choices of schools your child can attend.

College Expenses

The plans also greatly curtail your eligibility for other financial aid. The plans are typically a poor deal that locks you into one state's educational institutions.

2. College savings plans allow contributions to an account, which the student can use for educational expenses. Mutual funds are the most common investment account for these plans. Each state that has a plan typically offers more than one investment option. The plans usually include a portfolio of stocks and bonds for which the percentage of asset allocations changes to become more conservative as the student ages, fixed shares of stocks and bonds, or possibly individual portfolios with varying investment alternatives.

The 529 Plan earnings and withdrawals are free from federal taxes when used to pay educational expenses <u>after high school</u>.[7] Parents, grandparents, relatives, friends, or even organizations can open up 529 Plans for students. Monies from 529 Plans can be used to pay the following post-high-school educational expenses: room and board, tuition, books and supplies. Some states may also offer additional income tax deductions for contributions to the accounts—state treatment of contributions, earnings, and withdrawals varies. Each state sets its own contribution limits under federal regulations. The 529 Plans are popular because they allow large sums to be saved for educational expenses. These plans have no income eligibility requirements, and they typically offer mutual funds from which you can choose to invest. Many 529 Plans have funds that are composed of stocks, bonds, and cash equivalent investments—the mix of the investments

---

[7] Through 2011, unless renewed by Congress.

College Expenses

becomes more conservative as the student gets older in order to protect the assets. The 529 Plans have proved to be popular because they provide a way to save large amounts of money to pay college expenses while receiving tax breaks on investment gains. Some parents move from one state to another and wish to transfer funds to the other state's 529 Plan—several states have imposed taxes on such moves. No two 529 Plans are exactly alike. Compare alternatives when selecting plans—look at loads, expense ratios, investment results, restrictions on withdrawals, rollovers, and any restrictions on the beneficiary's age or residency. Research the plans like you would before purchasing mutual fund shares. For more information concerning 529 Plans, including investment costs and performance, visit www.Savingforcollege.com. Also visit www.collegesavings.org for links to your state's plans and other information. You can contribute funds to both Coverdell ESAs and 529 Plans. You can move funds from Coverdell ESAs to 529 Plans; however, to move funds from a 529 Plan to a Coverdell ESA, you must sell the shares, pay any taxes that are due, and then put the funds into the CESA.

For those students requiring financial assistance in attending college, there are numerous sources of aid. Schools most often compute what your family can afford to contribute toward the student's education based on total household income. Most public universities do not consider home equity or retirement accounts when considering the family contribution. High-income families can expect to pay the full cost of the student's education—regardless of savings. The expected family contribution (EFC) is the amount of money the school will expect the family to contribute toward the costs of tuition, fees, and room and board. The EFC is in essence the amount the family should be able to pay

College Expenses

toward education expenses. The EFC takes into consideration the family's income, assets, and overall financial circumstances. The Federal Student Aid website at www.studentaid.ed.gov has worksheets listed under "publications" that calculate the expected family contribution (or telephone 1-800-433-3243 to receive by mail).

Each college that offers the student admission will send a financial aid award letter—providing the student has completed the necessary financial aid paperwork. One of the first steps is to complete the "Free Application for Federal Student Aid" (FAFSA). The FAFSA is the form used to apply for federal Title IV financial assistance. Most schools and states also use the FAFSA form to award assistance from their local student aid programs. The FAFSA must be completed annually—suggestion: complete it as soon after January 1 as possible—financial assistance is on a first come, first served basis. The FAFSA requires information concerning family income, taxes paid in the prior year, assets, family size, number of family members attending college, and so on. Your tax records will be audited to verify the accuracy of the information completed on the FAFSA. You can get a FAFSA form from your school or you can complete an online FAFSA form at www.fafsa.ed.gov. The FAFSA form is used to generate a Student Aid Report (SAR) and the EFC is calculated. The EFC calculation can vary from school to school; however, all schools use a federally approved formula. Some schools may use an institutional formula. Each college has its own deadline for completing financial aid applications—visit www.finaid.org for links to postsecondary school financial aid office contact information and other valuable information concerning student aid. The student may qualify for as much financial assistance as is needed to close the gap between your family's EFC and the total cost of attending the school. Ask your school how they

College Expenses

determine your financial need. More expensive schools typically have a greater availability of funds to close the financial gap.

The U.S. Department of Education has a lot of valuable information at www.ed.gov. Also, be certain to get a copy of "The Student Guide—Financial Aid from the U.S. Department of Education" at http://studentaid.ed.gov/students/publications/student_guide/index.html. The U.S. Department of Education has the following student financial aid (SFA) programs:

1. Federal Pell Grants: Grants are monies you do not have to repay. Federal Pell Grants are available only to undergraduate students who have yet to earn a bachelor's or professional degree. These monies are not available to graduate students.

2. Federal Direct Student Loans (Direct Loans): Loans are monies you borrow that are repaid with interest charges. These are low interest loans available to students and parents and are lent by the U.S. Department of Education. Direct loans offer the following:

   a. Direct Stafford Loans (Direct Subsidized): Subsidized loans are awarded based on financial need, and the federal government pays interest (or subsidizes) the loan until you begin repayment.
   b. Direct Unsubsidized Stafford Loans (Direct Unsubsidized): Unsubsidized loans are not awarded based on financial need. Interest charges begin when the loan is disbursed and continue until the loan is paid in full.

3. Federal Family Education Loans (FFEL): These are low interest loans available to both students and parents that are lent by private lenders such as banks, credit unions, and savings and loan associations. You cannot receive both direct loans and FFEL loans for the same enrollment period.

   a. Subsidized Stafford Loans
   b. Unsubsidized Stafford Loans

College Expenses

To locate a lender, contact your state's guaranty agency. You may telephone the Federal Student Aid Information Center at 1-800-433-3243 for contact information on the guaranty agency that serves your state. The interest rate on direct loans and FFEL loans is variable (it is adjusted each year on July 1) with a maximum ceiling rate.

4. Direct Program Loans for Parents (Direct PLUS Loans): These loans allow parents to borrow for dependent undergraduate students who are enrolled at least half time. Get an application from your school's financial aid office. The loans are made by the U.S. Department of Education.

5. Federal PLUS Loans (FFEL PLUS Loans): FEEL PLUS loans allow parents to borrow for dependent undergraduate students who are enrolled at least half time. These loans do not require evaluation of your financial need. You cannot apply for both direct PLUS loans and federal PLUS loans for the same child during the same enrollment period. The interest rate on PLUS loans is variable and adjusted each year on July 1 with a maximum ceiling rate. Contact your state's guaranty agency to find a lender.

6. Direct Consolidation Loans: These loans consolidate all federal student loans so the borrower can make only one payment per month. Most federal student loans and PLUS loans can be consolidated. There are 3 types of direct consolidation loans:

    a. Direct Subsidized Consolidation Loans
    b. Direct Unsubsidized Consolidation Loans
    c. Direct Plus Consolidation Loans

    The interest rate is variable with a maximum ceiling.

College Expenses

7. FFEL Consolidation Loans: FEEL consolidation loans consolidate several types of federal student loans with varying repayment schedules into one loan with one monthly payment. FFEL consolidation loans are available through lenders such as banks, credit unions, and savings and loan associations. There are 2 types of FFEL consolidation loans:

   a. Subsidized
   b. Unsubsidized

   The interest rate charged on FFEL consolidation loans will be the weighted average of the all the loans being consolidated.

8. Federal Supplemental Educational Opportunity Grants (FSEOG): These monies are not available to graduate students. These funds are for undergraduate students with exceptional financial needs. FSEOGs do not have to be paid back. This campus-based program is administered by the participating school's financial aid office.

9. Federal Work-Study (FWS): These programs allow undergraduate and graduate students to work and earn money while attending school to help pay for education expenses. This campus-based program is administered by the participating school's financial aid office. The FWS salary will be at least the federal minimum wage.

10. Federal Perkins Loans: This campus-based program is administered by the participating school's financial aid office and offers low interest loans for both undergraduate and graduate students with exceptional financial need. Your school is the lender, and the government supplies the funds.

Visit the www.nelliemae.org website for information concerning loans for parents, undergraduates, graduates, and professional students. The site also has information on

College Expenses

current interest rates on loans. Many of the loans are the prime rate + 1% or lower. You can also apply for loans at www.salliemae.com.

Campus-based program aid for FSFEOG, FWS, and federal Perkins loans depends on your financial need, the amount of aid you are receiving, and the availability of funds at the school. When the funding is gone for that school year, no more funds are available until the following year—suggestion: check with the school, which sets its own deadlines for applications, and apply early.

In addition to federal programs, you can check out state and local programs such as the following:

1. State Student Incentive Grant Program (SSIG): This program is jointly funded by the U.S. Department of Education and individual states. The individual state might have its own name for this program. Individual states set their own eligibility criteria and amounts and determine their own application process for this program.

2. Companies often have assistance for employees' education expenses.

3. Community organizations, civic groups, religious organizations, clubs, professional groups, and other groups often have educational aid.

4. Your Veterans Affairs office might have assistance if you are a veteran or dependent of a veteran.

5. Scholarships: Visit www.fastweb.com and www.salliemae.com for information concerning scholarships.

6. Check with your high school guidance counselor concerning student aid.

7. Your local public library should be an excellent source of information on state and local sources of educational aid.

College Expenses

The following is a time guideline to help in your preparation for post-high-school education:

Age/Grade Level	Post-High-School Education Preparation Suggestions
Birth	Start an education savings plan. Make systematic contributions to the plan from the beginning until the student begins his or her post-high-school education.
1st–8th Grades	Take challenging courses in anticipation of the high school classes that will best prepare the student for his or her post-high-school education. Work on test taking skills and developing strong study skills.
9th Grade	Determine the student's possible career interests and determine the type of education required to gain employment in career preferences. Talk to your high school guidance counselor concerning an outline of high school courses to take in preparation for career choices. Take challenging courses. Get involved with school extracurricular activities and community activities—colleges prefer well-rounded students.
10th Grade	Take the Preliminary Scholastic Assessment Test (PSAT) and/or the National Merit Scholastic Qualifying Test. Visit possible post-high-school education schools and stop by their financial aid offices to discuss applications, paperwork, deadline dates, etc.
11th Grade	Narrow the list of post-high-school educational institutions to the student's top choices. Obtain admission forms, financial aid applications, and any scholarship forms. Explore financial aid from federal, state, and private sources. Your high school counselor should be able to help with state and local sources. The U.S. Department of Education can help with federal sources. Take the Scholastic Assessment Test (SAT) and/or the American College Test (ACT).
12th Grade	Meet with your high school guidance counselor early in the year to discuss post-high-school educational plans. Complete at least one federal financial aid form (e.g., FAFSA) and any other necessary financial aid forms. Submit applications to several colleges for admission, scholarships, and financial aid, paying close attention to all deadline dates. Apply to several institutions in case application to the top one or two choices results in rejection.

"*We all 'have knowledge,' as you say. This 'knowledge' breeds conceit; it is love that builds. If anyone fancies that he knows, he knows nothing yet, in the sense of knowing. But if a man loves, he is acknowledged by God*"—1 Corinthians 8:1–3. "*Do not be conformed to this world but be transformed by the renewal of your mind, that you may prove what is the will of God, what is good and acceptable and perfect*"—Romans 12:2 (Revised Standard Version). "*Happy* [is] *he who has found wisdom, and the man who has acquired understanding; for wisdom is more profitable than silver, and the gain she brings is better than gold*"—Proverbs 3:13–14.

Weddings

Chapter 30
Weddings

More marriages collapse over financial problems than for any other reason. It is important to discuss any preexisting debt before your marriage. Any significant debt issues including the amounts, monthly payments, due dates, interest rates, and so on, should be fully disclosed to and by your future spouse. As with all your financial dealings, it is best to be truthful up front. Not disclosing your debt issues before the wedding can severely damage the trust factor in your marriage. The best solution is for each person to pay off his or her debt before the wedding. If that is not possible, then you will have to decide as a couple who will be responsible for the debt once you are married. Will the debt be the sole responsibility of the spouse that incurred the debt, or will the married couple pay off the debt jointly? Many financial planners recommend a prenuptial agreement, which determines how the debts will be handled. Creditors can use a premarital pack to determine whether to target one spouse or both in pursuing debt collection.

Equally important as discussing preexisting debt problems before the marriage is discussing how the debts were incurred. For example, legitimate reasons for excessive debt might include educational expenses, unexpected medical expenses, parental support, and so on. If the debt was incurred through lack of financial discipline and impulsive spending on nonessential items, it likely will indicate a continuation of the same spending behavior after the marriage.

Weddings

In addition to preexisting debt issues, a couple should have serious discussions on how they will manage their finances once they are married and become one economic unit. Ask yourselves which accounts will need to be closed, which accounts will need to be opened, will the accounts be owned jointly or separately, who will pay the bills, and so on.

Next, the couple should begin discussions on the wedding and agree on wedding costs. Suggestion: do not start your married life together under the burden of excessive wedding debt. Keep in mind that financial problems are the number one contributor to divorce rates. Also, any costs saved on wedding expenses can be used toward immediate or future financial goals that help to increase your couple's portfolio. Wedding costs do not build your couple's portfolio.

Bride's magazine has a website at www.brides.com that has numerous wedding resources for planning local weddings. According to *Bride's* magazine, the average cost of weddings is around $19,000.

To help with your wedding budget, open the SS37 Calculator-Wedding Costs.xls.

1. Open the "SS37 Calculator-Wedding Costs.xls"; see Figure 30.1.
2. Click "Yes" to enable macros, if necessary.

Figure 30.1

Weddings

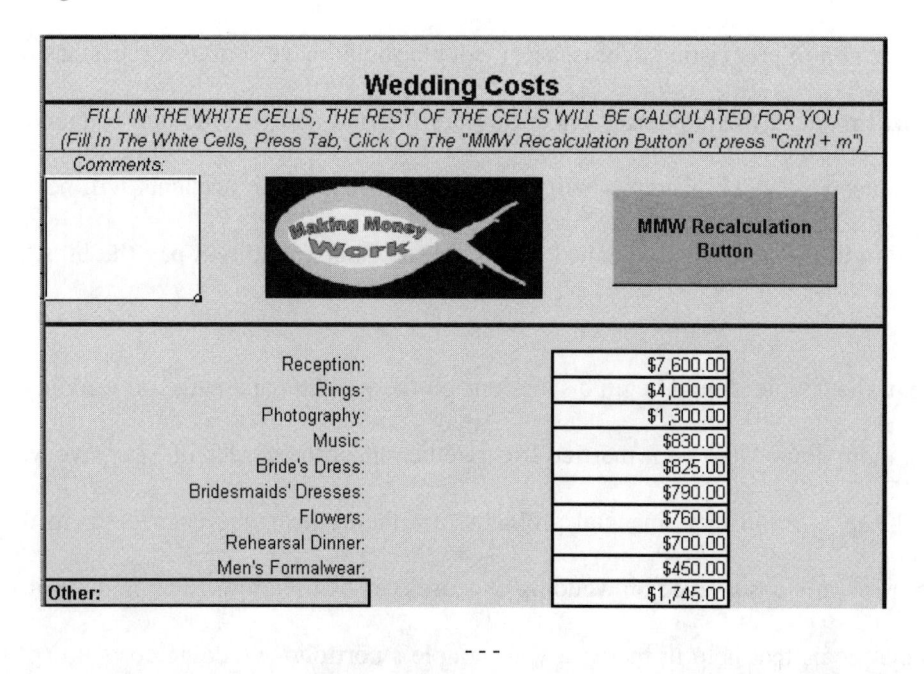

Wedding Costs

FILL IN THE WHITE CELLS, THE REST OF THE CELLS WILL BE CALCULATED FOR YOU
(Fill In The White Cells, Press Tab, Click On The "MMW Recalculation Button" or press "Cntrl + m")

Comments:

[MMW Recalculation Button]

Reception:	$7,600.00
Rings:	$4,000.00
Photography:	$1,300.00
Music:	$830.00
Bride's Dress:	$825.00
Bridesmaids' Dresses:	$790.00
Flowers:	$760.00
Rehearsal Dinner:	$700.00
Men's Formalwear:	$450.00
Other:	$1,745.00

- - -

Other:	$1,745.00
	$0.00
	$0.00
	$0.00
	$0.00
	$0.00
	$0.00
	$0.00
	$0.00
	$0.00
	$0.00
Total Wedding Budget:	**$19,000.00**

3. After reviewing the example, fill in your own personal information in each white cell (you may tab from one white cell to another).
4. After completing the information in all of the white cells, press "Tab" and then click on the "MMW Recalculation Button"—the spreadsheet will make the remaining calculations for you.

Jesus Christ said, "*In the beginning, at the creation, God made them male and female. For this reason a man shall leave his father and mother, and be made one with his wife; and the two shall become one flesh. It follows that they are no longer two individuals: they are one flesh. What God has joined together, man must not separate*"—Mark 10:6–

Weddings

9. "*Love is patient and kind; love is not jealous or boastful; it is not arrogant or rude. Love does not insist on its own way; it is not irritable or resentful; it does not rejoice at wrong, but rejoices in the right*"—1 Corinthians 13:4–6 (Revised Standard Version). "*There is nothing love cannot face; there is no limit to its faith, its hope, and its endurance. Love will never come to an end*"—1Corinthians 13:7–8. God is love. Where love is, God is. Keep God in your marriage to keep love in your marriage.

Life Insurance

Chapter 31

Life Insurance

The main purpose of life insurance is to provide income for your dependents in case either you or another family breadwinner dies prematurely. Insurance needs normally decline as dependents grow up and become independent and as the assets in your portfolio increase. In later life, few people need permanent life insurance if they have taken proper steps in building their own savings and investments and have well-managed debts. The biggest mistakes most consumers make when purchasing any type of insurance product is overestimating their potential risks and buying too much insurance or not buying enough insurance and buying too much of the wrong type of coverage to suit their needs. Buy coverage that insures against a broad range of risks and purchase only enough insurance protection to insure what you cannot afford to cover outside of the assets in your own portfolio. For example, many insurance companies sell accidental death insurance. It is highly unlikely that the policyholder will die in an accident. If you need life insurance at all, it does not matter whether you die in an accident or not—your funds are better spent in just purchasing life insurance that provides coverage in the event of your death under any circumstances.

Determine what your life insurance needs are before purchasing any life insurance product. Purchase only enough life insurance to cover your needs from a company licensed in your state. Purchase only life insurance products that you can afford. Purchase a life insurance product that suits your needs—comparison shop among several different

Life Insurance

companies. Check your coverage to make sure it is still adequate every three years or whenever there is a change in your family status such as the birth of a child, a marriage or divorce, a death, assumption of extra debt, the purchase of a home with a mortgage, and so on. Before committing to a life insurance policy, read it and make certain that you understand all aspects of the policy.

Insurers charge premiums to consumers in return for death benefit protection. The premiums from consumers are accumulated in reserve accounts and then invested by the insurer in securities, real estate, and other financial investments for growth. From these investments, the insurer eventually pays death benefits to beneficiaries. Life insurance death benefits pass tax-free to beneficiaries.

Insurers offer four primary types of life insurance policies:

1. Term life insurance
2. Whole life insurance
3. Universal life insurance
4. Variable life insurance

Term life insurance protects against an early death and is well suited for younger people. Term life provides death protection over a specified period of time such as 5, 10, or 20 years—the policy pays if the insured person dies within the time period covered by the policy. The insurer promises to pay a death benefit, or sum of money, to the insured's beneficiary in the event that the insured person dies. While term life insurance has no savings component, it provides the most insurance coverage per premium dollar. For example, a whole life insurance policy with a savings feature can easily cost 5 times the premium of a term life insurance policy. You can compare insurance cost alternatives by dividing the cost by death benefits (per thousand dollars—for example: a term policy that

Life Insurance

costs $300/year divided by $100,000 in death benefits = 0.003 x $1,000 = $3.00 cost/thousand). A whole life policy that costs $1,300/year divided by $100,000 in death benefits = 0.013 x $1,000 = $13.00 cost/thousand). The insurance company collects premiums from policyholders. Term insurance premiums go to pay for the death benefit, the administration costs, and the insurance company's profit. The death benefit is determined by statistical life expectancy tables that show the odds of a person's dying at a given age within a certain number of years. Term life insurance policies are particularly well suited for people with young children. As the children age and are no longer dependent, you can cancel the term policy if it is no longer needed. With term insurance, as the age of the insured increases, so does the life insurance premium. Term life insurance premiums normally start low but increase every year or every few years on a predetermined schedule. Term policies have no savings component (although small dividends might be paid on some policies) and no cash value (or savings feature). Renewable term life insurance allows you to renew your term insurance policy without having to take another physical examination in your older years or show evidence of insurability—the premiums rise each time you renew the policy. Look for a term policy that has an annual renewable clause until you reach age 65. Level term life insurance provides fixed premiums for a certain number of years while the death benefit remains unchanged. When the level term time period terminates, the policy premiums rise sharply. Decreasing term insurance has a death benefit that decreases over its term—for example, the policy might start with a death benefit of $100,000 of insurance coverage that then decreases by $10,000 per year for 10 years. Increasing term insurance has a death benefit that increases over its term—for example, the policy might start with a

Life Insurance

death benefit of $100,000 of insurance coverage that then increases by $10,000 per year for 10 years; the premium will also increase each year. After 20 years, only around 9% of term policies still remain active. A. L. Williams Insurance (purchased by Primerica Financial Services) had a huge impact on the insurance industry using the motto "Buy term and invest the difference."[1] That meant to purchase lower cost term insurance versus more expensive whole life policies and invest the difference in investments such as mutual funds that would often generate more savings than whole life. If you have the discipline to invest the cost savings between term and other insurance products and wisely choose stocks, mutual funds, bonds, and money market assets on your own, you will likely have considerably more savings in your future years. In addition, investing on your own gives you more control over savings accounts.

Whole life insurance policies fix the premium and death benefit when the policy is issued, in addition to the cash value in many cases. Whole life insurance thus is considered to be "permanent insurance." Permanent insurance protects your beneficiaries from an unexpected death, and it protects from future uninsurability. Whole life insurance premiums are substantially more expensive than term insurance rates, especially during the policyholder's younger years. Whole life policies usually have level or constant premium payments as long as the insured lives, which protects against the premiums becoming prohibitively costly as the insured ages—as might happen with term insurance. The cash value (or savings feature) is the amount you would receive from the policy should you decide to cancel it. The cash value rises according to a preset schedule shown

---

[1] Liberty University, www.liberty.edu, *"Art Williams: God's Entrepreneur"*.

Life Insurance

in the policy. The insured can usually borrow against the cash value amount while the policy is in force. While the cash value might be considered a sort of forced savings plan, the returns typically are much less than other savings vehicles. Insurance companies often tout insurance policies as investment accounts, savings accounts, or retirement plans—the typical investment returns (often less than 2% with an average of 5%) make them poor choices as savings vehicles compared to investments you can make on your own in stocks, bonds, and other money market assets. However, insurance policy earnings are not taxed while the policy is in force. Dividends may be paid on some whole life policies. After 20 years, only around 13% of all whole life insurance policies are still in force. Whole life insurance policies bring in more revenue for the insurance companies and more sales commissions for the insurance agents than term policies. If you require permanent insurance and can afford the higher premiums, then whole life policies might be suitable for your needs—more so than term insurance.

Universal life insurance is basically term insurance plus a savings fund. The cash value is based on current short-term interest rates, and it fluctuates. Universal life policies guarantee a minimum interest rate along with maximum mortality and expense charges. With universal life insurance, the death benefits can vary (within limits) at the discretion of the policyholder. Premiums are fairly high but can vary at the discretion of the policyholder. A portion of the premiums with universal life policies pay for the death benefit, a portion goes toward the administrative costs (e.g., sales commissions, overhead, and profits), and the balance goes toward low-risk financial investments with the rate of return being set by the insurance company. The rate of return is typically lower than general market rates. Universal life insurance premium rates are usually lower than

Life Insurance

whole life premiums. Universal life typically does not pay any dividends. With universal life, the cash value grows at a variable rate, which depends on several factors including the interest rate paid on the cash value—the insurance company can change the interest rate. The insurer is obligated to pay only its guaranteed values—if interest rates are low, the guarantee values may be all you will receive.

If you do decide to purchase whole life insurance or universal life insurance, you should plan to do so for the long haul. Around 50% of all buyers of whole life policies and universal life policies drop them within 5 years—well before any substantial buildup of equity accumulates in the cash value. When buying cash value policies, you need to make a 15 to 20 year minimum commitment to them. If you think you cannot continue the policy that long, then you are better off not purchasing the policy to begin with and just purchasing term insurance. Cash surrender value is the portion of the accumulated savings, which you get to keep should you choose to cancel the policy. You have to pay taxes on the cash surrender value. Surrender charges can take a significant amount of your accumulated savings. For example, if you cancel the policy in the first year, as much as 100% of your entire accumulated savings could be lost to surrender charges. If you cancel during the second year of the policy, 85% of accumulated savings could be lost. If you cancel during the third year of the policy, 55% of accumulated savings could be lost to surrender charges, and so forth until the 20th year when surrender charges phase out.

Interest sensitive whole life—sometimes called "current assumption whole life" or "excess interest whole life"—insurance policies actually resemble universal life policies more so than traditional whole life policies. Interest sensitive whole life policies use two interest rates—a lower guaranteed rate and a higher current rate. Unlike universal life

Life Insurance

insurance policies, interest sensitive whole life policies usually have fixed versus flexible premiums. Premiums are high. With interest sensitive whole life policies, typically no dividends are paid, and the cash value can vary. In most cases, universal life policies are better buys than interest sensitive whole life policies.

Variable life insurance policies have the key features of whole life such as fixed premiums (which are high) and minimum death benefits (which can vary, but never dip below the minimum). With variable life insurance policies, the cash value and death benefits above the minimum can vary because policyholders control the investment of their cash values among stocks, bonds, and money market securities. The cash value will vary depending on the investment results in the underlying accounts. Variable life policies typically pay no dividends.

So which insurance policy is right for you? As with most financial decisions, that depends on your own personal needs. When assessing those needs, you should look at factors such as your number of dependents and anticipated years of dependency, your age, cash reserve assets (or emergency fund), amount of debt, current size of investment portfolio, income level, number of years before retirement, and so on. Key considerations are how much life insurance you need, and what is the most cost effective way to obtain the insurance coverage.

Several different agencies rate insurance companies according to financial strength—they each have their own grading system.

Figure 31.1 Rating Agencies—Insurance Company Financial Strength Grading System

Life Insurance

Rating Agencies—Insurance Company Financial Strength Grading System				
A. M. Best Company	**Fitch Ratings**	**Moody's**	**Standard & Poor's**	**Weiss**
A++	AAA	Aaa	AAA	A+
A+	AA	Aa1	AA+	A
A	A	Aa2	AA	A-
A-	BBB	Aa3	AA-	B+
B++	BB	A1	A+	B
B+	B	A2	A	B-
B	CCC	A3	A-	C+
B-	CC	Baa1	BBB+	C
C++	C	Baa2	BBB	C-
C+	DDD	Baa3	BBB-	D+
C	DD	Ba1	BB+	D
C-	D	Ba2	BB	D-
D		Ba3	BB-	E+
E		B1	B+	E
F		B2	B	E-
		B3	B-	F
		Caa	CCC	
		Ca		

Figure 31.2 Website Addresses for Rating Services

Website Addresses for Rating Services	
Rating Service	**Website Address**
A. M. Best Company	www.ambest.com
Fitch Ratings	www.fitchratings.com
Moody's	www.moodys.com
Standard & Poor's	www.standardandpoors.com
Weiss	www.weissratings.com

You want to buy a policy only from insurance companies that are financially sound, so choose one that has the highest financial strength ratings such as the A. M. Best Company's A++ rating. Choose an insurer rated secure by at least 3 of the 5 rating companies. State guaranty associations are organizations comprised of all the insurers conducting business in your state. They collectively chip in to help keep the promises of any troubled insurer. If your insurer gets into financial trouble, the state guaranty association may make good on your policy. All 50 states have state guaranty associations, and they usually limit death benefits, cash values, and annuity amounts—generally up to

Life Insurance

$100,000 in cash value and $300,000 in death benefits. Choosing the highest rated insurance companies to begin with helps to minimize the risk of collecting on your policy.

Ratings reveal nothing about the quality of insurance policies. Neither do ratings reveal anything about the fairness of the insurance company in dealings with its policyholders. Comparison shopping different companies and policies is a must. You can compare insurance policies by obtaining information from the insurance companies, agents, your state insurance department, and via the Internet. Try www.insure.com ("Insurance shopping made fast and easy") to estimate your needs, obtain quotes, get your state's insurance department's address information, and obtain other information on various insurance policies such as life, health, auto, homeowner's, condo and renter's, and dental. Also, the Insurance Information Institute www.iii.org has valuable information concerning life, health, auto, home, business, disability, and other items relating to insurance. You might also call the National Insurance Consumer Help Line at 1-800-942-4242, which provides free information and referrals on life, auto, and home insurance. Check with your local Better Business Bureau to check complaint records against your possible insurance carrier.

To estimate your life insurance needs, please open the SS38 Calculator-Life Insurance Needs.xls.

Figure 31.3 SS38 Calculator-Life Insurance Needs

1. Open the "SS38 Calculator-Life Insurance Needs.xls."
2. Click "Yes" to enable macros, if necessary.
3. After reviewing the example, fill in your own personal information in each white cell (you may tab from one white cell to another).
4. After completing the information in all of the white cells, press "Tab" and then click on the "MMW Recalculation Button"—the spreadsheet will make the remaining calculations for you.

Life Insurance

Life Insurance Needs

FILL IN THE WHITE CELLS, THE REST OF THE CELLS WILL BE CALCULATED FOR YOU
(Fill In The White Cells, Press Tab, Click On The "MMW Recalculation Button" or press "Cntrl + m")

Comments:

[MMW Recalculation Button]

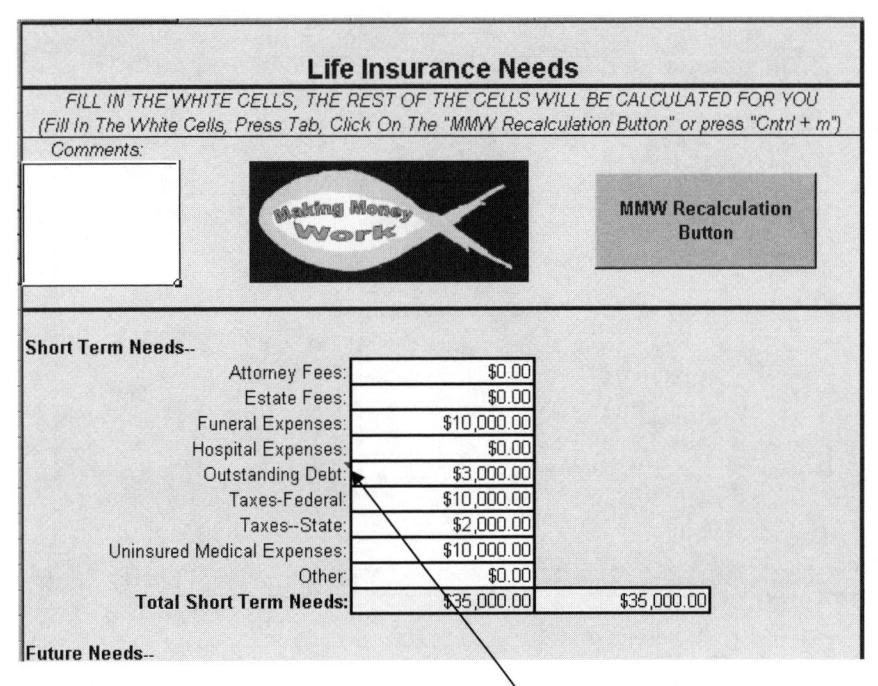

Short Term Needs--

Attorney Fees:	$0.00
Estate Fees:	$0.00
Funeral Expenses:	$10,000.00
Hospital Expenses:	$0.00
Outstanding Debt:	$3,000.00
Taxes-Federal:	$10,000.00
Taxes--State:	$2,000.00
Uninsured Medical Expenses:	$10,000.00
Other:	$0.00
Total Short Term Needs:	$35,000.00 $35,000.00

Future Needs--

Note: View each of the comments indicated with a small red triangle (by placing your cursor over the appropriate cell) for information concerning the numbers to be inputted.

- - -

Future Needs--

Current monthly living expenses:	$5,000.00
Future monthly living expense % estimate:	75%
Future monthly living expenses:	$3,750.00

Expected monthly income--

Living family members income:	$2,000.00
Pension Income:	$0.00
Social Security:	$1,400.00
Other monthly income:	$0.00
Total Expected Monthly Income:	$3,400.00
Anticipated Shortfall Between Future Needs And Expected Monthly Income:	$350.00
Annual Shortfall:	$4,200.00
Number Of Years You Wish To Cover Annual Shortfall:	17
Total Shortfall:	$71,400.00

Survivor's Future Expenses--

Total Shortfall:	$71,400.00
Child Care:	$30,000.00
Education-College Fund:	$78,000.00
Education-School Expenses:	$96,000.00

- - -

Life Insurance

Education-School Expenses:	$96,000.00
Emergency Fund:	$22,500.00
Housing Fund:	$0.00
Other:	$1,000.00
Total Survivor's Future Expenses:	$298,900.00 — $298,900.00
Total Short Term and Future Needs:	$333,900.00
Current Assets--	
Cash:	$2,500.00
Savings Accounts:	$10,000.00
Retirement Accounts:	$60,000.00
Stocks:	$8,000.00
Bonds:	$2,000.00
Mutual Funds:	$8,000.00
Insurance-Life (Currently Owned Policies:	$100,000.00
Insurance-Mortgage:	
Real Estate:	$40,000.00
Pension--Lump Sum Benefit:	$0.00
Other:	$0.00
Total Current Assets:	$230,500.00 — $230,500.00

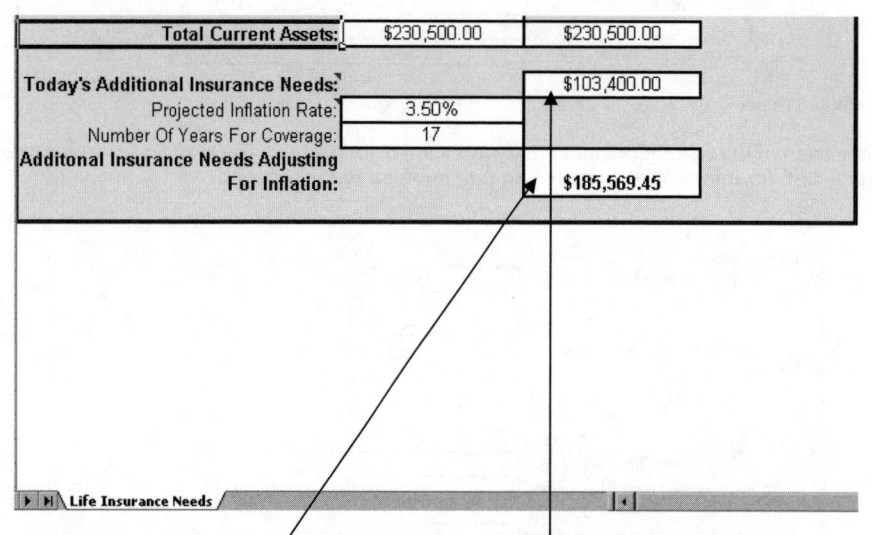

- - -

Total Current Assets:	$230,500.00 — $230,500.00
Today's Additional Insurance Needs:	$103,400.00
Projected Inflation Rate:	3.50%
Number Of Years For Coverage:	17
Additonal Insurance Needs Adjusting For Inflation:	$185,569.45

Note: The calculator estimates your insurance needs in today's dollars, and it calculates your insurance needs adjusting for inflation.

The best life insurance you can get is absolutely free. The acceptance of Jesus Christ as your personal Lord and Savoir is the ultimate life insurance policy—it guarantees you life eternal. The Apostle John said to the church "*I write these things to you who believe in the name of the Son of God so that you may know that you have eternal life*"—1 John 5:13 (New International Version). The key word in that scripture is "know"—not to

Life Insurance

guess, not to think, not to hope, and certainly not to doubt, but to know. Eternal salvation is God's promise to the believer—you never have to be concerned about payment on that "death benefit!"

Health Insurance and Disability Insurance

Chapter 32

Health Insurance and Disability Insurance

Health insurance is expensive but absolutely necessary to protect you from the potential enormous costs of major medical care. Around 50%[1] of the people that file for bankruptcy had medical problems and expenses. Without health insurance, all of your assets can easily be depleted through major medical expenses. Most major employers offer group health insurance to their employees. If you are able to choose from several insurance plans, you should compare the costs and benefits of each one in order to select the best fit for your situation. Check to see whether your doctors participate in the plan and how the plan deals with chronic diseases. Get references concerning the plan from friends or other coworkers—are they satisfied with the plan? Check with your local Better Business Bureau for the complaint record on the insurance company. Your state's insurance commissioner might supply you with information concerning a specific insurance company and its policies. Check the financial rating of the insurance company with the major insurance rating agencies—listed in Chapter 30, "Life Insurance," Figure 30.1, "Rating Agencies—Insurance Company Financial Strength Grading System"; and Figure 31.2, "Website Addresses for Rating Services."

Traditional health insurance typically has 3 main components:

1. Hospitalization—which usually covers all services for defined expenses while in the hospital.
2. Medical-Surgical—usually has a deductible (e.g., the insured typically will pay around 20% of the fee) and covers services such as doctor's visits and treatments.

---

[1] *New York University Law Review* 1999 statistic.

Health Insurance and Disability Insurance

3. Catastrophic–Major Medical—is added protection to the lifetime limits normally set on hospitalization and medical-surgical plans and covers expenses in prolonged illnesses.

Read your insurance policy carefully—if there is something you do not understand, get someone to explain it to you. Know what is covered and what is not covered.

Many employer group insurance policies may give you the option of using a health maintenance organization, or HMO. Membership in HMOs is growing rapidly. When considering an HMO, compare the insurance premium costs and the difference in copayments for doctor visits or hospital care versus traditional health insurance options. Check the HMO's list of approved doctors and hospitals: Where are they located? Are they in a convenient location for you and your family? What are their hours of operation? Can you use doctors outside the HMO network—if so, are there extra costs involved? Compare the HMO benefits to the traditional health insurance benefits—are there limits on coverage for certain conditions? Understand the conditions and benefits of the HMO policy—for example, you usually must have prior approval before going to a specialist or hospital (unless it is a life threatening emergency). Sometimes before selecting an HMO, or sometimes after selecting the HMO, you must select a primary care doctor—a family practitioner, an internist, or perhaps a pediatrician. Check the doctor's credentials and background by visiting the doctor's office; interviewing the doctor; getting references from neighbors, friends, or coworkers; and so on.

Many large employers offer tax advantages on health care spending accounts for medical expenses. Employees must estimate the amount of money they wish to have taken out of their payroll check before taxes for their medical expense fund for use on medical expenses not covered by insurance. The estimate should be conservative because

Health Insurance and Disability Insurance

of the federal government's "use it or lose it" regulation. If the funds are not used for medical expenses during the plan's calendar year, then you forfeit any remaining funds. The money placed in these "flexible benefit plans" escapes income tax and Social Security taxes. During the course of the plan's calendar year, as you incur medical expenses not covered by your insurance, you reimburse yourself with money from your flexible spending account. Let's say you historically incur around $2,000 per year in out-of-pocket medical expenses not reimbursed by your insurance coverage. To be conservative, you only agree before the start of the plan's calendar year to put $1,500 into your flexible benefit plan. The $1,500 of pretax money in the plan could save the following:

Figure 32.1 Flexible Benefit Tax Savings Example

Pretax Dollars Saved	Assumption Based on $1,500 in a Flexible Health Care Spending Account
$420.00	Assuming a 28% federal tax bracket
$93.00	Assuming 6.2% on Social Security taxes saved[2]
$21.75	Assuming 1.45% on Medicare taxes saved
$90.00	Assuming 6.0% state tax
$624.75	In total tax savings

Suggestion: invest the tax savings each year and put the money in your own retirement savings accounts. This federally approved tax break strategy turns a tax liability into a portfolio-building asset. In our example, if you invest the $624.75 annual tax savings each year into an IRA or other tax-deferred retirement account that averages 8%, in 30 years you will have an additional $70,773.69 saved for your retirement without having an additional penny taken from your pay! It just takes some work up front to determine a

---

[2] Keep in mind that this may slightly lower your Social Security income in the future; however, the immediate benefit gain typically outweighs the loss.

Health Insurance and Disability Insurance

conservative estimate of your medical out-of-pocket expenses by reviewing prior year actual expenses and projecting upcoming expenses. It also requires some homework in researching an investment vehicle that will have a reasonable rate of return. It also requires the discipline to make the investment with the money you save that would otherwise have gone to taxes anyway. That is what successful investing entails—work, proper research, and discipline to act on it. Yet only around 19%[3] of eligible employees that have access to flexible benefit accounts are utilizing them—that is a pity.

Congress approved the Consolidated Omnibus Budget Reconciliation Act in 1985—otherwise known as COBRA—and it requires employers with 20 or more employees covered by group health care to offer health insurance coverage to employees in the event they go from full-time work to part-time work, are laid off, or they retire. In essence, COBRA is a federal law mandating that former employees be offered to continue the same group benefits once group coverage has been terminated. The employee—not the employer—pays COBRA health coverage premiums. The premium may include up to a 2% administrative fee. COBRA coverage may extend health coverage for up to 18 months. If the employee dies, the benefits may be extended to the surviving spouse for up to 36 months. Former employees have 60 days to decide whether or not to enroll in COBRA. COBRA coverage might be an alternative to bridge the gap between employers or until new permanent health coverage takes effect, which can take up to 6 weeks. Once COBRA coverage has been exhausted in 18 months, you may be able to obtain coverage under HIPAA—The Health Insurance Portability and Accountability Act of 1996.

---

[3] Source: Foster Higgins 1997 research.

Health Insurance and Disability Insurance

COBRA health coverage is expensive—often the employee can find better rates elsewhere. HIPAA coverage costs may be even higher than COBRA coverage; however, preexisting conditions cannot be excluded. You can find out more about COBRA and HIPAA at www.cobrahealth.com. Another option might include short-term medical policies, which last up to 6 months—normally between 30 and 185 days. Short-term policies do not cover preexisting conditions and cannot be renewed.

Group health insurance policies typically have better benefits than individual health insurance policies. If your employer does not offer health insurance coverage, or if you are self-employed, you might be able to join an organization that offers the opportunity to purchase health care coverage in a group plan. Individual health insurance policies can be purchased from an insurance company, agents working for an insurance company, or independent brokers who represent the insurance company. Individual policies are expensive, and the costs depend on a myriad of factors such as the applicant's age, health, gender, amount of the deductible, and so on. If you have preexisting health issues, it may be difficult to find coverage at all. If you do find coverage, the policy may have preexisting condition limitations, which excludes coverage or stipulates that the insurance will not pay for preexisting conditions for a certain time period. Check the policy for time conditions such as the amount of time you have to make a claim and the length of time the policy is in force—most policies are in force for six months to a year. Check the policy to see if there is a waiting period before benefits begin. Check the policy for your renewal rights. There are numerous Internet sites that will allow you to compare costs on different health care plans; however, due to the complexities of health care coverage, advice from an insurance agent is a good idea. Compare at least three different

Health Insurance and Disability Insurance

companies/policies before purchasing. Review the following chart as a comparison basis when selecting medical policies:

Figure 32.2 Better Than Average Coverage for Traditional Health Care Insurance

Better Than Average Coverage For Traditional Health Care[4]	
Coverage	**Amounts and Limits**
Dental injuries	80% covered
Doctor's visits (in and out of the hospital)	80% covered
Home health care	80% covered
Lab fees and X-rays	80% covered
Mental health/substance abuse treatment	100% of inpatient service (up to 30 days) plus limited outpatient therapy
Private duty nurse care	80% covered
Semiprivate hospital room	100% covered for 120 + days
Surgical fees	100% covered

Medicaid is a program that provides medical assistance to individuals and families who have low incomes and limited resources. The federal government sets the general guidelines for Medicaid programs; however, each state sets its own specific regulations and also administers the Medicaid program. Federal and state governments jointly fund the Medicaid program. You can find out more about Medicaid requirements at www.cms.gov—the Centers for Medicare & Medicaid Services.

Medicare is the federal health insurance program usually for persons who are 65 years of age and older. To qualify for Medicare, you typically must have 40 or more quarters—10 years—in which you paid Medicare taxes through your employment. Medicare coverage consists of 2 parts:

1. Hospital insurance protection
2. Medical insurance protection—which costs $58.70/month (as of 2003)

---

[4] Source: Bureau of Labor Statistic survey. Kiplinger's Personal Finance Magazine, *Looking at your insurance coverage (Make sure you get only what's needed)* article.

Health Insurance and Disability Insurance

Medicare recipients may need supplemental insurance to pick up where Medicare stops. Supplemental insurance usually pays the deductibles and copayments required by Medicare. You can find out more about Medicare at www.medicare.gov, including a "Medicare personal plan finder" that includes available local area plans and a comparison of those plans. Medicare does not cover injuries or illnesses sustained while outside of the United States. Before traveling abroad, you should check your health insurance coverage—supplemental Medicare insurance or other health insurance policy—to see what type of coverage is provided while you are outside the United States.

Disability insurance is important to protect income earners and their dependents. Life insurance will protect dependents in the event of your death; however, if you are disabled and unable to earn income, without disability insurance, you and your dependents could be without income. Every income earner should have disability insurance coverage. Medical insurance companies often offer a disability policy along with their medical insurance policy. Disability policies typically cover 50% to 70% of your salary in the event you become disabled—the payments are generally tax-free. If your employer's disability policy covers less than 60% of your income, supplement the policy with one you purchase on your own to cover 60% to 70% of your income. Disability policies should not be cancelable and should guarantee the same amount of coverage at the same premium each year until you reach age 65. Disability insurance policies usually have benefit terms of 2 years, 5 years, to age 65 (the most common one), and lifetime. The benefit period is the maximum length of time the insurance company will pay the disability benefit. Benefits should continue until you reach age 65. Disability policies

Health Insurance and Disability Insurance

should have adjustments for inflation—or cost of living increases. Get a disability policy, which pays in case you are not able to work in your profession, not one that just pays in the event you are not able to work at all. Be certain you understand the policy's definition of a disability. Disability policies typically have 30-, 60-, 90-, 180-, and 365-day elimination periods, or waiting periods. The longer the waiting period, which is the time between the onset of the disability and the arrival of the first benefit payment, the lower the premium. Decide how long you could last with no income on your own reserves before selecting an elimination period. You are much more likely to need disability insurance than other types of insurance.

Figure 32.3 Insurance Risk Ratios

Type of Insurance	Risk Ratios (Chances of Filing a Claim)[5]
Homeowner's Insurance	1000 to 1
Automobile Insurance	250 to 1
Life Insurance	100 to 1
Income Insurance	4 to 1

Disability insurance and protection against lost income is one of the most important insurance coverages an income earner can have and should be a priority—at risk is your potential remaining lifetime earnings.

Most medical records are in the files and databases of individual medical facilities. The Medical Information Bureau (MIB) is the nation's largest medical record keeper. It is a nonprofit organization that keeps files on millions of Americans from data supplied by

---

[5] National averages per given year. Source: Raymond James.

Health Insurance and Disability Insurance

hundreds of insurance companies. The MIB generates reports that the insurance companies use to decide whether or not they will issue policies to applicants and what the premiums will be. The MIB reports will include information such as chronic conditions, illnesses, high-risk activities or sports, poor driving records, and so on. MIB maintains records for seven years. If you were refused coverage for health, life, or disability insurance because of information in your MIB report, you can get a free copy of the report; otherwise, you must pay a small fee (around $8.00) to obtain one. The MIB address information is as follows:

Medical Information Bureau
P.O. Box 105
Essex Station
Boston, MA 02112
617-426-3660

"*Then shall your light break forth like the dawn and soon you will grow healthy like a wound newly healed; your own righteousness shall be your vanguard and the glory of the Lord your rearguard*"—Isaiah 58:8.

Automobile Insurance

Chapter 33

Automobile Insurance

Most states require licensed vehicle owners to be insured. Since your liability exposure is enormously high, you should carefully review the amount of insurance coverage that will suit your needs—that may be more than the minimum coverage required by your state. Do not skimp on auto liability insurance—especially if you have sizeable assets to protect. Review your policy (or policies) annually to make sure you are not overinsured or underinsured. Different insurance companies might charge widely different prices for similar coverage, so comparison shopping is a must—at least 3, preferably 6 different quotes from financially sound insurance companies is best. Many factors affect your automobile premium costs. Your driving record is one. Do not speed or drive carelessly—for your safety and the safety of those around you. Another reason not to speed is that speeding tickets dramatically escalate the cost of your automobile insurance premiums. Insurance companies conducted research on California drivers and determined that those with 1 speeding citation in a 3-year period had a crash rate 50% higher than drivers who had no citations. The insurance company can refuse to renew your coverage for getting 1 speeding ticket. For those drivers who had 2 or more citations, the crash rate doubled. One speeding ticket would increase your premium around 27% from the base premium. A second minor conviction would increase your premium another 40%, and you might loose any good-driver discount. With a third conviction, you might pay 63%

Automobile Insurance

more than the original premium.[1] Over a 3-year period, that can cost you thousands of dollars extra in premium costs—much more than the cost of the tickets for the moving violations. If you are a teenager or young adult, these increases can be double or triple. If you've gotten 3 speeding tickets within 3 years, the insurance company can cancel your policy. Clearly, the best solution is to develop safe driving habits from the beginning.

The type of vehicle you drive partly determines your insurance premium rates. Insurance Services Office Inc. in New York is a nonprofit corporation that assigns a rating to every make and model vehicle. The rating is based on the vehicle's cost, theft history, and accident history. Vehicles that are stolen more often than others, vehicles that are more easily damaged than others, and vehicles that are involved in more accidents than others are assigned a greater risk rating. Insurance companies review the risk ratings for vehicles and charge higher premiums as their risk increases. Driving an expensive, high-performance car will cost considerably more in insurance premiums than driving an average car—possibly 2 to 3 times higher. Before making a new car purchase, it is best to check on insurance rates for the new make and model. Driving vehicles equipped with safety devices such as antilock brakes and air bags for both the driver and passenger will reduce premiums. A model that has done well in crash tests and has low bodily injury claims will have lower premiums. Check the Insurance Institute for Highway Safety website at www.hwysafety.org for crash test and safety information on the vehicle make and model. Having a younger driver at home will increase your premiums dramatically. Younger drivers (especially male drivers) tend to have more accidents, so the insurance

---

[1] Source of statistics: MSN Money article by Chris Solomon, *It pays to avoid a ticket—or fight one*, 2003..

Automobile Insurance

companies charge higher premiums for them. Statistically, 15% of drivers under age 25 are involved in accidents. These accidents account for 29% of all accidents and 26% of all fatal accidents. Older, married drivers tend to have fewer accidents and pay lower premiums. Married people usually pay less in premiums than single people. Driving a lot of miles each year will increase your premium—policyholders who drive less than 7,500 miles per year typically qualify for a discount. The use of public transit or carpooling can lower your premiums. Some policies charge more for city drivers than for suburban drivers. Some states allow insurance companies to charge more on auto policies for those consumers who have poor credit histories—based on studies that show people with poor credit histories tend to have more claims and claims with higher dollar amounts.

Auto insurance should be purchased to protect you against expenses that you cannot afford to pay yourself. A deductible is the amount of the loss per claim the policyholder agrees to pay. The higher the deductible, the lower the premium cost to the policyholder. By raising your deductible from $250 to $500, you can reduce your premium by 10% or more. Take the highest deductible you can afford. Do not file claims you can absorb yourself. Many insurers raise rates after you file a claim. Before filing a claim, ask yourself if the dollar amount received is more than the projected increase in insurance premiums over the next 3 years—if it is not, you are better off financially paying the expenses versus filing the claim. Also, the fewer claims you have, the better. The idea in keeping premiums low is to depend on the insurance company only for major losses.

Taking an authorized defensive driving course can lower your premiums by 5% to 15% for up to 3 years. If everyone on your policy has no moving violations or accidents in 3 years and has completed a 6-hour safe driving course, you may qualify for a good-

Automobile Insurance

record discount of at least 10%. Having an approved alarm system installed on your vehicle can save you 5% to 10%. You can lower your vehicle insurance premiums by combining all your vehicles, trailers, and recreational vehicles under one policy and getting a multivehicle discount. Also, auto insurers that offer homeowner's insurance and/or life insurance will often give you a discount for purchasing multiple policies from them—multiple policies from the same company can save you 10% or more. If your teenage high school student or college student child maintains a good academic record (e.g., a B average or better), the insurance company may give you a good-student discount—usually around 10%. If your son or daughter goes to college more than 100 miles away without a vehicle, your insurance company may give you a discount. If your children drive the vehicle less than half the time, put them on your policy—it is less expensive than purchasing separate policies. Occasional drivers are less expensive to insure than principal drivers. Check with each potential auto insurance company to find out what discounts they have available and the requirements for each.

Auto policies typically have the following components:

1. Bodily injury liability: If the accident is your fault, this insurance covers medical treatment, rehabilitation, lost income, and/or funeral costs for another driver, passengers of the other driver, your own passengers, and pedestrians. Bodily injury liability insurance also covers legal costs and any settlements for nonmonetary losses such as "pain and suffering." This is the most necessary coverage to protect you against financial ruin in the event you are sued as the result of an accident. Each state sets liability coverage up to certain limits. If you have assets to protect—a home, savings, and a well-paying job, you should purchase a bodily injury liability with limits of at least $100,000 per person and $300,000 per accident. If you have substantial assets to protect, consider $250,000 per person and $500,000 per accident. Only purchase the minimum required by your state if you have a low-paying job and few assets. Monetary limits are the amounts the insurance company will pay after each accident. Insurance coverage limits can vary from a low of your state's requirements to $500,000 per person and $1 million per accident. Often, the state's required limits

Automobile Insurance

are well below your potential losses in the event a court rules you owe more as the result of an accident—if that happens, you might have to use your other assets to pay the suit. Obtaining supplemental insurance such as an umbrella policy might be a more cost-effective way to increase your insurance coverage versus purchasing additional amounts of bodily injury liability insurance. For example, an umbrella policy for $1 million that covers losses above and beyond the coverage you have under auto and homeowner's insurance usually costs around $200 per year.

2. Property damage liability: This is the companion coverage to bodily injury liability. Property damage liability covers the repair of other people's vehicles or property that is damaged under your policy coverage. Each state sets the required property damage limit, which is usually around $15,000 per accident (some as low as $5,000). Insurers might sell up to $100,000 worth of this coverage. Once again, the state minimums might not come close to covering potential losses—consider a $1 million umbrella policy as a supplement if you have assets to protect. You should likely get $50,000 worth of property damage liability coverage on each vehicle. Bodily injury liability and property damage liability coverage is sometimes expressed together as a string of numbers in your policy. For example, "100/300/50" would mean $100,000 per person, $300,000 per accident, and $50,000 property damage per accident.

3. Medical payments coverage, or Med pay: This coverage is usually optional and covers physician's expenses, hospital bills, rehabilitation expenses, some convalescence services, and some funeral expenses for you and your passengers regardless of who was at fault in the accident. It also covers household members injured as pedestrians by motor vehicles. Coverage is sold without a deductible in increments of $1,000 or $5,000 up to $25,000. Your existing health insurance probably provides enough coverage; however, if you are not covered elsewhere, or if you have high health insurance deductibles and copayments, you may wish to purchase this additional coverage; $5,000 per car for people with good health insurance should suffice, with a recommended limit of $25,000. Some people choose to get this coverage to protect against medical expenses for passengers who might not have any other coverage on their own.

4. Personal injury protection, or PIP: This pays for medical expenses, in-home assistance, a portion of lost wages, and funeral costs to you and your family members regardless of who is at fault in an accident. PIP is mandatory in states with no-fault insurance. It is optional in other states. In some states, PIP coverage might include a deductible. Suggestion: if you have good health, life, and disability insurance, purchase only the minimum required by the state for PIP coverage.

5. Uninsured and underinsured motorist coverage: This coverage pays for medical expenses, rehabilitation costs, funeral expenses, and losses from "pain and suffering" caused by a hit-and-run driver, a driver without any insurance, or a driver without sufficient insurance. It covers you and your family members while in a vehicle, riding bicycles, or as pedestrians. This insurance is mandatory in most states and essential coverage to have. Limits are similar to bodily injury

Automobile Insurance

liability. Suggestions: if available, purchase at least $100,000 per person, $300,000 per accident, and $50,000 in property damage.

6. Collision and comprehensive: This is optional insurance coverage. Collision covers vehicle accident damage regardless of who was at fault. Collision deductibles range from $50 to $2,500—the higher the deductible, the lower the costs. Comprehensive covers vehicle damage from windstorms, flood, fire, vandalism, losses from theft, and so on. Comprehensive deductibles range from $0 to $2,500—the higher the deductible, the lower the costs. Suggestions: take deductibles $250 and higher (e.g., $500) to lower premium costs, or if your vehicle is 5 years old or older and is a low- to mid-priced car, consider dropping collision and comprehensive coverage altogether. A rule of thumb to use is if the collision premium cost per year is 10% of the vehicle's current value, then drop the coverage and save the premium expense.
7. Uninsured motorist property damage, or UMPD: This covers damage to you and members of your household for damage to your property by someone without insurance or someone without sufficient insurance to pay the cost of damages. UMPD has no deductible, covers less than collision insurance, and is far less expensive than collision insurance. Suggestion: where available, purchase UMPD coverage only if you do not have collision coverage.
8. Rental car reimbursement: This coverage pays for a car rental while your vehicle is being repaired from an accident. Suggestion: purchase this coverage only if you have one vehicle and no other alternative means of transportation.
9. Towing: This coverage is for towing charges in case your car breaks down or after an accident. Suggestion: decline this coverage and join an auto club such as AAA that offers towing among its other services.
10. Glass breakage: This covers your comprehensive deductible when your vehicle's glass is damaged. It may add 15% to 20% of the cost to your comprehensive coverage. Suggestion: if the premium cost is more than a few dollars per year, decline this coverage.

Thirty-six states have state insurance departments that provide free comparisons on auto insurance policies. You can contact insurance companies, agents, and brokers to research policies and their costs. The quality of service an insurance company gives on policy claims is difficult to assess; however, you can call your state's insurance department to get its record of consumer complaints against a potential insurer. Compare that number to the number of complaints against competing insurance companies to get an idea of their service levels.

Automobile Insurance

For assistance in comparing possible policies open the SS39 Calculator-Vehicle Insurance.xls.

Figure 32.1 Vehicle Insurance Policy Comparison Worksheet

1. Open the "SS39 Calculator-Vehicle Insurance.xls."
2. Click "Yes" to enable macros, if necessary.
3. After reviewing the example, fill in your own personal information in each white cell (you may tab from one white cell to another).
4. After completing the information in all of the white cells, press "Tab" and then click on the "MMW Recalculation Button"—the spreadsheet will make the remaining calculations for you.

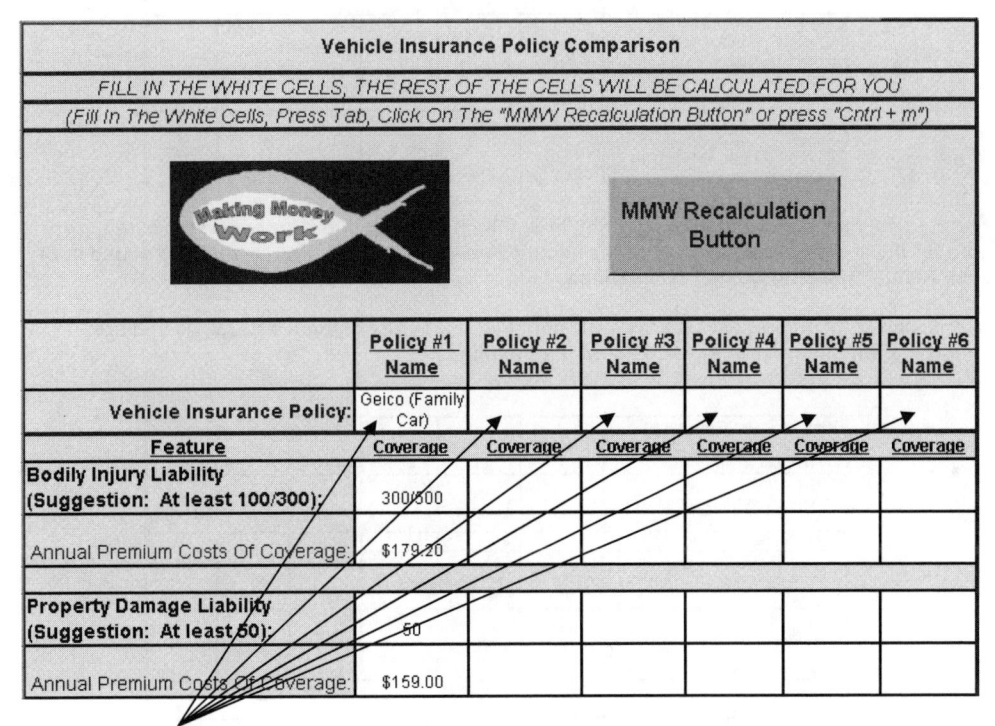

Vehicle Insurance Policy Comparison

FILL IN THE WHITE CELLS, THE REST OF THE CELLS WILL BE CALCULATED FOR YOU
(Fill In The White Cells, Press Tab, Click On The "MMW Recalculation Button" or press "Cntrl + m")

Feature	Policy #1 Name	Policy #2 Name	Policy #3 Name	Policy #4 Name	Policy #5 Name	Policy #6 Name
Vehicle Insurance Policy:	Geico (Family Car)					
	Coverage	Coverage	Coverage	Coverage	Coverage	Coverage
Bodily Injury Liability (Suggestion: At least 100/300):	300/500					
Annual Premium Costs Of Coverage:	$179.20					
Property Damage Liability (Suggestion: At least 50):	50					
Annual Premium Costs Of Coverage:	$159.00					

Note: There are six columns in which to compare your personal insurance quotes—suggestion: if you have a current policy, look at the "declaration page" (the policy document that lists the coverage you have and the cost for the coverage), type the information in the Policy #1 column as a starting point for price quote comparisons.

- - -

Automobile Insurance

Medical Payments (Recommended Limit Of $25,000):	$25,000.00
Annual Premium Costs Of Coverage:	$28.40
Personal Injury Protection:	Not Required
Annual Premium Costs Of Coverage:	$0.00
Uninsured And Underinsured Motorist (Suggestion: At least 100/300):	100/300
Annual Premium Costs Of Coverage:	$134.60
Uninsured Motorist Property Damage (Suggestion: At least 50):	$250 Deductible
Annual Premium Costs Of Coverage:	$0.00
Collision (Suggestion: The highest deductible you are comfortable with):	$500 Deductible
Annual Premium Costs Of Coverage:	$279.60
Comprehensive (Suggestion: The highest deductible you are comfortable with):	$250 Deductible

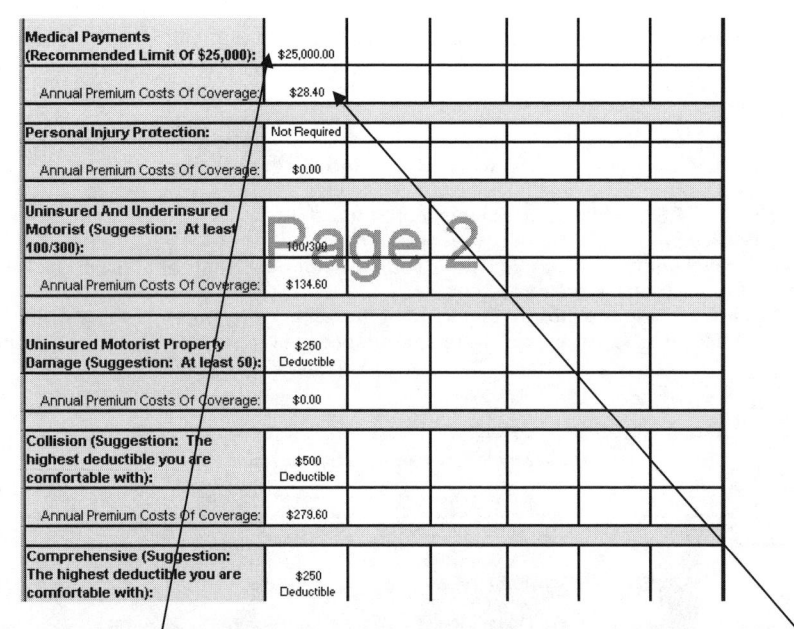

Page 2

Note: Record your policy detail description in the first line of each category and the actual price quote for the annual premium cost on the second line—only the price quotes will be added in the "Total Annual Premium Costs" calculations.

For collision and comprehensive coverage, consider taking the highest deductible you are comfortable with in order to save costs on the premiums.

- - -

Comprehensive (Suggestion: The highest deductible you are comfortable with):	$250 Deductible
Annual Premium Costs Of Coverage:	$114.60
Rental Car Reimbursement:	No
Annual Premium Costs Of Coverage:	$0.00
Towing:	No--Member of AAA
Annual Premium Costs Of Coverage:	$0.00
Glass Breakage:	No
Annual Premium Costs Of Coverage:	$0.00
Other:	None
Annual Premium Costs Of Coverage:	$0.00
Total Annual Premium Costs:	**$895.40**	$0.00	$0.00	$0.00	$0.00	$0.00

Page 3

Vehicle Ins. Policy Comparison

As you are obtaining price quotes, remember to ask for a list of special discounts.

Automobile Insurance

When contacting insurance companies, find out what type of policy they are quoting for you:

1. Substandard rates (more expensive) or nonstandard
2. Standard rates (average cost)
3. Preferred rates (best cost)—can save up to 50%; always try to get the preferred rate

Nonstandard insurance is a market that insures high-risk motorists such as people who have had several accidents—the cost is normally 30% to 40% higher than standard rates. Standard rates are for normal customers. Preferred rates are for motorists who have stellar records in driving, payment history, claim history, and so on.

For more information on auto insurance, visit the Insurance Information Institute website at www.iii.org. Also, for auto insurance quotes, you can visit www.insure.com. If you are not accepted by the insurance company, find out why and attempt to correct any problems your might have—for example, an error on your credit report or auto insurance report. The Comprehensive Loss Underwriting Exchange (C.L.U.E.) is an electronic database that has become the standard source that auto insurers use in deciding whether or not to accept new policyholders. The C.L.U.E. report lists all claims you've made with any insurance carrier during the last 5 years. If you are denied coverage, you are entitled to receive one free copy of your C.L.U.E. report. It is best to order a copy of your C.L.U.E. report before applying for auto insurance to clear up any corrections beforehand. For a small fee (e.g., around $9.00), you can get a copy of your C.L.U.E. report from ChoicePoint at www.consumerdisclosure.com.

Insurance companies differ on their underwriting standards; if one places you below the type of policy for which you feel you should qualify (e.g., a standard rate versus a

Automobile Insurance

preferred rate), call additional insurance companies. For example, some insurance companies might require 5 years worth of driving experience versus others that ask for only 3 years. In most states, insurance carriers have the right to drop your coverage during the first 60 days—for example, if you obtain a policy and later the company discovers you had accidents or violations not reported on the application. After the first 60 days, the insurance company might drop your policy after a claim in the event it discovers something such as a teenage driver in your household you failed to report to them.

Fifty to sixty percent of automobile renters are already covered through their own insurance policies. Check with your insurance company prior to renting an automobile to see what insurance coverage you have on car rentals. If it is adequate, waive the optional coverage the car rental company might try to sell you. If traveling abroad and renting an automobile, it is usually best to purchase the car rental company's insurance—including collision and loss damage waiver—since most domestic policies do not cover international car rentals. If you do not have your own vehicle insurance policy, then you will want to get the car rental company's insurance coverage. Also, many credit card companies offer free car rental insurance when the rental car is purchased using their credit card—check with your credit card company about this rental car insurance coverage.

In the event of an accident, be a "good Samaritan" and attend to people's injuries. Call 911 to get the police on the accident scene and request a police accident report. Obtain the names and addresses of all drivers, passengers, and witnesses. Get all license plate numbers, insurance companies, and insurance identification numbers. You will also want

Automobile Insurance

to keep track of all accident-related expenses for possible reimbursement such as lost wages, rental car costs, telephone bills, line item repair bills, and so on. Photograph the damages and keep a copy of all the paperwork.

Open the SS40 Vehicle Accident Report.xls.

Figure 32.2 Vehicle Accident Report

	Vehicle Accident Report			
Date Of Accident:				
Time Of Accident:				
Insured Vehicle:	Ford			
Year/Make/Model:	2003/Ranger/XLT			
Vehicle Identification Number (VIN):	1RICK14C4LAR29252			
License Plate Number:	KEJ-1262			
State:	NC			
Insurance Company:	Geico	Phone Number:	1.800.841.3000	
Person To Contact:	Dan S. Orndoff	Phone Number:	x338	
Insurance Co. Policy #:	4006-85-33-08			
Owner's Name--	Street, City, State, Zip Code	Driver's License #	State	Phone Numbers
Accident Information				
Driver's Names--	Street, City, State, Zip Code	Driver's License #	State	Phone Numbers

Suggestion: fill in the information you will need in the event of an accident; however, for identity theft reasons, leave any personal information blank until the accident report is needed just in case of a theft or in the event your vehicle is stolen.

- - -

Passenger Names--	Street, City, State, Zip Code	Other Information	Phone Numbers
Injured People--	Street, City, State, Zip Code	Extent Of Injuries	Phone Numbers
Witnesses--	Street, City, State, Zip Code	Other Information	Phone Numbers
Property Damaged--			

393

Automobile Insurance

Property Damaged-- Owner's Name--	Street, City, State, Zip Code	Other Information	Phone Numbers
Insurance Company:	Policy #:		
Property Description (For vehicle, make/model/year/state):		(If vehicle) License Plate #:	
Property Damaged-- Owner's Name--	Street, City, State, Zip Code	Other Information	Phone Numbers
Insurance Company:	Policy #:		
Property Description (For vehicle, make/model/year/state):		(If vehicle) License Plate #:	
Property Damaged-- Owner's Name--	Street, City, State, Zip Code	Other Information	Phone Numbers
Insurance Company:	Policy #:		
Property Description (For vehicle, make/model/year/state):		(If vehicle) License Plate #:	

Page 3

Description Of Accident--	City Or Town	Street Name Or Route Number	Intersection With
Location of Accident:			
Where Can Accident Vehicles Be Seen?:			
Description Of Accident:			
Diagram Of Accident:			

Page 4

Vehicle Accident Report

Suggestion: once you have completed the mandatory information you'll need in the event of an accident, print out a copy of the "Vehicle Accident Report" and keep it in your vehicle's glove box. The report will help to eliminate some of the confusion on needed information in a potentially stressful situation.

Automobile Insurance

After compiling your information from an accident, notify your insurance company as soon as possible. Do not authorize repairs on your vehicle until you receive approval from your insurance carrier—your insurance carrier will likely want to send out an adjuster to inspect the damages prior to restoration. If a claim is brought against you as a result of the accident, your insurer will represent you.

"*Suddenly there appeared chariots of fire and horses of fire, . . . and Elijah was carried up in the whirlwind to heaven*"—2 Kings 2:11. God loves righteousness. In all of history, only Enoch, Elijah, and Jesus Christ were righteous enough that God chose to take them to heaven in both physical body and soul. "*Righteousness shall yield peace and its fruit be quietness and confidence for ever*"—Isaiah 32:17. Nurture your body and your soul; however, remember your body is just the vehicle through which your soul travels until the opportunity to spend eternity with God. Claim God's promise of eternal life not by accident but by exercising your free will of accepting God's grace. The best "insurance" is God's "assurance" of life eternal!

Chapter 34

Homeowner's/Renter's Insurance

Homeowner's insurance pays for damages or losses to your home or belongings. Renter's insurance pays for damages or losses to your belongings. There are 3 basic categories for home insurance policies:

1. HO-1 (Homeowner's 1)—provides basic protection for occurrences such as lightning, fire, hail, glass breakage, burglary, theft, vandalism, and so on. It covers your home and personal property.
2. HO-2 (Homeowner's 2)—provides additional coverage for catastrophes such as electrical surge damages, roof collapse from ice or snow, frozen pipe damage, and so on.
3. HO-3 (Homeowner's 3)—provides even more comprehensive coverage on all risks to your house except flooding and earthquakes. It includes reimbursement for trees and shrubs.
4. HO-4 (Homeowner's 4)—provides basic protection for renters. It covers personal property and liability.

"Actual cash value" is insurance that pays the current market value of the personal property in a loss, not what it would cost to actually replace the property. Replacement cost coverage insurance pays the actual cost to replace the property new as opposed to the depreciated value of the asset. Get replacement cost coverage versus actual cash value coverage on homeowner's and renter's insurance to avoid possible tremendous losses from depreciating assets—for example, for a stolen TV costing $1,000 several years ago, you might only receive a few hundred dollars under an actual cash value policy. The same TV might be replaced at today's price of $1,100 under the replacement cost coverage policy. Replacement cost coverage policies typically only cost around 10% to 15% more than actual cash value policies and, in the event of a claim, will pay much larger sums. Ask if your replacement value coverage has recovery caps—or maximum

Homeowner's/Renter's Insurance

covered amounts. Purchase guaranteed replacement coverage, which covers the total costs of replacement, versus standard replacement coverage, which may have replacement costs limits. Get replacement cost coverage not only for your home, but also for the contents of your home. Riders are documents attached to your insurance policy to add benefits that are not covered by the basic policy. For example, you might have an additional rider to your policy with an extra premium charge to cover expensive jewelry, silverware, collectibles, heirlooms, and so on, that are excluded from coverage in the basic policy. "Scheduling" a particular item means that the item is covered via insurance without the normal deductible. For example, if you have a $2,000 pearl necklace scheduled on your insurance policy, which has a $500.00 deductible, and the necklace is stolen, the insurance company will reimburse you the $2,000 value of the necklace, not $2,000 less $500 for a $1,500 reimbursement. Each item scheduled requires an extra annual premium charge.

Find out what insurance discounts are available. Insurance policies might offer special discounts for dead bolt locks, home security devices such as monitored burglar alarms, fire extinguishers, sprinkler systems, fire and smoke alarms, nonsmokers, upgraded electrical systems, upgraded plumbing systems, senior citizen discounts at age 50 or older, and so on. Most insurance companies offer extra discounts when you have multiple policies with them—for example, both homeowner's coverage and automobile insurance. Discounts can cut your policy premium costs by up to 35%; ask your agents for a list of all possible discounts.

As with all insurance, your goal is to get the right insurance coverage in the right amount—neither to underinsure nor to overinsure. Review your policy annually to keep

Homeowner's/Renter's Insurance

your coverage in line with what you own. Understand the policy terms, policy limits, what is covered, what is not covered, and what might be depreciated. Review and keep all copies of mailings from your insurance company—they could have important notifications of policy changes. Get a policy that covers windstorm damage—some policies exclude it. Get your insurance agent to explain anything you do not clearly understand. Ideally, homeowners should purchase enough coverage to provide 100% reimbursement (80% of current value as a bare minimum) for total reconstruction of their home—in case it is completely destroyed. Inquire about inflation-adjusted options, which raise your coverage in order to keep pace with increases in local building costs. Do not include the value of your lot or land—it is uninsurable under a homeowner's policy. While normal homeowner's policies do not insure for losses from flood or mudslides, the Federal Emergency Management Act administers federal flood insurance for those living in vulnerable areas. This insurance is sold through most insurance companies. Contact your local government to find out if your home is in a flood zone. You can get an idea of what your home is worth by the resale prices of similar homes in your neighborhood. Your county courthouse makes the sell prices public information. To get a more accurate estimate, you might consider hiring a professional appraiser to appraise your home. Appraisers are adept at judging the home's market value. To get a better idea of the replacement value of your home, you can measure the dimensions of your home and multiply that by the cost per square foot of current construction builders in your area—add in another 15% for costs that can affect the price of rebuilding such as debris removal, permits, architect fees, and other related costs. Insure your home for the replacement value—not its original cost.

Homeowner's/Renter's Insurance

Raise your deductibles to the highest amount with which you are comfortable. This not only saves you money on yearly premiums, but it keeps you from filing claims on small amounts that you are better off handling out of your own resources. Claims might cause your insurance premiums to escalate. Or worse yet, if you have too many claims within a certain period of time, the insurance company might cancel your policy. When you apply to another company, they will ask if you've been denied insurance from any other company. A cancellation from another company might cost you a whopping 300% increase in annual premiums! By raising your deductible on a typical policy from $250 to $500, you can save around 12% on the annual premium costs. By raising your deductible on a typical policy from $250 to $1,000, you can save around 24% on the annual premium costs.

Most homeowner policyholders have insurance coverage up to $300,000 in the event someone is injured on their property or in the event someone in their household causes injury or damage outside the home. If you have assets in excess of $300,000, you should consider purchasing an umbrella policy to protect against a liability suit that could target your assets. A $1 million umbrella policy can be purchased for only a few hundred dollars in annual premiums. If $1 million is not enough to cover the difference between your normal homeowner's (or auto) liability policies, your insurance carrier might insure up to $10 million under an umbrella policy. In the event of a claim, your homeowner's, auto, or boat liability policies exhaust their coverage limits first before the umbrella coverage is used.

Thirty-six states have state departments of insurance that will help you with free comparisons of homeowner's policies and insurance company rates. They may also

Homeowner's/Renter's Insurance

provide you with complaint records against the individual insurance companies, which can give you a feel for their customer satisfaction levels. If you live in a state that does not provide these services, you will need to conduct your own research—use the methods cited earlier for other types of insurance coverage. Be certain to compare numerous homeowner's or renter's policies at different companies. Also, be certain to check the insurance company's financial standing using the rating agencies—A. M. Best, and so on (see Chapter 31, Figures 31.1 and 31.2), before making any purchase.

In preparation for possible homeowner's or renter's insurance claims, you will need to have proof of your home's contents. Refer to the SS31 Calculator-Household Inventory Form.xls you already completed. The total amount can be your guide regarding the amount of homeowner's or renter's insurance you'll need to protect your home's contents; however, keep in mind that you will need to adjust your insurance coverage annually to account for inflation. In addition to the SS31 Calculator-Household Inventory Form.xls information, save receipts for all of your purchases as proof of ownership for the insurance adjuster. In addition, make a video of your home's contents or take pictures of all of your contents. For special items such as expensive jewelry or oriental rugs, you will need to get a certificate of its value from a jeweler or antiques expert. The cost of the appraisal is miniscule in comparison to the potential insurance claims losses. Keep copies of the insurance policy, household inventory, receipts, and videotape (or pictures) in your safe-deposit box and with a relative or friend. A copy of this information is kept outside the home in case the home and its contents are destroyed in a fire or some other catastrophe. Give a copy of the videotape (or pictures) to your insurance company for safekeeping.

Homeowner's/Renter's Insurance

If you have property damage, take immediate steps to prevent further damage—for example, if a water pipe bursts, turn the water off at the main cutoff valve and take measures to clean up spilled water to prevent further damage to the flooring and subflooring. Keep all receipts for emergency repairs and turn them in to your insurance carrier. Also, save receipts for any out-of-pocket expenses the damage might have created—for example, hotel bills if the damage results in the home being temporarily uninhabitable. Record the damage with a video camera or photographs. Secure items as necessary to prevent further damage. As soon as possible, notify your insurance company to make an appointment for the claim's adjuster to view the damages. Obtain claim forms and file them with your carrier.

If your insurance company is unresponsive to your claim or you cannot resolve differences over your insurance matters, contact your state's insurance commissioner's office to see what assistance it might be able to give you regarding a settlement. The state's insurance commissioner's office cannot force the insurance company to pay an individual claim; however, they can carry much weight in dealing with insurance companies to get issues resolved. The state's insurance commissioner's office can fine an insurance company or take other punitive action against carriers that have histories of denying claims or underpaying claims.

Jesus Christ told his disciples, "*'In My Father's house are many mansions; if it were not so, I would have told you. I go to prepare a place for you. And if I go and prepare a place for you, I will come again and receive you to Myself; that where I am, there you may be also. And where I go you know, and the way you know.' Thomas said to Him, 'Lord, we do not know where You are going, and how can we know the way?' Jesus said*

Homeowner's/Renter's Insurance

to him, 'I am the way, the truth, and the life. No one comes to the Father except through Me'"—John 14:2–6 (New King James Version). Jesus Christ died for our sins. Christ prepared the way to your heavenly home (a "mansion" unlike anything we can comprehend here on earth)—the cost prepaid in its entirety, insured and guaranteed by God for all those with faith and trust in God. Jesus Christ also said, "*The words that I speak to you I do not speak on My own authority; but the Father* [God] *who dwells in Me does the works. Believe Me that I am in the Father and the Father in Me*"—John 14:10–11.

Long-Term Care Insurance

Chapter 35

Long-Term Care Insurance

Long-term care insurance may pay for some or all home health care, nursing home care, assisted living, respite care, adult day care, care management services, and help with "activities of daily living" for people with disabling conditions such as long physical illnesses, mental impairment, or physical disabilities. "Activities of daily living" include getting from a bed to a chair, walking, remaining continent, using a toilet, bathing, dressing, and eating. Traditional medical care tries to improve the medical condition of the patient; however, major medical insurance, Medicare, and Medicare supplemental insurance usually will not pay for long-term care. Long-term care attempts to help patients live their lives with their present conditions. In essence, long-term care insurance is a costly form of disability insurance.

Long-term care insurance can be very expensive and is not for everyone. The decision to purchase a long-term care insurance policy depends on a number of variables such as your health status, predicted future health status, age, retirement goals, income, and assets. If you already have a long-term health problem, it is likely that you will not be able to find a policy that will cover you. Some insurance companies will sell you a policy for a preexisting condition but will not pay benefits for long-term care related to the condition until after a certain period of time—such as 6 months. Long-term care insurance policies usually do not make sense for people with few assets to protect or for people who have many assets who could afford to cover their own long-term care needs. If your net worth is less than $150,000, you are better off depleting most of your own

Long-Term Care Insurance

resources[1] and then using Medicaid to fund long-term care needs versus purchasing a long-term care policy. Contact your state department of social services, office on aging, or Medicaid office for the specific rules in your state. Long-term care insurance does not make sense for people who cannot afford the premiums. If your assets are over $2 million, you should be able to pay your own long-term care needs. If you wish to protect assets from $150,000 to $2 million for heirs, you might consider a long-term care insurance policy if you can afford the premiums. Premium costs for long-term care insurance should not exceed 5% to 7% of your income.

As with health insurance, you must make premium payments each year to maintain your coverage. Premiums have been known to escalate up to 800%! If you think your future income will de-escalate and do not think you will be able to keep up with escalating premiums, do not purchase long-term care insurance. A guaranteed renewable long-term care insurance policy means the insurance company guarantees your right to renew the policy—it does not mean you can renew the policy at the old premium price. The premium may escalate over time as the insurance company pays out more claims and larger claims—the insurance company raises premiums to their policyholders in a state as a group. No individual can be singled out for rate increases.

Figure 35.1 Statistics to Help You Decide If You Need Long-Term Care Insurance and What Kind

Statistics	Remarks
Less than 1%[2]	Less than 1% of people in the U.S. under age 65 receive nursing home care.
4%[2]	4% of people age 75 to 84 live in nursing homes.
19%[2]	19% of people age 85 and older live in nursing homes.

---

[1] Your state may have provisions that allow the spouse to keep some assets, income within specific limits, and the family home.
[2] November 2003 statistics from *Consumer Reports*.

Long-Term Care Insurance

83 years of age[2]	The average age of admission to a nursing home.
25%[2]	25% of 65-year-olds fail the physical for long-term care insurance.
33%[2]	33% of 75-year-olds fail the physical for long-term care insurance.
66% of people 65 or older in 1990[3]	Will never go to a nursing home or will spend less than 3 months in one.
13% of women[3]	13% of women will spend 5 years or more in a nursing home.
4% of men[3]	4% of men will spend 5 years or more in a nursing home.
94%[2]	94% of nursing home patients receive help with bathing (make sure bathing is included as one of no more than two activities of daily living requirements).
5.6% annual increase[4]	5.6% annual increase in nursing home charges estimated from 2004–2008.
8% annual increase[4]	The annual rate of nursing home care has been increasing at 8% per year for the last several years.
466% increase in premiums for age differences[5]	A plan that costs a 50-year-old $1,625 per year will cost a 60-year-old $3,100 annually and a 70-year-old $7,575 annually.[2]
90%[2]	90% of all people age 65 who have entered a nursing home stay less than 5 years.
2 ½ years[2]	The average length of time a nursing home resident stays in the home.
$96–$420 per day[2]	Current day rates for nursing home care in the United States (plus 20% for uncovered drugs, supplies, and special services).
$181 per day[6]	Average rate for a private room in a nursing home ($63,712 per year).
$18.00 per hour[2]	Average home-health aid charge per hour.

The first step is to assess your individual situation and determine if it warrants the risk and expense of obtaining a long-term care insurance policy. As you age, your chances of needing nursing assistance increase—hence, as you age, your long-term care insurance premiums increase. If you buy a policy too early, there's a chance the care you might need will be excluded from the policy—for example, today's assisted-living facility care was not covered by long-term care insurance policies written 15 years ago, so if you buy a policy at age 40, the coverage could be useless when you need it at age 83 (the average age for admission to a nursing home).

---

[3] Kemper, P., & Murtaugh, C.M. (1991). Lifetime use of nursing home care. The New England Journal of Medicine: 324 (9): 595–600.
[4] National Association of Insurance Commissioners, *A Shopper's Guide to Long-Term Care Insurance,* Kansas City, MO, 1999, page 18.
[5] Derived from statistics in the November 2003 *Consumer Reports*.
[6] Survey by Metropolitan Life Insurance, 2003.

Long-Term Care Insurance

If you are between the ages of 55 and 60 and have a chronic condition that could prove incapacitating over a long period of time—such as diabetes—or a family history of requiring long-term care, consider purchasing a long-term care insurance policy. Your doctor should be able to give you some insight into the state of your physical needs in the future and whether it is likely you will require long-term care. At age 60, look closely at long-term coverage needs and assess whether your situation warrants the need for coverage. Most people who might need long-term insurance should purchase it around age 65. If you try to purchase a policy after age 70, you may not pass the physical to obtain coverage or the premiums might be prohibitively expensive.

Policies have elimination periods or waiting periods of 0, 20, 30, 60, 90, or 100 days during which you must pay for the long-term care out of your own resources. The elimination period is similar to a deductible (the higher the deductible, the lower the premium) in that the longer the elimination period, the lower the premium. Suggestion: pick a policy with a 30-day elimination period. A 90-day elimination period premium might be around 15% less than a 30-day premium; however, it is usually a better buy when you factor in the rising cost of health care and the potential benefits you might receive. For example, using the $181 (average cost per day for a private room in a nursing home), assuming you purchase a policy at age 65 and need it to enter a nursing home at age 83 (the average age of admission to a nursing home) or 18 years later, and a 5.9% annual increase in nursing home costs, the future rate per day would calculate as follows:

$181 x (1 + 5.9\%)^{18}$ = $507.93.

Long-Term Care Insurance

Use the SS15 Calculator-Compound Interest.xls to compute your individual cost, interest rate, and time projections. So, the $181 cost today in our example will become around $507.93/day when you will likely need the coverage. 90 days – 30 days = 60 days x $507.93 = $30,475.80. You can then compare that to your premium cost (as an example, say the premium cost averaged $7,575 dollars per year x 18 years = $136,350 paid in premiums at a 15% increase (difference between the 30-day and 90-day elimination periods) = $20,452.50. $30,475.80 - $20,452.50 = $10,023.30 saved. You will want to find out if your policy requires another elimination period for a second stay in a nursing home.

Obviously, due to the increasing cost of health care, it is vital that you select a policy that adjusts for the increasing care costs (note the 5.6% and 5.9% projected increase in nursing home care statistics in Figure 35.1). The inflation adjustment benefit may increase your premium payment 25% to 40%. The younger you are when you start the policy, the more important it is to add inflation protection. Inflation protection normally comes in 1 of 2 ways:

1. Automatically: The insurance company uses simple (the benefit increases by the same dollar amount each year) or compound rates (the dollar amount of the benefit goes up each year) and increases the daily benefit each year by a fixed percentage (typically 5%) for the life of the policy or a certain period of time such as 10 or 20 years. Compounding provides greater benefits.
2. Special offer: This allows you to increase your benefits periodically, for example, increasing them every 3 years—if you increase your benefits, your premium increases. If you decline your option to increase your benefits 1 year, you may not get another opportunity to do so.

Most policies have specific benefit periods in the range of 1 to 6 years—although some policies may offer lifetime coverage with extremely high premiums. Remember from the chart above that the average length of time a nursing home resident stays in the nursing

Long-Term Care Insurance

home is 2 ½ years. A 4-year benefit period should help to reduce premiums while providing adequate coverage for most people.

The Health Insurance Portability and Accountability Act of 1996 (HIPAA) may give some people who buy certain long-term care insurance policies some income tax advantages based on their age. Policies that meet the HIPAA requirements are called tax-qualified long-term care insurance contracts or qualified contracts. In addition, your state insurance department might supply you with information concerning additional state tax advantages under these plans. If you have a qualified long-term care insurance policy and you itemize your tax deductions, you might be able to add the premium cost to your other deductible medical expenses. If the total medical expenses exceed the current year excluded percentage (presently at 7.5%) of your adjusted gross income, you may deduct the excess amount of the excluded percentage (e.g., 7.5% of AGI) and your actual current year medical expenses from your taxes. For example, if your AGI is $50,000, up to 7.5% is not deductible—7.5% x $50,000 = $3,750. If your medical expenses + qualified long-term care insurance premium = $8,000, then you would be able to deduct $4,250 from your taxes ($8,000 - $3,750 = $4,250). To qualify as qualified contracts, the policies must meet certain federal standards. They must be guaranteed renewable, cover only long-term care services, cannot have a cash surrender value, and include a number of consumer protection provisions. Benefits paid from qualified long-term care insurance policies are generally not taxable as income. Long-term care insurance policies that are not qualified may be taxable as income.

Policies may be packed with restrictions that keep you from collecting on long-term care. Some policies only pay benefits for services received from state-licensed facilities,

Long-Term Care Insurance

some policies exclude certain facilities from benefit payment (which could include some state-licensed facilities), and some policies may pay benefits in only some of the state-licensed facilities. Policies may cover only a portion of the total care expenses. Understand the policy's "benefit triggers," which is when the insurance company decides to pay benefits. Benefit triggers may be in the policy under a section called "Eligibility for the Payment of Benefits" or "Eligibility for Benefits." For example, the policy typically pays benefits when you cannot do a certain number of activities of daily living—for example 2 of the 6. Long-term care policies may cover nursing home care, home health care, and personal care in your home; assisted living facility services; adult day care center services; and/or other community facility services. Most policies will exclude mental or nervous disorders—other than dementia—alcohol or drug addiction, war injuries or illnesses, government covered treatment, and attempted suicide or self-inflicted injuries. Long-term care insurance policies can be complicated and difficult to understand. Be certain to read the entire policy and get clarification on any points you may not understand.

Indemnity or per diem plans pay the full daily nursing home benefit selected regardless of the actual charges incurred; however, the policy only pays up to a set dollar amount. Indemnity plans could leave you short of money for long-term care expenses if those expenses exceed the limit of your policy. Reimbursement plans pay just the actual charges you incur up to the selected daily benefit. The insurance company decides if you are eligible for benefits and if those benefits are eligible for coverage. This may be referred to as the expense-incurred method of paying benefits.

Long-Term Care Insurance

Some policies allow you to add a nonforfeiture clause, which allows you to cancel your plan but still recoup money you've paid in premiums on daily long-term care expenses up to the amount you paid in—inflation is not covered, even if you chose the inflation protection initially. Without a nonforfeiture clause, you will receive nothing upon canceling your policy, even if you've paid premiums for 20 years prior to the cancellation. The addition of the nonforfeiture clause might increase your premium by 10% to 100%. Some policies may offer pooled benefits that cover more than one person such as both a husband and wife—these policies typically have a total benefit limit, which applies to all covered individuals on the policy.

If you've decided that a long-term care insurance policy is right for your situation, call facilities where you might receive care to get an idea of the present costs involved. Knowing the anticipated cost will help you in narrowing your choices for a policy. Call your state department of insurance, which will likely provide you with a list of approved long-term care insurance companies and plans for your state. Long-term insurance companies must be licensed in your state to sell policies. Your state department of insurance may also provide you with a great pamphlet called "A Shopper's Guide to Long-Term Care Insurance" written by the National Association of Insurance Commissioners (NAIC). The "Shopper's Guide to Long-Term Care Insurance" has worksheets to help you assess cost needs, compare policies, and to help you select coverages that suit your needs. The NAIC website is www.naic.org. The NAIC consists of the chief insurance regulators in each state, and its primary responsibility is to protect consumers' interests. You may also file insurance complaints with the NAIC.

Long-Term Care Insurance

You can get long-term insurance policies through private insurance companies, insurance company agents, through the mail, through employer group policies (which may offer a discount and allow employees to pay premiums with pretax dollars), through a life insurance policy, or through membership in an association. Policies can vary dramatically. Comparison shopping among different policies is a must in order to get the coverage that best fits your needs—compare benefits, facilities, coverage limits, excluded items, and costs. Be certain to check the insurance company's financial standing using the rating agencies (see Chapter 31, Figures 31.1 and 31.2)—select an insurance company that has 1 of the top 2 ratings. One good policy for long-term care insurance is sufficient.

Is long-term insurance coverage right for you? As with all other financial decisions, only you can answer that question. You may never need long-term coverage, you may need it for a period of time, or you may need it for the rest of your life. You will have to decide for yourself if the risks versus the cost warrant coverage. If you decide to get a policy, you will have to decide what balance of benefits versus cost and limitations you are willing to accept. Long-term care decisions are something of a gamble. While the future is uncertain, hopefully this information enables you to make a more informed decision.

Of course, God is the ultimate long-term care provider. The premium is at no charge to you. Jesus Christ said, "*There is no greater love than this, that a man should lay down his life for his friends. You are my friends, if you do what I command you. . . . You did not choose me; I chose you. I appointed you to go on and bear fruit, fruit that shall last; so that the Father may give you all that you ask in my name. This is my commandment to*

Long-Term Care Insurance

you: love one another"—John 15:13–17. Jesus Christ willingly went through the crucifixion to pay your debt for sins so that you can commune eternally with God. My friend, that is THE LOVE of the ultimate long-term care provider. When your physical body can no longer continue in this world, God will care for the believer's soul eternally.

Chapter 36

Other Insurance

We've already discussed the insurance most people should have or seriously consider—life, health, disability, homeowner or renter's, vehicle, and possibly long-term care insurance.

There are many types of insurance that most people do not need—credit life insurance, trip cancellation insurance, flight insurance, life insurance for children, collision insurance for old vehicles or rental cars, cancer insurance, mugging insurance, mortgage insurance, event or trip cancellation insurance, automobile extended service contracts, home warranty contracts from builders, rain insurance, baggage insurance, job-loss insurance, appliance or extended warranty insurance, contact lens insurance, and pet health insurance. U.S. consumers waste billions of dollars every year on either duplicate insurance or insurance that costs more than it's worth. Insurance coverage can be redundant. For example, people might purchase insurance for which they are already covered such as rental car insurance when they are covered under their personal auto policy or credit card coverage. The cost of insurance is expensive, and you are better off insuring losses for yourself when possible. For example, you are typically better off saving and investing the funds you would have spent on unnecessary insurance policies—those too costly or with little chance of claims—and accumulating funds in your 3- to 6-month emergency fund in order to handle small losses. For example, flight insurance has a very low probability of a claim since planes are one of the safest means of transportation, and it is not needed if the passenger already has life insurance. Life

Other Insurance

insurance is insuring against loss of income in the event of someone's death—so it does not necessarily make sense to buy life insurance on your children if they have no income and have no dependents. Your homeowner's or renter's insurance may already cover baggage insurance.

Sometimes insurance coverage can be too narrow in scope to be cost-effective. You are better off avoiding policies that insure against just one risk such as mugging insurance—obtain a good comprehensive health and life policy instead. Policies linked to a purchase such as automobile dealership extended warranties or builder homeowner warranties often have fine-print exclusions, and your potential losses could already be covered by existing policies such as the original car manufacturer's warranty or your homeowner's policy. Check you present coverage before purchasing additional coverage. It could be that if you were undercovered on something, it would be less expensive to add to your existing policy versus purchasing another insurance product.

Credit life insurance is sold to pay off revolving loans in case the borrower dies before the final payment. Credit life insurance has received condemnation from consumer groups for years as being overpriced with little chance of consumers' collecting on claims. For example, a consumer might get a credit life insurance policy on a car loan at $10,000 that costs him $260 over 4 years when he could just purchase a term life insurance product and get a lot more coverage that costs less and is not restricted to just paying off the car loan. Credit life insurance is usually a good buy only for the elderly or terminally ill.

It is a mistake to try and insure against every type of loss possible. When considering insurance, if the likelihood of a loss is minimal and the benefits of the policy do not

Other Insurance

compare favorably with the premium costs, then you are probably better off without the policy—take the money and invest it in your own emergency fund to be used for losses.

Some people have taken out duplicate health coverage policies, which are a waste of money because most insurers limit reimbursement of claims to the total value of the loss, including reimbursements from other insurance companies. If you have good health insurance, you might not need the portion of your automobile insurance that covers medical in accidents. Collision insurance on a vehicle 5 years or older can be too costly to justify—if the collision insurance exceeds 10% of the vehicle's value, you should probably drop it. Cancer insurance policies are not needed if you have a good health insurance policy—it is too expensive to purchase health insurance one disease at a time. Mortgage insurance is sold to protect the lender on loan payments in the event you die before the loan is repaid; life insurance policies typically will provide more coverage at a lower cost than mortgage insurance, and they are not restricted to just paying off your home loan. However, your mortgage lender might make mortgage insurance a requirement of the loan. Appliance insurance and most extended warranty insurance products are prohibitively costly for the amount of benefit you might receive—do not insure for losses that you could comfortably afford yourself. Health care costs for pets are usually low compared to humans, and in most cases pet owners should be able to fund their own pet care. Avoid insurance for noncatastrophic needs such as contact lens insurance and rain insurance.

In essence, you can be overinsured just as you can be underinsured. Eliminate duplicate coverage. Eliminate coverage you do not need. Use the savings to purchase coverage you do need. Use the remaining savings to help build your emergency fund or

Other Insurance

savings so you can self-insure against small losses. View insurance as protection against financial losses you could not afford on your own. Buy insurance that comprehensively or broadly covers you against catastrophic dollar losses.

People are paying billions of dollars per year on insurance premiums for products they do not need. In the end, the only insurance product anyone will need is God's assurance of life eternal, and that cost is free to the sinner. And yet, there are those who choose to reject their right to repent of their sins and accept God's grace. "*In the last days there will come men who scoff at religion and live self-indulgent lives, and they will say: 'Where now is the promise of his coming? Our fathers have been laid to their rest, but still everything continues exactly as it has always been since the world began'*"—2 Peter 3:3–4. "*There were heavens and earth long ago, created by God's word out of water and with water; and by water that first world was destroyed, the water of the deluge. And the present heavens and earth, again by God's word, have been kept in store for burning; they are being reserved until the day of judgement when the godless will be destroyed. . . . it is not his will for any to be lost, but for all to come to repentance. But the Day of the Lord will come; it will come, unexpected as a thief. On that day the heavens will disappear with a great rushing sound, the elements will disintegrate in flames, and the earth with all that is in it will be laid bare*"—2 Peter 3:5–10. We are all sinners; God wants you to be repentant of your sins and accepting of His love and grace. Do not waste your greatest opportunity. "*We have his promise, and look forward to new heavens and a new earth, the home of justice*"—2 Peter 3:13.

Wills, Trusts, and Estate Planning

Chapter 37

Wills, Trusts, and Estate Planning

Survivors are likely to encounter problems upon your death unless you take action to protect and transfer your assets according to your wishes with a will, living trust, or other arrangement that transfers your assets to your beneficiaries or heirs in the manner of your choosing. Without these preparations, your state's intestacy laws dictate who receives your assets and what they receive. To die intestate means to die without a will or arrangement for the settlement of your estate. State intestacy laws usually grant your assets to your closest family members; however, they are distributed by a formula, which can be very different from the distribution you would have preferred. The other negatives of dying without a will or other arrangement for your assets are that much of your property could be lost to legal expenses, taxes, or other costs that could have been avoided with the proper preplanning. For example, if you die without a will, the probate court might assign a court-appointed administrator. The administrator would settle the estate. The administration of the estate will likely be more complicated than the guildelines set by awell-prepared will, and that will cost more money. If you die with a will, you are said to have died testate.

A will, or last will and testament, states to whom—the beneficiaries—you wish each part of your estate to go once you are deceased. You can also name contingent beneficiaries in your will in case your beneficiaries die before you do. The will should appoint an executor—if the appointee is a male—or an executrix—if the appointee is a female—to probate the will. An executor or executrix—sometimes referred to as the

Wills, Trusts, and Estate Planning

administrator or personal representative—is someone who carries out or executes your wishes. Some people might also choose to appoint an independent coexecutor who could help to resolve disputes among family members—the coexecutor could be a bank or trust company. The executor or executrix you choose can be a trusted person, a bank, or some other financial institution. The executor or executrix manages the assets in the estate until they are distributed, prepares the tax returns for estate and inheritance taxes, and prepares the income tax returns on any earnings received by the estate before the assets are distributed. You should also name an alternate executor or executrix in your will in case the first executor or executrix is already deceased or incapacitated upon your death or simply is not up to the task of executing the will. State law normally dictates the specific manner in which a will should be written and witnessed—including any changes to the will. In most states, the owner of the will must sign it in the presence of at least 2 witnesses. Contact an attorney to make certain your will adheres to your state laws. Individual state laws can vary significantly on a multitude of specifics; be certain to choose a lawyer who is well versed in your state's will and trust specifics—or better yet, choose a lawyer who is an expert in estate planning. Even if you complete your own simple will, it is a good idea to have a lawyer review the wording to make certain it adheres to state requirements and in effect will execute your wishes as you intend. A will has no effect until you die. If you have changes such as marriage, the birth of a child, the death of a beneficiary, a divorce, a change in the size of your estate, your wishes change, you move to another state, or there are changes in the tax law, you should update your will. Probate court is the court procedure that determines the validity of your will and accesses the value of your assets and oversees the administration of the will by the

Wills, Trusts, and Estate Planning

executor or executrix. Probate court oversees the payment of claims against the estate and the distribution of remaining assets to the beneficiaries. Everything you own that is not distributed through a trust or by the naming of an account beneficiary—for example, a life insurance policy—is probate property. Insurance is not subject to probate proceedings. Insurance policies are paid to beneficiaries free of income taxes and usually free from the decedent's—the deceased person's—creditor claims. Having assets avoid probate court does not mean that those assets avoid taxes.

A basic will includes the following:

1. Your legal name
2. Your address
3. Your will's executor or executrix (and secondary executor[s], executrix[es])
4. Your wishes for guardian care of your dependents
5. Your wishes for the distribution of your assets to your beneficiaries
6. Your signature and date
7. 2 witnesses—signatures and dates

Without a will, a state court will decide who will be the guardian of your dependents. Most married couples have simple reciprocal wills in which each spouse's individual will is a "mirror image" of the other spouse's will. It is usually better to leave assets to beneficiaries in percentages to avoid conflicts that might arise by leaving specific dollar amounts. For example, what happens when you've written in your will that you wish to leave a specific relative $10,000 in a savings account, and the funds have been spent upon your death? You can also avoid disputes when leaving specific items to specific people by adding the simple words "if owned by me at my death." That simple phrase can eliminate countless headaches for an executor charged with giving a certain family heirloom to a specific relative when the heirloom was sold to pay medical bills for the deceased prior to death. The probate of a will can take 6 months, although the trustee can

Wills, Trusts, and Estate Planning

begin distributing property immediately after the deceased person's death. A will does not have any control over the disposition of property outside of probate. Nonprobate property can include life insurance policies and retirement plan beneficiary designations. A will is public record once it is probated. A will has no effect until you are deceased. Some people use other arrangements such as trusts to protect their assets while they are still living in the event of a disability such as a dementia that could leave them mentally incapacitated yet still alive.

A trust is an arrangement where the owner of the property—called a grantor, settlor, creator, donor, or trustor—transfers legal ownership to a trustee—someone else or an institution, who holds or manages the property (called the trust principal or corpus) for the benefit of the beneficiary. The beneficiary owns the property, but the trustee has control over it for a certain period of time—for example, until a dependent child reaches legal age. A trust helps to avoid probate and challenges to your will. A trust can be a substitute for a will; however, a trust disposes only of property that has been transferred to it. Regardless of what a will might say, a trust distributes the property held in the trust according to the terms of the trust. Likewise, the naming of beneficiaries on insurance and annuity contracts and retirement accounts override terms in a will. Trust can be used to manage assets for dependents until they reach a certain age. Trusts can be used to provide income for a spouse. Trusts can be used to benefit beneficiaries during their lifetime and then pass the remaining assets on to another beneficiary upon their death. There are many different types of trusts. Trusts have 2 main categories:

1. Those created while the grantor is still alive
2. Those created upon the death of the grantor

Wills, Trusts, and Estate Planning

The assets of any trusts that you control are subject to income taxes just as though there was no trust at all. <u>To keep property out of your taxable estate</u> using a trust or not, <u>you must give up both control over the property and the right to receive personal benefit from the property</u>.

Some people use a living trust as an alternative to a will. In a living trust, an individual's assets are transferred to the trust while the person is alive, and a trustee manages the assets. The trustee can either be the individual or a trusted agent appointed by the individual. While the individual is still alive, the trust becomes effective. Living trusts can be used to transfer assets or benefit heirs before you die. When the grantor dies, the assets in the trust are transferred to the beneficiaries without going through probate. A living trust can be changed or revoked anytime while the individual is still alive. A living trust can be one of the following:

1. Revocable
2. Irrevocable

Revocable living trusts are in effect during your lifetime and can be changed in any manner whenever you want or revoked at anytime before your death. Revocable trust assets pass to your beneficiaries after your death and avoid probate. A cotrustee is assigned and might take over in the event of your disability to manage the assets. This type of trust allows you to include complex details and arrangements for your assets. Upon death, the revocable living trust becomes irrevocable or unchangeable.

The trustee controls an irrevocable trust. Once assets are placed in an irrevocable trust, you loose control over them and cannot get them back. Irrevocable trusts can be created while you are alive or after your death through terms outlined in a will or other personal

Wills, Trusts, and Estate Planning

trusts. Once created, irrevocable trusts cannot be changed or revoked. Taking out insurance policies can help your beneficiaries tremendously if you have a sizable estate with nonliquid assets and expect sizable taxes upon your death. Life insurance can provide tax money so your beneficiaries do not have to liquidate noncash assets. For example, people may choose to have all ownership rights in their life insurance policies transferred to an irrevocable trust. Upon death, the trust and not your estate is the beneficiary of the life insurance proceeds. That way, the proceeds from your life insurance policy are not included in your estate for tax purposes. The individual who owns the life insurance policy gives up all rights of ownership including the right to borrow against the cash value and to assign the policy to another person. The transfer to an irrevocable trust of life insurance policies must be completed 3 years prior to your death or the proceeds will be included in your taxable estate. If an insurance policy is owned by the decedent as opposed to a spouse, dependent, trust, or other beneficiary, the proceeds are included in the decedent's estate for federal estate tax purposes. If the ownership of the insurance policy is by the irrevocable trust, the insurance policy proceeds are kept out of the taxable estate. Insurance policy proceeds paid to the decedent's estate are subject to the decedent's creditors. Life insurance proceeds are income tax-free to the recipient. Life insurance proceeds are estate tax-free if properly owned by a trust or third party. Life insurance proceeds owned by the decedent (or if the decedent has rights in the life insurance policy) will be included in the estate for estate tax purposes. You should name both primary and secondary beneficiaries on life insurance policies and retirement plans—if you do not, that money will likely go into

Wills, Trusts, and Estate Planning

your estate at death and be distributed according to your will, or by your state's legal formula if you have no will.

Testamentary trusts become effective when you die—they are set up through directions in your will and require that your will be probated.

A credit shelter trust keeps assets out of the estate of the surviving spouse and may spare your spouse a heavy tax burden. A credit shelter trust still gives the surviving spouse substantial access to the assets in the trust. Once the surviving spouse dies, the remaining assets in the credit shelter trust are disbursed to beneficiaries.

A spendthrift trust can own, manage, and invest assets for the benefit of children. The spendthrift trust can eventually distribute assets to the children when they become more mature, or make installments to them. A spendthrift trust can be set up under a will or any other trust established while you are living. The biggest advantage of a spendthrift trust is that you can protect your children from recklessly spending your assets by naming trustees who will be responsible for those assets.

You might also leave property through other means such as a business contract—for example, you might have a predetermined business contract to offer a business partner the opportunity to buy out your value in a jointly owned company. Stipulations in business contracts will override will stipulations.

A living will (or "advanced directive for health care") states your medical wishes in the event you become comatose or unable to speak for yourself. With a medical power of attorney (or health care power of attorney), you select a person to make medical decisions for you in the event you become incapacitated and unlikely to recover. A living will and medical power of attorney allow your wishes to be executed and prevent the possible

Wills, Trusts, and Estate Planning

spending of your assets to pay for costly medical treatment that might have little or no chance of succeeding. A standard power of attorney (or financial power of attorney) allows you to select someone to make financial decisions for you if you become incapacitated. A "letter of instruction" tells your family your desires regarding funeral plans, obituary information, and other instructions, which are not covered by other documents.

You should start your estate planning process by completing an inventory of all of your assets with an estimate of each asset's value. Also, complete a list of all debts you owe. Subtract the debts from the assets to get your estate value. The information you previously completed in the following should give you most of the data you will need:

1. SS31 Calculator-Household Inventory Form.xls
2. SS33 Calculator-Portfolio Allocation.xls

Also, be sure to include any other items such as the following:

1. Insurance Policies
2. Vehicles
3. Boats

Conduct your estate plan based on the size of your estate. You need to understand the federal estate tax laws in order to minimize the impact of taxes on your estate. Know the federal estate tax laws, gift tax, and generation-skipping transfer tax regulations. Currently, the estate tax shrinks through 2009, is eliminated in 2010, and returns again in 2011—unless Congress decides to make further changes to it. If the giver is deceased, the federal government may impose an estate tax. If the giver is alive, the federal government may impose a gift tax. Many states also impose similar taxes. Another tax that might be imposed on your estate is the "generation-skipping transfer tax" (GST tax). The GST tax

Wills, Trusts, and Estate Planning

was created to keep wealthy people from leaving assets to grandchildren instead of children in order to escape paying estate taxes twice on the same assets. The GST tax is automatically imposed at the highest federal estate tax rate and is in addition to the gift tax or federal estate tax owed on assets given to the second generation.

Figure 37.1 Current Federal Estate, GST Tax, and Gift Tax Rates[1]

Year	Federal Estate Tax Exemption (Unified Credit)	Generation-Skipping Transfer Tax (GST Tax) Exemption[2]	Gift-Tax Exemption	Maximum Tax Rate For Estate, GST Tax, & Gift Taxes Combined
2003	$1 Million	$1.12 Million	$1 Million	49%
2004[3]	$1.5 Million	$1.5 Million	$1 Million	48%
2005	$1.5 Million	$1.5 Million	$1 Million	47%
2006	$2 Million	$2 Million	$1 Million	46%
2007	$2 Million	$2 Million	$1 Million	45%
2008	$2 Million	$2 Million	$1 Million	45%
2009	$3.5 Million	$3.5 Million	$1 Million	45%
2010	Unlimited (Tax Repeal)	Unlimited (Tax Repeal)	$1 Million	0% 35% on Gift Tax Only (in excess of the $1 million exclusion). Estate & GST Tax Eliminated
2011	$1 Million	$1.38 Million	$1 Million	55% (Estate & GST Tax Reinstated)

Note that while the estate and gift taxes are scheduled to be repealed in the 2010 calendar year, they are reinstated in 2011—it is likely that Congress will make additional changes before then. In general, an individual can "give" $1 million to other individuals over their lifetime free of gift taxes. The gift amount is "unified" with the estate tax—the value of the gift reduces the amount that eventually can be excluded from estate taxes. It may

---

[1] Source: The Vanguard Group—"Plan Your Estate."
[2] Estimate for 2003 and later.
[3] The deduction for family-owned business is repealed.

Wills, Trusts, and Estate Planning

make sense to give assets to beneficiaries while you are still living as opposed to paying higher taxes as part of your estate upon your death.

Figure 37.2

IRS Calculations on Estate Taxes[4]				
Taxable Gift or Estate		**Tentative Tax**	
From	**To**	**Tax On "From" Column**	**Tax Rate on Excess or Amount Above Unified Credit**
$0.00	$11,000	$0.00	18%
$11,000	$20,000	$1,800	20%
$20,000	$40,000	$3,800	22%
$40,000	$60,000	$8,200	24%
$60,000	$80,000	$13,000	26%
$80,000	$100,000	$18,200	28%
$100,000	$150,000	$23,800	30%
$150,000	$250,000	$38,800	32%
$250,000	$500,000	$70,800	34%
$500,000	$750,000	$155,800	37%
$750,000	$1,000,000	$248,300	39%
$1,000,000	$1,250,000	$345,800	41%
$1,250,000	$1,500,000	$448,300	43%
$1,500,000	$2,000,000	$555,800	45%
$2,000,000	$2,500,000	$780,800	49%
$2,500,000	$2,500,000 +	$1,025,800	50%

You can use the chart in Figure 37.2 to estimate your estate taxes. For example, if your taxable estate were $2.3 million, you would fall between the $2,000,000 to $2,500,000 categories; $780,000 in taxes on the first $2,000,000 + 49% on the excess ($2.3 - $2.0 = $300,000 x 49% = $147,000) = $927,000 owed. This calculation is for taxable estate assets only—fortunately, there is some estate tax relief with the unified credit or federal unified estate and gift tax credit.

Assume it is the 2004 calendar year and you have $2 million in total assets you've left to your beneficiaries: $1.5 million is free of federal estate taxes with the unified credit;

---

[4] Source: 2003, SaveWealth.com.

Wills, Trusts, and Estate Planning

however, your estate will have to pay taxes on the excess—$2 million minus the $1.5 million = $500,000 x 48% (maximum tax rate) = $240,000 in taxes due for estate tax, GST tax, and gift taxes combined. For most families, estate tax planning is not a concern; however, if your family has combined assets over $1 million in value (or $1.5 million in 2004), you need to consider estate tax planning. Usually, the IRS requires cash payment of estate tax liabilities within 9 months of the date of death. These funds typically come from 4 sources:

1. Cash reserves
2. Loans
3. Liquidation of assets from the estate
4. Life insurance proceeds

Be certain your estate plan does not leave your beneficiaries in the position of having to sell investments or other assets to pay taxes at the wrong time because of a shortfall in liquid reserves.

The marital deduction allows one spouse to give to the other spouse (if you are U.S. citizens) any amount of assets free of gift or estate tax; however, you should be mindful of not wasting the one time federal unified estate and gift tax credit or unified credit on the first spouse to die—the problem arises when the second spouse dies. For example, assume a married couple has a $4 million estate. The first spouse dies in the 2006 calendar year, and the second spouse dies in the 2008 calendar year. Since the current law for the 2006–2008 tax years protects up to $2 million from federal estate taxes, Figure 37.3 outlines what would happen taxwise if the couple had established a credit shelter trust (or bypass trust) versus just leaving everything to the surviving spouse:

Wills, Trusts, and Estate Planning

Figure 37.3

Estate Example	Example Without a Credit Shelter Trust	Example With a Credit Shelter Trust
Total Estate	$4 million	$4 million
1st Spouse Dies in 2006 ($2 Million Federal Estate Tax Exemption)	$4 million left to the surviving spouse	$2 million left to the surviving spouse in a marital trust controlled by the surviving spouse. $2 million left to the credit shelter trust available to the surviving spouse as needed.
2nd Spouse dies in 2008 ($2 Million Federal Estate Tax Exemption)	$4 million - $2 million estate tax exemption = $2 million taxable x 45% (2008 estate tax rate) = $900,000 estate taxes due!	No estate taxes due.

In our example, the estate of this couple without a credit shelter trust would have to pay $900,000 in estate taxes. With a credit shelter trust, no estate taxes would be due because both spouses utilized the full $2 million federal unified estate and gift tax credit[5] available to each spouse. That's $900,000 extra dollars the estate can pass on to the couple's children or other beneficiaries. Without trusts, it is likely that only one spouse's estate tax credit can be utilized. The credit shelter trust must be established while both spouses are married and still alive. Often, a credit shelter trust is set up so the surviving spouse can receive income from the trust or even principal. To ensure that each spouse can use his or her entitled estate and gift tax credits, it may be necessary to split assets by retitling them from one spouse's name to the other's name. The estate plan's effectiveness can be negated by failing to retitle assets.

You can reduce your estate taxes and state death taxes by starting a gifting program while you are alive. If you have sufficient income from part of your holdings and would like to reduce estate taxes after your death, consider giving while you are still alive. The

---

[5] The IRS does not allow nonresident aliens of the United States to utilize the federal unified estate and gift credit.

Wills, Trusts, and Estate Planning

federal gift tax exclusion allows individuals to give up to $11,000[6] to as many beneficiaries as they desire per year without paying federal gift tax. If you are married, you can give as a couple up to $22,000 per year to any individual without gift tax implications. Giving every year can significantly reduce the implications of estate taxes after your death. Gifts in unlimited amounts to qualified charities may also be exempt from gift tax and give you current income tax deductions. Reducing your estate down to the unified credit allowable limits greatly reduces the future tax bite—for example, if you give to a nonprofit organization as opposed to just leaving money in your taxable estate, you potentially could save the following: 48% estate taxes + 28% income taxes to a beneficiary (other than a nonprofit organization) = 76% of every dollar going to taxes as opposed to 100% of the dollars going directly to a charity.

You might be able to contribute up to $55,000 or $110,000 for married couples in one year to a Section 529 college savings plan or prepaid tuition plan on behalf of another person—possibly a grandchild.[7] You can reduce your estate by paying directly to educational institutions or to medical providers any amount toward another person's expenses. Give any amount to your spouse—if your spouse is a U.S. citizen. Giving strategies that reduce the size of your estate can help to reduce your estate tax liabilities.

How you set up your accounts becomes important once you are deceased. Most couples have their home, checking accounts, savings accounts, and possibly their stock accounts set up as "joint tenants with right of survivorship" (JROS). JROS means that

---

[6] $11,000 is the limit in 2003—the limit is adjusted periodically for inflation.
[7] For gift tax purposes, contributions over $11,000 are prorated over 5 years. You will be required to file gift tax returns.

Wills, Trusts, and Estate Planning

each of the 2 or more "tenants" or owners of the property have equal and undivided interest in the asset. With a JROS stipulation on an account or asset, the decedent's share automatically shifts to the surviving joint tenant(s) at the moment of death. Nothing a will or trust says affects the automatic transfer of property with a JROS stipulation. For example, a mortgage deed with "William Hauser Roop" and "Sue Rowland Roop" "joint tenants with right of survivorship" means that in the event of William Roop's death, ownership of the home is automatically transferred to Sue Roop. Without the JROS stipulation, the property becomes part of William Roop's estate and the disposition of the property could be different than what William Roop had intended. Without prior arrangements in a will, trust, or other arrangement, the property could be divided among various beneficiaries. Also, your spouse may not have immediate access to funds in your checking account without the JROS stipulation. In just about every situation, using joint accounts saves no federal tax; 50% of property held jointly with a spouse is included in the decedent's estate for estate tax purposes.

Estate planning is the accumulation of assets, conservation of those assets, and the distribution of assets according to your wishes. Estate planning should consider 2 key elements:

1. The nature of the assets in your estate—which assets go to which beneficiaries?
2. The characteristics of your beneficiaries—can they handle the assets or not?

A good estate plan passes on the assets without needless legal aggravations. Your estate consists of all your assets such as personal items, jewelry, vehicles, stocks, bonds, mutual funds, savings accounts, retirement accounts, and other investments, land, real estate holdings, home, household belongings, insurance policies, and so on. A good estate plan

Wills, Trusts, and Estate Planning

insures that your family's needs are met and your assets are distributed in a timely manner to your beneficiaries or organizations while minimizing the taxes, fees, and work involved in settling your estate. Estate planning helps to determine how the ownership of your assets will pass to your beneficiaries when you are deceased—some property may pass to beneficiaries through a will, some property may be held in a trust, some property may be owned by you, some property may be owned by your spouse, and some property may be owned by both spouses. An essential part of estate planning is making sure the right beneficiaries are named. In estate planning, you should give as much attention to ownership and title designations of your property as you do to beneficiary designations. Assets can be passed to your beneficiaries either after your death or before your death through a myriad of alternative ways. Financial planning is an ongoing process. Financial planning involves budgeting, investing, insurance, retirement savings, taxes, and life goals such as achieving educational goals and home ownership. As your situation changes with events such as moving to another state, additions to your family, deaths in your family, changes in assets, changes in tax laws, and so on, you must review and update your financial plan accordingly. Everyone needs to do estate planning—it is not just for the wealthy.

Legal work in wills, trusts, and estates comprises some of the most complex and difficult areas of the law. Your attorney will likely charge more for work in these areas than others. Families often use a team of people to develop their estate plans such as an insurance agent, a financial planner or investment manager, a trust officer, a tax accountant, and an estate lawyer. An attorney is the only person licensed to draft legal documents. The estate lawyer should be well versed in your state's tax laws since laws

Wills, Trusts, and Estate Planning

can vary significantly from one state to another—what works in one state may not work in another state where you own property. To get names of qualified estate planning professionals in your area, ask trusted friends and coworkers for recommendations of financial and legal advisers. You might also check the American College of Trust and Estate Counsel's website at www.actec.org for information on lawyers in your area and more information on wills, trust, and estate planning. Check his or her credentials and choose a bona fide specialist—someone who has been specializing in estate planning for at least 5 years. A mistake in selecting the right estate planning attorney can cost your family thousands of dollars when your estate is settled. Estate planning specialists should be able to provide you with an estimated cost of their services based on the size and complexity of your estate .

To assist you in your preparation for your meeting with an estate planning attorney, please open the SS41 Calculator-Estate Planning Worksheet.xls.

Figure 37.4 Estate Planning Worksheet

1. **Open the "SS41 Calculator-Estate Planning Worksheet.xls."**
2. **Click "Yes" to enable macros, if necessary.**
3. **Fill in your own personal information in each white cell (you may tab from one white cell to another).**
4. **After completing the information in all of the white cells, press "Tab" and then click on the "MMW Recalculation Button"—the spreadsheet will make the remaining calculations for you.**

Wills, Trusts, and Estate Planning

Estate Planning Worksheet

FILL IN THE WHITE CELLS, THE REST OF THE CELLS WILL BE CALCULATED FOR YOU
(Fill In The White Cells, Press Tab, Click On The "MMW Recalculation Button" or press "Cntrl + m")

Comments:

MMW Recalculation Button

Assets--	Value/or Equity	Legal Name Currently On Account/and or Beneficiary
Bank Accounts:		
Bonds:		
Business Interests:		
Cash:		
Certificates of Deposit:		
Home (Primary Residence):		

Is the account in your name, your name and your spouse's name (if so, does it have "JROS" on it?), or is it set up in some other manner?

For example: "Bruce Morgan Fricke and Sherri Hayden Fricke JROS"

- - -

Home (Secondary Residence(s)):		
Investments (Other):		
Life Insurance:		
Mutual Funds:		
Personal Property:		
Real Estate (Other):		
Retirement Accounts:		
Savings Accounts:		
Stocks:		
Other Assets:		
Total Assets:	$0.00	

Debts--	Amount Owed	Legal Name Currently On Account
Business Loans/Debts:		
Home Loans:		

Note: Life Insurance policy owner's name and beneficiary's name.

Note: Vehicles, boats, jewelry, artwork, etc.

Wills, Trusts, and Estate Planning

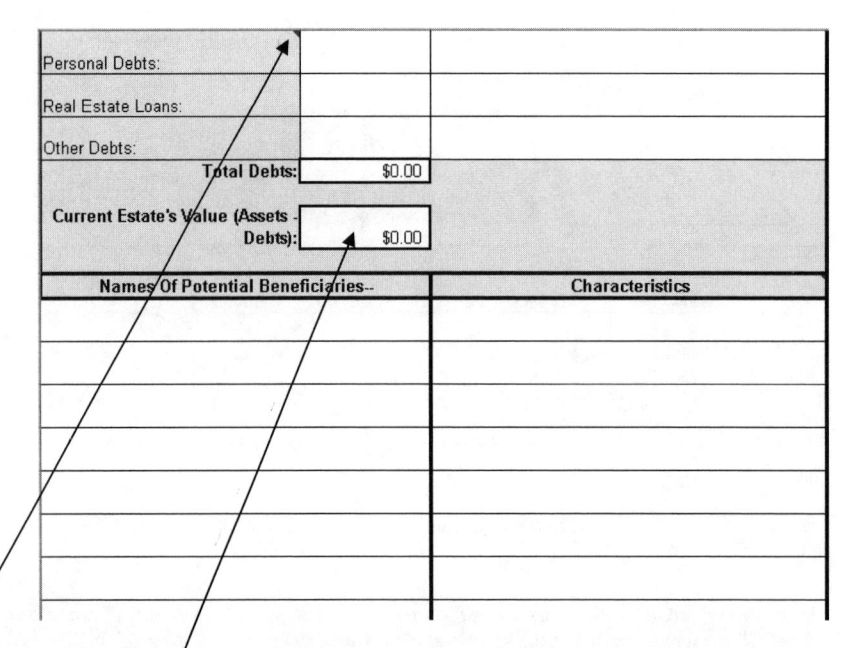

Personal Debts:		
Real Estate Loans:		
Other Debts:		
Total Debts:	$0.00	
Current Estate's Value (Assets - Debts):	$0.00	
Names Of Potential Beneficiaries--		Characteristics

Note: Vehicle loans, boat loans, jewelry debt, artwork debt, credit card debt, etc.

The "Current Estate's Value" is important information—it will help to determine what types of estate planning measures you may wish to pursue.
Characteristics for potential beneficiaries might include "minor dependent child," "spouse and a responsible adult," "nonprofit organization," or "educational institution."

There are 2 of these worksheets available for your use.

This should give you a good starting point on assessing your estate plan needs and help to point out necessary changes regarding retitling assets and so on.

Your estate plan information should be kept in a safe place that is easily accessible to your survivors. You will need to notify your executor or executrix where he or she can find your estate plan information in the event of your death so that the process of transferring your assets can begin. To assist you in preparing your estate plan information recap, please open the SS42 Estate Plan Information Recap.xls.

Figure 37.5 Estate Plan Information Recap.xls

1. Open the "SS42 Estate Plan Information Recap.xls."
2. Fill in your own personal information in each white cell (you may tab from one white cell to another).

Wills, Trusts, and Estate Planning

Estate Plan Information Recap

Comments:

Assets--	Account #/Policy #	Phone Number/and or Email Address
Checking Account:		
Boat Titles:		
Bonds/or Broker Accounts:		
Cemetery Deeds:		
Certificates of Deposit:		
Homeowner's/Renter's Insurance Policies:		
IRA's/or Broker Accounts:		

- - -

Life Insurance Policies:		
Mortgages Receivable:		
Mutual Funds/or Broker Accounts:		
Notes Receivable:		
Pension Funds:		
Property Deeds:		
Savings Account:		
Stock Certificates/or Broker Accounts:		
Vehicle Insurance Policies:		
Vehicle Titles:		
Other Assets--	Account #/Policy #	Phone Number/and or Email Address

- - -

435

Wills, Trusts, and Estate Planning

Debts--	Account #/Policy #	Phone Number/and or Email Address
Boat Loans:		
Business Loans/Debts:		
Credit Card Debt:		
Home Loans:		
Real Estate Loans:		
Vehicle Loans:		

Other Debts--	Account #/Policy #	Phone Number/and or Email Address

- - -

Estate Contact	Name/Company Name/or Institution	Street Address	City/State/Zip	Phone Number/Cell Phones	E-mail Address
Accountant					
Attorney					
Banker					
Business Partner					
Executor or Executrix (Primary)					
Executor or Executrix (Alternate)					
Family Contact					
Financial Adviser					

- - -

Wills, Trusts, and Estate Planning

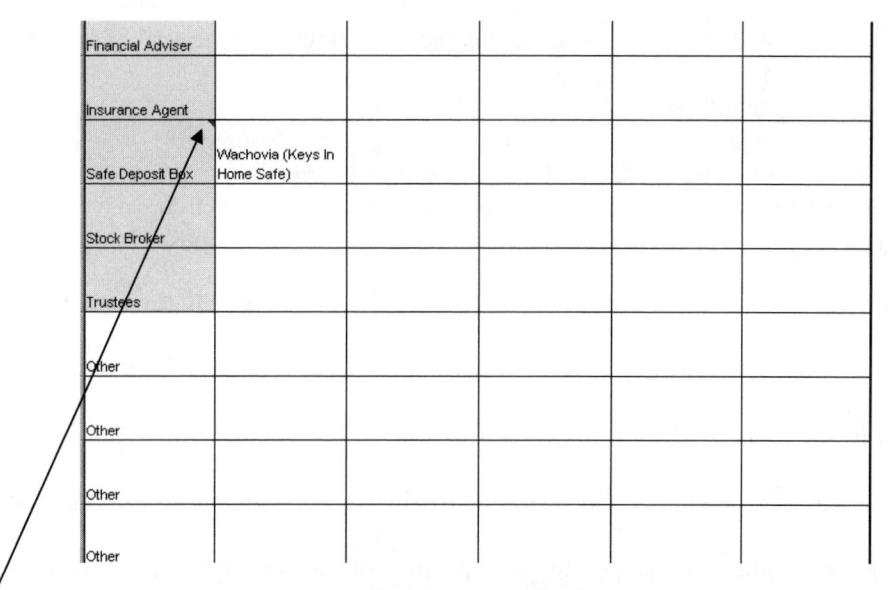

Financial Adviser					
Insurance Agent					
Safe Deposit Box	Wachovia (Keys In Home Safe)				
Stock Broker					
Trustees					
Other					
Other					
Other					
Other					

Note: Include information about the location of the keys for the safe-deposit box.

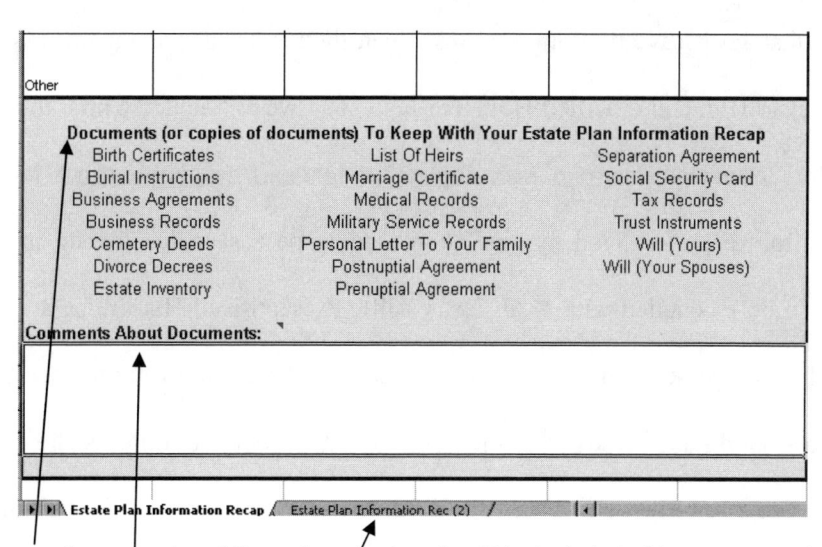

- - -

Other				

Documents (or copies of documents) To Keep With Your Estate Plan Information Recap

Birth Certificates	List Of Heirs	Separation Agreement
Burial Instructions	Marriage Certificate	Social Security Card
Business Agreements	Medical Records	Tax Records
Business Records	Military Service Records	Trust Instruments
Cemetery Deeds	Personal Letter To Your Family	Will (Yours)
Divorce Decrees	Postnuptial Agreement	Will (Your Spouses)
Estate Inventory	Prenuptial Agreement	

Comments About Documents:

\ Estate Plan Information Recap / Estate Plan Information Rec (2) /

These documents—or copies of these documents—should be included with your estate plan information recap and accessible to your executor.

In the "Comments About Documents" section, include any special instructions to your executor such as "Original birth certificate in safe-deposit box at bank."

There are 2 worksheets for "Estate Plan Information"—one for your spouse.

437

Wills, Trusts, and Estate Planning

In the book *The Will of God*, Leslie D. Weatherhead states that the will of God can be broken down into the following:

1. "The intentional will of God—God's ideal plan for men"
2. "The circumstantial will of God—God's plan within certain circumstances"
3. "The ultimate will of God—God's final realization of his purposes"

In essence, God's intentional will is for us to have the best in our lives. Circumstantial will involves man's free will to choose to do the right thing, to have faith and belief in God, and to love our neighbors, or we can choose to reject God's love, do the wrong things, and hate our neighbors. God's ultimate will always wins out—regardless of the "bad things that sometimes happen to good people" or the consequences of man's poor choices. The example Leslie D. Weatherhead uses is that God's intent or "intentional will" was that Jesus save us from our sins. Even though Jesus was innocent, some men chose to reject Him and crucified Him. Through sin, "we all" nailed Christ to that cross. Except for Jesus/God, no one is completely righteous (without sin). Humanity is estranged from a perfect God by sin. There had to be a sacrifice for sin in order for humanity to be reconciled with God. Jesus willingly sacrificed His life as a ransom for sin—all the past, present, and future sins of everyone. Three days after the death of Jesus on the cross, God raised Jesus from the dead so that the believer might share eternal life with God. The risen Messiah has already forgiven us for our sins. God's "ultimate will" allows those that confess their sins and have faith and belief in God to be forgiven. "*For God took the sinless Christ and poured into him our sins. Then, in exchange, he poured God's goodness into us!*"—2 Corinthians 5:21 (Living Bible). So, regardless of the pain, hurt, and suffering that might occur in God's "circumstantial will" due to man's evil inclinations, accidents, or other misfortune, God's "ultimate will" is accomplished

Wills, Trusts, and Estate Planning

through the sacrifice of Christ. The choice is yours—you can allow misfortune or circumstances to drive you further from God, or you can exercise your free will to allow misfortune or circumstances to draw you closer to God. The Rev. Joe Peabody liked to say, "God can use what He would not choose" if you only allow Him to do so. Hopefully, your choice will be to draw closer to God under all circumstances.

Being a Christian requires more than just a commitment to God. Being a Christian is surrendering your will to the will of God. No one in his right mind wants to endure pain and suffering. Jesus was well aware of the horrible agony and indignity that went along with death by beating, crucifixion, and being stabbed in the side by a Roman soldier's lance. "*Then came the day of Unleavened Bread, on which the Passover victim had to be slaughtered*"—Luke 22:7. During the Last Supper with His disciples, Jesus said, "*How I have longed to eat this Passover with you before my death!*"—Luke 22:15. Shortly before Judas betrayed Jesus and had the chief priests, the officers of the temple police, and the elders arrest Him, Jesus and His disciples made their way to the Mount of Olives. Jesus told His disciples, "*Pray that you may be spared the hour of testing*"—Luke 22:40. Jesus prayed himself, "*Father, if it be thy will, take this cup away from me. Yet not my will but thine be done*"—Luke 22:42. Jesus willingly surrendered His will in an earthly body to God's will. Jesus was obedient to His appointed role as the Messiah ("the anointed one") chosen by God as Savior from sin for all mankind. God's prophet Isaiah prophesized the sacrifice of the Messiah around 700 years before the crucifixion of Jesus by saying, "*He was despised and rejected by men, a man of sorrows, and familiar with suffering. Like one from whom men hide their faces he was despised, and we esteemed him not. Surely he took up our infirmities and carried our sorrows, yet we considered him stricken by*

Wills, Trusts, and Estate Planning

God, smitten by him, and afflicted. But he was pierced for our transgressions, he was crushed for our iniquities; the punishment that brought us peace was upon him, and by his wounds we are healed . . . the LORD has laid on him the iniquity of us all"—Isaiah 53:3–6 (New International Version).

Like Jesus, you should surrender your will to God's will, and great things will ultimately happen. It is not God's "intentional will" that you suffer; in fact, God would rather you be spared the test. However, if you are tested, remember that pain in this world is temporary; life with God is eternal—the ultimate victory already won through Christ. God does not want you going through life feeling guilty about the crucifixion; God wants you to go through life feeling appreciative of Christ's sacrifice so that you might live life more abundantly. It is for the guilty that Christ willingly chose to die—that we might be forgiven. "*We had the sentence of death in ourselves, that we should not trust in ourselves but in God who raises the dead*"—2 Corinthians 1:9 (New King James Version). The death of Jesus on the cross replaces the believer's eternal death because Christ died to sin in our place. "*For to this end we both labor and suffer reproach, because we trust in the living God, who is the Savior of all men, especially of those who believe*"—1 Timothy 4:10 (New King James Version). Preparation for death prepares you to live. Exercise your free will by surrendering to God's will. Put your trust in God by placing your faith and belief in the resurrected Christ, and in so doing lay claim to your estate in God's Kingdom. An estate free of cost to you, with no taxes, no creditors, and no mortgage—the price paid for by Christ.

Identity Theft

Chapter 38

Identity Theft

Identity theft is the fraudulent use of your name and information by someone else to obtain credit, merchandise, or services. Identity theft occurs when someone steals your personal information such as your name, address, Social Security number, date of birth, a credit card number, or other personal information and uses that information to apply for loans or credit cards. The thief then makes purchases and typically has the bills sent to a false address so the fraud goes undetected for a longer period of time. The FBI states that identity theft is the fastest growing white-collar crime in America. The Federal Trade Commission conducted a survey and found that nearly 1 in 10 Americans have been victims of identity theft in the last 5 years. Thieves get personal information by stealing credit and bank cards; stealing mail; rummaging through trash; obtaining personal information shared on the Internet; buying information from employees who work at businesses that have personal or financial information; stealing information from databases or commercial websites that are not adequately protected and contain personal data such as credit card information; fraudulently obtaining credit reports; peering over people's shoulders as they punch in access codes, passwords, or personal identification numbers (PINs) in public places; and other means. Credit card fraud is the most common identity theft. Some thieves have stolen personal information and used it to take out home loans on the victim's house—they normally apply for small enough loans to avoid intense scrutiny and cash the loan check before the victim receives a mortgage payment book in the mail.

Identity Theft

Identity thieves only need 3 pieces of vital information to open credit or bank accounts under your name or to drain your existing accounts:

1. Your legal name
2. Your Social Security number
3. Your date of birth

Federal laws place caps on monetary losses to identity theft victims; however, even in routine identity theft cases, it take victims an average of 2 years to clear their names. Victims may spend 30 to 60 hours resolving identity theft credit issues.

Individuals should take measures to prevent identity thieves from obtaining personal information. Businesses and financial institutions should use encryption and better systems to prevent theft. There should be internal computer security levels to help prevent employee theft of personal information—only the most trusted employees with the highest security clearance should have access to confidential data. Individuals should install firewalls and virus detection software on their personal computers to help protect information. Turn your computer off or unplug the Internet connection when you are not using it to help discourage hackers. Use passwords or personal identification numbers that are at least 8 characters long—the longer the password or PIN, the more difficult it is for a thief to decipher. Memorize your user IDs and passwords so they cannot be stolen —only keep written documentation of IDs and passwords in extremely secure places such as a bank safe-deposit box. Never disclose personal information such as your Social Security number or birth date on Web pages or resumes. Do not use email to send personal data that could be used in identity theft. Never respond to an unsolicited email request for your personal information. Unless you initiated the transaction, never disclose personal information that could be used in identity theft. Do not give anyone who has

Identity Theft

emailed you or telephoned you personal data without verifying the legitimacy of the person/company independently of the encounter. Remove and destroy hard drives on personal computers before discarding them or use hardware shredding software to destroy personal information. Destroy floppy disks or CDs that contain personal information before discarding them.

If you do not own a paper shredder, buy one. Use the shredder to destroy any documents you are planning to discard that a thief might use to obtain credit or access to your accounts such as wage statements, medical statements, bank account or broker account statements, credit card statements, preapproved credit card offers, bills, insurance correspondence, receipts, or any other documents that might have sensitive information on them. You can call the "Credit Reporting Industry Pre-Screening Opt-Out Number" at 1-888-567-8688 to stop preapproved credit offers from being mailed to your home for a period of 2 years or permanently. Calling the "Opt-Out Number" prevents the credit agencies from giving your personal information to credit card companies, which prevents preapproved credit card solicitations from being mailed to you. You must provide the "Opt-Out Number" with your Social Security number in order for them to access your records. When paying by credit card or debit card, try not to let the business employee disappear from view in order to avoid "skimming." Skimming is when dishonest employees use handheld magnetic card readers to copy information from the magnetic strip on your card. Always be careful to get your card back from employees when paying bills. Be certain to safeguard credit card receipts, debit receipts, and ATM receipts—never toss them into a public trash receptacle; shred them before discarding them. Replace regular mailboxes with locked mailboxes. Personally deliver sensitive

Identity Theft

documents such as bill payments and checks to the U.S. post office for mailing. Use direct deposit for checks whenever possible. After closing a bank account, destroy all unused checks. Secure all checks in a safe place. When ordering new checks, pick them up in person as opposed to having them mailed to your home. Do not carry sensitive information with you unless it is absolutely necessary—leave your Social Security card, government ID, birth certificate, passport, and other information in a locked secure place until needed. Only carry in your wallet or purse the bare essential information you will need at the time. Shield keypads with your free hand when using ATMs, phones, computers, or other devices in public places where an identity thief might peer over your shoulder. Avoid using cordless phones when conducting sensitive business since identity thieves might be using eavesdropping equipment to steal your information. Do not put your Social Security number on your checks.

Review your credit reports at least once per year from the 3 major credit bureaus—Equifax, Trans Union, and Experian. Your credit report contains your Social Security number, a listing of your account numbers (present and past), employers (present and past), and your overall credit score. Once again, the contact information for the major credit agencies for credit reports is listed in Figure 38.1.

Figure 38.1 Major Credit Agencies

Name	Address	Phone	Website
Equifax Information Services LLC Center	P.O. Box 740241 Atlanta, GA 30374	800-685-1111	www.equifax.com
Experian National Consumer Assistance Center	P.O. Box 2002 Allen, TX 75013	888-397-3742	www.experian.com/consumer
Trans Union LLC Consumer Disclosure Center	P.O. Box 1000Chester, PA 19022	800-888-4213 (if entitled to a free report—order via mail or online for a paid report)	www.transunion.com

Identity Theft

Monitor each charge and transaction on all credit card statements or other financial statements to insure that they were made by you. Immediately check on any unexplained bills. Keep a list of your credit cards, bank accounts, and other financial information including account numbers, expiration dates, customer service numbers, and fraud telephone numbers in a secure location. You might even make photocopies of all the credit cards, your driver's license, or other information you might carry in your wallet or purse in the event it is stolen. That will make reporting missing or stolen information easier and quicker. Immediately report any loss or theft. The Federal Trade Commission (FTC Identity Theft Hotline: 1-877-ID-THEFT or 1-877-438-4338) investigates interstate and Internet fraud. The FTC has a "Complaint Input Form" on its website at www.consumer.gov/idtheft. The FTC "Complaint Input Form" is an excellent way to get organized for the process of handling identity theft with all those individuals and companies that need to be notified. If the theft involves stolen mail, you will also need to file a U.S. Postal Service "Mail Fraud Complaint Form" at www.usps.com/postalinspectors/fraud/MailFraudComplaint.htm.

Telephone one of the major credit agencies if you suspect identity theft to file a fraud alert—that agency will then notify the other 2 agencies for you.

Figure 38.2 Major Credit Agencies "Fraud Alert" Phone Numbers

Identity Theft

Name	Phone #'s in Order to File "Fraud Alert"
Equifax Information Services LLC Center	800-525-6285
Experian National Consumer Assistance Center	888-397-3742
Trans Union LLC Consumer Disclosure Center	800-680-7289

The credit agencies will then place a security alert on your credit file to inform merchants, banks, credit unions, retailers, other credit lenders, and other businesses to the possibility of identity theft on your accounts. A fraud alert asks merchants not to allow new credit without your explicit approval. Your name will be removed from direct mail offers for credit. You will also be able to get a free file on your credit history for 3 months following your call to the first credit agency.

Contact your local law enforcement officials regarding any theft. A police report can help clear up your credit history from the unauthorized use by identity thieves. A police report is useful when dealing with the merchants or businesses involved in the stolen goods or services.

Notify the merchants, retailers, banks, the financial institution, credit card company, or any other business that the thief used to steal money, goods, or services in your name—supply them with a copy of the police report and/or the FTC complaint affidavit. Immediately close all accounts that have been used by thieves. Choose new passwords and PINs for all your other accounts as a precautionary measure.

For more information about identity theft, visit the Identity Theft Resource Center (ITRC) at www.idtheftcenter.org and the Privacy Rights Clearinghouse website at www.privacyrights.org.

Identity Theft

Beware of the ultimate identity theft. If Satan (the Devil) was bold enough to tempt[1] Jesus, then Satan is certainly bold enough to tempt you. Satan is often referred to as the "deceiver" or the "tempter" and for good reason. Satan tries to steal your identity as one of God's children and your inheritance of eternal life with God. Satan tries to keep you from accomplishing God's will for your life while you are on this earth.

In preparation for his ministry on earth, "*Jesus was then led away by the Spirit into the wilderness, to be tempted by the devil. For forty days and nights he fasted, and at the end of them he was famished. The tempter approached him and said, 'If you are the Son of God, tell these stones to become bread.' Jesus answered, 'Scripture says, "Man cannot live on bread alone; he lives on every word that God utters."' The devil then took him to the Holy City and set him on the parapet of the temple. 'If you are the Son of God,' he said, 'throw yourself down; for Scripture says, "He will put his angels in charge of you, and they will support you in their arms, for fear you should strike your foot against a stone."' Jesus answered 'Scripture says again, "You are not to put the Lord your God to the test."' Once again, the devil took him to a very high mountain, and showed him all the kingdoms of the world in their glory. 'All these,' he said, 'I will give you, if you will only fall down and do me homage.' But Jesus said, 'Begone, Satan! Scripture says, "You shall do homage to the Lord your God and worship him alone."' Then the devil left him; and angels appeared and waited on him*"—Matthew 4:1–11.

This scripture points out several messages for us. Satan knew Jesus was the Son of God, and he tried to stop the forthcoming ministry of Christ through deceit and deception.

---

[1] While Jesus was tempted, Jesus was without sin.

Identity Theft

Satan tried to destroy God's purpose for Jesus. Satan wanted to stop Jesus from accomplishing God's will that we be saved from our sins. Satan knows the Bible and twisted scripture for his own evil purposes. Jesus rebuked Satan with the proper meaning of God's Word.[2] As Jesus was prepared for spiritual warfare, you must prepare. Like Jesus, you should pray and study the Bible so when you are tempted by Satan to do the wrong things, or make the wrong choices, you will be able to rebuke Satan with God's Word and then move on from temptation to accomplishing God's purpose for your life. Christians who are not steeped in the Word expose themselves to opponents in the fallen world, the flesh, and the evil one—they succumb to fear and forget to love God as God deserves to be loved, and they may not treat their fellow man with the love that Christ commands. Seek God's Word until it pierces bone and marrow—read it, hear it, understand it, live it, and have a deep, abiding, intimate, personal relationship with Christ. "*Hear, O Israel, the Lord is our God, one Lord, and you must love the Lord your God with all your heart and soul and strength*"—Deuteronomy 6:4–5. Experience God, think what God thinks, feel what God feels. Oswald Chambers once said, "The root of all sin is the suspicion that God is not good."[3] Satan attempts to utilize doubt, fear, worry, stress, anxiety, bitterness, confusion, depression, disappointment, disillusionment, envy, frustration, greed, guilt, gossip, hate, hopelessness, hostility, hurt, ineptness, jealousy, being judgmental, loneliness, lust, being neglected, being overwhelmed, pity, feelings of powerlessness, pride, rage, regret, sadness, sorrow, feelings of superiority, terror,

---

[2] Paraphrase from Bill Roop, Norcross First United Methodist Church Library Room Emmaus Reunion Group.
[3] An interview question with Josh McDowell, Morgantown Bible Church, MBC Family: *This is Your L-Wife-Part II*, 3/2/2003, www.morgantownbible/church.com, peter6.htm.

Identity Theft

ungratefulness, vanity, and feelings of vengefulness to steal God's joy and peace in our lives. Do not allow Satan to steal your joy and peace. Do not allow Satan's deceit to convince you that God does not love you. Do not allow Satan to deceive you into not accomplishing God's purpose for your life. Do not allow Satan to steal your identity as a child of God. Do not allow Satan to steal your promise of eternity with God. When facing a life crisis, instead of only focusing on how big your problems are, concentrate on how big your God is.

When tempted, Gary Fleck's[4] grandmother liked to say "get thee behind me Satan!" She knew that God's purpose could not be fulfilled to its fullest while carrying the excess baggage Satan might try to place in her life. When tempted, do not walk but run from the temptation. When the Apostle Peter tempted Jesus by trying to get him to avoid the upcoming suffering and death by crucifixion, Jesus replied, "*Get behind Me Satan! You are an offense to Me, for you are not mindful of the things of God, but the things of men*"—Matthew 16:23 (The Soul Care Bible). Jesus would not be tempted to avoid suffering at the expense of God's will that we be saved from our sins.

There is an old adage that says, "God is good, all the time. All the time, God is good." God is infinitely good—believe it and receive your inheritance now!

---

[4] Gary Fleck is a former neighbor of the author.

Grace, Faith, Purpose, and Peace

Chapter 39

Grace, Faith, Purpose, and Peace

Grace is unmerited, unearned, and a nonrepayable favor from God. While you receive God's grace for free, grace does not come without cost. Grace came at a great cost—it came at the expense of Jesus Christ's death on the cross. It was God's ultimate sacrifice for our sins. Jesus Christ is the emancipator from slavery to sin.

Grace is

> **G**od's
> **R**edemption
> **A**t
> **C**hrist's
> **E**xpense

so that you might enjoy life abundantly and eternally.

God loves you so much; He was willing to die for you—there is no greater love than that! Bruce N. Fisk states, "To proclaim 'the message of the cross' . . . is to insist, in defiance of human logic, that God has used the grisly death of Jesus to inaugurate a new age of salvation. . . . Christ's humiliating defeat was (incredibly) God's glorious triumph."[1] God's grace is sufficient for all of your needs!

---

[1] Bruce N. Fisk, *Interpretation Bible Studies, First Corinthians*, pages 9–10.

Grace, Faith, Purpose, and Peace

As the Rev. John Newton would say, that truly is "amazing grace."

```
    A
    M
G R A C E
    Z
    I
    N
    G
```

"The Lord has promis'd good to me,
His word my hope secures;
He will my shield and portion be,
As long as life endures.

Yes, when this flesh and heart shall fail,
And mortal life shall cease;
I shall possess, within the veil,
A life of joy and peace."
—John Newton (excerpt from the hymn "Amazing Grace," first edition, 1779)

"*Out of his full store we have all received grace upon grace; for while the Law was given through Moses, grace and truth came through Jesus Christ. No one has ever seen God; but God's only Son, he who is nearest to the Father's heart, he has made him known*"—John 1:16–18. "*The grace of the Lord Jesus be with you all*"—Revelation 22:21.

That life of joy and peace is available to you, right now. It is your inheritance from God! The "evil one" may try to deceive you into nonbelief or doubt about claiming your inheritance; however, **"the One"** guarantees your inheritance. Just as there is a heaven, there is a hell. Hell is total separation from God. Choose to confess your sins, ask for

Grace, Faith, Purpose, and Peace

forgiveness of your sins, and accept Jesus Christ—"the Lamb of God"—as your personal Lord and Savior.

God is the Father, the Creator, and the Provider. God is Spirit. Jesus Christ is the Son of God, the Redeemer, and the Savior from our sins. The Holy Ghost is the Holy Spirit, the Sustainer, and the Indwelling Spirit. At Pentecost, the descent of the Holy Spirit on the apostles strengthened them in preparation for a life of accomplishing God's Will. At last, the Holy Spirit came to be with them, within them, and upon them. God, Jesus Christ, and the Holy Spirit, for the scientifically minded, can be thought of as three forms of the same thing—similar to ice, water, and steam. In other words, God is all three.

Your soul can be described as everything about you except your physical body. Does an atheist have a soul? Yes, every human being has a soul. What then differentiates the atheist from the Christian? A Christian has faith and belief in God and in His Son, Jesus Christ. This exercise of religious faith and the choice to accept God's love results in living your life better now—more in accordance to what God's will is for your life. Just as there is a bit of God in everyone, there is also the potential for good and evil in everyone. A Christian makes a conscious effort to choose right over wrong. It does not mean that you will be perfect—only God is perfect. It does mean that you will make an honest attempt to live your life to the best of your ability according to the teachings of Jesus Christ. A life of prayer, study, and service, which enhances God's Kingdom. A life of growing and becoming more God-like. A life that may not always live up to your full potential, but forgiven by God when you fall short and when you ask for His forgiveness. A life that is constantly seeking improvement. In so doing, you are preparing your soul for a human death. This, then, is the meaning of life—preparation of the soul for the

Grace, Faith, Purpose, and Peace

physical death of your body through worshiping God. Your soul is the only possession you have that cannot be taken away by death. Through God's gift of free will, your soul is the only possession over which you have ultimate control.

Reason and intellect can only carry you so far; ultimately, it is a question of faith. "For belief begins where knowledge and proof have their limit."[2] Do you believe in God? If so, you shall share life eternal! Your eternal communion with God begins immediately in your present lifetime. By faith in God you shall receive life eternal—not by works, not by good deeds, and not by service—although those are important to the nurturing of one's soul. "*Hold the faith that Jesus is the Christ, the Son of God, and that through this faith you may possess life by his name*"—John 20:31. Intellectual reasoning can carry us only so far; divine truth and faith can carry us home. Faith itself is a gift from God. "*Jesus asked his disciples, 'Who do men say that the Son of Man* [Jesus] *is?' They answered, 'Some say John the Baptist, others Elijah, others Jeremiah, or one of the prophets.' 'And you,' he asked, 'who do you say I am?' Simon Peter answered: 'You are the Messiah, the Son of the living God.' Then Jesus said: 'Simon son of Jonah, you are favoured indeed! You did not learn that from mortal man; it was revealed to you by my heavenly Father*"—Matthew 16:13–18. If your religious faith needs strengthening, ask God for it, and God will grant your request, for God is indeed a generous giver of faith and all else; God refuses no one. "*Without faith it is impossible to please him* [God]; *for anyone who comes to God must believe that he exists and that he rewards those who search for him*"—

---

[2] Werner Keller, *The Bible As History*," page 437.

Grace, Faith, Purpose, and Peace

Hebrews 11:6. "*Even gold passes through the assayer's fire, and more precious than perishable gold is faith which has stood the test*"—1 Peter 1:7.

God is love. God loves you. God loves you enough to send His very best—His Son, Jesus Christ. So, smile; through the death and resurrection of Jesus Christ, both today and tomorrow whisper joy.

Do more than just commit to God; surrender to God. Once you have surrendered your will to God, God's will becomes much more evident in your life. God blesses each individual with unique gifts only bestowed to that particular person. Every person is infinitely valuable, every person is unique, and God has specific purposes for each individual. Humility is the key to obedience, and obedience is the key to the heart of God. To be humble is to understand that God is God and you are not—salvation can only come from God. If you obediently surrender to God, God is able to utilize your gifts to accomplish great things. If you choose not to be obedient to God's will, then your gifts may not be fully utilized, or God's purpose for your life may go unfulfilled. God gives special gifts unique only to you; what you do with those gifts is your gift back to God. Gifts are for God's glory and purpose. Your limited gift to God can yield unlimited results by God. There is a difference between knowledge and wisdom. Knowledge is mental recognition. When mental recognition moves to the heart and is manifested into action to serve, knowledge becomes wisdom. "*But if any of you lacks wisdom, let him ask of God, who gives to all men generously and without reproach, and it will be given to him*"—James 1:5 (New American Standard Bible). True wisdom is not just informed knowledge; it is knowledge that has been transformed by the Holy Spirit. Don't just be informed about God's love; be transformed by the Holy Spirit. When the Holy Spirit

Grace, Faith, Purpose, and Peace

transforms you, God's sacred purpose for your life can be achieved. God is not looking for people of greatness; God is looking for people who recognize the greatness of God. When you obey God, you worship Him.

God's gift of grace cannot be bought. Peter admonished, "*Your money perish with you for thinking God's gift can be bought!*"—Acts 8:20 (Living Bible). "*Do not love the world, nor the things in the world. If anyone loves the world, the love of the Father is not in him*"—1 John 2:15 (New American Standard Bible). "*Then he [Jesus] said to them, "Watch out! Be on your guard against all kinds of greed; a man's life does not consist in the abundance of his possessions*"—Luke 12:15 (New International Version). Christ has no time for those who are simply trying to store up treasures here on Earth. Wealth can be lost instantly. In the end, it does not matter if you die a billionaire or a pauper—only how you answer THE QUESTION from Jesus, "*Who do you say I am?*"—Matthew 16:15, and whether or not you've done your best to fulfill God's purpose for your life. Rick Warren states, "The purpose of your life is far greater than your own fulfillment, your peace of mind, or even your happiness. It's far greater than your family, your career or even your wildest dreams and ambitions. If you want to know why you were placed on this planet, you must begin with God. You were born <u>by</u> his purpose and <u>for</u> his purpose."[3] You are to live your life to honor and worship God. Worship God by doing everything in your life for and with Jesus. We are saved to serve. Serve out of gratitude for what Christ did for you on the cross. Through Christian serving, we make an investment in eternity.

---

[3] Rick Warren, *The Purpose Driven Life*, page 17.

Grace, Faith, Purpose, and Peace

Being a good steward of your finances is just one aspect of worshiping God. God will entrust more spiritual blessings to those who are responsible with their worldly wealth. Worldly wealth is left behind upon your death. Spiritual blessings are the true wealth. Spiritual blessings last forever. There will be no financial accounts in heaven; however, there will be an accounting of your life and the use of the time, talents, and treasure God has entrusted to you. We were put on this earth to serve like Jesus served, to give more than you receive. Do good because God is good. Do good to bring glory to God by pouring love into all of your service. Live with Jesus in every thought, habit, and expression. The Rev. John Wesley (founder of the Methodist Church) said, "Do all the good you can, in all the ways you can, to all the people you can, as long as ever you can."[4] A Christian should be alive to the pain and suffering prevalent in this world today—a Christian should have a willing heart and desire to do something about it. For example, "*His mother called him Jabez because, as she said, she had borne him in pain. Jabez called upon the God of Israel and said, 'I pray thee, bless me and grant me wide territories. May thy hand be with me, and do me no harm, I pray thee, and let me be free from pain'; and God granted his petition*"—1 Chronicles 4:9–10. God wants to richly bless you so that you in turn can be a blessing to others.

If you kneel before God, you can stand before anyone. There is a great peace that comes from knowing that you are under God's control and not your own. Do your best to make the soundest financial decisions you can. Be willing to forgive yourself and others for mistakes. Trust that God is the one in ultimate control; control of your finances and,

---

[4] Norcross First United Methodist Church bulletin, Norcross, Ga., August 24, 2003.

Grace, Faith, Purpose, and Peace

more importantly, control of your salvation. Allow God to enrich your life through a deep, meaningful, personal relationship with Christ. Jean Danner, prayer evangelist, was inspired by God to write, "This is a mighty weapon when I take Christ down from the cross—His death a precious gift of redemption for me—the price paid by one who committed <u>no sin</u>. *But* . . . I must <u>take</u> the gift—take the crucified Christ and embrace Him until I am crucified with Him! Then every barrier, every argument and reasoning Satan has built so skillfully to keep me from a deeper, more perfect knowledge of Jesus Christ is completely demolished. . . . Then I can enter my Promised Land here on Earth. Filled to the brim and overflowing with the Holy Spirit—the promise of scripture and my soul never being in want! The peace that passes understanding."[5] The Bible says, "<u>*Do not be anxious about anything, but in everything, by prayer and petition, with thanksgiving, present your requests to God. And the peace of God, which transcends all understanding, will guard your hearts and your minds in Christ Jesus*</u>"—Philippians 4:6–7 (New International Version).

When you do not make God your number one priority in life, your life's priorities make living precarious at best. You may even reach a point of total disequilibrium like a pendulum precariously perched on a point:

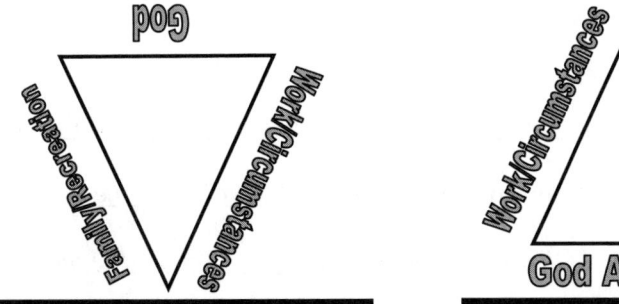

---

[5] Jean Danner, Praying Grace class handout and email to author, Norcross First United Methodist Church, 2003.

Grace, Faith, Purpose, and Peace

When you choose to make God your number one priority and the base of your life, your life can have equilibrium. God's foundation can give you peace in all of life's circumstances.

In the beginning of this book you were asked, "What do you think God felt" as He witnessed the crucifixion of Christ? God felt love. He felt unconditional love for you. God felt so much love that He willingly died on the cross for you so that you could spend eternity with Him! Max Lucado said in *He Chose the Nails* that "on the eve of the cross, Jesus made his decision. He would rather go to hell for you than go to Heaven without you." Can you feel that love? When you know you are loved, you are set free to love others. Be a conduit of God's love. Take God's love and use it to make this world a better place than it was before you came. And remember, life is not ended by physical death, only changed for the better through God's unconditional and unending love. "*For God would not be so unjust as to forget all that you did for love of his name, when you rendered service to his people*"—Hebrews 6:10. "*So now, since we have been made right in God's sight by faith in his promises, we can have real peace with him because of what Jesus Christ our Lord has done for us*"—Romans 5:1 (Living Bible). May your investments in loving your fellow man grant you God's peace that is endlessly profitable to your soul.

God said, "*Behold, my servant shall prosper, he shall be lifted up, exalted to the heights*"—Isaiah 52:13. God said to Moses, "*Thus you shall bless the people of Israel: you shall say to them, The LORD bless you and keep you: The LORD make his face to shine upon you, and be gracious to you: The LORD lift up his countenance upon you, and give you peace*"—Numbers 6:23–26 (Revised Standard Version).

Grace, Faith, Purpose, and Peace

"*The grace of the Lord Jesus Christ, and the love of God, and fellowship in the Holy Spirit, be with you all*"—2 Corinthians 13:14.

Making Money Work

Soli Deo Gloria
(Glory to God Alone)

"*Praise God, from whom all blessings flow; . . . praise Father, Son, and Holy Ghost.*"—Thomas Ken, 1674

God said, "**Be still, and know that I am God.**"—*Psalms 46:10 (King James Version)*

Amen (I Agree!)

If God has used this book to help you grow spiritually and if God has used this book to help you make better informed decisions concerning your finances, please email the following website address to your relatives, friends, and colleagues so that they might purchase their own copy:

www.MakingMoneyWork.us

Order Form

Be a Spiritual Champion; Be a Financial Champion!
Give the Gift of *Making Money Work—A Christian Guide for Personal Finance* to Your Relatives, Friends, and Colleagues
Check Your Local Bookstore or Use This Order Form

☐ Yes, please mail _____ copies of *Making Money Work—A Christian Guide For Personal Finance*.

☐ Yes, I am interested in having Bill G. Page speak to my church, club, association, school, or organization. Please send me information.

Number of Books Ordered	x	Cost/Book	=	Total
_____	x	$39.99	=	$ _____
_____	x	North Carolina Residents Must Include 7% Sales Tax (e.g., 1 book @ $39.99 x 7% = $2.80 NC sales tax) for each book ordered	=	$ _____
1	x	$10.26 Shipping and Handling for the first book ordered	=	+$ 10.26
_____	x	Plus $5.01 Shipping and Handling for each additional book ordered after the first book	=	+$ _____
Grand Total (Book(s) + Sales Tax + Shipping and Handling):			=	$ _____

Name:	
Shipping Address:	
City, State, Zip Code:	
Country:	
Phone or Cell Number:	
Fax Number:	
Email Address:	
Organization:	
Where Did You Hear About This Book?:	
Payment Must Accompany Orders—Either Credit Card, Check, or Money Order	
Credit Card Name (Visa, MasterCard, or American Express):	
Credit Card Number:	
Exact Name on Credit Card:	
Expiration Date on Credit Card:	
Signature:	
Check Number or Money Order:	

Payment must accompany orders. Please allow 5–6 weeks for delivery.

Order Form

Make checks payable to "Making Money Work" and return this order form to

Making Money Work
P.O. Box 2605
Chapel Hill, NC 27515

www.MakingMoneyWork.us (Email this website address to others so they can order their own *Making Money Work* book/software program.)

Also, if you would like to donate suggestions or ideas on improvements for future revisions of *Making Money Work*, please complete the following:

Page Number	Chapter # or Worksheet #	Suggestions for Corrections, Additions, Improvements, etc.

I agree to donate the above suggestions for future revisions of *Making Money Work*.
Signature: _____ Date: _____

Scholarship Program

Be a Spiritual Champion; Be a Giving Champion!
Give the Gift of *Making Money Work—A Christian Guide For Personal Finance*. Support the Making Money Work Scholarship Program, Which Supplies Copies of the *Making Money Work* Book to Those Who Cannot Financially Afford to Purchase a Copy.

Make Your Contribution (Non-tax-deductible) Using This Form

☐ Yes, I would like to contribute to the *Making Money Work* scholarship program by paying the cost of a book(s) for someone who cannot financially afford to purchase one.

Send your contribution to Making Money Work, which will distribute the book to a scholarship applicant.

Select from one of the following:
☐ Give the recipient your contact information and your personal message below so that they might have an opportunity to respond to you.
—or—
☐ Give the gift anonymously.

Number of Scholarships	x	Cost/Book	=	Total
____	x	$39.99	=	$ ____
____	x	North Carolina Residents Must Include 7% Sales Tax (e.g., 1 book @ $39.99 x 7% = $2.80 NC sales tax) for each book ordered	=	$ ____
____	x	Shipping & Handling for each book will be paid by Making Money Work	=	+ $ 0.00
		Grand Total (Book(s) + Sales Tax + Shipping and Handling):	=	$ ____

Name:	
Address:	
City, State, Zip Code:	
Country:	
Phone or Cell Number:	
Fax Number:	
Email Address:	
Organization:	
Personal Message to Scholarship Recipient:	

Scholarship Program

Scholarship Payment—Either Credit Card, Check, or Money Order	
Credit Card Name (Visa, MasterCard, or American Express):	
Credit Card Number:	
Exact Name on Credit Card:	
Expiration Date on Credit Card:	
Signature:	
Check Number or Money Order:	

Make checks payable to "Making Money Work" and return this contribution form to

Making Money Work
P.O. Box 2605
Chapel Hill, NC 27515

www.MakingMoneyWork.us

Peace!

Bibiliography

Boyd, Gregory A., and Edward K. Boyd. *Letters From a Skeptic: A Son Wrestles with His Father's Questions about Christianity.* Wheaton, Ill.: Victor Books, 1994.

Fowler, James W. *Stages of Faith: The Psychology of Human Development and The Quest For Meaning.* San Francisco: Harper & Row, 1981.

Girzone, Joseph F. *Joshua.* New York: Macmillan, 1987.

Kushner, Harold S. *When Bad Things Happen to Good People.* New York: Schocken Books, 1981.

Moore, Thomas. *Care of the Soul, A guide for cultivating depth and sacredness in everyday life.* .New York, NY.: Harper Collins, 1992.

Naylor, Thomas H., William H. Willimon, and Magdalena R. Naylor. *The Search For Meaning.* Nashville: Abingdon Press, 1994.

Stanley, Thomas J. and William D. Danko. *The millionaire next door: the surprising secrets of America's wealthy.* Atlanta, Ga.: Longstreet Press, 1996.

Weatherhead, Leslie D. *The Will of God.* Nashville: Abingdon Press. 1972.

Index

12b-1 fees, 190, 191, 222

401 (k) plans, 119, 120

403 (b) plans, 120

529 College Savings Plans, 349

A.M. Best Company, 369

accumulation phase, 259, 262

acquisition fees, 330, 334

adjustable rate preferred, 148

adjusted gross income AGI, 108, 238, 244, 408

Aesop's fable, 82

Aggressive funds, 184

allocation, 51, 52, 140, 141, 149, 200, 303, 305, 306

American Savings Education Council, 94

amortization, 144, 153, 267, 273, 274, 275

annual percentage yield APY, 228, 229, 233

annuitization phase, 259

annuity, 117, 123, 234, 235, 241, 248, 259, 260, 261, 262, 263, 264, 265, 266, 369, 420

Average cost per share, 201, 202

balance sheet, 152, 154, 155, 286

Balanced funds, 184

BBB Wise Giving Alliance, 39

Before Tax, 109

benefits, 9, 21, 28, 34, 59, 86, 87, 99, 100, 101, 102, 105, 113, 195, 203, 241, 264, 265, 266, 363, 366, 368, 369, 374, 375, 377, 378, 397, 403, 406, 407, 408, 409, 410, 411, 414

Better Business Bureau, 41, 42, 62, 179, 317, 320, 370, 374

Bibiliography, 466

Bible, 7, 10, 11, 13, 16, 19, 24, 27, 66, 80, 116, 141, 208, 226, 230, 258, 266, 342, 448, 449, 450, 453

Blend funds, 183

bonds, 18, 83, 87, 110, 111, 112, 120, 121, 131, 136, 139, 147, 150, 154, 161, 162, 182, 184, 194, 209, 210, 211, 212, 213, 214, 215, 216, 217,

467

Index

219, 220, 221, 222, 226, 227, 260, 262, 288, 303, 304, 322, 347, 350, 365, 366, 368, 430

budget, 46, 51, 52, 54, 56, 59, 85, 271, 278, 359

capital gains, 33, 37, 113, 114, 186, 190, 193, 200, 204, 235, 262, 282, 292

cash flow, 146, 147, 159, 160, 162, 286, 300

cash value, 331, 364, 365, 366, 367, 368, 396, 422

centenarians, 23

Certificates of deposit CD's, 231

Chick-fil-A, 17, 18, 19

Christian, 6, 9, 12, 14, 15, 19, 20, 38, 116, 181, 439, 452, 455, 462

church, 9, 12, 17, 31, 37, 42, 43, 116, 372, 456, 462

closed-end funds, 185

Collision And Comprehensive, 388

Common Stock, 153, 155

compound interest, 66, 67, 68, 69, 70

Consolidated Omnibus Budget Reconciliation Act, 377

convertible preferred, 148

copyright, 477

Coverdell Education Savings Account, 348

credit card, 40, 46, 50, 60, 61, 63, 299, 300, 309, 310, 311, 312, 392, 413, 434, 441, 443, 445, 446

cumulative preferred, 148

current assets, 48, 49, 153, 154, 155, 156, 157

current liabilities, 47, 48, 49, 153, 155, 156, 157

Current Ratio, 155

debt, 44, 45, 46, 47, 52, 56, 57, 59, 60, 62, 63, 66, 96, 152, 155, 156, 162, 163, 219, 221, 228, 313, 358, 359, 363, 368, 412, 434

Debt consolidation, 59

debt ratio, 156

debt-to-equity ratio, 156

468

Index

deductibles, 53, 327, 331, 380, 387, 388, 399

Deflation, 77, 80

depreciation, 144, 154, 158, 161, 162, 314, 315, 330, 331, 334, 335

Disposition fees, 330

diversification, 112, 118, 131, 139, 149, 150, 182, 185, 186, 194, 213, 214, 215, 286, 304, 307

dividends, 120, 142, 144, 146, 147, 148, 151, 155, 159, 162, 172, 177, 184, 185, 193, 200, 201, 286, 287, 343, 364, 367, 368

Dow Jones & Co., 171

earnings, 63, 70, 81, 86, 99, 102, 104, 116, 118, 120, 123, 143, 144, 145, 146, 147, 148, 151, 157, 159, 161, 163, 164, 183, 215, 218, 235, 253, 259, 262, 286, 301, 305, 307, 350, 366, 381, 418

education, 32, 44, 96, 107, 240, 279, 343, 344, 345, 346, 347, 348, 351, 355, 356, 357

Equifax, 58, 332, 444, 446

Equity-income funds, 184

estate, 32, 37, 96, 247, 248, 417

estate planning, 417, 418, 419, 421, 422, 423, 424, 425, 426, 427, 428, 429, 430, 431, 432, 434, 440

Experian, 58, 332, 444, 446

faith, 3, 6, 14, 19, 29, 66, 106, 141, 219, 361, 402, 438, 440, 452, 453, 458

filing system, 290

First In, First Out, 202

Fitch Ratings, 216, 217, 369

fixed annuities, 260

formula, 67, 68, 69, 110, 119, 138, 222, 223, 228, 253, 271, 334, 335, 352, 417, 423

future value, 125, 253, 254, 255, 256, 278, 342

futures markets, 288

futures options, 148

Index

Gallup Organization, 30, 128

Gallup poll, 8

giving, 6, 17, 27, 29, 30, 31, 33, 34, 37, 40, 42, 66, 82, 97, 199, 222, 323, 419, 428, 443

Global Funds, 183

God, 1, 2, 5, 6, 7, 8, 9, 10, 11, 12, 13, 15, 16, 17, 18, 19, 22, 23, 24, 25, 26, 27, 28, 29, 31, 37, 42, 46, 66, 73, 74, 95, 97, 106, 107, 116, 132, 133, 141, 181, 208, 230, 258, 285, 296, 302, 307, 313, 342, 357, 360, 372, 395, 402, 411, 416, 438, 439, 440, 447, 449, 450, 451, 452, 453, 454, 455, 456, 457, 458, 459, 460, 461, 477

Goodwill, 38, 153, 154

Grace, 3, 5, 6, 7, 28, 310, 416, 450, 451, 455

Gross Domestic Product, 181

Gross Margin Percent, 158

Growth funds, 183, 184

Health Insurance Portability and Accountability Act, 377, 408

highest in, first out, 114

Holy Ghost, 6, 452, 460

Holy Spirit, 4, 6, 11, 16, 19, 22, 452, 454, 457, 459

homestead exemption, 279

hope, 13, 14, 22, 26, 63, 133, 361, 373, 451

Identity theft, 441

Income distributions, 186

income funds, 120, 130, 184

income statement, 157, 161, 162

Independent Retirement Arrangements
IRA's, 234

Independent Sector, 30

Index funds, 184

indexes, 79, 172, 272, 288

Individual Retirement Account
IRA, 69

inflation, 76, 77, 78, 79, 80, 87, 88, 92, 94, 124, 130, 131, 166, 173, 174, 213, 220,

Index

272, 286, 372, 381, 398, 400, 407, 410, 429

insurance, 45, 53, 101, 106, 120, 144, 179, 217, 234, 240, 241, 259, 260, 261, 262, 263, 271, 274, 279, 280, 281, 293, 294, 296, 300, 301, 312, 315, 326, 331, 362, 363, 365, 366, 367, 368, 369, 370, 372, 374, 375, 377, 378, 379, 380, 381, 382, 383, 384, 385, 386, 387, 388, 389, 391, 392, 395, 396, 397, 399, 400, 401, 403, 404, 405, 406, 408, 409, 410, 411, 413, 414, 415, 416, 419, 420, 422, 427, 430, 431, 443

interest, 9, 23, 45, 46, 50, 55, 59, 60, 61, 62, 66, 67, 68, 69, 70, 71, 72, 73, 74, 77, 79, 80, 107, 109, 110, 111, 112, 116, 118, 125, 126, 127, 130, 144, 147, 154, 157, 159, 161, 173, 174, 185, 193, 209, 210, 211, 212, 213, 214, 215, 217, 218, 219, 220, 221, 222, 223, 225, 226, 227, 228, 229, 231, 232, 233, 234, 241, 244, 253, 255, 260, 267, 268, 269, 271, 272, 273, 274, 279, 280, 282, 297, 299, 300, 301, 309, 310, 311, 312, 313, 314, 321, 326, 333, 334, 343, 353, 354, 355, 356, 358, 366, 367, 407, 430

Interest rates, 210

Internal Revenue Service, 32, 33, 40, 99, 108, 203, 236

Jesus Christ, 1, 2, 3, 4, 5, 6, 7, 8, 9, 10, 15, 18, 22, 24, 25, 27, 28, 29, 64, 65, 73, 80, 95, 97, 107, 116, 258, 285, 342, 360, 372, 395, 401, 402, 411, 412, 438, 439, 440, 447, 448, 449, 450, 451, 452, 453, 454, 455, 456, 457, 458, 459

JROS, 429, 433

justified, 6

Kelly Blue Book, 316

Index

Keogh plans, 120, 220
laddering, 214
Large-cap funds, 183
Last Will and Testament, 417
lemon laws, 317
liability, 55, 193, 312, 376, 383, 386, 387, 388, 396, 399, 478
life expectancy, 90, 91, 92, 240, 257, 263, 264, 266, 314, 364
liquid assets, 37, 47, 84, 156, 422
Living Trust, 417, 421
Long-Term Care Insurance, 403, 404, 408, 410
long-term debt, 60, 156
management fee, 188, 218
Medicaid, 102, 379, 404

Medicare, 99, 101, 102, 103, 104, 376, 379, 380, 403
Mid-cap funds, 183
money, 12, 15, 16, 21, 27, 28, 29, 40, 42, 44, 45, 46, 50, 53, 54, 55, 57, 59, 61, 63, 68, 70, 71, 72, 73, 74, 75, 76, 77, 80, 82, 83, 96, 97, 98, 100, 107, 108, 109, 114, 116, 118, 119, 121, 131, 133, 134, 135, 136, 137, 138, 143, 145, 147, 149, 150, 152, 154, 157, 159, 160, 161, 163, 165, 167, 174, 176, 178, 180, 182, 184, 185, 187, 189, 191, 192, 195, 198, 200, 201, 203, 206, 209, 210, 213, 214, 215, 220, 222, 227, 228, 231, 234, 235, 240, 241, 249, 250, 259, 260, 262, 263, 264, 266, 267, 271, 273, 277, 278, 279, 281, 282, 286, 289, 294, 298, 299, 300, 302, 303, 304, 308, 309, 310, 315, 321, 326, 327, 333, 335, 336, 339, 341, 347, 349, 351, 355, 363, 366, 368, 375, 376, 399, 409, 410, 415, 417, 422, 429, 446, 455
money factor, 333
Money Market Account, 227
Money Market Funds, 112, 227, 305

Index

monthly payment, 59, 267, 268, 269, 277, 328, 332, 339, 341, 355

Moody's Investor Service, 217

mortgages, 44, 218, 272, 273, 282, 286, 300

Mother Teresa, 26

mutual funds, 33, 83, 112, 120, 121, 130, 136, 149, 165, 182, 185, 187, 189, 190, 192, 194, 195, 197, 198, 200, 203, 208, 211, 215, 218, 228, 262, 287, 347, 350, 365, 430

NASDAQ, 171, 172, 173

National Charities Information Bureau, 37, 39, 42

National Fraud Information Center, 41

NAV, 186, 194, 198, 200, 215

Net Cash, 160, 161, 162

net income, 158, 159, 160, 161

Niebuhr, Reinhold, 13

Noah, 1, 84

No-Load, 191, 196

Oppenheimer, 128

Order Form, 462

participating preferred, 148

penny stocks, 135

Pension and Welfare Benefits Administration, 124

Personal-injury protection, 387

portfolio, 89, 112, 118, 123, 124, 125, 126, 127, 130, 131, 135, 137, 139, 141, 143, 146, 149, 150, 174, 175, 178, 181, 182, 184, 185, 186, 187, 192, 193, 196, 198, 200, 203, 213, 214, 215, 217, 221, 226, 262, 303, 304, 305, 306, 307, 322, 350, 359, 362, 368, 376

prayer, 8, 13, 23, 24, 25, 43, 452, 457

present value, 222, 223, 253

Property & Equipment, 153, 154

prospectus, 177, 187, 192, 193, 196, 215, 216, 261

quick ratio, 156

Real Estate Investment Trust, 286

473

Index

records, 33, 50, 100, 178, 196, 200, 201, 279, 282, 292, 332, 352, 370, 381, 391, 400, 443

residual value, 330, 331, 334, 335

retirement, 55, 69, 73, 82, 83, 84, 85, 86, 88, 89, 91, 92, 93, 94, 99, 100, 101, 102, 105, 106, 116, 117, 118, 119, 121, 123, 124, 125, 126, 128, 129, 131, 141, 149, 183, 209, 220, 234, 235, 238, 239, 241, 247, 248, 249, 253, 259, 262, 263, 264, 305, 306, 307, 351, 366, 368, 376, 403, 420, 422, 430

revenue, 146, 147, 158, 366

risk, 55, 69, 91, 110, 112, 118, 130, 131, 136, 137, 138, 140, 141, 145, 146, 149, 163, 180, 183, 184, 186, 194, 195, 198, 199, 209, 210, 213, 214, 216, 217, 219, 232, 260, 273, 275, 278, 280, 301, 304, 305, 366, 370, 381, 382, 384, 391, 405, 414

Risk Assessment, 140, 141

rollovers, 249, 351

Roth IRA, 235, 241, 242, 243, 244, 245, 246, 247, 251, 252, 253, 348

rule of 72, 71

Russell 3000 Index, 173

sales charge, 189, 198, 218

Sales loads, 190

sanctification, 7

saving, 10, 53, 55, 56, 73, 75, 80, 83, 95, 97, 123, 178, 205, 413

Savings Incentive Match Plans for Employees, 248

Scholarship Program, 464

Sector funds, 185

Simple interest, 67

simplified employee pension, 121

SEP, 236, 247

Small-cap funds, 183

Small-company funds, 183

Social Security, 86, 89, 99, 101, 102, 103,

Index

104, 105, 106, 108, 265, 296, 299, 376, 442, 443, 444

soul, 7, 8, 11, 15, 21, 22, 132, 395, 412, 448, 452, 453, 457, 458

Standard & Poor's Corporation, 217

Standard & Poor's 500, 129, 130, 138, 164, 172, 195

stewards, 16, 17, 27, 456

stock, 33, 34, 37, 79, 80, 83, 87, 96, 117, 118, 130, 136, 138, 142, 143, 144, 145, 146, 147, 148, 149, 150, 151, 152, 161, 162, 163, 164, 166, 167, 169, 170, 171, 172, 173, 174, 175, 176, 178, 181, 183, 184, 185, 186, 188, 195,

213, 215, 221, 222, 226, 275, 278, 286, 288, 301, 303, 429

Stock options, 148

Stockholders' Equity, 153, 155

straight preferred, 148

Supplemental Security Income Benefits, 102

Taxable Equivalent Yield, 111

taxes, 6, 32, 34, 37, 40, 46, 64, 84, 89, 99, 102, 104, 107, 108, 109, 110, 111, 112, 113, 114, 115, 116, 118, 120, 122, 131, 144, 167, 186, 193, 200, 201, 203, 204, 220, 235, 236, 240, 241, 249, 250, 257, 259, 271, 274, 279, 280, 286, 292, 314,

315, 334, 335, 348, 349, 350, 352, 367, 375, 377, 379, 408, 417, 418, 421, 422, 424, 425, 426, 427, 428, 431, 440

tax-free income, 111

tax-free mutual fund, 112

time-share, 284

tithing, 53, 82, 97

traditional IRA, 235, 238, 240, 241, 242, 243, 244, 248, 249, 250

Trans Union, 58, 444, 446

Trusts, 217, 286, 295, 417, 420, 421, 423, 428, 431

U.S. Department of Education, 353, 354, 356, 357

Index

U.S. Postal Inspection Service, 42

Uninsured And Underinsured Motorist Coverage, 387

Uninsured Motorist Property Damage, 388

Value funds, 183

variable annuities, 260, 261, 262, 263

vehicle, 13, 15, 83, 187, 208, 314, 315, 316, 319, 320, 321, 325, 326, 327, 328, 329, 330, 331, 332, 333, 335, 336, 339, 341, 342, 347, 377, 383, 384, 386, 387, 388, 392, 393, 394, 395, 413, 415

verses, 10, 11, 12, 24, 27

volatility, 168, 183, 195, 197, 198

Wall Street Journal, 135, 198, 204

warranty, 281, 317, 318, 323, 326, 327, 332, 342, 413, 414, 415, 478, 479

website address, 461

Weiss, 369

will, 1, 2, 5, 9, 12, 16, 19, 25, 82, 249, 292, 325, 335, 357, 395, 418, 419, 420, 421, 423, 429, 438, 439, 440, 454, 478, 479

Wilshire 5000 Index, 173

Working Capital, 157

Yield, 110, 111, 112, 212, 216, 220, 229

Copyright and Covenant Stipulations For *Making Money Work*

"*You shall not steal.*"—Exodus 20:15

Unauthorized copying or duplicating of copyrighted material is a violation of both the legal law and God's law. Your covenant with Making Money Work--herein referred to as MMW--© 2005 Willie Glenn Page, Inc. is to honor all copyrights on all materials in accordance with the guidelines and permissions authorized by MMW.

System Requirements: Microsoft Excel 2000 or later version and Microsoft Word 2000 or later, 24MB of hard disk space.

End user license agreement (herein referred to as EULA): Carefully read and understand all of the rights and limitations described in this EULA. Your use of the MMW printed materials/software is your confirmation that you agree with the terms in this agreement. Use involves installing, viewing, reading, copying, or otherwise using the MMW information. If you do not agree with the terms of this agreement, do not install or use the software or printed materials and return all materials unused in their original containers to your place of purchase along with proof of purchase for a refund. This EULA is a legal agreement between you and MMW for printed materials and software produced by MMW. The software/printed materials are licensed to the end user, not sold to the end user with your agreement to the terms in this EULA. This EULA is valid and grants the end user license rights only if the printed materials and software are genuine MMW products.

Except for brief quotations or reference used in critical articles, reviews, books, sermons, speeches, lectures, or other talks, no part of the MMW written materials or software may be reproduced in any manner whatsoever without prior written permission from the publisher. Please make sure quotes and references are accurate and receive the proper credit line—for example: "Copyright 2005 Willie Glenn Page, Inc." All copyrighted materials require prior permission before you may reproduce them. If you are granted permission to make copies, you must put on each copy these words: "Reprinted with permission from Making Money Work for use on [include the date you are actually using the material such as "December 25, 2006"]. Any unauthorized copying or duplicating of the MMW material in whole or in part without written permission of MMW is expressly prohibited.

With the exception of brief quotes and references, all rights of the MMW materials are reserved. No part of the materials may be reproduced or transmitted in any form or by any means including electronic, mechanical, photocopying, recording, or by any information storage and retrieval system without written permission from the publisher.

You may only install, use, access, run, or otherwise interact with one copy of the software on a single digital electronic device—such as a single computer, workstation, terminal, handheld PC, pager, smart phone, etc. The software may not be installed, accessed, displayed, run, shared, or used concurrently on or from different computers or any other digital electronic devices. You may transfer your copy to another CPU providing that the software is usable on only one digital electronic device.

You are only licensed to use one copy of the software. A separate end user license must be purchased for each separate computer on which the software is run.

You may install one copy of the software and keep the original media on which the software was purchased solely for backup or archival purposes. If the software is not installed on your digital electronic device, you may make one copy of the original media solely for backup or archival purposes. It is illegal to circumvent any copy protection technology employed in the software or to make unauthorized copies of the software or printed materials. You may not reverse engineer, decompile, disassemble, modify, adapt, translate, or create derivative works based on the software or printed materials. You may not separate the software for use on more than one computer—the software is licensed as a single integrated product. You may be held legally responsible for copyright infringements, which are caused by your failure to abide by the terms of this agreement.

Copyright and Covenant Stipulations For *Making Money Work*

You may not rent, lease, or loan the software or otherwise transfer the software to another user. You may not resell, or otherwise transfer for value, the software or printed materials.

In the event that you fail to comply with the terms and conditions of this EULA, MMW may terminate your rights under this EULA in which case you must destroy all copies of the software and/or printed materials and documentation.

This EULA does not grant you any trademark or service marks of MMW or of its suppliers.

You acknowledge that the software under this EULA is of U.S. origin and agree to comply with all applicable international and national laws that apply to software and printed materials including the U.S. Export Administration Regulations. In addition, you agree to comply with end user, end use country destination restrictions issued by the United States and other export authorities.

The limited warranty in these "Copyright and Covenant Stipulations" is the only express warranty made to you. No other express warranties created by any documentation or packaging or person including MMW and its suppliers are valid. The software and printed materials are provided as is with all faults. All other warranties and conditions, either express or implied or statutory are disclaimed—including but not limited to implied warranties, conditions of merchantability, fitness of a particular purpose, lack of negligence, lack of workmanlike effort, and lack of viruses. This EULA supersedes all proposals or prior agreements oral, written, or communicated in any manner between you and any representatives of MMW or its suppliers. There is no warranty or condition of title, authority, or noninfringement in the software or printed materials. MMW and its suppliers make no guarantee or warranty regarding the currentness, accuracy, reliability, use, or results of use of the software or printed materials. MMW and its suppliers make no guarantee or warrant that the software will meet your system requirements or that the software will be uninterrupted or error-free.

MMW and its suppliers are not liable for any special, incidental, or consequential damages whatsoever arising out of or in any way related to the use of or inability to use the software or printed materials. The user agrees that any references to specific companies or investments in the MMW printed materials and software are for illustrative purposes only and are not recommendations to purchase any specific investments or use any specific goods or services. The user agrees to accept full responsibility for investment decisions without any blame or consequences to either MMW or its suppliers for any losses including but not limited to loss of income, loss of profits, losses from investments, business losses, loss of data, losses from interruption of use, losses for personal injury, losses of privacy, losses for negligence, claims of third parties, and for any pecuniary or other loss whatsoever even in the event that MMW or its suppliers have been advised of the possibility of such damages. The user agrees that the MMW printed materials and software are intended to provide general information only without recommending any specific investments in any products, goods, or services. The user agrees to verify all calculations with financial institutions prior to making any financial decisions and to not hold MMW or its suppliers responsible for any errors in the use of the MMW calculators, the software, or the printed materials. The user agrees to contact a financial planner, attorney, tax advisor, and or financial advisor before implementing any financial strategy. The user agrees that the calculators in MMW and the printed materials are meant to provide a general idea on financial implications based on the amounts provided and that these estimates are to be verified with the user's lenders and/or financial institutions for accuracy. The user agrees that the calculators in MMW and the printed materials are not intended as Investment advice in purchasing or investing any specific goods, products, or services. In no event shall the liability of MMW or its suppliers exceed the actual amount paid by you for the software and printed materials.

MMW and its suppliers may use information you supply concerning the software and printed materials for its business purposes including product support and product development.

Copyright and Covenant Stipulations For *Making Money Work*

MMW or its suppliers own all title and intellectual property rights in the software and printed materials. The user owns only the disk(s), but MMW owns the software itself.

MMW and its suppliers reserve all rights not specifically addressed under this EULA.

This license allows the purchaser to display a copy of the software on a single computer with a single CPU at a single location as long as the user complies with the terms of this agreement.

Limited warranty: MMW warrants for a period of 90 days from the date of purchase of the software/printed materials that they perform substantially in accordance to their design and function under normal use and service and they are free from defects in materials and workmanship. No warranty or conditions of any kind are guaranteed after the stated warranty period—local jurisdiction limitations may apply. This limited warranty is only made to the first licensed user of the software/printed materials—there are no third party beneficiaries under this EULA. At the discretion of MMW and its suppliers (subject to applicable law), you will receive the following remedy for any defects:

1. customer service support to correct files, programs, or other issues,
2. replacement of defective items,
3. or return of the price paid for the software/printed materials (with original sales receipt and return of all original components to your place of purchase).

You will receive the remedy elected by MMW without charge with the exception of any expenses you might incur such as shipping or handling. If the replacement of defective items option is used, replacement items will be warranted for the remaining time left in the original warranty or for 30 days—whichever time frame is longer. This limited warranty is void if failure of the software/printed materials is the result of accident, abuse, abnormal use, misapplication, or virus.

Your covenant with MMW is a pledge to abide by and follow the stipulations in this agreement.